THE AVENUE

THE AVENUE

A History of the
Claremont Institution

Rachel Pollard

Denzille
Press
DUBLIN

First published in 2006 by
DENZILLE PRESS
Dun Laoghaire
Co. Dublin, Ireland
e-mail: denzillepress@yahoo.ie

ISBN (10 digit) 0 9553239 0 8
ISBN (13 digit) 978 0 9553239 0 4

Cover design by Caroline Harberd, Martello Press
Typesetting by Rachel Pollard
Printed by Colour Books, Dublin, Ireland

This publication has received support from the Heritage Council
under the 2006 Publications Grant Scheme
and from the Claremont Trust

AN
CHOMHAIRLE
OIDHREACHTA

THE
HERITAGE
COUNCIL

Dedicated to the memory of the Rev. C.E.H. Orpen, M.D.
and of the pupils of the Claremont Institution,
many of whom lie buried in unmarked graves
at St. Mobhi's Churchyard, Glasnevin, Dublin*

Av-e-nue.

* See Appendix 6

'Whatsoever thy hand findeth to do,
do it with all thy might'.
Ecclesiastes 9:10 (KJV)

The above verse was 'Our Motto'
adopted by the Claremont Institution.
It is depicted on a placard in the photograph
of the Carpentry Shop on the front cover.

National Institution at Claremont (near Glasnevin) for Deaf & Dumb Children of the Poor in Ireland; Supported by voluntary contributions.

The rent of this House, and 18.½. acre of land, and the Head Master's Salary amount, only to £ 203.11.6.

Lithographed at Allens Dame St Dublin, from a Sketch by Mr Humphreys. Head Master of the School.

Claremont, Glasnevin as at 1826 – sketched by Joseph Humphreys, first Headmaster
and lithographed by John Johnson, former pupil

On the Invention of Writing

Tell me, what genius did the art invent,
The lively image of the voice to paint?
Who, first the secret, how to colour sound,
And to give shape to reason, wisely found?
With bodies, how to clothe ideas, taught,
And how to draw the picture of a thought.
Who taught the hand to speak, the eye to hear,
A living language, roving far and near;
Whose softest noise outstrips loud thunder's sound,
And spreads her accents, through the world's vast round;
A voice, heard by the Deaf, spoke by the Dumb,
Whose echo reaches long, long time to come;
Whose dead men speak, as well as those alive –
Tell me, what genius did this art contrive?

Bellenger

CONTENTS

APPENDICES

Foreword

A pioneering venture in the history of Irish education, the National Institution for the Education of the Deaf and Dumb Poor of Ireland (commonly known as the Claremont Institution), was founded in 1816. Its founder, Dr Charles Orpen (1791-1856), was inspired by both educational and evangelical zeal, and he became the leader of the education of deaf children in Ireland.

Today Special Needs Education is in the forefront of Irish schools. The care and education of deaf children is a high priority and the integration of Special Education pupils into mainstream schools continues to gain support. It was not so two hundred years ago. Deaf children were neglected and were considered as 'mutes' and not capable of being educated. In the early nineteenth century a number of specialist institutions were founded, where deaf children could be housed and taught either 'sign language' or 'articulation' to enable them to communicate with the non-deaf. The Claremont Institution was such a school and it led the way in Ireland by developing methods and aids to assist deaf pupils to learn. It was a Protestant charitable institution supported by voluntary subscriptions and serving deaf children from all parts of Ireland. Public examinations of the pupils were held annually in the Rotunda Round Room in Dublin to demonstrate the success of the school and to collect further funding.

Charles Orpen was a medical doctor and, prior to the opening of the Claremont Institution, he had travelled widely in Europe visiting similar institutions. He was particularly impressed by the work of Abbé Sicard, head of the Institution for the Deaf and Dumb in Paris and author of *Cours d'Instruction du Sourd-Muet de Naissance*, a book widely used during the early years of Claremont. Orpen also visited institutions in Switzerland and Italy where the method of 'articulation' (learning to speak) was preferred to sign language, so that the pupils would be able to communicate in the wider world and not just with other deaf persons who were familiar with sign language. Orpen also was much influenced by the educational ideas of the famous Swiss educator, Pestalozzi (1746-1827), who was a pioneer of 'child-centred' education, based on the observation and experience of the children. John Synge of Glanmore Castle, Co Wicklow, a close friend of Orpen, was also a devotee of Pestalozzi and he published Pestalozzian educational charts for use in Ireland. Joseph Humphreys, who was the first headmaster of Claremont, was involved in the work of the Kildare Place Society, another pioneering Irish educational venture, which supported schools, printed textbooks and trained teachers in the new monitorial system of Joseph Lancaster of London (1778-1838). Thus in the early nineteenth century, educational ideas in Ireland were part of a broad European network and the Claremont Institution was the fourth deaf school of its kind in the British Isles - the others being in London, Edinburgh and

Birmingham. Voluntary efforts continued to lead the way, and in 1846 the Catholic Institution for the Deaf and Dumb founded its school for girls under the auspices of the Dominicans in Cabra, and in 1857 for boys at St Joseph's under the auspices of the Christian Brothers. In 1889 there was to be a Royal Commission on the Blind, the Deaf and Dumb of the United Kingdom and this was to be the first official recognition of the educational needs of such children.

As well as providing primary education, the Claremont Institution was concerned with the employment of the deaf children afterwards in such as domestic service, millinery and/or factory work for the girls, and farming, shoemaking and printing for the boys. In 1876 the Dublin Working Boys' Home was founded to provide accommodation for young men coming up to Dublin to work and in 1889 Miss Harding left a legacy to provide a technical school attached to the Home. A number of deaf boys, on leaving Claremont, went to live in the Harding Home and a chapter in the book traces its history. Another area where boys were encouraged to work was to become missionaries to the deaf at home and abroad as 'messengers of the Gospel'. The Dublin Protestant Deaf and Dumb Association held evangelical religious services using sign language, and it published a journal, *The Irish Deaf-Mute Advocate and Juvenile Instructor*.

The Claremont Institution was situated in Glasnevin in a fine purpose-built house, approached by a long avenue - hence the title of the book. Although it was well known in the area, it has been part of what the author calls the 'hidden history' of Ireland. Using the extensive records of the school, which are deposited in the National Archives, Rachel Pollard has produced a valuable historical study. The book gives not only an account of the life and work of the Claremont Institution itself, but also places the education of the deaf in the context of the history of Irish education. The book includes personal memoirs of past pupils and a range of contemporary illustrations. In 1943 the school moved to smaller premises in Monkstown and finally closed in 1978. However, with the support of the Claremont Trust and the Heritage Council, this book has brought back to life the remarkable story of one man's vision and of his pioneer work that brought education and self esteem to 'the children of silence'.

Susan M.Parkes, MA, M.Litt., FTCD
Emeritus Fellow and former Senior Lecturer in Education
Trinity College, Dublin.
August 2006

Introduction

As part of organizing a reunion for former pupils of the Claremont Institution in 2001, research work was carried out on the origins of the 'hidden school'. In 1928, Mr George Taylor, Headmaster, produced his version of the history of the Institution, which was Ireland's first public school for educating the deaf, founded in 1816. The Governors, however, decided not to incur any expense in printing it, and Mr Taylor's plan was abandoned. Now, this plan is revived and brought into completion in the production of this book to document, for perpetuity, the story of the 'hidden school.' Owing to its geographical location, the Institution was spatially cut off from the world - situated in a large demesne, surrounded by trees and bound by the Claremont river, with the tree-lined Avenue, half a mile in length, stretching out to the outskirts of the village of Glasnevin. Psychologically and historically, it was and is 'hidden' from the sight of the educationalists and historians. The Institution had been established for the class which the world wants to erase from memory and from sight - the deaf.

The Claremont Institution might have already been referred to, though briefly, in text-books covering the education of the deaf in Ireland. There has been proliferation of Deaf Studies, already recognised as an academic discipline in several universities world-wide, in Trinity College Dublin and elsewhere. With Irish Sign Language amongst foreign languages as part of Adult and Continuing Education, this forms a catalyst for raising awareness of the existence of Irish Deaf History. Even if that is so, the real purpose of this book is to record the circumstances of how this Institution came into being; and to bring to life the stories told by the deaf pupils with regard to the distinct lifestyles experienced during the nineteenth century Ireland.

Efforts have been taken to ensure that the book is, on one hand, approachable and succinct for the lay reader and, on the other hand, informative and detailed for the academic historian or educationalist. In order to provide the context for the book, it is appropriate to include extracts from letters composed by the pupils, portions from some letters and lecture notes by the school's founder - Dr Charles Orpen, and from other relevant articles produced during the nineteenth century. That way, one can form the mental picture of how daily life at Claremont had been experienced. In regard to usage of terminology when referring to deaf people in the book, the words 'deaf and dumb' and 'deaf mute' were of common usage during the nineteenth century and earlier. Most deaf in those days were actually without speech unless they had been taught articulation which was, until the 1880s, the preserve for those from wealthy or cultured families. In order to avoid repeating the lengthy official title of the Institution - *National Institution for the Education of the Deaf and Dumb Poor of Ireland*, I shall refer to it as the 'Institution', and to the Managing Committee of the Institution as the 'Committee', and after its incorporation under the Commissioners of Charitable Donations and Bequests in 1887, as the 'Board of Governors' or 'Governors'.

The Institution is not my Alma Mater; it provided the means of education for my husband, Henry, whose story, together with another from a former pupil who entered Claremont in the final decade of the nineteenth century, shapes the prologue for this book. Certainly, the Claremont Institution, as with any educational or charitable institution, owed its establishment to the key persons – the indefatigable Doctor Charles Orpen, Mr. Joseph Humphreys, the first headmaster, and Thomas Collins, the first pupil, whose letter to the monarch of the United Kingdom touched the hearts of not only those in his time but also nowadays. Dr Orpen had expended so much of his time, money and energy in the service of deaf and hearing people at home, in England and in South Africa, that his life-story deserves a major part in the book.

While information on the origins of Deaf education in general might be brief, the intention is to draw the reader's attention to the history of deaf education executed within the walls of Claremont, Dublin. This book contains interesting information, for those with a leaning towards local history and genealogy, on the physical locations of the Claremont Institution – Smithfield in the city of Dublin, Glasnevin near Dublin and Monkstown in south of Dublin. For those wishing to visualize the social life in the early nineteenth-century Dublin, this book contains extracts from letters by pupils describing the events and incidents that occurred within and outside Claremont. The progress of the Institution is covered from its beginnings in Smithfield, after its move to Glasnevin and then in Monkstown. The struggles of the Institution on the educational, administrative, financial and religious levels are described in detail. Once the public became aware of Claremont's existence with the resultant increase in the number of deaf children admitted to receive secular, religious and vocational instruction, the Institution managed the influx through the expansion of the school in 1823 and in 1844.

Also covered in the book are the teaching methods of the deaf adopted, namely articulation (or speech therapy, as it is known today) and sign language – the visual/gestural means of communication generally used by deaf people from the beginning of civilization. Included are illustrations of two sets of the manual alphabet – the English two-handed and the Spanish one-handed, designed by Mr Joseph Humphreys. The stone plates for printing these alphabets had been seen by Henry and are still missing – it is very much hoped that these rare artifacts would surface one day. The Institution could not survive without finance, and this is covered in a chapter addressing the various means of generating revenue, including a tiny sum of money donated by a little girl for the benefit of her compatriots, who were 'deprived of the faculties of hearing and speaking'. One motive behind the establishment of the Institution was to enable, by provision of temporal and vocational education, the deaf children become more self-reliant and less a burden on the 'Union' (forerunner of the city or county council). The other motive was to lead the spiritually uneducated deaf into personal knowledge of their Saviour, Jesus Christ. This Institution was established at a time when the Evangelical Movement was gathering momentum in

Ireland. The outcome of religious education received at Claremont was the emergence of the deaf missioners whose vocation was to bring the Gospel to the deaf in their own language – signs and 'finger-spelling'.

This book contains the accounts of some of the pupils after they made their way down the Avenue for the last time to go into the world. Some succeeded in employment, others took the boat to England, America, Canada and Australia, while some fell by the wayside, into destitution and crime. Among those who were noticed upon admission into Claremont as having possession of 'talent for drawing' are profiled in this book, and their achievements in visual arts remain 'hidden'. Another 'hidden' element of the deaf community needs revelation – Deaf women. One particularly stands out – Charlotte Elizabeth Tonna, where some of her literary works are being reprinted under the title, *Irish Recollections*. Up to the 1880s, the profession of teaching the deaf was the masculine domain, since it was perceived that usage of sign language in the classroom required 'extensive amount of energy' and therefore unsuitable for the 'weaker sex'. This did not apply in the case of Claremont, where a former female pupil, from Cork, was retained as an assistant teacher in 1824 – making history, as far as could be known, of being the first deaf female teacher in the United Kingdom. Owing to their inferior status in the social class system, some deaf women endured hardship and ill-treatment, since they were at a disadvantage of having had received, when young, inferior education at Claremont. Time allocated for their education in class was, on a daily basis, three hours less than that for the deaf male pupils. Even inequality extended to salaries of male and female teachers, and then to hearing and deaf teachers, the latter having received less pay.

The final chapter takes on a different character, where it covers the history of another Dublin institution which, like Claremont, also disappeared into the 'mists of time' – the Dublin Working Boys' Home. This provides the shelter not only for the hearing boys leaving school and going to Dublin for apprenticeship and employment, but also for some of the former pupils of Claremont. It details the origins of the Home, the facilities provided within the confines of the 'Harding' and the profiles of some of its former residents after they passed through the doors of the building in Lord Edward Street for the last time.

In conclusion, it is hoped that this book will open the 'Avenue' in your mind's eye, and let your eyes follow along the incline of the gravelled Avenue, lined with elm trees, loved by Mr Joseph Humphreys, across the bridge spanning the little river where the boys played in the water, floating on a door and making an 'island' with sods, and see the crumbling façade of the building, with the portico-flanked door, receiving the deaf children into a new world – education, enlightenment and enduring friendship for the time to come.

Rachel Pollard
July 2006

Acknowledgements

First of all, Henry and I want to express our most grateful thanks to the person who has been our mentor and co-researcher for the past several years. Without his help, inspiration and encouragement, we would not have proceeded with the research work, which leads to the end-product, the book itself - Anthony J. Boyce, Doncaster, England. Thanks are also due to the members of the British Deaf History Society for their assistance in many ways.

We wish to express our most sincere gratitude to the Heritage Council and to the Governors of the Claremont Trust for financial assistance towards the publication of this book, which is vital for documenting the history of this Institution for posterity.

We would like to acknowledge the assistance from the following in our research work on this 'hidden', yet important part of Irish history: Aideen Ireland, Gregory O'Connor and Elizabeth McEvoy, archivists, and the staff of the National Archives of Ireland; Joanna Finegan and the staff of the National Library of Ireland; Máire Kennedy and the staff of Dublin City Library and Archives in Pearse Street, the Librarian of the Royal Irish Academy; Dr Raymond Refausse, Dr Susan Hood, Mary Furlong and Heather Smith of the Representative Church Body Library, Muriel McCarthy of Marsh's Library, the Librarian of Mercer's Library, Mary Shackleton of Religious Society of Friends' Historical Library, Mary Malone of Ballitore Library and Quaker Museum in Ballitore, Co. Kildare, Joan Johnson of Friends' Meeting House, Waterford, Susan Parkes, Archivist of the Church of Ireland College of Education. Thanks to the Librarian of the John Rylands Library of Manchester University, Mary Plackett and Susan England of the Royal National Institute for Deaf People Library, London, Michael Olsen of Gallaudet Archives, Washington D.C., the Librarian of Linen Hall Library, Belfast, Colin Scudds of Dun Laoghaire Historical Society, Patience Pollard of Edenderry Historical Society, the Librarian of Cape Town University Library, the Archivist of the Church of the Province of South Africa, Belinda Gordon of the Museum in Colesberg, South Africa, Irene Keogh of Friends of the Rotunda, and Patrick Wolohan of Claremont Avenue, Glasnevin, Dublin.

We wish to acknowledge the relatives and descendants of those who had links with Claremont - the founder, the staff and the pupils of the school in Glasnevin - Michael Orpen in Cape Town, Richard Orpen in Port Elizabeth, Paddy Orpen in Cradock, South Africa; Russell Clayton in Vancouver, Canada for information on French Pascoe; Gary and Lynn Switzer for information on the Switzer family of Rathkeale, Co. Limerick; Frank Ferris (nephew of Miss Harriet Ferris); Allen Williams (son of Charles Conrad Williams), Maureen Wood (daughter of Tom Carpenter) and Penny Turner (daughter of Betty Bateman).

Thanks are due to those for sharing their stories, memories and photographs of their schooldays and thereafter - the two surviving former pupils of the Claremont Institution in Glasnevin - Dennis Steenson and Stella Platts; and to the former pupils of the School at Monkstown – Margaret Anderson (née Eager), Alan Coulter, John Cummings, Doreen Deacon, Eric Deacon, Wendy Hawe, Cyril and John Hobson, James Horan, Edward McAuley, Claire McIlwrath (née Gilmore), Ruth O'Reilly, Iris Pearson, Henry Pollard, Norman Rankin, Maureen Reid (née Clawson), Adrienne Ring, Martha Smith (née Horan), Myrtle Stewart (née Henry) and Lesley Valentine. Thanks also to Mrs. Vera Finlay (sister of the late Wilfred Neil), and to the former teachers, Mrs. Jane Bleakley and Mrs. Mee Choo Thoeng Kelly. For information on the Dublin Working Boys' Home, we thank Sam Atkinson, the Hickey brothers and, particularly, Golding Kidd for his generosity with his time and practical advice. Thanks to Ian Duthie for his assistance with transcribing the tape recording of 'Memories', and to the Rev. Kevin Dalton, Daithi Ni Maoichoille and Patricia Arnold of the Claremont Trust for their assistance.

Many thanks are due to David Breslin, who provided useful information on Irish Deaf History, particularly on the former pupils of Claremont, who had gained distinction as artists and to Carmen Martin for communication services in Irish Sign Language. Regarding the research work on the deaf and hearing missioners, we would thank the following: Vera Telford for information on her late husband, the Rev. John Telford, the caretaker of St Luke's Church, Douglas, Cork, on the Rev. F.A. Elliott, Tom Lewis, Secretary of St Matthew's Church, Irishtown on the Rev. V.J.Walker; and Paul McManus, Milford, Co. Armagh, regarding Charles Radcliffe's employer, McCrum Wilson Mercer Ltd.

Many thanks are owed to Etain Murphy of Monkstown, Co. Dublin, for her support and encouragement in preparing this book. We happened to bump into each other at Dun Laoghaire Public Library, researching on the same subject matter – herself on the Parish Church of Monkstown, of which history she had produced an excellent book, and myself on 'Carrick Manor', the home of the Claremont Institution / School from the 1940s to its closing years. For practical and moral support, we want to thank Dorothy Jack, Eimer Harding, Mary McLarney and Orla Ryan. Also thanks to Gerry Finn for editing and proof-reading the manuscript and to Edward McCready for his assistance with graphic design. Thanks to Sean Griffin for his opening story. Also thanks to many deaf and hearing individuals, who are too numerous to list here, for their encouragement and advice.

Lastly but not the least – many thanks to Henry, who has been of enormous help in the massive task of culminating seven years' research work to produce this book, particularly for his work of tedious, mind-numbing scanning of newspaper reports!

Prologue

'We, who are men of the world, know that a good uniform
must work its way with the women, sooner or later.'
Pickwick Papers, *Charles Dickens*

One Sunday, while attending church service with her deaf pupils at Monkstown Parish Church, Miss Ferris, headmistress of the Claremont Institution, noticed, with concern, that groups of pupils from other schools in Monkstown – girls from the Hall School and boys from Brook House School – sitting in pews allocated to them, they presented an orderly appearance, wearing neat uniforms. Shortly afterwards, Miss Ferris issued a letter to parents that the children must be supplied with a new outfit of school uniform before returning to school.

In the evening before the day of his return to school after the summer holidays, Henry, aged six years, watched with embarrassment while his mother attached labels, with his name written in black ink, to each item of clothing, even his vests and underpants. It was the Hungry Fifties in Ireland and he was the only person in his family issued with brand new clothes. His brother and his two sisters had to wear second-hand, ill-fitted clothes. His mother had reluctantly asked her mother-in-law, Granny Pollard, for some money to obtain the requisite outfit of clothes for Henry. In due time, the Claremont boys were kitted out with black flannel coats, black caps with peaks for summer and calm days and black berets for winter and rainy days, grey sweaters, white shirts, knee-length grey shorts, grey socks and black shoes. The girls wore black flannel coats, black berets, black gym-slips, white blouses, grey socks and black shoes. On the following Sunday, Miss Ferris was suitably pleased as she cast her eye upon the orderly row of her pupils, neatly lined up in the pew in the West Gallery of Monkstown Church.

Henry Pollard with his Da, on his first day at school

1

Part One

How the Story Starts

A Letter to the King

When I walk past the crown-topped monument to King George the Fourth near the East Pier in Dun Laoghaire Harbour, my thoughts sometimes stray northwards across Dublin Bay to the hill at Glasnevin called Claremont and I think of the true story of Thomas Collins and his impossible dreams.

Sixteen-year-old Thomas Collins had followed the visit of the King to Ireland from the pages of the *Dublin Evening Post* that Mr Joseph Humphreys, headmaster of the Claremont Institution for the Deaf and Dumb, had pinned up for his pupils to read.

The King had arrived on 12 August 1821, his birthday, by a mail packet ship and disembarked in the little fishing harbour of Howth – to the surprise and disappointment of all the dignitaries waiting in forlorn ceremony for the Royal Yacht to dock in Dunleary. Thomas Collins, writing in his journal, also registered his bitter disappointment:

GEORGE IV

'I went to the Park to see the king and the military review last Saturday, it was very pretty. The soldiers marched very well, and the artillery very handsome. I did not see the king for the crowd was very great and they pushed me, very much, but I saw the King's carriage which was most handsome. I think I saw him bowing to the people but I am not certain.'

Thomas made bold to write to the King and besought his bemused benefactor, Dr Charles Orpen, to deliver it to the Post Office in Sackville Street. Thomas wrote:

'My Dear George,

I hope I will see you when you come and see the deaf and dumb pupils. I am very sorry that you never did come and see them; I never saw you. The boys and girls are much improving and are very comfortable here. Are you interested in seeing the deaf and dumb? I am very much pleased with writing a letter to you. I want to get a letter from you. Would you like to see me at Claremont? I am an orphan and a very poor boy. God will bless you. Do you know grammar, geography, bible, arithmetic, astronomy and dictionary? I know them very little … I am thinking of everything and to be polite to every one. I have been at school four years and a half. I am sixteen years of age. I am very delighted that I am improving very much; perhaps I will be an assistant in the deaf and dumb school one day.

Where were you born? I was born in Dublin. Would you like to correspond with me? What profession are you at? I never saw you. I am very anxious to see you indeed; and would like to see the King of England very much.

I am, your affectionate friend,

Thomas Collins, Claremont, Glasnevin, near Dublin.'

It was unreasonable, even for optimistic Thomas to expect a special visit from the King of England. Was it an illusion then, when early in the morning of the day of the King's departure from Ireland, a bright yellow carriage emblazoned with the royal arms rolled up the Avenue that led up to Claremont House? Dr. Orpen and Mr Humphreys, with uncontained excitement and pride, hurried the bewildered Thomas to the front parlour. There, Sir Benjamin Bloomfield, Private Secretary to the King, in response to a letter, which had greatly affected His Majesty, presented Thomas Collins with an envelope inscribed with his name. Silently, the gentlemen watched the boy as he brought the letter to the window and, fingering the red seal bearing the royal crest, with glowing eyes compared it with the coat of arms on the door of the coach standing outside the front door. Thomas made signs for scissors to be brought so that he could cut off the wax carefully, keeping the royal imprint intact.

And what message was in the letter? Did it matter? Thomas Collins had not been forgotten; he had been recognised, and he had been heard by one of the monarchs of the United Kingdom. Yet, barely thirty years later, he died and was buried in the churchyard of St Mobhi in Glasnevin, situated at the end of the Avenue stretching across the wide terrain of the Claremont demesne. No monument or marker commemorates him.[1]

My First Day at Claremont

David John (Jack) Stanton

Born in Dublin on 13 September 1899, I lived in the upstairs rooms above my father's shop in 67 Lower George's Street, Kingstown. He runs a fruit and vegetable shop, and I have four brothers and one sister. When I was twenty-one months old, I fell ill from 'water on the brain'[1] and consequently became deaf.

It was a mild day in September 1906 when my father and I took the tram, No. 8 from Dalkey, which stopped outside my home. When approaching Monkstown, I could see, from the upstairs section of the tram, the moored yachts bobbing up and down in the Coal Harbour. Next came the village of Blackrock, and I watched out for the ancient stone cross in the middle of the little square. It had a strange, deadpan face. Turning the corner, the tram approached the large park, where I could see the bubbling fountain, the snowy white swans and the bandstand, with the army band making music. Suddenly, I realised I could no longer hear music, and the clangs and twangs made by the tram clattering along the steel tracks. Soon, the landscape changed from green, leafy suburbs to grey, tall Georgian houses of the city. After crossing the wide bridge spanning the Liffey, thronged with horse-carts, bicycles and passer-bys, we reached Sackville Street.

We changed for the No. 13 tram about to depart from Nelson Pillar. I craned back my head as far as I could, to see the face of the maritime one-armed hero perched on top of the Corinthian column. My father picked up my brown suitcase and parked it on the seat of the tram, and I sat beside him. Cranking and struggling uphill, the tram made its way northwards to Glasnevin. After passing the Botanic Gardens, the tram reached the junction close to Delville House and there we got off. Passing the 'Ink-bottle' school-house, we walked up Ballymun Road until we came to the police barracks at the corner of Claremont Avenue. Turning left and proceeding up the narrow road, we came before a pair of stone pillars, flanking the steel gates.

After my father stated the purpose of our visit, the lodge-keeper opened the gates, and we walked up the Avenue, the golden, dry leaves crunching under our feet.

Soon, the Dutch elm trees on both sides of the Avenue started to envelop us, and I could feel the hairs rising on my neck. My hand, in my father's hand, trembled, and my father assured me with words, 'It's alright, Jack.' I could not hear his soothing voice, but his kind yet weary expression assured me. After what it seemed miles of grey gravel, we approached the front of the building, which was to be my home for the next seven years. The door was surrounded by a portico and two columns. At the right side was a house with bow-fronted windows, and a greenhouse erected against the wall at the ground level. At the left side was a long building annexed to the house, stretching from the porch, with many windows at two levels. Glancing at one of the upper windows, I spotted the face of a young boy, watching us. Then my father approached the door and rang the bell. The door opened, and the girl servant asked what our business was. Then we were led into the dark, cold hall, and then into a small room. We were told to take our seats, and a few minutes later, a slim, moustached man entered the room. He introduced himself as Mr George Taylor, the headmaster. He looked at me, and then smiled. Slowly and steadily, he mouthed: 'Hello, Jack. Welcome to Claremont.' I could not understand him, so he moved his hands towards his chest, indicating a gesture of welcome. Slowly, I relaxed and gave a tiny smile, wondering who was that little boy looking out of the window, with the anticipation that we would have good times together in the years to come.

Thomas Henry Pollard

I was born on 12 December 1942 in a little cottage in Co. Kildare, close to the River Boyne, up the road northwards from Edenderry, Co. Offaly. At the age of four, I fell into a ditch and became seriously ill. I could have died but for the doctor who performed a lumbar puncture, removing the spinal fluid pressing on my brain. When I awoke on my sick-bed, I was startled to see the faces of my mother, granny and aunt speaking to me - soundless. Thus I entered the silent world.

In April 1948, on the coach to Dublin, accompanied by my father, a farmer, I glanced out of the window of the coach. Stretched out for miles were the dark, rich-brown bogs, broken then and there by small holdings of fir-trees, gorse and heather. Approaching the capital city, I spotted the obelisk erected so long ago as a monument to the Iron Duke, surrounded by trees in the Phoenix Park. Soon, we arrived at O'Connell Street, and instantly, my father headed for the nearest pub, to satisfy his thirst with a pint of

Guinness, and a bottle of lemonade for me. Peeping out of the window of the pub, I watched the guards with huge, white gauntlets, directing the traffic across the wide bridge. Then it was time to catch the electric tram to Dun Laoghaire. I was excited when I saw the sea for the first time as we approached Merrion. Fascinated, I watched the white breakers, the mail-boat and the sea-gulls beneath the silver-grey sky.

Arriving at Blackrock, we got off the tram, and walked up the steep road towards Monkstown. Looking up the long, tree-flanked straight road, I stared at the huge, dark structure of exotic design. It was the parish church of Monkstown[2] with Moorish turrets. I shuddered while I glanced at the dark, gothic windows, the grey stone steps and the gloomy, huge buttresses. Soon, we passed Hewett's shop and the drapery store cum post-office until we arrived at the square house, surrounded by walls. My father lifted the brass knocker on the front door, and shortly a young maid opened the door. We entered the dim, narrow hallway dominated by an enormous grandfather clock, and we were shown into a little room. Then an elderly lady, elegantly dressed with a brooch at her neck, entered the room. My father arose and inclined his head slightly, and he removed my cap from my head. She introduced herself as Miss Harriet Ferris, the headmistress. Then she looked at me, with a twinkle in her eye, saying to me, 'How are you, Harry?' I blushed, and said nothing, knowing instantly that she would stand no nonsense from me.

Once the formalities were over, Miss Ferris took me by the hand and brought me to the classroom, where a small group of children, of varying ages, were seated around the table. There was only one boy called Dennis — much taller with a mop of dark brown hair and wearing round spectacles. The oldest girl, her name being Iris, beckoned to me, and said, 'I'll look after you, alright?' I sat beside her, and Miss Ferris walked to one of the two blackboards in the classroom. It was a square board propped on the easel and the other was a vertical 'conveyor-belt' blackboard, salvaged from the old school at Glasnevin. Using chalk, Miss Ferris wrote, 'His name is Henry Pollard. He is from Co. Offaly.' She mouthed the words, and the children imitated her, with much effort, repeating the sentences, until she was satisfied with their speech.

Soon, Miss Ferris dismissed the class, and we went outside to play. In the front of the garden was a lawn with a gravelled drive-way, and on the left was a large orchard with thirty apple trees. They looked pretty with pink blossoms, and the sight made me feel a little better. Then Miss Ferris gathered us together, putting us in 'crocodile' order and led us to the West Pier in Dun Laoghaire Harbour. For the first time, I smelt the salty air, with the pungent scent from the decaying seaweed – so different from the coconut-like fragrance of the yellow gorse close to my home.

3

Children of Silence

'a disenfranchised exile from society'
- Dr. Orpen

Before the industrialisation of Britain, families were expected to care for their children, only if they were productive once they passed the threshold of childhood which was far lower than today. When they reached the age of seven or eight, children took on the adult roles in production and responsibilities at home and outside. To this effect, children with disabilities, including deafness and muteness, were considered unproductive. Some deaf children were either sent away to monasteries and nunneries, or forced out of homes and these survived by begging or undertaking menial tasks.[1]

Deafness was most often described as an affliction that isolated the individual from the Christian community, where the deaf was existing in spiritual darkness and beyond the reach of the Gospel. These metaphors of darkness and ignorance had been used in speeches at public meetings, charity sermons and annual meetings as part of drawing attention of the public to the plight of the 'unfortunate creatures' and 'objects of pity'– the deaf. The speakers and orators placed an emphasis on the tragedy of the 'children of silence' who were in danger of being left in an uneducated condition, in an earnest effort to tug at the heart-strings and, to this effect, loosen the purse-strings for the 'distinct and strongly marked class of human beings' for which educational institutions had been established during the late eighteenth and nineteenth centuries.[2]

Superstitions regarding the Deaf
Until the early nineteenth century, among the lower orders in society, there were many superstitions regarding the deaf who were believed to be otherwise gifted as 'visionaries'. This idea was generally compounded, particularly by strolling dumb beggars, dealing in fortune-telling, magic tricks, juggling and thieving. In 1821, Mr Humphreys, headmaster at Claremont, wrote to Dr Charles Orpen regarding a pupil who ran away from the Institution, recommending that he not be readmitted as he had been of bad example to other pupils, and that he had been regularly trained by his mother in the falsehoods of fortune-telling, in the exercise of his agility as a tumbler (acrobat) at fairs and in thieving. In 1832, Mr Buckingham, lecturing in Dublin on the Mutes of the Oriental countries, said that deaf mutes in the East were used as silent spectators and witnesses of 'deeds of villainy' and that they were compelled to be executioners for the tyrant to whom they were enslaved, by strangling the victims with either the bow-string or the dagger. He said that he was pleased that that was not the case for the deaf children, where they were at last receiving education and becoming 'enlightened.'[3]

Muteism was often assumed; and many impostors had been detected in this character. In the Dublin newspapers during the 1820s, there were notices warning the public of impostors, where hearing men pretended to be deaf. Dalyell, in his book, *Darker Superstitions of Scotland*, says, 'In this country the faculty of prediction has been associated with the dumb; and, as of old, it originated from a vision. The devout connected some communication with the Deity, or with the ethereal world, during suspension of human faculties. Thence Daniel, in a vision, 'became dumb'; and Zacharias, a priest, was speechless for nine months from having seen a vision in the temple.' The popular terms for deaf people were: deaf and dumb; dummy; the silent people; the deaf mute; and in the Irish tongue, *bodhar agus balbh* – 'deaf and dumb'.[4]

Sir William R. Wilde

Sir William Robert Wilde, father of the famous Oscar Wilde, playwright and poet, was a prominent oculist and aurist. Fellow of the Royal College of Surgeons in Ireland since 1844, he attained a large practice and edited the *Dublin Journal of Medical Science*. As Commissioner of the Census of Ireland in the year of 1861, he produced detailed reports on his observations on the deaf and dumb, making frequent references to the statistics maintained on the deaf and dumb since 1851.[5]

Sir William Wilde was the first teacher of aural surgery in the English-speaking world.[6] As founder of St Mark's Eye Hospital, Dublin, he had been appointed in 1851 as Oculist and Aurist to the Claremont Institution, as well as to the Roman Catholic Institution for the Deaf and Dumb, Cabra. He commented, 'As to whether blindness or deafness is the greater calamity, and it is asserted that loss of sight is a greater privation than that of hearing; but with this I do not agree, for we know that the memory of objects affords greater consolation to the blind than the memory of sounds does to the totally deaf. In a spiritual point of view, congenital deafness is the greater affliction, for the child so born remains shut up within himself, and without great educational efforts, his understanding must for ever remain undeveloped, hearing being the chief instrument for psychological advance, while sight is only necessary for physical objects. The blind, however, meet with more sympathy from society, probably because deafness is not accompanied by any apparent physical defect.'[7]

The Case of the Deaf blind Girl

Sir William Wilde said, 'We had in Ireland some years ago a case of a deaf, dumb and blind girl, whom I have frequently seen and examined; she was a congenital mute and had lost her sight, in infancy, from ophthalmia. She was well forward and remarkably intelligent; her intelligence was, however, converted into cunning by the training and artifices of an exceedingly clever mother, who made a livelihood by showing her as a monster, and who resisted every means taken by benevolent persons to provide an asylum and suitable education for her child. The girl had rather a placid expression of countenance, delicate hands and an exquisitely delicate sense of touch, so that she could tell any portion of her mother's dress by feeling it, even when held by another. She was fond of sewing, but the most remarkable feat was that of the reading of her needle, by placing the needle between two of her lower teeth and laying the thread on the tip of her tongue, and with one or two latent motions, she managed to pass it through the eye of the needle.'

'For several years this poor child was exposed by her heartless parent, during the most inclement weather, by the wayside, in some of the outskirts of Dublin; there she might be seen sitting for hours, with a placard attached to her breast setting forth her infirmities, and receiving the occasional alms from the passer-by; while the mother lingered at some distance, watching the result. When I last saw her, she and her mother were inmates of the South Dublin Union Workhouse, where the poor girl died in 1847. At that time arrangements were being made at Belfast[8] to have her instructed, but before they were completed, the mother absconded with the little girl.'[9]

The Role of the Benedictines in Deaf Education[10]

The first attempt to instruct the deaf in a systematic manner was made by **Juan Petro de Ponce**, *(see picture)*, a Benedictine monk, at the monastery of San Salvador, Oña, in Spain, around the middle of the sixteenth century. It was related by Morales, the historian, that he taught the two deaf sons of a Castilian nobleman, to read and write. It was stated that these persons could understand by sight the motions and expressions of the lips and that they also spoke. Later autobiographical details revealed that he educated many more deaf mutes; some were taught Latin, others Latin and Greek, and to understand Italian. One of them went on to receive the orders of priesthood.

De Ponce died in 1584, and his system appears to have been followed up by his countryman, the Benedictine monk, Juan Pablo Bonet, who published, in 1620, a book on the Mode of Teaching the Deaf and Dumb. This work displayed the one-handed manual alphabet which had then been adopted, with some alterations, in several countries in Europe and in North and South America.[11]

Attempts of Introducing Deaf Education to Ireland
In the early 1800s, James Robertson, a Benedictine monk (name in religion: 'Gallus'),[12] came to Dublin. He found there a number of deaf and dumb children, and proposed to the Government to establish and direct a national school for the children's instruction using the Abbé Sicard's plan. But his proposal was not successful, and his project fell to the ground.[13] He had been tutor to leading families in Ireland, and later, a teacher of French in Maynooth College, a Catholic seminary for those entering the priesthood. It was through his stay in Ireland that the most extraordinary episode in Robertson's life took place. Through the Duke of Richmond, Lord Lieutenant of Ireland, he was recommended to Sir Arthur Wellesley, the future Duke of Wellington, at that time Chief Secretary for Ireland. In 1808, disguised as a commercial traveller, Robertson went to the French-occupied Danish islands, where Spanish troops were stationed under the command of the Marques de La Romana, to whom he communicated the arrangement for British ships to transport the troops to Spain to take part in the Peninsular War against the French. The operation was successful, and he was named as 'Romana Robertson'.

Robertson went to the Benedictine seminary in Regensburg, Germany. In May 1816, he set up a school for the deaf, and also, on the monastery premises, a school for blind children. These initiatives did not prosper, though Robertson was later termed 'Vater der Blinden Jugend' (Father of Blind Youth), and is recognised as the initiator of education for blind people in Bavaria, Germany.

Where did the Irish Deaf go for education?
In the late eighteenth century and in the early nineteenth century, there had been instances of some Irish deaf persons who had received education, such as Sampson Towgood Roch and Samuel Close, both of whom maintained business in art. In Co. Monaghan in north of Ireland, John Burns, who had learnt to read and write before the age of ten, came to the attention of a clergyman who instructed him in the principles of religion. Having had two children, whose mother died young, he supported the family and himself by writing a book, *A Historical and Chronological Remembrancer*. Published in 1775, it had over 1,000 subscribers, and consequently John Burns had taken the place of being the earliest known Irish deaf author.[14]

Asylum for the Deaf and Dumb, Old Kent Road, London

At the beginning of the nineteenth century, there were establishments for the educa-
tion of the deaf in Britain: an Academy initiated by Mr Thomas Braidwood in
Edinburgh, and the Asylum for the Deaf and Dumb in Old Kent Road, London, under
the management of Mr Watson. At the latter, there were records of deaf pupils from
Ireland.   The first Irish pupil was William Rountree from Cork, admitted on 9
February 1816, and he died in 1820.   On 3 February 1819, John Clancy, from Dublin,
was admitted, and he also died in 1824.   Ten years later, another boy from Cork,
Alexander McCallum, was sent to London and was discharged on 30 March 1833.[15]

Around ten to twelve Irish deaf[16] had attended the College for the Deaf and Dumb
in Rugby, England, which was established by Mr Henry Brothers Bingham for the
upper classes.[17]   One of them was William Joseph (Willy), son of William Smith
O'Brien (1803-1867), leader of the Young Irelanders and sentenced to transportation to
Australia for his attempts to overthrow the British administration in Ireland. Willy
was born deaf on 31 March 1839, and when he was six years old and became difficult
to control. His father obtained advice from Dr Tait who said that Willy should be
admitted to a private school for the deaf in Rugby. The school fees were expensive,
and William Smith O'Brien had to ask his mother, Lady Charlotte Smith, for assistance
and she agreed to pay for transport, room rental and the cost of school outfit, while
William Smith paid for tuition fees. Willy attended Rugby School on 27 April 1845,
where he remained until 1860.[18] In the British Census of 1851, the list of occupants at
the Rugby School showed two Irish-born persons: William Joseph O'Brien, scholar,
and Miss A. Twigg, visitor to the school. This lady was a regular subscriber to the
Claremont Institution.

In 1854, at the annual meeting of the Claremont Institution, Sir Joseph Napier,
M.P., said that 'he had been highly gratified at the truly beautiful language and ideas
frequently to be met with in essays written by the deaf and dumb boys of the Rugby

School.' He went on to say that 'it was boys of such imagination as the one who had written that book who would have been treated by the law of Romans as idiots, and would still have been so by our law.'[19]

In the Annual Report of 1817 of the Institution for the Education of the Deaf in Birmingham, England, was an extract with the following details from the Dublin newspapers referring to the deaf:

> *Dublin Press* – 'No description can possibly convey an accurate idea of the habits customs and manners of this singularly interesting and savage race.'
> *Evening Paper* – 'We can say that these evidently are a genuine partly not like some of the Paddy Murphy Indians who before now have been palmed off on an intelligent public.'
> *Freeman* – 'To such as have not seen them, description can convey no full idea of what they are; they are genuine bushmen and continue to attract numerous and respectable audiences.'

In the year of 1812, Dr De Lys and his friend, Alexander Blair, carried out their experiments in teaching a deaf girl named Jane Williams, how to read and write, by means of signs. After giving lectures and demonstrating the deaf girl at the Birmingham Philosophical Institution, a committee was formed to establish an institution for the deaf in that city.[20] This initiative provides the 'Avenue' for the deaf in Ireland from the condition of 'ignorance' into 'enlightenment', as will be explained in the next chapter.

Institution for the Deaf and Dumb, Birmingham, England, established in 1812, which provided the catalyst for the systematic education of the deaf to be introduced into Ireland in 1816. Two of the Principals of this Institution had previously spent some time at the Claremont Institution, Dublin – Louis du Puget and Arthur Hopper.

4

The Doctor Who loved the Deaf

'Truly, he was a good man'
E. LeFanu

Charles Edward Herbert Orpen, the youngest of three sons, was born in the city of Cork on 31 October 1791. His father, Francis, was curate of St. Peter's, Cork, and in 1792 he was promoted to the rectory of Dungourney, Co.Cork, where he resided in the vicarage presented by the Earl of Shannon, whose demesne of Castle Martyr was within four miles of the village. His second son, Sir Richard, said, in his memoirs, that his father was a brave, courageous man during the Rebellion of 1798, while at Dungourney. At the vicarage, he built a porch to the entrance-door with port-holes for musketry, and had iron bars put to the windows. Every night, the rector had laid ready for use on the table, a loaded blunderbuss and several fire-guns. On his appointment to the parish of Douglas, near Cork, he moved his family back to the city.

At the age of sixteen, Charles was so affected by the powerful preaching of Dr. Quarry, rector of St Mary's, Shandon, Cork, that he decided to give up the theatre and other amusements, which most young people would have pursued at that stage of their lives.[1] In the first decade of the nineteenth century, the Evangelical Movement had begun to make itself felt in Ireland, and Dr Quarry was one of the adherents of this movement.[2] Charles soon learned that Christianity was not a system confined to forms and restrictions, but that it was based upon the principle of love – love, gratitude and reverence for God, and active benevolence towards his fellow-men.

Even though Charles wanted to take holy orders like his father and his grandfather, his mother arranged for him to be apprenticed to a Dublin doctor. However, he chose to take his studies under Dr Gibbings in Cork. Upon completion of his apprenticeship, he applied for examinations at the Royal College of Surgeons in Dublin, but Dr Gibbings was not a licentiate of the College. Surgeon Todd kindly offered to take on Charles, and after the second apprenticeship of five years, he passed the examination. The profession had been linked with the barbers from early times and only achieved independent status in the late eighteenth century, a step symbolised by the establishment of Royal Colleges in Edinburgh in 1778, Dublin in 1784 and London in 1800. The study of basic relationships between organs and structures was acquired largely through apprenticeship attained in the late eighteenth century by six months to a year in London, Edinburgh or Dublin. It was then customary, though not mandatory, to obtain a licence from one of these colleges.

In 1812, Charles went to Edinburgh and London to finish his medical and surgical studies and in the following year he was conferred with the degree of M.D. Soon afterwards, he made a tour through the South and West of England, to examine hospitals, prisons and factories. Dr de Lys in Birmingham gave him the first report of an institution for the education of the deaf and dumb, which was recently established there. During his residence in London and Edinburgh, Dr Orpen had never heard of the existence of such establishments in those capitals. He said:

> 'so ignorant was I as to the wretched state of the deaf-mute when uneducated, and the importance and interesting nature of their instruction, that I took so little interest about them as not to visit the school in Birmingham at that time. On looking into the report, however, I found it had originated from a few lectures on the subject, and the exhibition of a little girl, whom Dr de Lys and his friend, Alexander Blair, had partially educated for the purpose. I know that no such school had ever existed in Ireland; and it occurred to me, that I might perhaps, at some future time, be able to apply the same means to this same end, for the good of my own country'.

In the year 1814, he was struck down three times by typhus fever, caught while engaged in his professional duties. During his convalescence, he prepared lectures and lessons suitable for deaf children. Enquiries were made in Dublin for a deaf child at the Foundling Hospital and at Bedford Asylum for Orphans attached to the House of Industry. Several deaf children were found at both places, and a nine-year-old boy was selected, as 'being the most neglected of all'. Dr Orpen took him home.

'At the first visit I saw in Thomas Collins timidity - the result, perhaps, of his ignorance why he was singled out from the rest of the boys at the school which he attended, but at which he had not learned anything. The second time I saw him, he was brought into the room where there were several other gentlemen present. He entered pale and downcast, but when the master, who could understand his signs, told him that he was to go away with me to my house, where he should be taught to read and write, and speak, and be well clothed, and comfortably lodged, his eyes instantly glistened with delight, his cheeks flushed, and his every gesture was gaiety and liveliness. He raised his head, and stood erect and tall, as if he then felt for the first time that he was a man, rational, and like his fellows, educable and seemed so delighted, intelligent and animated, that no person could have recognised in his enlivened air and sparkling eyes, and glowing cheeks of joy - the little, timid boy that had just before been led into the room.'

After three months, Dr Orpen succeeded in teaching Collins the pronunciation of the letters, syllables and words, and the boy by then knew a large number of nouns and adjectives, and a few verbs. Dr Orpen delivered his lectures at the Rotunda Assembly Rooms, Dublin, on his experiments of educating the deaf, supported by exhibitions where Collins demonstrated his skills in writing, mathematics and articulation. A crowded audience, who had never witnessed such an exhibition, was caught up by the enthusiasm of Dr Orpen who pleaded for those who could not speak for themselves, and most left the Rotunda with the impression that something must be done. 'See him,' were Dr Orpen's words, in referring to the desperate position of the deaf, 'see him in his own country, a wretched alien, unpitied by his compatriots - even in his own home by his family, a despised and neglected shame, eternally alone, a disfranchised exile from society.' In May 1816, subscriptions were received, a committee was formed, and a temporary plan of the school was drawn up and adopted. Eight boys were admitted, and applications for admission poured in. Dr Orpen said, 'when the Institution was established, I, of course, relinquished my little pupil to it.'

Dr Orpen taught in the school himself, in addition to his professional duties. His friend, Mr Joseph Humphreys, at his suggestion, was sent to Edinburgh to learn the system of teaching for the deaf under the guidance of Mr Kinniburgh, until he became competent to take charge of the school. During his daily visits to the school-room and looking on the group gathering around him, Dr Orpen said, 'These are the children whom the Lord hath given me.' Desirous of extending interest beyond Dublin, he went to some of the major towns in Ireland, accompanied by his two most intelligent pupils, William Brennan and Thomas Collins, and repeated his lectures with great success. He afterwards visited England with the same object.

In 1817 and 1818, Dr Orpen, accompanied by his brother, went on a tour of the Continent, travelling in France, Italy and Switzerland, with the purpose of visiting the institutions for the deaf, and making himself acquainted with the mode of instructing the deaf. His contact with the **Abbé Sicard**, *(see picture)*, successor to the Abbé de l'Epée, founder of the Institution for the Deaf and Dumb in Paris, and his pupil, Massieu, was the most interesting part of his tour. Dr Orpen had read about Sicard and Massieu, the latter having, at the age of thirteen, learnt the alphabet in two days. When visiting foreign schools, Dr Orpen's previous observations were confirmed regarding generous feelings of affection amongst the deaf. The pupils valued education and interaction with others. He often saw the pupils at Claremont gather around one newly admitted, and encourage him to dry his tears, lead him through all the rooms, garden and grounds of the Institution, show and explain to him pictures and objects, and correct his imperfect signs. While visiting the Institution for the Deaf in Bordeaux, he acquainted himself with the instructor, the Abbé Goudelin, who said to Dr Orpen about to depart, 'I look on you as a friend and though I am a Frenchman, and you an Englishman (sic), though you are a Protestant, and I am a minister of the Catholic Church, yet I cannot look upon our separation and difference, but on our union in heart and spirit. I embrace you as the friend of the objects of our common solicitude.'[3]

In Italy, Dr Orpen visited the Deaf School in Milan, under the superintendence of the Abbato Carlo de Bonis. One of the pupils gave him, before he left, a copy of the manual alphabet, engraved by himself, begging the doctor to present it, on his return to Ireland, to the Institution for the Irish pupils. During the first ten years after the Irish Institution was established, Dr Orpen maintained contact with the Institutions for the Deaf in Genoa and Milan, exchanging annual reports and pamphlets. Among the reports sent by the Institutions of these Italian cities were samples of engravings created by the pupils. Also received from the Institution in Paris was Sicard's work, *Cours d'Instruction d'un Sourd-Muet de Naissance*, which had been consulted during the early years of the Irish Institution.

In Switzerland, Dr Orpen visited the school for the children of the poor, established by the educational reformer, **Johann Heinrich Pestalozzi**, *(see picture)*, whose system had been adopted by Dr Orpen's friend, John Synge, High Sheriff of Roundwood, Co. Wicklow, for the school for children of his tenants. On Synge's recommendation, Lord de Vesci established a school on his estate in Abbeyleix, Co. Laois, with Monsieur Louis du Puget, disciple of Pestalozzi, as assistant (who later received training on instructing the deaf at Claremont and then became Principal of the Edgbaston Institution for the Deaf in Birmingham). Nature was the only book with which the deaf were familiar and Pestalozzi developed a system of intellectual and moral education suited to the observation and experience of the children. Engravings were provided, representing the objects with which the children were familiar, and the lessons consisted in naming the parts, and describing their structure and use. One day, the master presented to his class an engraving of a ladder, and a little boy exclaimed that there was a *real* ladder in the courtyard - why not talk about it rather than about the picture? When an engraving of a window was displayed, the boy again exclaimed that the window is in the school-room, and not in the courtyard. These observations were reported to Pestalozzi, who decided that the boy was right, saying, 'The reality is better than the counterfeit; put away the engravings, and let the class be instructed by means of real objects. Thus a widespread system of education had its origin in the wise remarks of a little boy.

In his article on Pestalozzi, Dr Orpen said, 'his manner being so kind and attractive, I was able to feel and speak and act, as if by long familiarity and co-operation. My heart never understood so well, until intimate with Pestalozzi. If you wish anyone to love you, said he to me one day, you must first love him; there is no way of teaching love to another, except by loving him. I now understand the mystery of Pestalozzi's immense influence over his pupils, and over all who came near him; it was nothing but his imitation of God's conduct in loving us first.'[4]

On a subsequent visit to Monsieur Naef, master of the Deaf-Mute Institution at Yverdun, in the Pays-de-Vaud, Dr Orpen learned that it was possible to guide the deaf into the knowledge of God, and into comprehension of the truth of salvation and of a future life. Dr Orpen's observations while visiting the Continental deaf schools and study of Pestalozzi's system were put into practice. He wrote several articles detailing his observations, which were published in 1828 in a book entitled, *The Contrast between Atheism, Paganism and Christianity, illustrated, or the Uneducated Deaf and Dumb, as Heathens, compared with those who have been Instructed in Language and Revelation and taught by the Holy Spirit as Christian.* This edition, consisting of 1,000 copies, was published at Dr Orpen's expense; and on finding that when between 500 and 600 copies were either sold or given away, the receipts were sufficient to cover all expenses. The remaining copies were dispersed all over the world in order to draw attention to the condition of the deaf. He sent them, through the various Missionary Societies of Great Britain, the United States and the Netherlands, to their missionary stations throughout the world. Another edition was produced in 1836 under the title, *Anecdotes and Annals of the Deaf and Dumb,* which contained illustrations of the engravings by a deaf pupil, John Johnson.

Returning from his travels in 1818, Dr Orpen commenced his medical practice and later on, he was appointed Medical Inspector by the Lord Lieutenant in consequence of the fierce spread of typhus fever, which prevailed at the time throughout Ireland and in many other parts of Europe. His duty was to visit the poor of the city of Dublin, in a wide district stretching from north to south. Duties included daily medical and surgical visits to the poor in their own houses at all hours and in every kind of weather. The years 1818 and 1819 meant labour, constant danger and repeated illness. Not only the patients suffered, but also the medical attendants. His observations were recorded in the pamphlet entitled *Address to the Public on the State of the Poor of Dublin.*[5]

'I have,' Dr Orpen said, 'visited several thousand houses in which not less than forty or fifty people live, sometimes twelve individuals occupying one room. Numbers also lived at the rear of the houses usually occupied by stables. The entrance was usually by a ladder outside. I stepped into a small room less than twelve feet square, in which seven, eight or nine persons, lay scattered on different parts of the floor, without bedding or furniture, all dressed in rags and all ill of fever. I had to step over several of them who could scarcely move, before I could reach the others to feel their pulses. Every article of furniture and of clothing, even the father's tools of trade, had gone to the pawnbroker's. In the end I was laid up with typhus fever for twenty-one days; I still feel the effects. I could tell the names of a dozen young medical men who had died from similar causes, and of others disabled for life.'

'Not only disease was due to overcrowded and unhealthy dwellings, but from the darkness of the staircases, accidents continually occur to the aged, the infant and the drunken. The window and the hearth tax excluded all ventilation, as the landlords avoided taxation by blocking up the fireplaces and windows. Lack of change of clothes prevented any ventilation of clothes or of skin. No whitewashing or scouring could prevent infection while the purifying of their clothes and cleansing of their skins was neglected. I could fill your whole paper, several days in succession, with details of the excessive misery of the poor in Dublin. I have frequently found poor people lying in cellars, without any bed or bedding, except an old hamper torn down at the sides with a little decayed straw in it, in which the individuals lay crumpled up, with their knees bent up to their chins like those of a dog on a frosty night. I have often found persons near death, in a wretched room, totally alone, sometimes with no clothing but a piece of baize. It has happened hundreds of times, when ordering some medicine from the dispensary, where the bottom of an earthen jar or old crock was used as kettle, saucepan or drinking-vessel. The poor could not afford to purchase milk to make whey for taking medicine with; occasionally the doctors had to buy milk for their patients. None but medical men know the real state of the poor.'

Signature of Dr C. Orpen, when he was Secretary to the Institution

In the year of 1831, in a letter to the Lord Lieutenant,[6] Dr Orpen, in his role of Surgeon and Physician to the Richmond Penitentiary (part of the House of Industry), put forward his suggestions of provision of clean water to serve that Institution which was to be converted into a Cholera Hospital. He said that the water, obtained from the Canal harbour, was stagnant and full of the filth of turf boats and their crews, and, therefore, exceedingly bad and, in the summer months, unfit for drinking, so bad that the convicts and patients refused to use it, and the officers of the House were obliged to get it filtered. He petitioned for the formation of large temporary filtering machines, by means of hogsheads (barrels) filled with sand and charcoal, sufficient for the supply of drinking water to the establishment, about which he had unsuccessfully tried to draw the attention of the Inspectors of Prisons.

As well as engaging in medicine, Dr Orpen spent some time in analysing the Irish Bible, having subscribed to the Hibernian Bible Society. He highlighted the flaws in the Irish Bible, in the form of a letter entitled *Errors of the Irish Bible* to the Editor of the *Christian Examiner* in 1830. He had referred, for comparison purposes, to several Irish dictionaries in the Library of Trinity College Dublin and in Marsh's Library. In short, he favoured the usage of the English translation of the Bible for introducing and searching the Scriptures. In addition to his literary discussions and debates, he lent his support to the anti-slavery campaign established in England by Mr Wilberforce.

On 10 December 1823, Dr Orpen married Alicia Frances, widow of the Rev. Cowan who died a few months after his marriage. She made a most amiable and affectionate companion, with whom he enjoyed many years of domestic happiness. She bore him seven sons and, in 1833, a daughter, Susannah, was born, bringing joy to the family. Sadly, she died at the age of four from scarlatina, and was buried with her father's mother, Mrs Susanna Orpen, in St George's Cemetery, Whitworth Road, Dublin. In 1838, a daughter, Alicia, was born and she was adored by her parents and her brothers.

Despite his successful medical practice and numerous engagements in Dublin upon his time, Dr Orpen continued to maintain links with his family and friends in Cork, as evinced in his letters to his friend, Humphreys. He said, 'I still feel the want of my friends in Cork to make me happy, though I know that the God of all comfort is as much present here as there.' He felt that a great deal of our happiness depends on our being with those we love. 'When deprived of them, or absent from them, we feel unhappy'. In 1815, when he was struck by fever, he was recuperating when he received news that his beloved sister, Cornelia, died from consumption at the age of twenty-two years. His grief at not having been with her for a last farewell was profound, as noticed by his friend. 'Dear Humphreys,' he said, 'our house is now desolate indeed'.

In 1840, Dr Orpen, having disapproved of the educational system generally used for boys where it focussed on academic training, decided to give up his practice in medicine and move his family to England, to set up a school in Birkenhead and send his sons to the Pestalozzian School in Worksop, Nottinghamshire.[7] The Committee of the Institution presented him with a parting gift, a copy of Bagster's Polygot Bible, containing on each page the sacred text in eight languages. He had collected for the Institution between 50,000 and 60,000 pounds, and also expended hundreds of pounds out of his own pocket. About fifteen hundred poor deaf children had already been educated, and had gone to their homes, well instructed in reading, writing and works of different kinds, to be a help instead of a burden to their families, and enlightened by Scriptural knowledge. If the time, exertion and money, which he had voluntarily bestowed on the Institution for the Deaf and Dumb, had been turned to his own advantage, he might have amassed a considerable fortune in his profession. Among the tributes afforded to him was one from one of the first physicians in Dublin (unnamed), 'Dr Charles Orpen was universally esteemed and respected as a warmhearted Christian philanthropist.' Sir Richard Orpen, in his letter to a friend, said of his brother Charles, 'he was the most nobly generous fellow.' [8]

Crest of the Orpen Family
at Ardtully Castle, Co. Kerry
(author's photograph)

FAMILY TREE
OF THE ORPEN FAMILY

Richard Orpen married Isabella Palmer - had issue including the eldest son who was:

Thomas Orpen, born in 1696 in Killowen, Co. Kerry, died in 1767,
- married Agnes Herbert in 1722; was rector of Kenmare, Co. Kerry
- Had issue of 13 children - the youngest being:

Francis Orpen, born 1747, married Susannah Millerd in 1780, died in 1805
Curate of St. Peter's, Cork; rector of Dungourney, Co. Cork in 1792,
and of Douglas, near Cork.

- Had issue as follows:
(1) Arthur George Orpen
(2) Richard John Theodore Orpen (1788-1876) *
(3) **Charles Edward Herbert Orpen (1791-1856)**
(4) Susannah Maria Frances Orpen
(5) Emilia Grace Caroline Orpen
(6) Rebecca Newenham Millerd Orpen
(7) Cornelia Orpen

* Sir Richard J. T. Orpen married Elizabeth Stack in 1819
  - Had issue of six sons and five daughters, including:

  Arthur Herbert Orpen married Anne Caulfield in 1861
  - Had issue of four sons and one daughter, including:

  Major Sir William Newenham Montague Orpen, R.A.
  - who had gained great distinction as an artist, having had an official position as artist during the Great War (1914-1918), and had painted portraits of military commanders and statesmen.

Sources: *The Landed Gentry*
Burke's Peerage
The Orpen Family - Goddard H.Orpen (1930)
Chart of the Orpen Family Tree - Michael Orpen, Cape Town (2004)

Major Henry Charles Sirr

Alicia, Dr Orpen's wife, *(see picture below)* was daughter of Major Henry Charles Sirr, *(see picture)*, the Town Major of the City of Dublin.[9] He gained notoriety for arresting and wounding Lord Edward Fitzgerald during the 1798 Rebellion. His efforts to suppress evil literature, promote temperance, foster the Irish language, and alleviate distress by helping to found the Mendicity Institute, led to a change in public opinion towards him. He was a sheriff's peer in Dublin Corporation, Governor of the Claremont Institution for the Deaf and Dumb, the Royal Hibernian Military School and the Royal Irish Institute for Promoting Fine Arts of Ireland. He used to reside in Cullenswood, Ranelagh, having retired from Town Major in 1826, but was permitted to retain his apartments in Dublin Castle.

He had been a most efficient chief of police for 28 years and was notorious for his methods he employed. He had arrested all the heroic leaders of the United Irishmen between 1787 and 1803, including Lord Edward Fitzgerald, who was arrested on 25 August 1803. This was not the result of his own zeal or initiative, but by direct orders of his superiors, either Chief Secretary or the Under-Secretary, acting on information given by the officers.

He was interested in the Irish language and the antiquities of the country, he was taught by Major General Vallancey who came to Ireland in the mid eighteenth century, as a British officer of engineers. While on military surveys, Vallancey met so many Irish speakers that he devoted much of his time to the study of the Irish language, early history and antiquities. Between 1791 and 1826, Sirr contacted in Dublin many bi-linguists. His wife, from an Anglo-Irish family, acquired the Irish language from the local peasantry in Co. Westmeath. It was well known to Dubliners detained in the Castle in 1803 that some of the Major's men spoke to one another in Irish.

An eminent banker and philanthropist, James Digges La Touche, not only spoke Irish but afterwards taught it to his own children. The Major was co-founder of the Irish Society for Promoting Scriptural Education in the Irish Language. After his retirement, he collected ancient Irish gold ornaments and artefacts, acquired after his death by the Royal Irish Academy and now in the National Museum of Ireland (400 objects). Ironic and contradictory about Sirr, he was responsible for the martyrdom of Irishmen during the years of 1798 to 1803 and yet he collected mementos of ancient Ireland. He could be condemned for his activities as a Government official but yet praised for his work as a connoisseur of early Irish art.

He died on 8 January 1841 in Dublin Castle from a heavy cold, and was buried in St Werburgh's Church, almost opposite Christ Church Cathedral, Dublin.

Richard John Theodore Orpen

Richard was Charles' brother and in 1817 he accompanied him on the Grand Tour of the Continent. As mentioned in Mr Humphreys' letter to Mary Leadbeater, Richard was 'disappointed with the remains of antiquity, and disgusted with the superstition of the people and tired of looking at pictures, and anxious to get home. He always anticipates too much, he was disappointed on his first visit to Killarney.' Mr Humphreys later wrote, 'Richard's (letters) are much more lively and furnish a greater display of the character and manners of the people than Charles. Richard is not so religious as Charles; Charles is not so good an observer nor so philosophical as Richard.' Like his brother, Richard took special interest in Thomas Collins and gave him a present of a pocket-watch and wrote a poem for the boy to recite at the public meetings to demonstrate his progress in articulation.

Richard was made Life Member of the National Institution for Education of the Deaf in Ireland, and he, as a barrister, had a large and prospering practice upon which he had to expend his energies. In 1860, he was elected President of the Incorporated Law Society of Ireland, and in 1869 he was knighted. He married Elizabeth Stack in 1819 and made his home in Dublin.[10] From 1849 onwards, after purchasing Ardtully Castle, near Kilgarvan, Co. Kerry, the family spent long periods in Kerry. Several of his sons followed him into the legal profession, one of whom, Arthur Herbert, was father of the celebrated painter, Sir William Orpen, who spent some time at Ardtully. Sir Richard Orpen died in 1876, and was buried in Mount Jerome Cemetery, Dublin. Ardtully Castle had fallen into decay, but the Orpen crest can be still seen on one of the turrets.

Ardtully Castle, near Kilgarvan, Co. Kerry - the home of Sir Richard J.T. Orpen
(Author's photograph)

Pascoe French - Dr Orpen's deaf cousin

According to a letter[11] from Joseph Millerd Orpen to a newspaper in South Africa, his father, Dr Orpen, had educated his own first cousin, Pascoe French, who had 'good means but was born deaf and dumb.' He became a great sailor and senior member of the Royal Yacht Club of Cork, where he and Dr Orpen were born.

Pascoe French was mentioned in a magazine produced for the deaf community in the United States[12] as follows: 'The funeral of Mr Pascoe French, the well known deaf and dumb yachtsman, who died at his residence, Marino, Queenstown,[13] on Sunday morning, 24 September 1893, took place on 26 September, when he was interred in the Old Churchyard, Queenstown. The deceased gentleman was the senior member of the Royal Cork Yacht Club, which he joined in 1834, and since then he has had a most successful career in the yachting world, having won more than most yachting men for the last half century.'

5

The Clergyman Who served his People

"I believe all the (people in South Africa) are equal in God's sight'
- Rev. Charles Orpen

During his stay at Birkenhead, Dr Charles Orpen's plan of a school for boys did not succeed. The task of overseeing a number of unruly boys turned out to be more difficult than anticipated, so he abandoned the project, and resumed his medical practice with considerable success. Dr Charles Orpen's fourth son, Joseph Millerd,[1] commented that his father, having moved the family of seven sons and one daughter to Birkenhead, had inaugurated several charitable works, such as the Lying-in Hospital in Birkenhead. Joseph was to have studied medicine, but found the prospects of sheep farming and life in South Africa so tempting that he decided to emigrate, taking two of his brothers with him. Two of his elder brothers, Frank and Charles, had already gone there before him, attracted by the reports of a cousin, William Dixon, farming in the Northern Cape.

They bought a farm in the Colesberg district, since land and stock were cheap. Dr Orpen intended to set them up in farming, as he had independent means from property in Ireland. There were many openings for enterprising young men in South Africa, since the professions, medicine and law, were overstocked in Ireland and England.

Colesberg *painted by Thomas Baines in 1850*

Early in 1848, Dr Orpen, who was then 57 years of age, decided that he would emigrate to South Africa with his wife and the remaining children, to join his sons. As his early desire for entering the Church had not departed from him, he decided to follow in his father's and grandfather's footsteps, to become a clergyman and not to practise his profession of medicine for gain. Bishop Sumner, afterwards Archbishop of Canterbury, and some other Bishops introduced him to Dr Gray, who was then in England and had been consecrated Bishop of Cape Town. Impressed with the references from the Bishop of Cashel, the Very Rev. Daly, and other distinguished friends of Dr Orpen, the Bishop decided to receive him as a candidate for ordination, as he was well qualified by university education and was familiar with Hebrew, Greek and Latin, which he used for conversation with Italian priests while on the tour of hospitals and of schools for the deaf.

On 12 January 1848, the Orpen family started their voyage to the Cape of Good Hope. He had arranged for packing and delivery of some of the furniture and his large collection of books (which was later donated as part of the establishment of a public library in Colesberg). On 11 March, Dr Orpen and his family reached Cape Town. Sir Harry Smith, the Governor of the Cape, received him well, in consequence of Lady Combermere's letter of introduction. This lady was the daughter of Dr Orpen's first tutor in Cork, Dr Gibbings. On 26 April 1848, they reached Port Elizabeth, and in July 1848 the family arrived at their destination – Colesberg.

Christ Church, Colesberg, of which Rev. C.Orpen was the first rector
(Author's photograph)

The population of the parish numbering around 15,000 comprised mostly ethnic groups: English, Scot, German, Dutch Afrikaaneers and Hottentots. The number of males in that area considerably exceeded that of females. No minister of the Church of England had ever resided in or probably visited this wild district, before Dr Orpen's arrival. The village contained around 500 inhabitants. The country was mountainous with the roads incessantly winding up and down. There could not be a single house or wagon after hours of travelling, which was dangerous at night, owing to the wild animals prowling about. The summers were very hot, and the winters, when it rained, very cold. Dr Orpen described his house as 'a thatched house, without a single ceiling, and the floors only beaten earth. Yet for such a house, without any garden or out-offices, no presses, fireplaces or conveniences, I pay as much as I did for a very handsome house in a very handsome square, or for an excellent house in an excellent street, in which I lived, either in Birkenhead or in Dublin. In torrential rain, all the bedrooms filled with a flood of rainwater in about five minutes, which roused us out of bed, and it was five weeks before the mud floors were dry again. But by God's mercy and blessings, neither my wife, children, nor myself, suffered any illness, though some of us were obliged to walk about and work in the water to remove it.'

After his arrival at Colesberg, he preached twice on Sundays in the court-house, since there was no English church there, only a large Dutch Reformed church, a small Methodist church and a new chapel for the Kaffirs, Hottentots and Zulus, established by the London Missionary Society. On 12 November 1848, Dr Orpen was ordained by the Bishop, Dr Gray. At the public meeting in the court-house, the Bishop recommended that a collection be made for a church, and another for a stipend for the Rev. Orpen, who later on set up a system for the relief of the sick and poor, the opening of the public library, as well as taking an interest in the schools.

Hot-ten-tot.

In one of his letters to Ireland, Dr Orpen revealed his partiality to the deaf, 'I wish we had two deaf and dumb servants, they would be invaluable here, as it is almost impossible to get servants in the town; there were only about five white servants; the people are all too independent to be servants. They live very cheaply, as beef and mutton are only a penny or more a pound. Also shops and all clothing, tea, coffee and sugar are cheaper than in England. The Chief Constable has a deaf and dumb Kaffirman whom he caught in the woods in the last war but one. He has had him ever since and he is an excellent servant, sober, honest and faithful. Many of the Kaffirmen and women are fine-looking people, and very few drink. I believe all the Kaffirs are originally Arabs (Ishmaelites); the Hottentots are, I believe, a degraded colony of Chinese, who settled in this colony a thousand years ago. This is my theory. There are not more than ten or twelve Roman Catholics here, all Irish discharged soldiers.'[2]

Kaf-fir.

At the end of 1850, he received a letter from Ireland regarding the death of his first and favourite pupil, Thomas Collins, at the age of 45 years. His reply was, 'Poor Collins! I expected from my brother's letter that he would not recover. Pupil first, master afterwards!'

In the Cape Colony, which occupied three or four times the extent of Britain, there was no hospital except one at Cape Town – 800 miles away from Colesberg. In all the country towns and villages there were very few midwives, which accounted for the high number of women and infants who died in childbirth. The death of wives was so frequent that it was common for farmers to marry three or four times. 'I met one,' said Dr Orpen, 'who was married to his sixth wife by the Roman Dutch law. If either husbands or wives are the survivors, they are entitled to half of each other's property.' Dr Orpen's medical skill was much appreciated, and his services were sought from great distances. 'One day,' he wrote, 'I rode about 75 miles between 10 o'clock in the morning and twelve o'clock at night, to see a man who had accidentally shot himself in the arm and shoulder. In my younger days, when in Italy, I rode about the same distance in one day, with fresh horses every ten miles, but now in this country, with a broiling sun and no inns, I had only one horse for the whole ride, and no roads at all, except for tracks across the while country'.

After falling ill, Dr Orpen felt that moving from excessive heat of summer and cold of winter in Colesberg to Port Elizabeth, being close to the sea, might be beneficial. On 5 April 1855, Dr Orpen, his wife and daughter, and his son, Richard, left Colesberg, travelling by two ox-wagons, with two teams of oxen, fourteen in each. On 14 April, they arrived at Graaf Reinet and Dr Orpen was too ill to proceed. High prices of hiring a wagon, the cost being £52, delayed travel plans for another twelve days. Then they continued their journey, and after nine days, the Orpen family arrived at Port Elizabeth.[3]

Dr Orpen said in his letter, 'I was so weak when I got into the wagon that I could scarcely walk. There is nothing so medicinal as living, sleeping and travelling all day by ox-wagon without springs.' As soon as he came into the damp atmosphere near the sea, he felt quite better. Lack of vegetables, which had been part of his diet before he moved to Africa, he assumed, had been injurious to his health. On arrival at Port

Elizabeth, he was seen by a doctor, who diagnosed excessive physical and emotional fatigue, since he had been anxious about his financial matters, resulting from his failing health which compelled him to leave Colesberg with the resultant decline in his income, as he had to give up the salary of his chaplaincy to his replacement. He then decided that he would return to Ireland; this was welcomed with joy by his Irish friends and relatives. In his final letter, he reflected upon what he had done, and what he should have had done. He turned to the unfailing source of his comfort: 'However, God has pardoned my sins, I trust, for Christ's sake.' His final words were, 'God bless Dr Gordon (who married Dr Orpen's sister), and yourself, Richard and Emmanuel, and all at George's Street and Ardtully, and all friends, and remember us all to whoever kindly enquires about us.'

A letter from Dr Orpen's son, Henry, brought the sad news to Ireland. It announced the death of his father, which took place on 20 April 1856. He was buried in St Mary's Anglican Cemetery, Baakens River, Port Elizabeth, and his grave was marked with an impressive obelisk, with an inscription outlining his achievements as 'Philanthropic founder of the National Deaf & Dumb Institution of Ireland at Glasnevin, Dublin, of the Infirmary in Birkenhead, Cheshire, and Promoter of other charities and First Minister of Christ Church, Colesberg in this Colony. He was a faithful servant of Christ, and a loving husband and father. Precious in the sight of the Lord is the death of his Saints.'

As for Ireland acknowledging Dr Charles Orpen's contribution, in his own words, 'for the good of my own country', there is 'no marble to perpetuate his name, no inscription to record his Christian virtues; this Institution (namely the Claremont Institution) forms the noblest tablet to his memory.'[4] Nevertheless, the author of this book strongly feels that Dr Charles Orpen, who had made it possible for the deaf in Ireland to receive intellectual and religious education - the key to their physical and spiritual welfare, deserves some lasting memorial. Therefore, this book meets this need.

Inscription on the monument at Dr Orpen's burial-place at St Mary's Cemetery,
Baaekens River, Port Elizabeth, South Africa
(Author's photographs)

The brief extracts from the letters of his own children exhibit the unselfish character of the good man more than anything that could be said by others. He hardly ever thought of himself; it was hard to get him to think of himself. In the midst of intense suffering, he took refuge in prayer. He remembered every one of his loved ones in prayer. 'Truly, he was a good man.' If there were failings in this good man, which in any degree impaired his usefulness, and for a time prejudiced some against him, they are to be attributed to slight eccentricities and a defect in judgement.[5]

At the annual meeting in May 1856, it was stated that 'it was Dr Orpen who first aroused the public mind in this country to the necessity for providing instruction for the afflicted deaf-mutes. Through trials, dangers, and difficulties did he persevere in the good work until he achieved the establishment, early in the present century, of this 'Association for Promoting the Education of the Deaf and Dumb Poor of Ireland'. Through the munificence of the public, whom he deeply interested in his benevolent object, he was enabled to purchase this handsome place, where we are now assembled, and opened in June 1816, this National Institution for the accommodation of 120 deaf and dumb children. Amid the cares of a laborious profession, and the claims of an extensive practice, it continued to be his delight and duty to foster the infant establishment, enlarge the area of its operations, and ensure its permanence. Few were aware of what he attempted, and of all he achieved; few knew how patient and persevering were his exertions, how untiring and energetic his efforts as a truly Christian philanthropist.'

Rev. C. Orpen's seven sons in South Africa

1. Francis Henry Samuel
2. Charles Sirr
3. Arthur Richard
4. Joseph Millerd
5. Richard John Newenham
6. Henry Martyn Herbert
7. Theodore Robert Morrison

Their sister, Alicia, had also emigrated with them. She married John Murray of Grahamstown. Her mother, Alicia Frances Orpen, died on 4 December 1869, and was buried in the Church of England Cemetery, Grahamstown.

6

The Quaker who taught the Deaf

'He liked to converse with the Deaf and Dumb'
- David Holmes, a pupil

Joseph Humphreys, son of Joshua and Patience, nee Dobbs, was born in Cork on 3 December 1787. Historical accounts on the Religious Society of Friends referred to some Quakers receiving formal education at Newtown School, Waterford, while others were sent to a school in Ballitore, Co. Kildare, managed by Abraham Shackleton, whose grand-daughter, Mary Leadbeater, is Joseph Humphreys' aunt and author of *The Annals of Ballitore*, which referred to the deaf female twins, the Murphys, one of whom supported herself and the family through baking bread for sale at Ferns, Co. Wexford. As the charming village of Ballitore was on the route from Dublin to Cork, Mr Humphreys and Dr Charles Orpen often stopped there to visit the 'Friends'.

Joseph Humphreys and Charles Orpen, as young boys, met at a grocer's shop in the main street of Cork where the owner was interested in minerals, coins and fossils. The boys had discussions on their collections, and afterwards, young Humphreys invited his new friend home to look at his coins. When hearing of Dr Orpen's death in South Africa in 1856, the impression of that first meeting was still fresh on Humphreys' mind, 'Charles Orpen's face was one of the most beautiful I ever saw.' He could not speak of him without emotion and he treasured the following letter from Dr Orpen in which his appointment as headmaster to the Claremont Institution was announced.

'Claremont is taken – it is a noble place that I must say. You will have one of the most elegant places around Dublin – and it has the finest view. I am preparing a triumphant report. I rejoice in the prospect both for you and for the deaf & dumb. Dearest Joseph, what a noble task is yours, and how blessed, yet how awful! God grant you His grace ever! Everyone is delighted with Claremont. We take possession in a few days. An auction will be of the furniture, garden tools, &c. We intend to purchase some things for you; but much will remain to be done when you arrive. So hasten, but do not hurry. Receive my best love and friendship, my chiefest and earliest friend, Charles.'[1]

Mary Leadbeater wrote, 'Joseph Humphreys introduced to us his friend, Dr Charles Edward Herbert Orpen, a native of Cork, whose indefatigable labours have established in Dublin a school for the deaf and dumb, to whose instruction he devotes himself. He is a well-looking young man, engaging in countenance and modest in manners, concealing rather than exhibiting the strength of his understanding and the play of his wit.'

Statue of Mary Leadbeater at Ballitore, Co. Kildare
(Author's photograph)

During 1817, in his letters to some of the Friends[2] in Ballitore, Humphreys wrote:

14 May 1817

'I have heard that my three Friends got home safe, I want to know whether Sarah was annoyed by a certain man, to whom she was polite (by mistake) in the boat, and I also want to know, if Lydia will be likely to see Dublin before the 27th of this month.   On that date is to be the General Meeting of the Deaf & Dumb. North, one of the first orators, will speak, and I expect many other speeches. The exhibition of paintings is near opening and will close early; the General Meeting of the Society for Promoting Education of the Poor in Ireland will take place. The Deaf & Dumb School is removed to a house[3] near the House of Industry and the Governors of the House of Industry have lent them beds and bedsteads and sent the boys them, and will clothe them. Victuals - they are not, therefore, put to the expense of buying bed-linen and will not want much except coarse towelling.'

'I went this morning with Orpen to visit them and his talk was chiefly about you (*Mary Leadbeater)* and tell Sarah she is a favourite of his, but lest she might be too proud of this; he likes Deborah better. I hope in my next letter to send copies of an address written by a member of the D&D Committee.'

28 May 1817

'I hasten to give thee the earliest intelligence which circumstances would permit, of the meeting of the Deaf & Dumb Society - knowing that thou art interested in it - and being also fully aware of the very strong interest which is felt for its welfare by others of my dear friends in Ballitore.'

'We had, then, a very full and highly respectable Meeting; there were not fewer than a thousand persons present, and altho' we were disappointed that neither Phillips nor North were present, they being under the necessity of attending at the Courts; the Meeting went off very well. First, Dr Gordon read the report in the proper emphasis and good discretion. Next, Counsellor O'Donnell made a speech, which, in some of its parts, was extremely beautiful. I cannot recollect the order of the speakers but we had a short speech from Richard Orpen (the Doctor's brother), from each of the two Singers (Paulus Emiticus and Joseph), from Sankey (the writer of the appeal), and from James Digges La Touche. After speeches and thundered applause, then followed the Doctor (Orpen), but he had not proceeded far, before he found himself unable to proceed - until repeated clapping and cheering had allowed him time to recover a little and altho' his voice is so defective in strength, yet in the most crowded theatre heard such applause and indeed I think then deserved. Nevertheless, I could have wished that he had spared himself what I know is to him a great exertion, speaking in public.'

'I believe I have now told them as much as I can, at least as much as I can recollect of this meeting. Mary Shackleton was there and was much pleased. Some of the pupils were exhibited but we did not stay for that part of the Business; there is more satisfaction in being there at the School.

My dear love to thee all and especially to thyself,

from your friend, J. Humphreys'

In November 1815, Humphreys was in London when he applied to the Committee of the Society for Promoting the Education of the Poor of Ireland, known as the Kildare Place Society, based at 6 Dawson Street. He said, 'I am by birth and education an Irish man, bred up to regular habits of mercantile business and at present employed as Book-keeper in a respectable and well-known House here, but this business neither suits my wishes and my health, and I should prefer a place where I could be more generally useful. I beg to refer you to Richard John Orpen, my particular friend.' In May 1816, he was offered the position of Under-Secretary to the Society.[4]

In his letters Humphreys referred to Charles and Richard Orpen undertaking the Grand Tour in France and Italy, and to Dr Orpen's visits to the Deaf schools in France, Italy and Switzerland, the latter where Dr Orpen spent three months in Yverdun, 'copying several tracts of Pestalozzi's, of whom he gives a very high character'. In 1818, he wrote, 'Dr Orpen arrived with sermon; he could not stop at Ballitore (after leaving Cork).' He expressed his concern about the state of funds and probable expenses for the new establishment before considering acceptance of the situation as Superintendent of the Deaf school. He mentioned about two gentlemen visiting the Deaf School (in Brunswick Street) who were impatient for the immediate opening of the 'Establishment for the Deaf of the Rich.'

In October 1818, based upon Dr Charles Orpen's recommendation, Humphreys was offered and accepted the position of Superintendent of the Deaf and Dumb School on the same conditions as Mr Kinniburgh, principal of the Edinburgh Deaf and Dumb Institution, viz. annual salary of £100, to be provided with a house capable of receiving rich pupils, and be allowed £18 for the maintenance and education of each poor pupil, with the parents and friends of the poor pupils to clothe them. On 1 February 1819, Humphreys set out for Edinburgh to receive training from Kinniburgh at the cost of £150 to be paid by the Committee. Kinniburgh had already completed his apprenticeship under Braidwood, founder of the Academy for the Deaf in Edinburgh, and was, therefore, in a position to train others. During his time residing with the Kinniburgh family, Humphreys struck up a close relationship with some of the assistant teachers and pupils.

Qua-ker.

Alexander Atkinson, former pupil, wrote of Humphreys, 'he was in the full gait of his sect (Quakers), a dark brown coat, a pair of light drab breeches, a pair of clean whitish-grey stockings, and a pair of bright calf shoes - smartly fitted to a good-sized person. He held in his hand a new broad-brimmed hat. We learnt that he was from Cork, where his father was a respectable tradesman. His name was Joseph Humphreys, and he showed tastes and accomplishments both literary and scientific. He showed a new copy of *The Vicar of Wakefield* and had also a great skill in drawing, many humorous specimens of which he made on our slates. Mr Rattray was then about to leave us and Mr Humphreys made a punning satire which he shaped on a slate, into a figure of a 'rat' sitting in the middle of a 'tray'.

Edinburgh Institution for the Deaf and Dumb
Where Mr Humphreys obtained his training in the education of the deaf in 1819

'As fresh as the mountain air which he had just left, he talked about the incidents of his tour and criticised his collections of minerals and pebbles, as long as the usual Scotch dessert of whiskey toddy and nuts remained on the dinner table. Mr Humphreys continued to practise the system of teaching in every class. He received much assistance from Turner (deaf assistant teacher) whose quickness of mind and expression he often admired than the headmaster (Kinniburgh). He was not in haste to return to Dublin upon completion of his training, for he decided to tour the Highlands, and return home by the long east coast route from Aberdeen. He gave us a lively account of his journey, having managed to master our sign dialect and trying to amuse us. He lingered on, and he departed from Edinburgh, to our great regret, for London where he attended the annual gathering of the members of the Society of Friends from all parts of Great Britain and Ireland who, no doubt, hailed him as the first teacher of the Deaf and Dumb in our Sister Island (Ireland).'[5]

The Committee in Ireland paid the first instalment of training fees to Mr Kinniburgh and £30 to Humphreys to cover his expenses while in Scotland and England. In April 1819, he visited the deaf schools at Glasgow, Dundee and Aberdeen, and then London and Birmingham. On 28 May, the Committee received word from Mr Kinniburgh that Mr Humphreys had completed his training, and in the following month, Humphreys took charge of the Institution at Claremont, making the distinction of being the first superintendent of Ireland's first school for the deaf, and the fourth school for the deaf in the British Isles, namely Edinburgh, London and Birmingham. On 20 August, he married Mary Chandlee, a Quaker, and they had nine children. At least four of their children, listed under 'Life Members' in an Annual Report of 1839, had assisted in raising funds for the Institution.

At the start of his appointment, he had 16 pupils under his charge. The Committee had the onerous task of raising funds to pay the salaries of Humphreys and his assistants, as well as maintaining the large premises and lands, and feeding and clothing the increasing number of pupils. They organised the charity sermons, as well as collecting subscriptions and sending deputations to towns in Ireland and England. To this effect, Humphreys travelled all over the country, taking with him two of his best pupils to demonstrate the methods of educating the deaf. In 1822, he travelled to Liverpool, Manchester, Huddersfield, Bristol and Leeds. As well as collecting money for the Building Fund, these visits formed a catalyst for the formation of similar institutions for the Deaf in some of the above-mentioned towns. In September 1824, he wrote to a Friend in Ballitore:

'I am preparing for another journey to the Great City (London) and I can scarcely describe the feeling with which I look forward to this visit nor why I have them – I am going to seek for money for our Institution, not by public lecture – but private applications, as I suppose I shall be there for three weeks or a month.'

In 1828, he visited the institutions for the deaf in France and Switzerland, accompanied by Monsieur Louis du Puget, headmaster of the Birmingham Institution for the Deaf. Philip Geary, a pupil and then assistant teacher in Claremont, wrote of Humphreys, 'My master taught boys about France and Switzerland by his signs. He saw parts of France, which were very beautiful. I like to see my master telling us by his signs.' Humphreys' talents include drawing, Latin, French and German, which were advantageous for translating books covering the systems of instruction of the deaf adopted in France and Germany. His sketching skills were depicted in two works: the picture of Claremont used as frontispiece for Dr Orpen's book, *The Contrast*, and the 'Claremont Windows', engraved by a former pupil, John Johnson. The latter depicted the two manual alphabets: the English two-handed and the Spanish one-handed. During his management of Claremont, Humphreys had five deaf assistants under his charge - Thomas Collins, Philip Geary, Anne McCormick, Charlotte Riddall and Cecilia White. Humphreys continued his boyhood interest in mineralogy which was referred in a pupil's letter as 'bad stones and good stones and shells.' He exchanged his findings with some of his friends, including T. Crofton Croker, the most respected antiquarian, who took special interest in tobacco pipes, including three, which having been discovered at Claremont were contributed to his collection by his 'worthy friend, Mr Joseph Humphreys.'[6]

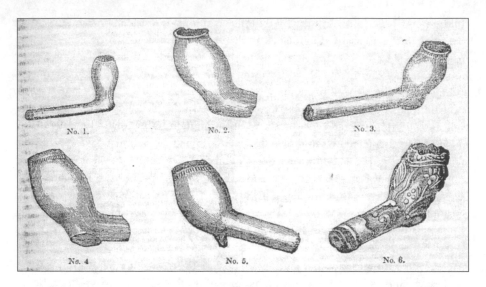

Collection of Tobacco Pipes by Crofton Croker, antiquarian and friend of Humphreys

In January 1820, he wrote to his aunt, 'Between frost and snow, we are weather-bound at Claremont. I was employed with the boys in making a huge Snowman who sits all pale and white in great state in our largest yard. Our dog was very noisy at him and the boys were highly delighted. Most of them are very fine lads, some of them as big as myself; we have also four girls.' Later on, he wrote, 'We have been living for the last few days in the world of spirits with my pupil Brennan, who has had a most extraordinary dream of the creation of the world and of the spiritual dwellings of heaven and hell, of the occupation of angels, and the power of the Supreme. I will continue through the parts of this Dream which I have endeavoured to obtain him in as connected a manner as I could.'[7] In his letter to a Friend, Mr Humphreys revealed problems regarding a Quaker employed at the Institution, 'Some in Ballitore blame me for E. Gough's leaving Claremont but I do not wish to enter into any indication of myself. She knows herself how and why she left this. My little ones are very stout. I think Maria's present admiration is the 'sounding gale' which prevails very much here. Nightly storms are dreadful. Alas for our fine elms; bid fair to lay some of their heads in the dust and we have already lost many of them.'

In the late 1830s, the task of managing Claremont became onerous, owing to the increasing number of deaf pupils, reaching 80, and this had affected Humphrey's health. Furthermore, this had been exacerbated by financial difficulties, with the Committee owing him over £300. This compelled him to borrow money from his Friends to buy food and clothes for the pupils and keep the school and demesne in reasonable repair. At one time, the boys had been ordered by Humphreys to clean the ponds in front of the school for provision of water for over 100 people, as it was too expensive to send out a horse and cart to the nearest river to draw the water.

In March 1833, Mr Humphreys wrote to the Committee, addressing their concern about his absences from Claremont:

> 'on the third day every week, I attend the Friends' meetings, which is over so as to allow me to be at home at half past twelve. As this is composition day, there is little need for me in the school, until the boys have written their letters and are ready for examination. One day each month, after the meeting for worship, is our monthly meeting (Quakers), which I attend and which lasts until three o'clock. I mean to be in the school regularly till two, when I go to town for provisions (food, clothing and necessities for Claremont). In addition, I have to prepare lessons for my own children. I hope to examine the pupils in arithmetic at least once a week. I can assure the Committee that the two hearing and the two Deaf and Dumb assistants are sufficient to keep a larger number of boys at work.'

In November 1833, the Committee proposed to appoint a confidential person to select the articles, regulate the prices and superintend the farming arrangements, all under Humphrey's direction.

In April 1840, he retired, at the age of 53 years, through ill-health and disagreements with the Committee over the administration of the Institution and the methods of religious education, since the Institution had to be managed, upon the insistence of the subscribers, on the principles of the Established Church (Church of Ireland). In May 1840, David Holmes, pupil, wrote, 'I am very sorry to see Mr Humphreys and all his family departing from Claremont to move to Kilmacow in Co. Kilkenny, near Waterford. He sold his effects by auction on 22 April. He could sign very plainly and comprehensively; the Deaf and Dumb could understand his signs extremely well; he used to allow the boys to go and pull the gooseberries after work every evening, and for this they loved him the more. He used sometimes to work in his flower garden and have some boys with him there, and he often told the boys the names of his flowers. He liked to converse with the Deaf and Dumb, and whenever he travelled to the country and came back, he used to tell us about many different and amusing circumstances. He used to allow us to go to the Zoo Gardens in the Park every summer. We used to be very happy and delighted with him, but now he is gone, and we are very sorrowful.'[8]

He died on 2 June 1859 at the age of 71 years, and was buried in the Friends' Burial Ground, Waterford. No headstone marks his burial place, while the locations of the interment of the members of the Humphreys family were recorded on the site-map of the Burial Ground.

7

The First Pupil of Claremont

'... the Lord led me to select him out of others ...'
- Dr Charles Orpen

According to the Institution's application book, Thomas Collins was totally deaf with an inflammation in one eye and was an inmate of Bedford Asylum for Children, part of the House of Industry. In an Annual Report some years later, he was mentioned as an orphan from the Foundling Hospital and he had one brother and one sister. The Foundling Hospital (which later became the South Dublin Union Workhouse) was founded by the Corporation of the City of Dublin in 1729 and was located in James Street.[1] It accommodated around 1,200 children and more than half of the children had died before the age of twelve. Abandoned babies were placed in a basket on a wheel at the door. These children, mostly illegitimate, were not only from Dublin, but also from several parts of the country, even England. Inevitably, there was no indication as to what was the birthplace of Thomas Collins.

In a letter in 1821 to his cousin, Thomas Collins wrote, 'I saw you before when I was an ignorant little deaf boy in your house. I am growing a big lad. Do you remember me? My parents are both dead. I am an orphan. My brother is a gardener for the deaf and dumb. My sister lives with him; he supports her at Claremont. My brother is married; he has one child. My mother took me away from your house. I was crying when I went to Dublin. I was a stranger with you. I remember to have seen you long ago; you were putting hay into a loft, and you let the fork fall in your lip, and it tore the flesh. I saw your wild cow, which ran at a woman, and tumbled her into a river, and then a board was put on the cow's face, to keep her from seeing people.'

His intellect being very good (having spent some time in the Lancastrian school at the House of Industry), of amiable disposition and a talent for drawing, Collins was selected, in December 1815, out of several deaf inmates by Dr Orpen who brought him to his bachelor home to try out the schemes of instructing the deaf. After some time, Collins learnt to write, read and pronounce a few words. During the year of 1816, Collins had been exhibited at lectures conducted by Dr Orpen at the Rotunda Assembly Rooms. According to a letter in July 1816, 'Doctor Charles Orpen exhibited a boy of about ten years of age who audibly counted to 100 and some of his copies in learning to write was given to the auditory, I have got two of them, the boy has been only four or five months under tuition and spoke distinctly and surprised the audience by his cleverness, I believe there were 400 persons present.'[2]

*Rotunda Assembly Rooms where Dr Orpen conducted lectures and exhibitions
on Education of the Deaf and Dumb in 1816 (Picture by James Malton, 1797)
(courtesy of Friends of the Rotunda)*

On 16 May 1816, he was admitted to the newly-formed Deaf School in the Penitentiary for Young Male Criminals in Smithfield. In 1822, the Committee appointed him as monitor over pupils during out-of-school hours, paying him ten shillings per quarter. He left on 30 May 1825, at the age of 20 years. From October 1825 to January 1826, Collins accompanied Mr Humphreys on deputation tours to London and other towns in its vicinity. A collection totalling £38 was made by some of his friends in order to bind Collins as apprentice to a printer, Mr Goodwin, Denmark Street, Dublin. Dr Orpen's brother, Richard, donated £10 towards the collection. In September 1832, Dr Orpen informed the Committee that Collins had not been able to find work at a printer in Dublin and that after trying Liverpool and London without success, he was considering of emigrating to America. Mr Humphreys consented to employ Collins as assistant teacher and printer for the Male Department of the Institution. With the number of pupils totalling 78 before the end of 1832, Collins commenced his position with a view of teaching articulation, the Committee to supply him with food and a small salary. Simultaneously, there was another deaf assistant teacher, Philip Geary, who died from consumption two years later, aged 24 years.

Collins was a special favourite with his patron, Dr Orpen. A week never passed without his spending at least one day with him. His warm feelings, his intelligence and his close attachment to Dr Orpen endeared him to the doctor's family, friends and acquaintances who often met him at Dr Orpen's home. The money given to Collins, it was given away to charity. Having accumulated a sum, he gave all to the Institution, so that his name appeared in the reports as a contributor. In order that more deaf children would benefit from receiving education, Collins went immediately to his little paint-box and took out a purse in which there were four ten-penny coins and one five-penny coin. He held out the four ten-penny pieces in one hand, saying, 'Four tens go to deaf and dumb.' He held the five-penny piece in the other, adding, 'Thomas five,' meaning that he would keep it for himself. The other day, he gave the remaining coin to a poor sick black man lying down in the street.

Collins had become famous for many years for his boldness in making contact with a monarch of the United Kingdom. The following report and his letter to King George the Fourth had been published in newspapers, periodicals and reports which contained issues relating to the welfare and education of deaf people.

The Visit of King George the Fourth to Ireland in 1821

'Among those who hailed the King's presence, there was one, a poor orphan boy, a deaf-mute - Thomas Collins, the first pupil of Claremont. From the moment he had heard of His Majesty's arrival, he wished to write to him. He actually wrote his letter on some gilt-edged paper, and directed to His Majesty, and put it into the post-office himself. (*The contents of the letter are reproduced in the first chapter of this book.*)

The King, although unused to being addressed by strangers through the medium of the post office, and to the familiar style in which this letter was written, was touched by its unaffected simplicity, but no more was heard of it till a short time before his departure from Ireland, when one day, the inmates of Claremont were greatly astonished to see one of the royal carriages drive up the avenue, and stop at the door. Sir Benjamin Bloomfield and the gentleman enquired for Thomas Collins, as they had been commanded by His Majesty, in consequence, they said, of a letter which had interested the King deeply. The gentlemen stood at the far end of the drawing-room, to observe the boy's countenance as he read the letter which they brought. The boy read the address, and turning the letter to open it, instantly perceived that the seal resembled those which he had seen on official letters from the Castle,[3] and guessed it was an answer to his letter to the King. He begged for scissors, that he might not break the seal; but none being at hand, he opened it most carefully. On reading the letter, which contained a draft in his favour on the King's banker for £10, he was in an ecstasy, which he testified so naturally by his words, countenances and gestures, that the strangers were delighted. The sum was put into the savings' bank, and afterwards laid out in apprenticing him to a printer, and thus did it happen that he found his constant occupation in the diffusion of language.'[4]

Collins' Watch stolen, leading to a Trial

The pocket-watch was a present to Thomas Collins from Dr Orpen's brother, and was precious to Collins. One day it was snatched by a woman, who was pursued by its owner and finally captured by a watchman. The trial afterwards followed, and a

report on its proceedings appeared in *Saunders'*
Newsletter, 1 February 1826, as follows:

Sessions Court, Green Street, Dublin
Yesterday came on before the Recorder, an interesting and curious trial, in which a deaf and
dumb boy was prosecutor. Doctor C. Orpen,
Secretary to the Deaf and Dumb Institution, was
sworn to interpret, and communicated the questions of the Court, of the Jury, and of the Prisoner,
partly by spelling the words on his fingers, and
partly by writing, to which the boy answered,

Watch.

both by speaking articulately and by signs. It was given in evidence that the boy's
name was Thomas Collins; that he was, until lately, a pupil of Mr Humphreys, a
master of the Deaf and Dumb School at Claremont, and is now an apprentice to
Mr. Goodwin, a respectable printer, in Dublin, and that he is totally deaf and until
taught to speak in that school, had been totally dumb.   His evidence was confirmed by the watchman, who apprehended the woman, and found the watch in
her possession, and by the interpreter, who proved that the watch had been given
by his brother to the boy some years since. Doctor Orpen also proved, that he had
known the boy ever since 1815; that he was detained at the Printing-Office till late
every evening; that his principles and conduct were excellent; and that he perfectly understood the nature of an oath, and the consequence of a lie. The prisoner
attempted an excuse, by stating that she was drunk, and that she had taken the
watch in her room, and not in the street, but these were distinctly contradicted on
oath by the boy. The Jury did not hesitate a moment in finding her Guilty; and the
Judge sentenced her to seven years' transportation.

The following letter, which was handed by the boy to the Recorder, after his examination (not viva voce) was over, explains the circumstances of the robbery:

Judge.

'To My Judge,
         I was standing, looking at a shop window and
things, last Monday week night, it was nine of the clock
in the evening, a wicked woman met me, and she
asked me. I said, 'I am deaf and dumb,' and by signs,
until she took away my watch and my fob-pocket, and
tore it off. She ran away into another street, into a
house; I followed her, with my eyes, immediately, and
ran after her. She ran into a house downstairs, into a
little back kitchen. She threw a candle down, out, with

her hand, to make dark night, and she pushed me. I fell down on my back on the ugly ground; my elbow and back were painful and blue. I got up dirty and caught her; she is very strong; I called a watchman. I said, 'come, come,' to take her to prison. She pushed my watch under the bed and hid it by sitting on the bed; the two watchmen found it by their search. It is very true - I swear true. I hope the Judge will not hang her. Will he give me my silver watch and my fob, and send her to be locked up in prison, or send her by ship to Botany Bay? I am Thomas Collins, a deaf and dumb orphan boy. Perhaps if a good minister will speak to her some things about God and Jesus Christ, she will be repentant and will become a good woman, and a minister will be better than a Judge; but if she will not be repentant, that the Judge will send her to hard work in Botany Bay.'

Eventually, Mr John Synge, a gentleman of large property and engaged in benevolent pursuits, took Collins to his home, Glanmore Castle, in Roundwood, Co. Wicklow. He was one of the Irish admirers of the Pestalozzian method and is grandfather of J.Millington Synge, the famous playwright. Collins' assignment was to superintend a printing press for producing educational charts and textbooks. These were used for 'diffusion of language' at the school established by Mr John Synge for the children of tenants on his estates.

In 1850, Dr Orpen, while in South Africa, received a letter from his brother, Emmanuel, that Collins was dying from consumption. When the doctor, hearing of the death of his favourite pupil, said, 'Pupil first, master afterwards!' According to the burial records of St. Mobhi's Church, Glasnevin, he used to reside at Nicholas Street, having died at the age of 45 years, and he was buried in the churchyard on 28 September 1850.

Nicholas Street, Dublin – where Thomas Collins used to live till his death
Christ Church Cathedral is in the background
(Author's photograph)

Part Two

The Claremont Institution

8

Claremont, Glasnevin

'Come, the day is fair,
The bees are humming in the air -
The sun is laving(sic) in the lake -
The fishes sporting near the brake -
So come and drink the balmy breeze,
By soft gales wafted from the trees.'[1]

(composed by a deaf 'lad', c.1832)

In the year of 1837,[2] the 'village of Glasnevin is pleasantly situated on the river Tolka, and though not more than two miles from Dublin, from its rural and retired appearance, it might be supposed far from any city. It has associations with the names of some celebrated Irishmen - Tickell, Addison, Swift, Delaney and Sheridan. Delville, formerly the seat of Dean Delaney, was the scene where distinguished literary men assembled to enjoy social intercourse, including Dean Jonathan Swift and his lady-friend, Stella. The Botanic Gardens occupy the ground which was once Tickell's demesne. Covering over thirty acres, it is laid out on scientific principles, and is provided with displays of splendid collections of plants, trees and foliage.' Near Cross Guns' Bridge was the turnpike gate, at which tolls had to be paid, and this provided a deterrent for potential visitors to Claremont and placed inconvenient expenses on the Committee members and officers of the Institution.

The Lindsays

In the early nineteenth century, Glasnevin House *(see picture)* and extensive lands became the property of the last Protestant Bishop of Kildare, Charles Lindsay. In July 1819, he, having donated £10 to the Deaf and Dumb Institution, was elected Vice-Patron. Bishop Lindsay's heirs sold a large tract of land to Glasnevin Cemetery in 1830. One of his heirs, Captain George H. Lindsay, a local magistrate, owned several portions of land, and had been Chairman of the North Dublin Workhouse, Brunswick Street.

Going north from the village of Glasnevin, along Ballymun Road, past the little road on the right side leading to St Mobhi's Church, on the left side is the avenue to the Claremont Institution. At the bottom of the Avenue was the Royal Irish Constabulary barracks until 1909. Further up the Avenue just before the stone pillars of the entrance to Claremont, on the left side was Glasnevin House - the home of the

Lindsays. For many decades, male members of this family were on the Committee and then Board of Governors of the Claremont Institution. Among them was Colonel H. Gore Lindsay, who in 1904 was unintentionally introduced to a deaf visitor, preparing a report on the Claremont Institution for *The British Deaf Times*. 'Following the directions given by a past pupil of Claremont, I had left the tram at Glasnevin and arrived, as I thought, at the Institution. Passing a picturesque lodge, around the door of which fluttered a number of doves, I found myself facing an old-fashioned house, standing within extremely pleasant grounds. Unsure if the house was the Institution itself, I rang the bell and entering through the open door, I stood in a hall hung with hunting crops, driving whips, and the paraphernalia of a sportsman. A man-servant appeared, and I wrote 'Mr Taylor, please?' upon my card. Then I was ushered into what was the 'den' of a hunting man. Eyeing the 'hunting fixtures' upon the table, it occurred to me that either educating the Irish deaf was remarkably a fine profession, or that hunting and driving must form part of Claremont's curriculum! My vision of a class careering across the country led by the Principal was broken by the entrance of a very upright old gentleman possessing a weather-beaten face, and walking with a slight limp. Anticipating interesting, perhaps startling 'copy', I shook hands cordially and started to finger-talk. The look of astonishment which overspread the old gentleman's face, told me at once that I had made a mistake, and explanations rapidly followed. I had entered Glasnevin House and the gentleman whom I commenced to interview as Mr George Taylor, principal of the Claremont Institution, was in reality Colonel Lindsay, squire of Glasnevin.

'Colonel Gore Lindsay (*see picture*) was a Scotsman by descent, and an old military man, having been through the Crimean war. He was an ardent sportsman and follower of hounds, while the close proximity of his Glasnevin estate to the Claremont Institution has led him to take considerable interest in the education and welfare of the deaf. For some years he has been a Governor of the Institution, and like all interested in the Irish deaf, he looks to the day when State Aid will be given to the work. Colonel Lindsay said that the new Chief Secretary had already been approached upon the question of a Grant similar to that made to England, Wales and Scotland, and had promised to bring in a Bill, which, once passed, will secure fair play for Ireland in this matter'.

According to Patrick ('Andy') Wolohan, whose descendants used to work in the service of the Lindsays and living in the cottage in Claremont Avenue opposite Glasnevin House, Major Hugh Lindsay was a former equerry to Queen Elizabeth. He had been killed in a skiing accident in 1988 at the Swiss resort of Klosters. He recalled some stories about Colonel Lindsay, particularly about the discovery by demolition workers of a pair of duelling-guns hidden behind the window-shutters in Glasnevin House. The Lindsays' property was requisitioned by the Government for various purposes during the Second World War. The house had fallen into decay and was listed for demolition. In November 1948, new offices were built for occupation by the Institute for Industrial Research and Standards, which were later renamed as Enterprise Ireland, a semi-state agency with remit of creating indigenous employment in Ireland.

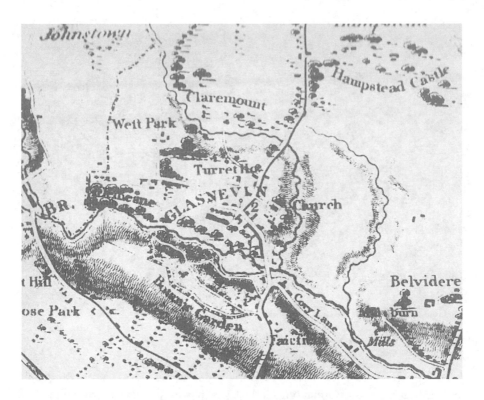

Glasnevin showing 'Claremount' – William Durcan Map, 1821
(courtesy of the National Library of Ireland)

Claremont

During the eighteenth century, Glasnevin was the seat of Lord Claremont, the Irish Postmaster General. In 1777, Benjamin Geal, a banker, took over Claremont and sold it to Mr Edward Hayes who then sold it in 1819 to the Committee of the Institution for the Education of the Deaf and Dumb Poor of Ireland.'[3]

In 1838, John D'Alton described Claremont as follows, 'Proceeding (southwards) from Ballymun to Glasnevin, in a sweet situation at the right, off the road is Claremont Deaf and Dumb Institution, founded in 1816. It is a large and commodious establishment, with 18 acres and a half of ground attached, for which £220 10s annual rent is paid. The house is beautifully situated in the midst of meadows and gardens, which are very tastefully laid out, and command very fine views of the expanse and the shores of Dublin Bay. The establishment contains schoolrooms and dormitories for 100 children, as poor boarders. The master also has accommodation for children of the richer class, who pay £50 per annum. The charge for pupils at the highest is £22 15s, but the majority are supported gratuitously.'

Claremont with Extensions at left side, c.1826

'Out of school hours the pupils are employed in useful works, contributing either to their health or to the formation of industrious habits; the boys in gardening, farming, tailoring, shoemaking, and other mechanical labours; the girls in needlework, housewifery, laundry work, and dairy management. A small printing-press is worked for the double purpose of employing the pupils and furnishing books for the general use of the deaf and dumb. The buildings, yards and grounds are so arranged, that the boys and girls in the Poor Establishment have distinct schoolrooms and playgrounds, besides the Master has entirely separate apartments and walks for his own family, and for private pupils of both sexes, who are either deaf and dumb, or afflicted with impediments in speech.'[4]

On 15 August 1822, Dr Charles Orpen wrote to William Gregory, Dublin Castle, that the Institution at Claremont had been unable to extend its benefits, owing to the increasing number of candidates seeking admission over the past two years. He said that the cause was the small school-room in the dwelling house which had prevented the Committee receiving pupils, and it became overcrowded, causing inconvenience for their health and their instruction. The present schoolroom was inadequate to receive about 40 scholars, which number was less than one-third of the candidates for admission. The specific modes used for teaching the deaf must be used, and the necessity of boys and girls having separate school-rooms, under the same ceiling, divided by a partition and supervised simultaneously by the instructors, made it crucial to have a larger building than would be required for ordinary children.[5]

Between 1822 and 1823, the extensions were erected, comprising the large wing annexed to the dwelling-house. The rooms in the wing were the School-room, the dining-halls and the dormitories. In 1829, further extensions were constructed to provide accommodation for assistant teachers. Later on, a porch was added to the west side of the Girls' school-room, providing a separate entrance. Owing to the establishment in 1846 of the Roman Catholic Institution for the Deaf, which superintended separate schools for deaf boys and girls in Cabra, Dublin, the number of pupils admitted to Claremont decreased. In the 1920s, the Inspector from the Commissioners of Charitable Donations and Bequests commented now and then on the dilapidated condition of the building at Claremont, recommending that a smaller building might be suitable, taking into account of the small number of pupils.

In 1921, the Lord Lieutenant's inspector reported that the 'dormitories, classrooms, lavatories, refectory and kitchen were faultless in their arrangements; lighting, ventilation and heating being exceptionally good, and the neatness and cleanliness of the whole Establishment were most praiseworthy. The number of children in the Institution on that date was 18, of whom 10 were boys and 8 were girls. The children were healthy in their appearance and neat in their dress'. Despite dithering efforts since the 1890s of the Board of Governors to consider moving to a smaller, more manageable building, the School continued to operate in Glasnevin.

In 1943, the Local Government Board issued an order for the buildings at Claremont to be requisitioned as a hospital for children suffering from tuberculosis, and the Committee of the Institution sold the buildings for £3,400. In 1972, the hospital was taken over by the then Eastern Health Board and the name changed to St. Clare's Home. The home currently provides residential accommodation and day-care services for the elderly.

St Mobhi's Church, Glasnevin

This is the church where the staff and the pupils of the Glasnevin School worshipped till the 1940s. In 1820, Colonel Gore of Glasnevin House obtained the pew in the Church for the use of the Institution, as landowners of Claremont. Up to 1896, around thirty pupils and a few former pupils had been buried in the churchyard, including the first pupil, Thomas Collins, in 1845. There was not a single headstone to mark any of the burial places of these deaf individuals.

Mr. Edward James Chidley, headmaster, was buried in February 1881. His son, John, who died in 1882 at the age of twenty-two years from typhus contracted on his medical studies, was buried with his father, and a plaque to his memory was erected inside the church above the vestry door. The last burial of a pupil from Claremont was Janet Marshall in March 1896. She died at the age of eleven from consumption.

Also in the churchyard lies the Rev. George Carroll, incumbent of St. Mobhi for over forty years, who was on the Committee of the Claremont Institution for many years. He had carried out religious instruction for the pupils and prepared them for confirmation at St. George's Church, Hardwicke Place, Dublin, which was the place of worship of Dr Orpen, his brother, Richard, and their families, when resident in North Great Georges Street. At the back of the churchyard of St Mobhi was the family plot of the Gore-Lindsay family, who used to live at Glasnevin House, which was adjacent to Claremont. For almost 100 years, the Lindsays were on the Committee, with the last one being Colonel Henry, who died in 1914, a friend who for many years took a keen interest in the welfare of all in Claremont. He occasionally took part in the prize-giving ceremonies at the School Sports Day every September. Some of the male pupils joined the parish group of Boy Scouts assembling in the parish school, which used to be called the 'Ink-bottle' because of its distinctive shape. Most of the deaf children attended Sunday School, participating in the outings and picnics arranged by the parishioners.

According to the Applotment of the Parish in 1825, the Claremont Institution for the Deaf and Dumb, being in possession of a large house and eighteen acres, paid three pounds at the rate of eight pence in the pound, which was rather high in those days.

James Foulston, headmaster from 1845 to 1855, had his two children baptised at the church in 1850 and in 1854. On 21 April 1862, at the Easter Vestry, Edward J. Chidley was appointed churchwarden along with Captain Lindsay, as overseers of public houses, deserted children and as officers of health. On 9 May 1870, Benjamin H. Payne, pupil and then teacher at Claremont, was appointed one of the Select Vestrymen.

In April 1881, at the Easter Vestry meeting, Edward W. Chidley, son of the late E.J. Chidley, was appointed as church-warden, and then as Diocesan Synodsman. In 1885, Thomas J. Chidley and Joseph Keating, teacher from Claremont, were added to the list of Vestrymen. On 3 January 1888, a letter was received by the Select Vestry from Edward W. Chidley, tendering his resignation as trustee of Parochial Funds in consequence of leaving the Parish.

In May 1888, there was discussion about replacing the Baptismal Font with that 'in possession of the Headmaster of Claremont. The latter originally belonged to the Parish Church, and it was proposed to get estimates from stonecutters to repair the proposed font'. However, it was found impossible to restore the old font, and instead a new font was obtained from W.Harrison, stonecutter of Brunswick Street, Dublin, at the cost of £10.

In November 1908, the male pupils and teachers at Claremont offered to build a new oak pulpit for the church, submitting designs which were then approved by the Vestry. In the following year, the pulpit was erected, along with a brass plate acknowledging the contribution of the Claremont Institution. In December, the Rector recommended that a new hymn board be created, following a similar pattern as that used for the pulpit. It was presented as a gift to the church by Mrs Taylor, wife of the Headmaster. Mr Taylor was secretary on the Vestry from May 1904 until his retirement in 1928. In 1910, the oak screen at the organ chamber was executed by the pupils for a sum of £10. The designs for the carved panels were submitted to and approved by the Archbishop of Dublin. It was announced at the Annual Meeting in May 1908 that the pupils of Claremont were commissioned to make the four panels for the new pulpit in the church in Thornton, Leicestershire, England.

9

The Early Years of the Institution

'to provide a permanent Asylum for those outcasts of society, who now find
within the walls of Claremont, a shelter and a home'

- Annual Report, 1834

The House of Industry

In June 1773, a Committee of the Corporation for Relief of Poor of the City of Dublin was formed to erect in their district a House of Industry to provide for four classes: disabled men, disabled women, male beggars and 'strolling women.' A site was obtained at the north-eastern side of Channel Row, now North Brunswick Street, with an old disused malt-house. Two large houses in Channel Row were taken by the Corporation, and fitted up for reception of the poor of Dublin, and applications to the House of Industry were received from all over Ireland. The buildings of this Establishment, which contained the lodging-rooms, dining-halls, weaving-shops, workshops and the apartments of several officers, formed a hollow square. In the centre of the south side was the entrance with the porter's lodge, and opposite to it was a building, containing the board-room, secretary's office and other apartments, through which was the passage to the interior square, which formed the Bedford Asylum. This is where Dr Orpen found his first pupil, Thomas Collins.

Bedford Asylum for Industrious Children

Some of the children admitted came from the 'remotest parts of the (United) kingdom.' They included former Charter School children set adrift by masters to whom they were apprenticed and who then became homeless. (Charter schools were set up by the Incorporated Society, established in 1701, to provide education, based on Protestant principles, for children of the poor). This building was adapted to receive, lodge, feed, educate and occupy the children. The officers' apartments separated the male from the female part of the Institution. There were separate dining-halls and school-rooms for boys and girls, with smaller rooms for nurses, with sufficient accommodation for 300 boys and as many girls, on the ground floors. There were workshops for the grown children of each sex. To prevent communication between the sexes, they not only ate and slept in different apartments, but were separated into two distinct yards, by an enclosed board-walk leading to the officer's apartments.

Many of the older children in the House of Industry were employed on weaving, hosiery, comb-making and tailoring, with the proceeds of their produce funding their maintenance, after the superintendents in charge of children's training had taken their share of the income.

*Penitentiary for Young Male Criminals
 in Smithfield*

The Penitentiary, under charge of the House of
Industry, opened in 1801 for reception and
reform of young male criminals under fifteen
years of age. Some were convicted without trial
for theft and violent crimes; others were apprentices escaping from masters or were misbehav-
ing. Those getting into crime were sent in by parents. Many boys were sent in for eloping from
the Charter Schools or for offences in these
schools. As for the fate of the young males

imprisoned there, some were either sentenced to transportation, pardoned by the Lord
Lieutenant, enlisted into the Army or the Navy or transferred to the House of Industry
for good conduct.

Deaf and Dumb School in Smithfield

In the year of 1816, there were 21 deaf, male and female, among the inmates of the
House of Industry[1]. On 18 May of that year, at a public meeting in the Rotunda, with
Lord Massy in the chair, the National Institution for Education of the Indigent Deaf
and Dumb in Ireland was established to provide means for their education. Dr Orpen,
secretary of the newly-formed Committee, appealed to the Governors of the House of
Industry, who granted the use of two rooms in the Penitentiary, one room as a school-
room and the other as a dormitory, for ten children. The Governors consented to provide food for the pupils until the Committee could raise sufficient funds. Eight boys
were admitted, and the number soon increased to 16, five being day-scholars. A visitor to the school-room where the deaf children were undertaking lessons said,

> 'The first thing that strikes a stranger on his entrance, is the silence which reigns
> in the room, so different from the buzzing noise which assails him in every other
> school; but there is nothing melancholy connected with this absence of sound; the
> faces of all the children around are remarkably cheerful and intelligent. They
> always feel great joy when they are taught to expect the arrival of a new scholar,
> and testify it by their faces whenever a stranger enters.'[2]

Dr Orpen did not intend to continue with educating his charges. Finding it difficult
to get a suitable master from England or Scotland, the Committee employed two
young men, Charles Devine, previously a monitor in the Lancastrian[3] School at the
House of Industry, and Frederick Mack, a pupil teacher from the Model School,
Kildare Place, Dublin.

During 1816, changes were made in the regulations governing admission to the House of Industry. The involuntary inmates (mostly 'sturdy beggars and disorderly women') were discharged to make way for a 'more destitute and deserving class', comprising four categories, namely the infirm and aged, the sick, orphan children and lunatics. The House of Industry therefore took on the character of the Poor Law Workhouse and a large complex of buildings including the Richmond Surgical Hospital and the Whitworth Medical Hospital. By April 1817, there were over 2,500 inmates, including nearly 900 children, and an additional 160 children in the penitentiaries.[4] Consequently, the Governors of the House of Industry asked the Committee of the Deaf School to remove the deaf boys from the Penitentiary immediately, as separate accommodation was required for children afflicted with 'scabbed head' (ringworm). In the following month, Dr Orpen located a house in Brunswick Street, renting it for one year at 30 guineas, with the pupils still boarded by the House of Industry, and the Deaf School was transferred there. In the meantime, the Committee was seeking suitable premises with sufficient space to accommodate an increasing number of pupils, with several deaf children, including girls, waiting to be admitted. Many letters and appeals had been received from wealthy people seeking admission for their deaf daughters.

Move to Claremont

In February 1819, an advertisement was placed in newspapers, seeking a house and grounds near Dublin, and after visiting five or six places, a house in Glasnevin was decided upon. On 27 April, the Sub-committee stated that they visited the demesne of Claremont and having considered it well suited to the purposes of the Institution, as it possessed a capability of being so divided as to afford 'ample room for two distinct establishments.' The advantages of Claremont, as told at the annual meeting in the following year, were 'air and beautiful exercise, and the facility of introducing trades, teaching agriculture and gardening, with pupils contributing towards their own support. Removal from the metropolis not only cuts off the interference and frequent intercourse of unsavoury persons, protecting the pupils from the dangers of immorality and vice in its various contaminating forms.'[5] The Committee offered the owner, Mr Hayes, Bridge Street, Dublin, a fine of £1,000 and rent of £220 10s 9d per annum. On 31 July 1819, the Institution moved from Brunswick Street to its new home – Claremont.

The Committee was committed to pay Mr Humphreys, when he returned from Edinburgh upon completion of his training, a sum of £100 a year and a house free of rent with the capacity of accommodating rich pupils. The building at Claremont comprised a dwelling-house and a few out-offices. The school was held in the house, leading to overcrowding and poor ventilation. In 1821, the Committee drew up a plan for the new buildings, to accommodate the increasing number of pupils, which was at that time 43. It was proposed to make alterations and construct an extension, in order to make the Institution complete in the Lodge, Schoolroom, dormitories, dining-hall, laundry, kitchen, hospital, etc. It was proposed to separate completely the males and females and also the Master's private and poor establishments.

Engraving of the Institution at Claremont by Clayton

To prevent absconding of some pupils, iron bars had to be fitted to the lower windows of the house, and a shoemaker was then placed in the lodge, as gatekeeper; who was to see that none of the pupils leave the Institution at improper hours; to attend to public visitors, admitting none except during the prescribed days and hours. It was intended to bind some of the pupils apprentice to him, to learn his trade. The violent storms of 1822 threw down many trees, which were sold or exchanged, for some hundred young trees to be planted in various parts of the grounds. These storms also considerably injured some parts of the buildings, especially the out-offices.

The crowded state of the old building, becoming daily more obvious, some friends to the Institution resolved, during the summer of 1822, to commence a separate fund, for building a new school-house, with a dormitory under the same roof. One friend offered (in order to enable them to commence the building without delay) to lend £400, free of interest or security, to be repaid when this fund exceeded that sum. In the meantime the subscription proceeded, still more promoted by a pamphlet, published anonymously by a friend to the Institution, entitled: *"An Investigation into the Principles, Management and Wants of the National Institution at Claremont, near Dublin, for the Education of the Deaf and Dumb Poor of Ireland - By an Observer"*. The Committee, finding the effect of the circulation of the first edition by the author, in increasing the building fund, printed another edition at the cost of that fund. The result was a further increase of contributions. Mr Humphreys reported that he had received encouragement from some friends, in several of the chief towns in the West of England, to visit those places with some of his pupils, for the purpose of collecting funds for the Institution, and especially for the new buildings, arrangements were accordingly made by the Committee for his executing this plan. A new large edition of the circular, as well as the third edition of the Investigation, and a second edition of the 6th Report, was printed for distribution in England, on 21 September 1822, in the St George Steam Packet, and arrived in Liverpool the next day. The owners of the packet granted them free passage, for which the Committee express their sincere thanks, as also to the captain, for his kindness, and personal attention to the boys during the voyage.

'Nothing (said Mr Humphreys in one of his letters) could exceed the kindness of the captain of the St George Steam Packet. The boys were quite well all the way; Brennan was comparing the waves, breaking all over the face of the ocean, to one thing or another; but his first idea was the best; 'They are laughing – glad – not quiet – happy'. Collins seemed to have changed places, or rather minds, with Brennan; for, although he was occasionally lively, as is usual with him, there was a generally a quiet thoughtfulness in his manner, and a constant reference, in all his expressions of wonder at the mighty element on which we were moving, to that almighty power, which with one breath called it into being. I but translate his signs, in this last expression; they were constantly repeated, as often as he looked around him, and then on the vessel and the passengers. He expressed his astonishment and his reverence; and reverted to the littleness of man, and then seemed to sink into himself.'

Having given a series of public lectures and examinations of his pupils in Liverpool, Manchester, Leeds, Huddersfield, Bristol, Clifton and Bath – in all of which towns he was received in the kindest manner – he returned to Claremont, on Saturday, 21 December, having been absent exactly three months. The total of collections received at lectures and examinations was £789, and after expenses of travelling, meals and hire of rooms, it came down to £668. One result of Mr Humphreys's visit to England was the establishment of Deaf schools in Liverpool, Manchester and Bath; according to some extracts from the newspapers of these towns.[6]

A letter by one of the two pupils while in Leeds on 27 October 1822, to his father follows, 'I was very much delighted with my journey, was in Liverpool, Manchester and now Leeds. One gentleman gave me one pound, and another pound to Collins. Another gentleman gave me an umbrella, and one to Collins, and gave us five shillings. I wondered at the people in England, more neat than in Ireland. All kinds of businesses are better than in Ireland, and people are richer. In Liverpool – a great many merchants and great deal of goods, and ships at dock. English horses were larger and stronger than the Irish horses. I saw many kinds of factories spinning cotton and weaving cloth, by the power of the steam. I think it would be better for you, Father, to work in Manchester than in Ireland. We have four meals in one day in England. The streets are very narrow and badly paved. I had seen the Blind Asylum in Liverpool, and we wondered at the blind women and girls who threaded needles with their mouths. We are always walking in the streets for getting money from the people for the Building Fund. We will go to Bristol soon. We lodge very comfortable, and we pay very little for our lodgings. I would like to live in England, because I am very pleased with seeing the English so neat.' The money collected at lectures in some of the large towns on behalf of the Claremont Institution and the lodgings provided for Mr Humphreys and his two pupils were looked after by some Quakers, such as Bewley and Neville, merchants in Manchester.

Visits to Claremont of Those involved in Education of the Deaf

From the time when the Institution was established, Dr Charles Orpen commenced correspondence with Institutions for the Education of the Deaf in London, Edinburgh, Birmingham, Glasgow, Aberdeen, Paris, Genoa, and in America – Pennsylvanian Institution in Philadelphia and the American Deaf and Dumb Asylum[7] in Hartford, Connecticut. On 29 August 1821, Mr Robert Kinniburgh, from the Edinburgh Institution, paid a visit to Dublin at Mr Humphrey's invitation. In July 1822, Mr Robert Taylor, master of the Aberdeen Deaf and Dumb School, came to visit the Institution and appeared much pleased with it. In September 1822, the Rev. John Townsend, founder of the London Deaf and Dumb Asylum in 1792, visited the Institution at Claremont and subscribed towards the Building Fund and brought for the Committee several documents regarding the Asylum in London.[8] In the same year, the Rev. James Marshall, secretary of the Glasgow Institution, visited the School at Claremont. He presented the Dublin Committee with the Glasgow report.[9]

Teachers at Claremont

There had been problems of retaining assistant teachers, as some of them had been induced by wealthy parents to leave the Institution in order to give private tuition to their deaf children. In May 1832, Mr Henry Overend, senior assistant, had been offered a situation, by Mr Pennefather, as tutor to his deaf son, Daniel. The other assistant, Mr Arthur Hopper, was then promoted to Senior Assistant, with salary raised to £52 per annum. To prevent the inconvenience and disruption to the educational management of the Institution, those about to become assistant

School-mas-ter.

teachers, were obliged to sign the engagement and give security of a large sum, to be bound for seven years to the Institution, which was the common policy adopted at the Institutions in England and Scotland.

The duty of the Headmaster in the school was not only personal instruction of all the pupils, including the superior classes and superintendence of the instruction of all, but also domestic economic management of the Institution. He had to order food, clothing and school materials for both rich and poor pupils. He had to assess each pupil's progress in education prior to removal from the Institution, and their potential to obtain employment, as well as attending to visitors to the School. On 22 August 1832, Mr Humphreys wrote to Dr Orpen that he had no means of providing the Institution with food supplies for another week, and on application to the Committee's office, he was told that there was no money. Over the three months, he was owed by the Committee a sum of over £100, and he needed another £175 for the remainder of the year, while the number of pupils reached 78.

School-room.

One of the Committee members visited the school and found all the male pupils employed, during school hours, in cleaning the pond outside the building and that these pupils had been in school for only six or eight days in a period of three weeks. Mr Humphreys explained that the water in the pond was stagnating, thus giving stench, and the water-pump was out of action. Nearly one hundred persons were without water for washing and other purposes. He had to send a horse and cart regularly twice a week to the river in Glasnevin for water, and had to send gangs of boys with the water carriage. For several weeks he had been incapable of attending to any business by ill-health and the various difficulties which he met in managing the affairs at Claremont, especially from the uncertain supply of money. In order to feed the pupils and the staff, he had to go to town to source and purchase supplies. The doctor advised him to take time off to go to the sea to restore his health. The Committee agreed that a steward be employed to take the administration of the farm out of Mr Humphrey's hands.

Hearing Female Teachers

Mr Humphreys was questioned by the Committee regarding the girls being deficient in education, which was, they presumed, to be due to lack of a hearing female assistant. The Committee informed Mr Humphreys that the girls should be taught arithmetic, and that some time each evening should be devoted to this purpose.

Interestingly, an advertisement appeared in a newspaper, announcing that 'two ladies, originally perfected in the system for the education for the Deaf and Dumb, with a view to instruct a member of their own family, are now in a position to receive into their house, situated in one of the healthiest parts of Dublin, a few Female Deaf and Dumb Pupils, not to exceed six in number, to be instructed in Reading, Writing, Arithmetic, Drawing, Fancywork, and every suitable female accomplishment, and while imparting the power of reading the Word of God, and of using the language common to their fellow-beings (sign language), they would endeavour to instil such principles of thinking and acting as would render them amiable as well as efficient members of society'.[10]

Dublin Day School for the Deaf and Dumb

In October 1824, a delegation from the Ladies Auxiliary Society, which included Miss Magee, sister of the Archbishop of Dublin,[11] informed the Committee of the Claremont Institution that they established a day school for deaf children in the city of Dublin, as a preparatory school for Claremont. This was set up in the Dorset Institution, Sackville Street, Dublin, under the tutorship of Mr Joseph White.[12] In May 1828, the Committee informed the Ladies conducting the Day School that the school-room at Claremont was not filled yet by boarders from the country parts of Ireland owing to lack of funds to support them, and that they would be in a position to admit day pupils if the Ladies Auxiliary Society would defray the expense of a caravan to ferry the children to Claremont from the city and back. In the following month, the Ladies' Committee replied that they declined the proposal owing to the difficulties of transporting boys and girls to and from such a distance unless attended by a master and mistress and to the expense of horse, driver and attendants. In 1840, the number of pupils attending the Day school since 1824 was 93, of whom 25 had been apprenticed. Out of 20 to 30 attending the school daily were 17 of the poorer children.[13]

In January 1830, an advertisement appeared in the *Dublin Evening Mail* announcing that 'a sermon will be preached by the Rev. Mortimer O'Sullivan,[14] Prebendary of St Audeon's at St Mark's Church on Sunday, 24 January, for the benefit of Dublin Day School for the Deaf and Dumb. Subscriptions received will be received by the Ladies of the Committee: the Countess of Roden, Viscountess Lorton, Lady Gregory, Miss Magee, Lady Shaw, Mrs Ruxton and Miss Kellett.' The first two ladies' husbands were earnest supporters of the Evangelical Movement. Among those who preached the charity sermons for the benefit of both the Claremont Institution and the Dublin Day School were the Rev. Richard Daly, later Bishop of Cashel,[15] the Rev. Dr C.M. Fleury, chaplain of the Molyneux Asylum for Blind Females, the Hon. and Rev. Edward Wingfield, and the Rev. John Gregg. The latter was considered to be the most popular preacher in Dublin and in 1862 he became the Bishop of Cork. His son, the Rev. Dr. R. Gregg, also Bishop of Cork following his father's death and then Primate of All Ireland, took an interest in the deaf and dumb in 1883 by becoming President of the newly-established Mission to the Adult Deaf and Dumb (Southern District of Ireland).

Private Seminary for the Deaf and Dumb in Dublin

In November 1825, Dr Orpen informed the Committee that Charles Devine, former assistant master at Claremont, was setting up, at 1 Strand Road, Dublin, a 'Private Seminary for respectable Deaf and Dumb children', to meet a need for such an establishment and that he, having attained ten years of instructing the deaf based on the Abbé Sicard's system, was 'enabled to guarantee to instruct pupils in a period less than that of the London Schools (for the deaf)'.[16] In 1829, Mr Devine moved, for better accommodation of his pupils, the Seminary to a house and grounds, comprising of fifteen acres, at Killininny, Firr House, about four miles from the city of Dublin.[17] On two occasions, in 1840 when Humphreys retired from Claremont and in 1842 when the Rev. Martin, successor to Mr Humphreys, resigned, Mr Devine applied for, and failed to obtain, the position as Principal of the Claremont Institution.

Belfast Day School for the Deaf and Dumb

On 25 April 1821, the Belfast Auxiliary Society was formed and subscriptions were raised to send Ulster's first pupil, John Vance, aged 13, from Ballymaconoghy, Co. Down, to Claremont.[18] Exactly ten years later, some gentlemen resident in Ulster expressed their desire of establishing a school for the deaf in Belfast rather than having to pay heavy travelling expenses in sending deaf children from parts of Ulster to Dublin. On 25 April 1831, Mr Samuel Gordon gave a series of lectures on the instruction of the deaf at the Lancastrian School-house in Belfast. He exhibited the progress of a deaf boy who had been educated at the Dublin Day School for the Deaf. Afterwards, a meeting was held for purpose of forming the Ulster Society for Education of the Deaf, Dumb and Blind. The founders had voiced their disapproval of Claremont's monopoly of education of the deaf. Mr Gordon said that he had been employed as 'usher at Claremont', but was asked by Mr Humphreys to sign a bond not to reveal the method of instruction of the deaf to anyone, which he refused. For that reason, he said, he was dismissed by Mr Humphreys.

On 2 May 1831, Mr Humphreys wrote to the Editor of the *Belfast Newsletter*, refuting claims of Mr Gordon, who had spent a few months at Claremont. He did not insist on Mr Gordon to sign an engagement, but he had to dismiss him for ill-treating some of the boys, one of them having blackened eyes, and another boy kicked brutally by Mr Gordon. Mr Humphreys went on to say that Mr Gordon asked him for a letter for Mr Watson, principal of the London Asylum for the Deaf, in order to apply for a vacancy at that school. However, in June 1826, Mr Gordon verbally attacked the Committee of the Claremont Institution at its Annual Meeting at the Rotunda, regarding the advantages of the Day School over the Boarding ('exile') School. Dr Orpen had publicly disputed Gordon's theory of the Day School by saying that many of the children attending the Dublin Day School were from the country and had to be lodged in various residences in the city, incurring costs for their maintenance.[19]

Problems at the Schools

In April 1832, one of the Committee members stated that he had visited Claremont and examined the head classes of boys and girls and found them 'miserably deficient even in their answers to the simplest questions.' He called upon the assistants to explain some questions to the pupils, but they were unable to answer. The explanation was that the 'education of the deaf and dumb required a much longer time to complete in comparison with that of those with full faculties, and that the usual hour for the school to start was ten o'clock in the morning. On the public visiting day, the children did not receive any instruction, and on Saturday, only two hours in the day were spent at school. We think, therefore, that three more hours in the morning should be added to the business of the day.'[20]

In the year 1835, there were two male hearing assistants in the Boys' school with one deaf assistant, Thomas Collins. They had 64 boys to instruct, and in all schools for the deaf in the United Kingdom, there was at least one assistant for every 10, 12, or 15 children in order to carry on educating efficiently. The Girls' school contained 36 pupils, with two deaf assistants, Anne McCormick and Cecilia White, without any hearing female assistant except for the work-mistress who taught only needlework. The Committee had been prevented for a number of years from engaging a hearing female assistant owing to lack of funds and suitable accommodation for a 'respectable young woman,' which were later resolved by further extensions at Claremont.

Teachers' Salaries

Prior to his departure in 1834, Mr Arthur Hopper's annual salary had been raised to £45 to compensate for extra duties. The salaries of other male assistants, Mr Whitsitt and Mr Webster, were increased to £20. These were to increase annually for five years in order to prevent them 'quitting the Institution and bettering themselves' by undertaking private tuition or obtaining posts at other schools for the deaf. The annual salaries of female assistants were, Miss Eliza Bates (hearing) £21, Miss Eliza Hobson (hearing) £15, Anne McCormick (deaf) £10 and Cecilia White (deaf) £6.

Overcrowding at Claremont

In 1834, the number of pupils reached the total of 100, and this necessitated further extensions at the cost of £1,000. In the meantime, six beds were placed in the girls' dining-room and two children had to share some beds. By October 1835, there were 120 pupils in the school and nine more elected and expected to arrive. Mr Humphreys was concerned about the decline in his revenue caused by all his private pupils being taken away during the construction of the extensions and alterations to the buildings of the Institution. As part of controlling the movements of the male pupils, two porters were placed at the door leading to the stairs and to the boys' school-room, and particular attention were used to keep the boys from disorder. The gates of

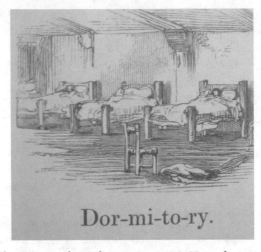

Dor-mi-to-ry.

Claremont would not be opened until half past eight in the morning. Mr Humphreys, his wife and his children had been insulted and threatened by some of the pupils. The pernicious moral effects upon the pupils were produced by the example of the conduct of the rich[21] during the Easter Monday breakfast and meeting of the Juvenile Association held at the School-room of the Institution in Claremont.

Great disorder and insubordination resulted from overcrowding where some of the girls had to sleep in a separate room at the other side of the yard without any supervision. Some of the girls admitted over-age or of bad conduct beat and struck their teachers and could not be controlled. This led to a requirement for a separate building for the female department, comprising dormitories, schoolroom, workroom, assistants' rooms and a clothes-room. A room was required for boys in wet weather when not at lessons, a room for their hats and boots, a washing-room with troughs, and a paved room opening into the boys' yard for breaking stones (which was the usual practice for male inmates of the House of Industry and other workhouses).

In May 1836, owing to the number of pupils at a total of 111 (59 boys and 52 girls), with 30 more about to be admitted, it was decided to obtain, funds permitting, two male hearing assistants and one female hearing assistant. The following alterations were to be carried out, in order to accommodate the new assistants: (1) a portion of the west end of the Boys' school to be cut off, by a temporary partition, for the two additional male assistants, (2) the provision of an additional room at the end of the boys' second bedroom for the present two assistants to occupy; (3) the extension of the new Building at the north end by a small addition three storeys high to provide an additional small dormitory for girls and as a bedroom for female assistants, and (4) a laundry and drying-room on the improved plan introduced in other Institutions such as the Magdalen Asylum, Baggot Street, Dublin.

It was decided to abolish the system, introduced in 1822 to prevent some parents sending their children almost naked to Claremont, of the pupils admitted to the

Institution with an outfit of new clothing and leaving with a similar outfit as it prevented the newly-arrived pupils from having uniform clothing which harmed the appearance of the school. Poor parents were not in a position to provide the obligatory outfit of clothing for their children. In order to raise funds for the Building Fund, Mr Humphreys made a deputation tour in England, visiting Bristol, Bath, London, Norwich, Leicester, Nottingham and Derby. This journey raised £183, and after allowing expenses for himself and the pupil for ten weeks, the proceeds came to £113.

Classroom in the Institution for the Deaf and Dumb, Birmingham
Boys at left and girls at right

Accommodation for the Pupils after Extensions

Two extensive Schoolrooms, united in the shape of 'L', were erected. The longer limb of 'L' was taken up by the schoolroom designated for poor boys only, 78 feet long, 20 feet wide and 14 feet high, with accommodation for 120 pupils. The shorter limb was taken up by the schoolroom for poor girls, 50 feet by 18 feet, capable of accommodating 80 pupils. The design of the layout of the Schoolrooms was such that Mr Humphreys would have a separate platform in the angle of the union of the two rooms for his private pupils, from which he could command a view of both schools, so as to inspect the pupils of both at the same time. He could teach the pupils either separately or all together, while the pupils of either part could not see those of the other.[22]

Each form and desk was to be long enough to accommodate ten pupils. The boys' dining room was 30 feet by 19 feet, to accommodate 80, and the girls' dining-room to accommodate the same number. The tables were used for needlework, so a separate workroom was needed. The boys' large dormitory was 78 feet by 19 feet, and contained 20 beds along each side with 10 down the centre, totalling 50 beds. The boys' small dormitory had 17 beds. The girls' dormitory was 80 feet by 18 feet; it contained 21 beds on one side and 23 on the other, totalling 44 of which one was occupied by the second Deaf female assistant, Cecilia White.

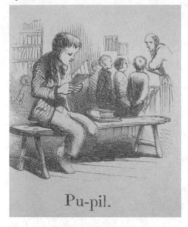

Pu-pil.

For 65 boys with 12 more to come in, totalling 77, there were three male assistants, but no deaf male assistant except on occasions when a senior pupil was employed as monitor to instruct the junior pupils. William Brennan was appointed Monitor in school and Thomas Collins to be monitor during out-of-school hours, with ten shillings every three months to be paid to each of them. They were to wear badges notifying their status on their left arms. It was recommended that the deaf assistants should not be fed as the pupils but separately, and rather better, to satisfy them and enhance their authority. A laundry was needed, similar to one at the Magdalen Asylum, to provide instruction in clothes-washing for the girls, as their only chance of obtaining employment after leaving the Institution.

End of Humphreys' Management

On 8 January 1840, Mr Humphreys tendered his resignation as Headmaster. In April, applications received from various candidates for the two situations - Headmaster and Superintendent - were conveyed to Dr Orpen for perusal in recognition of his great interest and length of time he acted as Secretary to the Institution. Among the applicants were *Charles Rhind*, assistant master of the London Asylum for the Deaf and Dumb; *Henry Overend*, formerly assistant master at Claremont; *George Clarke*, Incorporated Society (Charter School), Dublin; *Arthur Hopper*, former assistant master at Claremont;

Pre-cept-or.

Charles Devine, formerly assistant master at Claremont; *John O'Brien*, formerly second master at Birmingham Institution for the Deaf and Dumb; the *Rev. Charles Stanford*, curate of the parish of Glasnevin; and *John Birch*, Belfast Academy. On 22 April, the Rev. Charles Stanford was appointed Superintendent of the Institution. The new Headmaster was the Rev. John Martin, headmaster of the Ulster Institution for the Deaf, Dumb and Blind, Belfast.

10

Claremont – The 1840's

Ulster Institution for the Deaf, Dumb and Blind, Lisburn Road, Belfast

Since June 1836, the Rev. John Martin had been master of the Ulster Institution for the Deaf, Dumb and Blind, replacing Mr Collier, who took up the situation of headmaster at the Liverpool School for the Deaf. When the Rev. Martin left for Claremont in 1840, the vacancy in Belfast was filled by Mr Charles Rhind, assistant master for eleven years in the Old Kent Road Asylum for the Deaf and Dumb, London. The Rev. Charles Stanford, incumbent of Glasnevin from 1838 to 1845, was an eminent scholar and had held several positions in literary and academic circles before and after his engagement as Superintendent at Claremont.

However, as time went on, there had been much acrimony between the two clergymen. They could not see eye to eye on some matters dealing with domestic management, accommodation arrangements and religious instruction at Claremont. The Rev. Stanford, with responsibility for domestic economy of the Institution, refused requests for increase in salaries from both deaf and hearing assistant teachers, owing to scarcity of funds. By December 1840, there were seven assistant teachers, including two deaf females, Miss Anne McCormick and Miss Cecilia White.

Mr Hopper's Move to Birmingham
In January 1841, Mr Arthur Hopper, second Master, announced that he had been appointed Headmaster of the Edgbaston Institution for the Deaf and Dumb in

Birmingham. This was perceived as 'a national calamity' for the Dublin Institution, as he had been most efficient in his position as teacher of the deaf. During his time at the Birmingham Institution for more than 40 years, he produced a series of text books especially for the deaf, which were held in high esteem in the United Kingdom.

Three months later, the Committee, after considering the duties assigned to the situations of the Rev. Martin and the Rev. Stanford, agreed that the Rev. Stanford had the right of superintendence over the religious instruction in the School.

The Rev. Charles Stuart Stanford (1805-1873)
Superintendent of Claremont Institution (1840-1842)
(courtesy of Representative Church Body Library, Dublin)

In August 1841, Miss Bates resigned her position as Matron, and among the applicants for the vacancy was Mrs Martin, wife of the Headmaster, but she was not offered the post. In the following month, their daughter, Miss Martin, who had some experience with the deaf in Belfast, was appointed teacher in the Female School at a salary of twenty pounds per annum, washing included but not meals.

The following May, the Committee received a letter from the Rev. Martin requesting a conference regarding his duties and the education and charge of the pupils. The reply to him was that the Institution was the Church of England in its character, and accordingly the Committee authorised the Rev. Stanford to direct and superintend personally the religious instruction of such pupils as he might select, with the assistance of two of the teachers, from 10 to 11 o'clock on three days of the week. The Committee felt it was essential for the welfare of the Institution that the pupils and teachers should be taught to respect the Rev. Martin's authority in the School, and that the teachers should be informed that any disrespect on their part would be censured by the Committee.

Resignations of Dr Orpen, Rev. Martin and Rev. Stanford
In August 1842, Dr Charles Orpen resigned from the Committee owing to ill-health. An enquiry was held by the Committee as to how they had departed from the system so long in practice at the Institution and which had been recommended by Dr Orpen. In November 1842, the Rev. John Martin resigned. The Rev. Charles Stanford also tendered his resignation. In the following month, applications for the vacant situation of Headmaster were received, and among them was Charles Devine, Templeogue, County Dublin, who had a private school for the deaf at Fir House.[1]

Disorder at Claremont
During the inspection of Claremont in December 1842, the Committee was shocked to notice that the boys' schoolroom, as well as the boys themselves, was in a most filthy state, 'a disgrace to the Institution.' Mr Colgan, assistant master, had absented himself without leave and returned the next night through the window, the doors being locked at that time. The pupils were out of control; several windows had been wrecked, and the door-locks of the Institution torn off, the boys' yard destroyed and, with no security in place, the boys were able to go out and return whenever they pleased.

Mr and Mrs George Clarke, former Headmaster and Mistress of the Charter School in Kevin Street,[2] Dublin, were appointed Providore and Matron respectively, and, in due time, order was restored. Some changes to the dietary system were suggested, with more meat and vegetables, cultivated from the Institution's gardens. He arranged for some of the boys to be taught tailoring and shoemaking, two boys to be employed each day. After five applications for the vacancy of Headmaster, three from Dublin and two from Scotland, were received and read, the post was re-advertised in the newspapers in England and Scotland. By the end of 1842, Claremont was still without a Headmaster, with Mr Webster, Senior Master, taking responsibility for conduct of the junior teachers, while Mr and Mrs Clarke looked after the domestic administration of the Institution.

Yorkshire Institution for the Deaf and Dumb, Doncaster
(*reproduced from* The History of the Yorkshire Residential
School for the Deaf, 1829-1979 *by Anthony J. Boyce*)

James Cook

In June 1843, two members of the Committee paid visits to some of the Institutions for the instruction of the deaf and dumb in England, to enquire into the mode of education and general management. Two months later, after writing to Mr Charles Baker, headmaster of the Yorkshire Institution for the Deaf and Dumb, Doncaster, in regard to James Cook, teacher at that Institution, the Committee appointed James Cook as Headmaster of the Claremont Institution with a salary of £200 per annum with apartments and gardens. Prior to his appointment to Claremont, Mr Cook had been familiarising himself with the system of teaching the deaf for twelve years, eight of which he had been Assistant Teacher in the Doncaster Institution which was, at that time, one of the most flourishing Institutions in the United Kingdom. He had studied the systems adopted in the French and German Schools for the deaf, and, combined with a satisfactory personal interview, the Committee considered him as the best qualified person to fill the situation.

Mr Cook carried out a detailed survey of the educational system at the Institution in Claremont, and presented his recommendations to the Committee. He noticed that there had not been a systematic course, on every subject, particularly in language, which was all-important to the Deaf. He added that the use of signs, instead of finger-spelling, in the ordinary communication between the teachers and pupils not only kept the children in ignorance of many common phrases and idioms, but when they went into society, made them appear much more ignorant than they really were, and would present problems when taken on as apprentices. The deaf children had not attended church service, and were less interested in the service through not being able to follow the prayers and the sermon.

As for the girls, they were much more backward than the boys, owing to the shortness of the time allowed for instruction, which was three and half hours a day, five days a week. Mr Cook proposed to bring in the Bible as much as possible and wished the children to have no unpleasant associations, no ideas of difficulty or tasks connected with it, but to prepare them so that they might read it with pleasure and interest. Copies of Charles Baker's works, *Revealed Religion* and *Scripture Lessons*, had been ordered for this purpose.

He proposed to banish signs as much as possible from ordinary communication and to endeavour, as far as possible, to insist upon others carrying on all conversation by spelling, and to keep signing with the objective of explaining written language instead of being substituted for it. He wished to see the assistants enter into conversation with the children, show an interest in their pursuits, convey to them knowledge on the affairs of common life and show them the advantage of industry and acquiring a trade so as not to be a burden on others. He recommended that a boy of about fifteen years of age be engaged to enter readily into the feelings and pursuits of the children, and to make friends with them. Such a boy might be found from some of the public schools, and he should have a good English education. He also suggested that children on leaving the Institution should be supplied with a copy of the Bible and Prayer Book.

Largest number of pupils received by the Institution
In 1844, the number of pupils in the Institution reached 136, including those elected, for admission to Claremont, at the Annual Meeting of the Juvenile Association on Easter Monday of that year. That was the largest number of pupils ever in one year during the history of the Institution. However, the Committee had to turn away 42 candidates, owing to lack of funds and to limited accommodation of the dormitories. Charge of the Female Department had been given to the female assistants: Misses Simpson and Wood (hearing), and to the deaf assistants: Anne McCormick, Cecilia White and Charlotte Riddall. The male pupils were under the charge of two hearing assistant masters, Mr Colgan and Mr Preston. Miss McCormick received a gratuity of five pounds for her length of service and good conduct. In January 1845, building of an extension of dormitories for the pupils, and bedrooms and sitting-rooms for assistants commenced at the cost of £700. The donation of £300 was received from the Lord Primate towards the building funds, and Dr Charles Orpen had collected £200 for these purposes. Mr Cook appointed a former pupil, John Feeney, as assistant teacher. In October, a printing press was erected at the Institution for purpose of providing

training for some of the boys, and to produce lesson books, circulars, annual reports, etc. In December, the Committee entered into negotiation with the Secretary of the Ulster Society for the Education of the Deaf and Dumb with the effect of transferring to the Ulster Institution in Belfast any pupils who were from the North, and to cease having any auxiliaries in, or elect pupils from Ulster.

The following March, the Committee met at Claremont for the purpose of investigating charges that the system of religious instruction was not well suited to the children having regard to their capacities and that the Sabbath was not being strictly observed. On Sundays, a pupil was weeding and two of the boys were occupied in wheeling ashes into Mr Cook's garden. It had been the practice of Mr Cook to put aside damaged Bibles to be used by the boys for lighting fires in the school-room and in his own hothouses. Upon investigation, it appeared that Mr Cook had no vicious intention of burning the Bibles, but acted from lack of direction regarding use of waste paper.

The mother of a female pupil had called to the Committee's office to complain that Mr Cook had severely cut the girl in several places on the neck and face. Upon investigation, Mr Cook did not appear to have exercised undue severity on the girl in question. In March 1847, Mr Cook informed the Committee that he had been offered a position as headmaster of the Edinburgh Deaf and Dumb Institution.

Mr James Foulston and attempts of merging Male and Female Pupils

Mr Cook was succeeded in May 1847 by Mr James Foulston, teacher of the Doncaster Institution for the Deaf, at a salary of £150 per annum. There was an objection to his appointment, as he was considered too young and inexperienced for the situation of Headmaster. It was suggested that both male and female staff, during school hours, would remain in the same schoolroom and be under the constant control and vigilance of the Headmaster, and that the room used as the Girls' Schoolroom be converted into a general dining hall for all the pupils. However, this was rejected as dangerous to the moral well-being of the Institution. On 9 November 1847, Dr Orpen, founder of the National Institution of the Education of the Deaf and Dumb Poor of Ireland, announced his intention of emigrating to South Africa. At this point, the Institution at Claremont had reached the beginning of its end.

Deaf Children from the Army and the Navy

The Application Book, the Register and some of the Annual Reports revealed that some deaf children were sent, with or without financial support from the regiments or the Navy in which their fathers had served, to Claremont. Further details of some of these pupils are contained in Appendix 7.

View of Sackville Street, Dublin (Barker, 1835)
The Institution's office was located at No.16, on the right side of the street.
(courtesy of the National Library of Ireland)

Procedures for Admission

In order to have a deaf child admitted into the Institution, an application form had to be requested from the Committee. Particulars such as name, residence, date of birth, age, onset and severity of deafness, any physical defects, skills already attained, parents' occupation and financial situation, were entered, and the form had to be signed by the two persons who were to provide securities or bond. In effect, the child once admitted was bound to the Institution until either the term of education, usually four to five years in length, or the age of fifteen has been reached, before the child could be removed from the Institution and sent back to either the family home or the friends who had provided financial support for the child's education and maintenance. The average cost of educating and maintaining a pupil was £15 to £20 per annum.

Where no financial support could be obtained for individual applicants, funds were raised through voluntary contributions, in form of subscriptions from auxiliary societies, legacies, donations, collections at the public meetings, charity sermons and deputation tours. Contributions were called for by a collector or sent by post. Lists of the names of subscribers and amount of their contributions received were published in the Annual Reports. Subscribers of one guinea annually had the right to vote at the half-yearly election of pupils to the Institution. Those who donated larger sums were granted extra voting rights. At the elections, prospective pupils were chosen from the list of applicants.[3] Dr Charles Orpen referred, in his book, *Anecdotes and Annals of the Deaf and Dumb*, to bitter disappointment felt by the parents when their deaf children failed to get themselves elected.

He referred to an instance where a father and mother from County Clare who had three deaf children in a family of four, walked to Dublin with their deaf son, to try and procure admission into the Institution for the boy. Their journey came to nothing when they arrived at the offices of the Institution at 16 Sackville Street, Dublin. The funds of the Institution were insufficient to permit more admissions. His admission was postponed for another year, and he was soon to be of such an age. In most cases, it was at the age of twelve years, that the rules of the Institution must exclude him. Several applicants who had failed to obtain admission had no choice but to remain uneducated and thus perceived by their families and the public as a burden on the family and on society.

In the Annual Report of 1820, there was a List of Applicants declared ineligible owing to over-age, idiocy, forfeiture of election, or other causes, the oldest applicant being 23 years of age. Some parents of those who were over age offered to pay all expenses. Some of the pupils were supported by rich neighbours and nobility, including Lord Powerscourt and Lady Bandon. Mr Shirley, landowner of the Farnham estate near Carrickmacross, Co. Cavan, sponsored a deaf son of one of his tenants, by name of David Moncrieff.

The survey of the application forms (from 1861 to 1900) and the Register (from 1836 to 1900) showed that the average age of children admitted into the Institution was nine to ten years. In 1861, it was decided that a relaxation be made to one of the rules of the Society to lower the age of admission. When institutions for the Deaf were originally founded, their rules of admission were framed upon the supposition that it was premature to educate deaf children less than six years of age. However, an opinion to the contrary had been gaining ground among those having close acquaintance with the mental condition of infant deaf children, resulting in Claremont opening up to children of much earlier age.

Admitting Deaf Adults for Education

Due to the limited numbers of supervisory and teaching staff at Claremont required for adequate supervision of the pupils within the Institution and its surroundings which stretched across eighteen acres of cultivated and untended land, the Committee decided against admitting any uneducated deaf person over eighteen years of age. In addition, there was concern that adult deaf people would exert unfavourable influence on the younger deaf children. On 25 August 1852, the Rev. Griffith, chaplain of Cork Foundling Hospital, enquired whether the rules of this Society would admit deaf adults for instruction at a certain rate per annum. The Committee replied that the rules would not allow admission of pupils after twelve years of age. The following month, Cork Foundling Hospital wrote that the Governors were willing to pay any reasonable sum for the two deaf females. The reply was that adults could not be admitted.

The main source for obtaining information on occupations of parents who applied for admission of their deaf children into the Claremont Institution was the application form for admission. The range of occupations was diverse – whether it be a respectable position such as clerk or at the bottom of the social class such as beggar. The means of the parents or guardians were assessed based on the occupation or, if the applicant was a farmer, on the acreage of the land. In some cases, the landlords, the nobility and the gentry of the estates in which the deaf child resided would contribute towards all or part of the fees. Completed application forms had to be signed in presence of one or two members of the professional classes, most often either the clergyman or the doctor of the child's parish. Once the application form was signed by the parent or the sponsor, responsibility for the care of the child was transferred to the Committee of the Institution for the fixed term stated on the form.

Private Pupils and Parlour Boarders

The establishment was divided into two parts - one for reception of the deaf children of the poor, and the other for private pupils, who were taken into the care of the Headmaster and the Matron. Mr Joseph Humphreys offered 'tuition for private deaf and dumb pupils and for the cure of impediments in speech.'[4] The terms per annum stated were as follows:

Board, etc.	30 guineas
English Language Grammar and Writing	20 guineas
Stationery and books	2 guineas
Arithmetic	5 guineas
Articulation	15 guineas
Geography, Astronomy and History	12 guineas
Drawing and materials	8 guineas
Needlework	4 guineas
Washing	4 guineas

The privileges afforded to the private pupils were that each pupil was to have a separate bed, and live in all respects as a member of the Headmaster's family, and his wife was to take charge of the female pupils. At the Institution's office, the registers were maintained where details of the children admitted were entered, but not those of private pupils, as they were under the sole charge and responsibility of the Headmaster who retained most of the fees for their education and maintenance.

Among the private pupils was Acheson S. Colquhoun, who was listed on the British Census of 1861, for the Liverpool School for the Deaf, as teacher, at the age of 20 and his birth-place as Ireland. He continued to teach at Liverpool according to the 1871 Census.

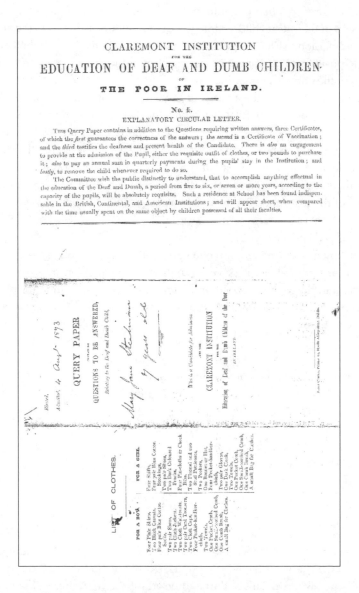

The first page of the four-page Application Form for admission on 4 August 1873 of a seven-year-old deaf girl named Mary Jane Steadman into the Institution. The page shows the list of clothes which had to be supplied upon her arrival at the School. Alternatively, one pound was requested in lieu of the outfit. The format of the application form has remained the same for over 150 years since the establishment of the Institution except for a few instances, such as the omission of the List of Clothes to be supplied by parents or sponsors for the pupil prior to admission.

2 *Questions to be answered, with Certificates of the truth of the Answers, to be signed*

No. 11.

QUESTIONS.	ANSWERS.

I. *Relative to the Child's Parents or Friends.*

1. Are the child's parents living or dead? — *yes*
2. What are the names of the child's parents or friends? — *John + Anne Steadman*
3. What is their Present Residence? Nearest Post Town? — *41 New Street. Dublin*
4. What are their characters? Occupations? — *Industrious + Deserving HH shoemaker*
5. What is the number of their children? and how many of them are Deaf and Dumb? — *three . one deaf-mute*
6. What have been, and are the pecuniary circumstances of the child's parents, relatives, and friends? — *poor*
7. What is the utmost sum the parents or friends could pay annually to the Institution for the board, lodging, clothes, and education, &c., &c., of the child? — *nothing*
8. Have they any rich neighbours, landlords, or others, who would be willing to engage to pay part, or the whole of these expenses of the child? What are their names? and what is the utmost that each and altogether would pay? — *No*
9. If the parents, or friends are unable to pay anything towards the child's support, will the Parish or Union contribute for that purpose? and how much?

II. *Relative to the Child.*

1. What is the child's name? Exact date of Birth? — *Mary Anne Steadman. 30th Augt 1866.*
2. Does the child live with her parents? if not, with whom, and how long? and how is the child now maintained? — *with parents*
3. Was the child deaf from birth? and if not, when and how was hearing lost? — *no, From scarlatina.*
4. Has the child been always Dumb? and if not, when and how was speech lost? — *deafness total.*
5. Is the Deafness total? and if not, does evince any sensation from loud noises? or does the hearing extend to the distinguishing of the sounds of the voice, when articulated with ordinary distinctness? — *No.*
6. Is the Dumbness total? and if not, does the power of speech extend to the utterance of intelligible words? — *Yes — No*
7. Is the child certainly not in any degree idiotic? and does discover a good natural intellect, by making signs, intelligible to those with whom has constant intercourse? and do those signs evince intelligence? — *intelligent*
8. Is the child's sight perfect? or has he any other bodily defect? — *1st Yes 2d No*
9. What has been, and is the child's general state of health? and is free from fits, and the evil, and at present from every symptom of chronic, acute, contagious, and cutaneous disease? — *good, yes*
10. Has the child had the Small Pox or Cow Pock? Measles? Scarlet Fever? Hooping Cough? — *yes, each..*
11. Has the child, as yet, received any education? — *No*
12. Has the child learned any manual trade, or labour? or ever been employed in any useful occupation? if so in what? — *No*
13. What appears to be the child's disposition? — *good tempered*
14. Has the child shown any particular talent, as for drawing, carving, mechanics, &c. — *No*

The Steadman family lived at 41 New Street, Dublin, and her father's occupation was a shoe-maker, his character being industrious and deserving. The family, with three children, was poor, and nothing could be afforded to pay for Mary's education and maintenance. Mary had become totally deaf after contact scarlatina (scarlet fever).

11

Claremont - The 1850's to 1880's

Upon the departure of Dr Orpen to South Africa in 1848, the light kindled by the Doctor in 1816 dimmed, and the Claremont Institution plunged into despair and darkness. Ireland was recovering from the effects of the Great Famine, and religious intimidation was on the increase, spurred on by the restoration of the Roman Catholic authorities to the religious, educational and social affairs affecting the populace of the country. The efforts of the Committee of the Roman Catholic Institution for the Deaf and Dumb were doubled since its establishment in 1846, with the opening of a school for deaf female Catholics, whose education and maintenance was administered by the Dominican Sisters at their Convent in Cabra, Dublin.[1] In 1849, Catholic deaf boys were taken under the charge of the Carmelite monks at Prospect Seminary in Glasnevin, and in 1857, the Christian Brothers agreed to take over education of deaf boys, after the new buildings were erected in Cabra, to accommodate the increasing number of deaf boys.[2] The Catholic priests, becoming aware of the existence of the Catholic Institution for the Deaf and Dumb, sought out any deaf parishioners with the intention of arranging for their admission into the schools administered by this Institution At that point of time, there were some Catholic pupils in the Claremont Institution, and in some cases, their parents were under duress by the priests, on pain of being denied access to the rites of their church, to withdraw their deaf children from Claremont and transfer them to Cabra.

The Shanahan Case

In 1843, Mrs Fisher, a lady from Charleville, Co. Cork, told the Roman Catholic parents, the Shanahans, who were at that time in the workhouse and had two deaf children, that she would arrange for their deaf daughter, Mary, to be educated at the Claremont Institution in Dublin. She assured the parents that no interference would be made in regard to her religion. In 1848, the deaf boy, Denis Shanahan, aged twelve years, was also sent to the Institution. In the following year, the father, Patrick Shanahan, having heard rumours from the neighbours that his deaf children were not being reared as Catholics, decided to travel to Dublin to see for himself. He had a confrontation with the officers of Claremont, when he tried to remove his children from the school. It had been pointed out to him that his children were, according to the rules of the Institution, under the care of the Institution until the expiry of the term, and that their mother had given her consent, having signed the application form. Then Mr Shanahan took legal action to take his son, Denis, out of Claremont.

In November 1852, Mr James Foulston, headmaster, was ordered by the court to give evidence that the mother of the pupil, Denis Shanahan, had given consent for her son to be admitted to Claremont. 'On personal examination in presence of the Counsel by Mr Justice Moore of Denis Shanahan for the purpose of ascertaining the free Agency and Wishes of the said Denis Shanahan as to his future residence and instruction and he having in reply to the several questions put to him through the *medium of signs* stated in writing his desire and determination to continue as such Pupil at said Institution until the expiration of the Term required for the completion of his Education according to the rules and regulations thereof.'[3] The boy was asked, by written communication, whether he wished to remain, up to the expiry of his term, at Claremont.

> 'Your father wishes to remove you from the Institution but you can go or stay whichever you please. Would you like to go home with your father?'
> The boy said, 'No.'
> 'Would you wish to remain in this Institution?'
> The reply was 'Yes.'

Then the court ordered that Denis Shanahan be 'remitted to the Care and Protection of the Managers and Head Master of said Institution at Claremont there to continue and remain in compliance with such his election and desire.'

When he commenced his headmastership, Mr Foulston carried out a detailed examination of the system of education adopted at Claremont and in January 1848, he presented his findings in a lengthy report to the Committee. While investigating into the general deficiency in the Girls' School, he noticed that the girls received one hour less of instruction than the boys. When asked why that was so, Miss Simpson, hearing teacher, said that a great part of her time was occupied in undoing what had been done by Miss McCormick, deaf assistant teacher. Mr Foulston referred to Lawrence Feagan, deaf and engaged as drawing teacher at the Institution, that he was uncooperative and was guided more by 'pecuniary motives, than by feelings of gratitude.' Addressing the qualifications for the teachers of the deaf, Mr Foulston observed that John Feeney, though efficient, disliked teaching while Cecilia White possessed only very moderate abilities but steady perseverance and willingness to improve. He felt that Anne McCormick got easily excited and became quite incapacitated for teaching, and that she had no teaching skills. In regard to Charlotte Riddall, she was very quiet, well-disposed and willing, but was deficient and could not teach much. In the year of 1848, the number of pupils in the Institution declined to 64, and the services of Anne McCormack and Charlotte Riddall were no longer required. Sir Richard Orpen, brother of Dr Orpen, wrote to the Committee expressing his concern about Miss McCormick's dismissal. He was sent an extract from the Headmaster's report regarding her incompetence as teacher. However, both McCormick and Riddall were retained until October 1851. Charlotte Riddall was boarded out in Co. Wicklow for a small payment, while Anne McCormick was granted a pension of £15 a year during her lifetime.

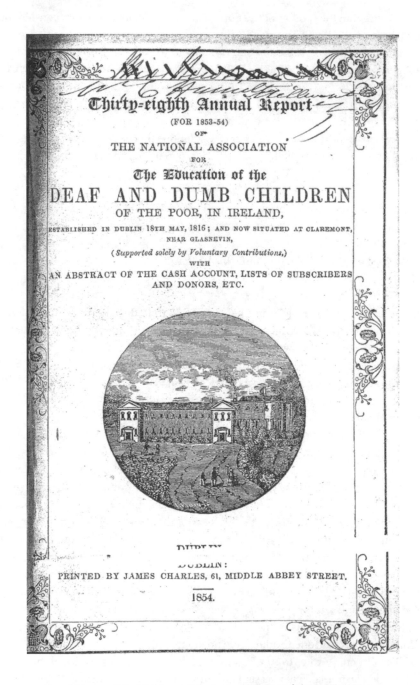

Front Cover of the Thirty-eighth Annual Report of the Institution
The vignette, depicting front of Claremont, was designed by Lawrence Feagan, former pupil

NATIONAL ASSOCIATION

For Promoting the Education of the

𝔇eaf & 𝔇umb 𝔓oor of 𝔍reland,

CLAREMONT, NEAR GLASNEVIN.

THE ANNUAL

MEETING

Will (D.V.) be held in the

INSTITUTION, CLAREMONT,

On *EASTER TUESDAY, APRIL 2nd, 1872.*

The Chair will be taken at 12 o'Clock

BY THE

RIGHT HON. THE LORD MAYOR.

THE PUPILS WILL BE PRESENT.

No Tickets required

J. Charles & Son, Printers, Abbey-street.

Notice distributed at churches in Dublin, announcing the forthcoming Annual Meeting of the Claremont Institution. The above was found at St Andrew's Church, Suffolk Street, Dublin (with thanks to Brian Lawson).

Mr Foulston was implicated in unfounded charges regarding misapplication of food and abuse of articles provided for use of the Institution, and several officers, including servants and the gardener, were severely reprimanded by the Committee.

In June 1852, Mr Foulston was granted leave of absence to attend the Conference of Headmasters of the Deaf in Doncaster. In the same month, the Committee held at Claremont an examination of Mr Foulston and the three hearing female teachers, Miss Simpson, Miss Carnegie and Miss Cooper. They found that, firstly, Mr Foulston had given instructions on several occasions to Miss Carnegie but only on one occasion to Miss Cooper; secondly, there were two sets of signs (i.e. sign language) in the Institution, Mr Foulston's and Miss Simpson's, leading to great confusion in the school; and thirdly, the head class of Girls had received no instruction from Mr Foulston. After deliberation, the following arrangements were made: no increase of teachers in the Boys' School; no decrease in the Girls' School; Miss Simpson and Miss Carnegie to take classes in the Girls' school, and that an 'Alphabet Class' be formed for Miss Cooper in the Girls' school, consisting of all the new pupils, both boys and girls. To meet the extra expense of the third teacher, Miss Simpson's salary was reduced from £30 to £20 per annum.

In 1855, Mr Foulston wrote a book entitled *Reflections on Education of the Deaf and Dumb*, with guidance for parents of deaf children. On 8 October, he resigned and left Claremont. He had asked for a letter of reference as part of his application for a position in the Asylum for the Deaf and Dumb, London. Later on, he engaged himself in the mission work among the Deaf and Dumb in his native city, Leeds. After ordination in 1882, he devoted himself to ordinary clerical duties in the diocese of Ripon. He died and was buried in Leeds.

Deputation to Institutions for the Deaf and Dumb in Great Britain
In December 1855, two Committee members, Dr John Ringland and Mr John Gelston, visited several Institutions for the Deaf and Dumb in Great Britain. In the preface to the Report on the Deputation, Dr Ringland said that 'they entered zealously upon the duty imposed upon them, and did not hesitate to undertake the inconvenience of leaving home in the depth of a most severe winter, and of travelling, within a fortnight, upwards of 1,200 miles, amidst great snow and most intense frost.' The Institutions (Principals in brackets) visited were Liverpool (Mr Buxton), Manchester (Mr Patterson), Birmingham (Mr Hopper), London Asylum (Mr T.J. Watson), Brighton (Mr Sleight), Doncaster (Mr Baker), Newcastle (Mr Neill), Edinburgh (Mr Rhind), Donaldson's Hospital in Edinburgh (Mr McDiarmid), Glasgow (Mr Anderson) and Belfast (Rev. Kinghan).

All the above Institutions, with one exception, admitted 'parlour boarders' (private pupils). At some schools, the Principal arranged the terms, out of which he paid the Institution a fixed sum annually for the board of each; at others, each boarder paid a fixed amount to the Institution, out of which the Principal received a percentage, whilst at others, the Principal received the whole of the revenue from pupils, who boarded at his private table. In the majority of the schools, eight was the minimum and twelve the maximum age for admission, and the pupils were retained from five to six years in the Institution. However, the Claremont Committee felt no need to alter the rule, namely to admit between the ages of six and twelve, while pupils, having reached the age of sixteen, were to be removed.

Separation of the Sexes

In the majority of the institutions visited, pupils occupied the same school-room, mingling in the same classes. The Deputation observed that in the London Asylum both sexes were in the same school-room, which was in the form of a right angle, one arm of which was occupied by boys, the other by girls, thus practically keeping them separate, while in the same room. With two exceptions (Edinburgh and Donaldson's Hospital), all the pupils, male and female, took their meals at the same time in a common dining-hall. But in all schools, there was a separate playground for each sex, and during that time, they were kept strictly apart. The principals of those Institutions 'highly approved of these arrangements and did not believe that any immorality had ever resulted'.[4] Based on these findings, it was recommended that the adoption of the system of permitting the children of both sexes to meet daily, under proper surveillance, in the school-room and dining-hall in the Claremont Institution.

Female Assistants employed in Institutions for the Deaf and Dumb

In 1855, there were no female teachers in Liverpool, Manchester, Brighton, Doncaster, Newcastle, Edinburgh and Glasgow. Mr Buxton (Liverpool) and Mr Baker (Doncaster) considered that 'male teachers better suited for instructing mutes, as the sign language, to be efficiently taught, demanded a greater amount of energy, as well as of physical strength and endurance, than in females.'[5] In eleven institutions visited, out of 52 assistants, seven were female, while of these seven, five were deaf and dumb. Dr Ringland and Mr Gelston felt that they 'could not avoid recommending that Male Assistants should be appointed to fill any vacancies which might arise among the female teachers at Claremont'. They added that 'one female, whether be an assistant or a work-mistress, should be at all times present with the girls, but more especially during the periods when the boys and girls were together.'

Deaf and Dumb Assistants

In the year of 1855, in the eleven Institutions in Great Britain, there were only twelve deaf assistants, seven male and five female. At Manchester, two male assistants, at Birmingham three female teachers; at London three male assistants; at Brighton one male assistant; at Donaldson's Hospital one female; at Glasgow, one male, and at Belfast one female assistant were deaf. The general doubt, expressed to Ringland and Gelston, was the suitability of the 'deaf and dumb appointed to any office of authority, on the ground that their ignorance of the world and its ways, deeming them unfit for carrying out duties of command over those subordinate to them, and of submission to those placed in authority over them.' However, there was some difference of opinion as to their eligibility for the situation of Assistant Teacher. Many Principals agreed that the deaf and dumb made good teachers, while others preferred hearing assistants. Some had procured 'especially intelligent mute teachers for junior classes'. All principals, however, agreed that the deaf were not suitable for the 'more advanced classes.' Putting the deaf assistant in charge of junior classes, it was believed, was proper as the deaf assistant had mastered the 'natural language of signs, as expressed by the countenance, gesture and attitude,' and therefore more useful for the arrival of new pupils. The conclusion, reached by Ringland and Gelston, was that the 'more advanced classes' should not be left to the instruction of a 'mute teacher.' Nevertheless, they said, 'we never doubted that the faculties of many of the deaf and dumb are capable of cultivation to the highest extent.'[6]

Arrangement of Classes

In 1855, the average number of pupils in each class, at the different Institutions in Great Britain, was fifteen. The number of classes was dependent on the number of teachers, the number of pupils and the financial condition of the Institutions. Ringland and Gelston recommended for adoption at Claremont the plan used at Liverpool. In that school, there were six classes and three assistants. Each assistant took two classes, Senior and Junior. The teacher had one class occupied receiving instruction at the slate, while the other was at their desks, writing and preparing their lessons. At fixed times, the two classes changed places, and thus all pupils were fully occupied, under his observation. It was agreed that time of the Principal of any Institution would be more occupied in general supervision of the school and in going from class to class, checking during the week on the progress of each class.

In the Classroom of a Deaf School as at 1855

Large slates were inserted on the walls around the school-room, three feet high and two feet from the ground. Pupils sat at the three sides of the long desk, all facing the teacher, with his back to the slated wall. A considerable number of maps were used, as well as a large terrestrial globe, suspended from the ceiling by weights and pulleys. All the Institutions were supplied with pictures, arranged around the walls of the school-room, which were 'very useful in deaf mute instruction.' The system of using such aids had long been employed at Claremont. It was recommended that a 'museum,' articles in common use, raw materials, manufactured commodities, natural history specimens, models and objects of interest, stored in a small cabinet, be obtained for Claremont.

Public Examination at the Rotunda on 11 November 1842

On the platform was a blackboard around which the deaf children stood. Each question was written on the board, and the children wrote the answers under the questions. A pupil, Thomas O'Malley, aged 14 and six years at Claremont, wrote that he learnt religion, geography, grammar, arithmetic, and the use of good things. 'What do you mean by good things?' The boy wrote, 'Minerals'. 'What are minerals?' 'Digging out of the earth'. 'Who made the earth?' 'God'. 'Who is God?' 'A spiritual eternal, invisible, all-seeing, just, holy and merciful'.

Mr Martin, headmaster, volunteered to explain the gestures of the children in making themselves explained in some answers. The boy was asked, 'what is merciful?' He rubbed the palm of his left hand with the fingers of his right – the gesture of 'blotting out'. When asked what was 'all-seeing', the boy looked about in every direction. When asked what is 'just', he held out his hands as if weighing something in each hand. When asked, 'what is a mediator?', he held up his hand, and opened out his first and third finger wide and then put up the second finger between them - to express a difference between two persons, and a third person coming between them and making them friends. A gentleman asked the boy, 'what is a river?', and the answer was written on the board, 'a current of fresh water'. 'Where is Petersburgh?' The boy wrote, 'in Russia.'

Thomas Dixon - the Deaf Messenger

Among the officers employed by the Institution was the deaf messenger, Thomas Dixon, who had been admitted to Claremont in 1828, his maintenance funded by Major Sirr, father of Dr Orpen's wife, Alicia. His duties were to convey messages between the school at Claremont in Glasnevin and the Committee's office in Sackville Street, Dublin. Several times each year, he put forward requests for replenishing of various articles of clothing, including a hat and 'great coat', as well as the 'Christmas box.' Mr Chidley, headmaster, informed the Committee on 8 April 1869 that 'the appearance of the pupils would be greatly improved by obtaining a proper hairdresser for eight shillings per quarter, as the hair of the boys is cut by T. Dixon in such a manner as very much disfigures them.' Occasionally, he was reprimanded for being 'out of order' and for opening the letters without permission. One time, he was reported to the Committee for being insolent to a gentleman riding along the road. It was decided to have him and Laurence Feagan, the deaf drawing teacher, boarded out with a respectable Protestant family in the city, to discourage contact with the female pupils and staff. In 1855, Mr Clarke, Providore of the Institution, complained of Dixon's conduct towards him when reproving him for wasting bread. Dixon was asked to apologize to Mr Clarke in the presence of the School, for his abusive letter about Mr Clarke, or he would be dismissed. On 2 May 1877, Thomas Dixon died at the age of 58, and he requested that his effects be given to the Claremont Institution, to which he had been of service for over forty years.

Edward James Chidley (1819-1881)
A man of cultivated mind and of amiable disposition, he was born in Worcestershire, on 15 March 1819. His father died before he was born and when his mother died, he was admitted to the London Orphan Asylum at the age of eight years, and remained there for five years. He was a brilliant scholar, and was recorded on the Roll of Honour, becoming a life member by his donation of fifty pounds. After leaving school, he spent some time at a solicitor's office, and then became a pupil teacher at the London Asylum for the Deaf and Dumb, under Thomas James Watson, and later senior teacher.[7]

Articulation or not?
Mr Edward Chidley entered into a debate on the subject of mechanical articulation. He had been for 20 years an instructor in the London Institution, in which articulation was taught. In 1856, when asked by the Committee of the Claremont Institution whether articulation was to be recommended as a part of the system of instruction, he answered in the negative, and the consequence was that articulation was not taught at Claremont. The exception he would make was in the case of deaf children of wealthy parents. Then Mr Chidley was appointed headmaster. He brought to his work an appreciation of the importance of language to his pupils. He was a free agent so far as the Committee of the Institution was concerned. At that time, the Institution had upwards of two hundred auxiliaries, most of whom were active at raising funds for the Institution. Each year, many meetings, including examinations of the pupils, were held by a clerical deputation, and at these examinations, the test of the pupils' proficiency was not language, but historical information. Before a pupil had made any progress whatever in composition or in reading the Bible for himself, he was expected to answer questions calculated to puzzle the skilled student of the Scriptures. This method of public examination was discomforting for Mr Chidley. While certain pupils, especially from the private class, gained some knowledge of language and arithmetic, the majority of the pupils were drilled to answer questions relating to the facts of Scriptural history and the history of England.

Mr Chidley's viewpoint on the practice of articulation and lip-reading was mixed; he felt that the 'combined system' (sign language and articulation) was a failure, and the 'pure oral method' (articulation and lip-reading without support of sign language) was doubtful. He was baffled about the rigid rejection of sign language by some instructors of the deaf. In his letters to the Committee, he gave detailed accounts of his efforts at sourcing apprenticeships and employment for the pupils when they completed their education, and of returning unemployable pupils to their homes. Pupils, unfortunate to be homeless and friendless, were either removed to the Union Workhouse, took the emigrant ship out of Ireland or turned to crime.

On 5 November 1856, the Inspector from the Endowed Schools Commission paid a visit to Claremont and his report was as follows. 'The general state of the Institution was very satisfactory. Pupils were examined in language lessons, geography and arithmetic, in all which a remarkable degree of proficiency was exhibited, thanks to the very efficient teacher, Mr E.J. Chidley. Pupils appeared healthy, and there was no vacant expression which is generally observable in the uninstructed deaf and dumb. Some defects in internal arrangements of the building were noticed; no water closets were provided, and urinal accommodation in the boys' dormitory was deemed unsuitable. Only one warm bath was available, not sufficient for wants of so large an establishment. A large plunge bath was out of order at the date of my visit.'[8]

In 1857, the number of applications for admissions to Claremont declined, and the number of pupils fell to under 60. Consequently, the estimate of cost per head was larger and this led to the Committee dispensing with the services of the Providore and Matron, and placing the entire management of Claremont under Mr Chidley, assisted by his wife. Finally, it was admitted that it was economical to amalgamate the Male and Female Schools, where both sexes of pupils could be under surveillance by the Headmaster, saving on costs of teachers.

The Headmaster had made arrangements for receiving into his own family a superior class of boarding pupils at the following rates: under 10 years £30 per annum, over that age £40 per annum. The Intermediate class of paying pupils at £25 per annum were to share the same table and the bedroom with assistant teachers. The third class was to pay £8 per annum to have same food as the indigent pupils and clothed in the same way.

After a short illness, Edward James Chidley died on 17 February 1881, leaving a widow, four sons and two daughters. His widow, Emma Mary, remained at the Institution as Matron, under the charge of her son, Edward William. She died on 9 April 1884, aged 54, and was buried with her husband in St. Mobhi's Churchyard, Glasnevin. At the annual meeting in June of that year, the Secretary said, 'for 25 years, our valued Matron, Mrs Chidley, devoted herself with untiring energy and zeal to the duties of her office, and her kindly attention to the pupils endeared her to them all. The Committee have appointed as her successor a lady of considerable experience in the domestic management of Institutions in England and Ireland.'

Edward William Chidley, B.A.

Having entered Trinity College Dublin on 12 October 1880, at the age of twenty-two, Edward William Chidley took up his father's mantle. He decided to introduce the oral system to Claremont. In April 1882, he asked for permission to go to London for six weeks with the object to learn from Mr Schoenthiel of the Jews' Home, Notting Hill, London. Some time later, two assistant teachers from Claremont were sent to London to receive training in the 'pure oral system'.

In 1883 he sought an increase in his salary, mentioning *'the anxieties of the place, the variety of the duties and the unremitting nature of the work.'* He pointed out that the existing arrangement of receiving private pupils at the rate of £40 a year, with one quarter being paid to the Committee, and £30 for feeding growing children, leaving nothing for their care, was insufficient. This was supported by letters from some of the English institutions of the deaf. He constantly complained about the dilapidated state of the building and the lack of a proper water supply which could be obtained from the public water-pipes ('Vartry water') which came as far as the entrance gates. He mentioned a need for *'30 yards of netting to keep the fowls out of the flower-ground; and the School-room, when the doors are open, is subject to draughts and this needs a green baize screen to protect against the cold.'* Some teachers applied for and received an increase in their salaries, while Mr Chidley only received, on rare occasions, some form of bonus, since he had the use of the house, garden and the farm-produce. He mentioned that, during his holidays in 1885, he visited the Institution for the Deaf in Paris which was 'converted' in 1880 (presumably to the oral system) under circumstances similar to those at Claremont. He said that Claremont's results of three years are *'little if at all inferior to theirs.'* He tried to introduce *'recreational amusement for children, a plain set of cricket for boys would keep their minds occupied and keep them from mischief'.* His attempts to improve the quality of life at Claremont were hampered by lack of finance.

On 14 October 1887, his resignation, together with that of Miss Crowley, teacher, were accepted. An advertisement was published for a Headmaster and Female Teacher, the former at a salary of £200 per annum with apartments, coal and light; the position of Female Teacher to commence at £36 per annum, with board and residence. In November 1888, Mr George Taylor was appointed Headmaster of the Claremont Institution.

Benjamin H. Payne

Born on 23 January 1847, he received his early education at Ranelagh School, Athlone, and, at the age of ten, became totally deaf after contracting scarlatina. In 1860, he went to Claremont, first as pupil, then pupil-teacher, and finally assistant teacher. He was popular with the pupils and, when the drawing teacher left, Payne deputised. His creation was the picture of Claremont which was then engraved by George McNaught, and the work used as a frontispiece for the Annual Reports since then.

He recalled his early days of hardship at Claremont where he received his very low salary, plain food and little time for leisure. The teaching staff had to observe rigid economics in fuel and lighting.

Mr E.J. Chidley stated with regard to Benjamin Payne who had been a salaried teacher since 1 January 1862 that by his steadiness and attention he had fully answered the expectation and that at sixteen years of age he was already able to render some important assistance and asked that the Committee would raise his salary from five shillings to seven shillings per month. In January 1873, he asked the Committee to increase the salary of 'our very deserving Assistant Teacher, Mr Benjamin Payne, whose services are valuable to the Institution, with 11 years training and experience at Claremont, and has acquired a remarkable skill in the sign-language.' He went on to say that Mr Payne was an excellent teacher and the influence he exerted over the pupils out of school tended to promote their good conduct.

On 10 December 1875, after 16 years' teaching at Claremont, Mr Payne tendered his resignation, having obtained the position as principal of the Cambrian Deaf and Dumb Institution at Swansea, Wales. He was chosen, after open competition with seven hearing candidates. In 1876, he married a former Claremont teacher, Florence Passant, of Slane, Co. Meath. They had lived in Swansea for 40 years before they retired. He was an eloquent signer, and his sign-name was the 'bible under his arm'. He was involved in the organisation of the British Deaf and Dumb Association, and he came to Ireland to assist with interpreting church services for the deaf in Dublin, Cork and Donegal.

In an article covering B.H. Payne's career, it was said that his word was law in the Cambrian Institution for the Deaf and Dumb, Swansea, and that there was good rapport between the Principal, the staff and the pupils. He conducted Divine Service for the adult deaf and dumb in the Institution every Sunday, and was a good friend and counsellor. He was a Vice-President of the British Deaf and Dumb Association. Both the manual and the oral methods were in use in his school. He believed in adapting the method to the pupil rather than the pupil to the method. He was broad-minded and liberal. Moreover, his literary style, as his essays evinced, was crisp, decisive, yet smooth and fluent. He had penned, in a poetic sense, the eulogy of the late Miss Wilhelmina Tredennick, Superintendent of the Ulster Institute for the Adult Deaf and Dumb in Belfast.[9]

He died on 20 August 1926 and was buried in the same grave as his wife who had died in 1921 at Suffolk. His only son, Arnold Hill Payne, having graduated from Oxford University, took holy orders and later on became Missioner at several Institutes for the Deaf and Dumb in Britain.[10]

Samuel Johnson (see picture)

According to the 1882 Annual Report of the Victorian Deaf and Dumb Institution, Melbourne, Australia, the Rev. Lowe, minister of Christ Church, St Kilda, who was visiting England, secured the services of an experienced assistant teacher for the school (Victorian Deaf and Dumb Institution). Samuel Johnson, who had for six years occupied the position of second master in the Claremont Deaf and Dumb Institution, Dublin. On 13 July 1882, Mr Johnson sailed in the *Sorrata* from Gravesend, England and arrived in Melbourne on 22 August. He had been assistant teacher at the Victorian Deaf

SAMUEL JOHNSON

and Dumb Institution for three years, when he became the Head Teacher, with his wife as Matron. He resigned to take up a position at the South Australian Institution for Blind, Deaf and Dumb. Mr Johnson threw himself into the cause of pupils at the Institution and also of those who had left. He conducted Divine services at the South Australian Blind, Deaf and Dumb Institute, and interpreted the speeches into sign language for the deaf.

Vere Henry Wintringham Huston[11]

He was born in Co. Armagh in Northern Ireland in 1868. On 7 November 1883, Mr Chidley, headmaster, recommended the young Huston as successor for a male assistance teacher about to leave. Mr Huston, appearing before the Committee, presented the testimonials from the Dean of Armagh and the Rev. Gibson, headmaster of King's Hospital, Dublin. He was engaged at the salary of £15 per annum with board and lodging. He was most respectable and a general favourite in the house. After one year, Mr Huston applied for extra pay during the absence of Mr Keating, teacher at Claremont. In November 1885, he gave notice to leave Claremont and take up a position in the Margate Institution for the Deaf and Dumb. He qualified as a Certificated (sic) Teacher under the School Board of London in 1897. He was the first Head Teacher of Ackmar Road Primary School for the Deaf, London, when the school opened on 31 January 1898. He was representative of the deaf schools on the National Union of Teachers. He assisted with the organisation of the International Conference for the Education of the Deaf in 1925, and set up the evening classes for the adult deaf. In July 1932, he retired from the Old Kent Road School for the Deaf, London, and on 21 April 1940, he died at the age of 72 years.

12

Claremont - The 1890's to 1940's

'The country should not forget that this was the pioneer Institution in Ireland.'
- *The Archdeacon of Dromore, the Ven. G. Hannon, 1936*[1]

George Taylor (1888-1928)

When Mr Taylor commenced his headmastership in 1888 at Claremont after transferring from the Institution for the Deaf and Dumb, Margate, near London, there were 35 pupils on the roll. By the end of 1900, the number arose to 40, dropping to seven at the time of his retirement in 1928. This particular period was difficult because of the wars at home (the Easter Rising of 1916 and the Civil War in 1922) and abroad (the Boer War and the Great War of 1914-18), depriving Claremont of its life-blood - young male teachers and financial support. Following the Disestablishment of the Church of

GEORGE TAYLOR.

Ireland in 1869 and the Land War in 1880, the Protestant population in Ireland constantly declined, and voluntary subscriptions, legacies and donations dwindled as a result.

To make the Institution self-supporting, the Board of Governors[2] organised for the Schoolroom and other rooms to be rented out for various purposes, particularly during the summer vacation. A Bazaar was held in the Schoolroom in aid of Glasnevin National School. In 1921, a letter was received from the secretary of Glasnevin and District Social Club asking for use of two rooms at a rent of £40 a year plus costs of lighting, fuel and cleaning, and it was decided to charge them the rent of £5 a month. A request was received from the local Chess Club for use of a room, and this was turned down. The local troop of the Girl Guides asked for use of the field for hockey games and their request was also refused.

As well as managing the school building, Mr Taylor had to balance the books for the large estate, with some of the acreage leased out for grazing and the rest for cultivation, producing potatoes, vegetables and fruit for the school. He had to ensure the neat appearance of the pupils by selecting and costing material for suits for the boys. Estimates had been received from reputable clothing suppliers such as Pim's and Arnott's, the latter which still retails in school uniforms to this day. In November 1888, on recommendation of the Ladies' Visitor Report, girls' winter cloaks in blue cloth pattern from Pim's were ordered at twenty-two shillings each, while in March 1889, boys' clothing were ordered from Arnott's; the material to be blue serge for jackets and waistcoats, and grey tweed for trousers.

On the night of 26 February 1903, the storm caused damage at Claremont. Slates and tiles were stripped off, gutters torn away, and two chimney stacks damaged, together with 34 broken panes of glass. Nineteen large elm trees and many smaller trees were uprooted, and the water main was burst in two places due to falling trees.

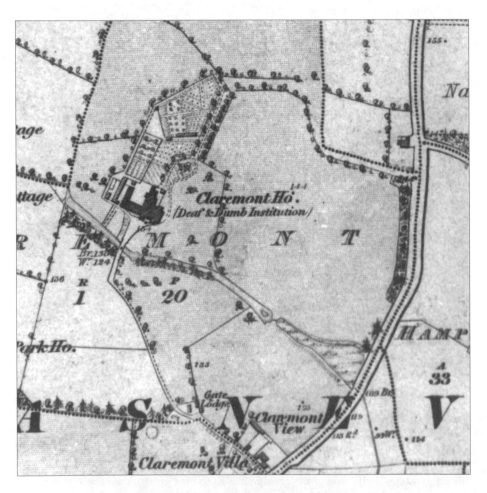

O.S. Map of 1842 showing the Claremont Demesne
with the farm and gardens at the back of the School

At the meetings of the Board of Governors, Mr Taylor had to report on the progress, more usually health-wise, of the pupils and teachers. When a new pupil could not be cured of *'dirty habits'* or found to be of *'weak intellect'*, he asked for removal of that pupil from the Institution. In 1889 he submitted to the Governors a plan of desks, *'as used for Oral classes in many Institutions.'* He reported of a female teacher resigning, after her complaining of *'loneliness and want of society after school duties.'* The school was isolated, two miles away from the city of Dublin, situated in a large expanse of farmland, with the half-mile long, tree-lined Avenue separating the Institution from the outskirts of the village of Glasnevin.

Census Returns of 1901 and 1911 on Claremont

The Census of Ireland returns of 1901 on the residents of the Claremont Institution in Glasnevin revealed that George Taylor, head of the household, put down 'Schoolmaster' as his occupation with 35 pupils under his charge. He was born in England, 43 years of age and married to Emily with seven children – five daughters and two sons. Miss Maud Adams, from Co. Cavan, was the Matron. The three teachers were the English-born George Bateman and John Wootton, and Elizabeth McConnell, from Carlow. The religion of the Taylor family, the matron, teachers and pupils was Church of England and Church of Ireland, except for the four Dublin-born domestic staff, being Roman Catholic. According to the 1911 Census returns, the teachers were Algernon Browne, aged 21 and from England, Elizabeth McConnell aged 29, and Stanley Taylor, the headmaster's son and aged 21. There were 22 pupils at the time of the census.

Teaching Staff at Claremont, 1904
Mr Wootton, Miss McConnell, Mr Taylor, Miss Jacobs, Mr Rowan

Fires at the Schools for the Deaf

In May 1856, the Strabane Institution, under the principalship of Mr George Downing, former teacher of Claremont, had been destroyed by fire, killing six deaf children. After an investigation, John Boyd, superintendent of the school, had been cleared of negligence. That Institution, established in 1845 with assistance of the Mrs. C.F. Alexander,[3] wife of the Bishop of Derry and then Primate of All Ireland,[4] continued in another building, though with a smaller number of pupils. In 1871, this Institution closed down and the remaining five pupils were transferred to Claremont on payment of £130. A further sum of £450 was paid as Endowment for the 'Derry and Raphoe Diocesan Ward,' with two Free Pupils to be always maintained in the Claremont Institution. At that time, the Ulster Institution for the Deaf, Dumb and Blind in Lisburn Road, Belfast, was under the management of the Presbyterian clergymen. In 1897, an application for admission of Mary Ann McKinney from Derry was received, and she was declared elected a 'free pupil of the Derry and Raphoe Diocesan Ward in the Claremont Institution.'

Male Pupils at Claremont c.1916
Third and fourth are Willie and Samuel Rothwell from Enniscorthy, Co. Wexford

At Claremont, on 25 January 1886, a fire had taken place in the Reading-Room of the Institution. Owing to the exertions of the teachers, it had been brought under control before much damage had been done. In the evening of 21 August 1893, between 7 and 8 o'clock, a fire broke out in some stores adjoining the Claremont Institution.

The stores, used as a receiving room for oil and wood, were connected with the main building by a passage. The Fire Brigade promptly went to the place taking with them a 'steamer'. Great difficulty was experienced by the firemen in procuring water. The yard pump was brought into requisition but the supply was very limited. Buckets of water were carried by the brigade men and some of the employees of the Institution, and thrown on the structure, which joined the Institution and the outhouses. After great difficulty, the main building was saved, but the store was completely destroyed.[5] Substantial damage was caused, and repairs were carried out at the cost of £213. The insurance company undertook to pay the expenses of the Fire Brigade. The Governors of the Institution drew the attention of the Inspector of the Royal Irish Constabulary to the *'great bravery shown by Constable Patrick Rogan, on the occasion of the fire at the Institution'*. The Secretary reported that £20 had been distributed among those who had assisted at the fire. Consequently, one of 'Miller's Concussion fire engines' at the price of £5 was obtained for the Institution.

In 1904, a deaf reporter for *The British Deaf Times* described the Claremont Institution as 'a large old-fashioned building, standing far back from the road, and surrounded by acres of field and pasture land. At present 33 pupils are being educated in the school, the method being oral in almost a pure form. There are three carefully graded classes, and the scheme of work is well planned.'

'The principal, Mr George Taylor, is a gentleman of wide experience possessing healthy, advanced views concerning the education of the deaf, but his work at Claremont is seriously hampered by the lack of State aid, from which all Irish schools for the deaf suffer. For instance, although no technical education is carried out at Claremont, Mr Taylor fully realises its vital importance for the deaf, and, given the means, would keep the lads at the Institution until the age of 21, when they could leave perfectly equipped for the daily world of adult life. Although he has a well matured plan of work ready and plenty of ideas, neither he, nor the Governors, could do anything until the Government deigns to wake up to the injustice of the present state of affairs'.

'In teaching the deaf, Mr Taylor's method is in most ways similar to that adopted in ordinary schools, and he echoes the views of many teachers of the deaf, that a teacher, before taking up work among the deaf, should have experience of teaching hearing children. After three years, and when the special language course for the deaf had been mastered, Mr Taylor continues the education of his pupils upon lines similar to those used in the case of hearing children. The same text-books, readers, geographies, etc. which are in use in National Schools, are used by the Claremont pupils. In teaching Scripture, the narrative form was used. Mr Taylor deemed this preferable to that of rote (question and answer), and maintained that story-telling preserved the connection of events and exercised the power of expression which is lacking in the deaf. The success of his systematic teaching is shown by the results his pupils had obtained at the annual Scripture examinations held by the Diocesan Board.'

Those considering of becoming teachers of the deaf were obliged to have had received either 'English education' or professional training on teaching children at the Kildare Place Model School administered by the Church of Ireland Training College. At one time, its Principal, the Rev. Kingsmill Moore, had been asked for advice in regard to sourcing suitable candidates for filling a vacancy at Claremont. When no suitable person could be found, the search had to be extended to include the institutions for the deaf in Great Britain. In April 1895, Mr A.M. Axe of Doncaster Institution for the Deaf was appointed teacher at the salary of £65 per annum with board and residence. To prevent possible resentment within Claremont, the salary of the assistant teacher, Mr Newburn, Irish-born, was increased to £50 per annum. In June 1906, Mr Taylor informed the Governors that:

> 'Three replies were received in answer to the advertisement for a Pupil Teacher. Of these only one is worthy of consideration, and he is a Presbyterian. My son, Stanley Taylor, aged 16 years, is anxious to enter the profession and I should like him to be trained here that I might supervise his further studies. He has already received instruction in advance of the general run of applicants for the position of Pupil Teacher and has the further important advantage of being quite conversant with the deaf and dumb, having been born at the Institution and had daily intercourse with the pupils. I trust the Governors will favourably consider my application on his behalf.'

His eldest son, Stanley, was appointed pupil teacher on 13 June 1906 at a salary of £12 per annum, with one month's notice. In February 1909, his father wrote, 'Stanley Taylor completed his three years as Pupil Teacher on 20 January 1909 and he is now entitled to an advanced salary. The College of Teachers of the Deaf requires candidates to have reached the age of 21 years before sitting examination (to become a certified teacher of the deaf). Stanley Taylor is now over 19 years of age and therefore cannot enter for this examination for two years.' On 13 January 1911, Stanley Taylor tendered his resignation, and emigrated to Canada, where he settled down in Winnipeg.

Walter Newburn and the Bicycle Incident

Walter's father, Johnston Newburn, Clerk of the Petty Sessions in Co. Westmeath, had died leaving a young family, and his mother was postmistress in Tyrrellspass. His brother and sister were taken under the care of the Masonic Orphan schools. Educated at Tyrrellpass, he had a good English education, and regularly attended Church, Sunday School, the Y.M.C.A., and was a member of Total Abstinence Society.

In January 1891 Walter Newburn started his teaching career at Claremont Institution as pupil teacher and two years later he became qualified to teach the deaf.

Male and Female Pupils at 1916, Miss Ferris at right

However, he became dissatisfied with the conditions at Claremont as seen in the following letters he sent to the Governors:

> 13 October 1898 - I regret to say I find it absolutely dangerous to my family's health to remain during the winter months in the cottage (in the estate at Claremont). The paper is falling off the wall with dampness, and I find it necessary to send my wife away to recruit her health owing to frequent colds from damp clothes. We cannot keep anything dry in the house.

> 12 January 1899 - I have had my present salary of £50 per annum for the past two years on which I find it very hard to live. Trusting you will give my application your kind consideration and support.

> 1 February 1899 - I beg to make application for the position of Senior Master of the Institution now vacant by the resignation of Mr Thompson. I am now 25 years of age and have been Junior Assistant for the past six years.

In January 1901, tyres of a bicycle in the Institution were found to have been punctured several times, and whenever tubes were replaced, they were again punctured. An investigation was held among the servants, and a housemaid said that she noticed Mr Newburn entering the house. On 5 February, the bicycle was sent for inspection to Mr Gamage, Cycling Outfitters, in Grafton Street, Dublin, and his findings were that the tube of the tyre had been maliciously punctured with a penknife or scissors. A few days later, Mr Taylor asked that an inquiry be carried out by the Governors into Mr Newburn's conduct with reference to the pupils, officers and servants at

Claremont, creating dissent between the officers and the Headmaster, and other serious matters complained of by the Matron. On 17 February, Walter Newburn resigned his position as Senior Assistant Master.

After his departure from Claremont, Newburn moved his family of three children, to various locations in the south of Dublin. In 1906, he started his college for the deaf at Castlewood House in Rathmines. The Irish Census of 1911 stated that his wife was Elizabeth Meredith, tutor. She was teacher at Claremont until June 1896 when she married Walter Newburn in the following November and they had eight children. They employed a deaf servant, Jane Collins, who had three deaf sisters, all of them from Kingstown and educated at Claremont. Between 1911 and 1913, he had a practice in elocution at 70 St Stephen's Green, Dublin, before changing addresses to Baggot Street, where he and his wife were 'tutors'.[6] After that year, no more could be found of Walter Newburn. It had been said that he had been elocution teacher at Eton College, but that has yet to be proved.

In 1889, the Institution received a bequest of the lands at Rathmullen, near Drogheda, which formed part of the Harpur Estate, which were then sold. to the Land Commission, releasing funds for the Institution to admit at least six pupils as 'free pupils' at a cost of £20 each pupil per year. Those from families of substantial means were admitted as 'intermediate' pupils at £25 per annum, and one of the privileges was to sit with the teachers at meal-times. In some counties (or 'Unions'), the Board of Guardians would contribute anything from £10 to £18 per annum towards the maintenance of deaf children from their own areas, after the Relieving Officer assessed the means of the applicants' parents, such as acreage, value of tillage and stock, and the wages earned. Sometimes, the father would be reluctant to apply to the Board of Guardians. Inevitably, this prevented some deaf children from being sent to school and, when reaching adulthood, they were unable to learn a trade, thus becoming a 'burden to their families and to society'.

Miss Ferris (Pupil Teacher), Miss Taylor (headmaster's daughter)
and Miss E. McConnell (Matron)

The First World War

At least five teachers, who had passed through Claremont, had responded to the call to active service in the Great War of 1914-18, including Stanley Taylor, who enlisted with the Winnipeg Grenadiers in Canada. The other former Claremont staff were R.J. Wootton (who left in 1911), Algernon.B. Browne (who left in 1913 to take a position in the Halifax Institution for the Deaf in Nova Scotia), B. Stewart and F. Bannister. Whenever a male teacher was unavailable, the Headmaster usually appointed the male oldest pupil as temporary supervisor of the school. Sometimes, the gardener would assist with supervisory duties, in order to allow Mr Taylor to take brief vacations or go out of school on business.

Former Pupils' involvement in the Great War

James Gibson, former pupil, joined the Royal Scot Fusiliers and was despatched to France. His degree of hearing combined with his ability to lip-read enabled him to pass his medical examination. He could speak well but with a peculiar accent. Before joining the army, he was twice arrested, in Dublin and in Belfast, as a German spy. He proved his connection with Claremont and in both places he was able to call friends to speak for him. Mr Taylor read out two letters at the meeting in 1917 received from a former pupil, Ernest Simpson, who was a private in the Canadian Expeditionary Forces.[7] Another former pupil, Patrick Dwyer, was also employed on Government work in Scotland.

Mr Taylor drew the attention of the Governors to the special work, in some of the English institutions for the deaf, for soldiers and sailors suffering from deafness caused by the war. The London County Council had arranged for classes in lip-reading for all soldiers afflicted in war service. He said that Claremont being the only institution in Ireland with lip-reading classes, he was prepared to give his services, free of charge, out of school hours, for soldiers and sailors in Ireland. Soldiers, whilst attending evening classes in England, had their pensions increased to the maximum at 27/6 per week and reimbursed for their travelling expenses.

The Easter Rising and the Civil War

In 1916, on Easter Monday, there had been some disturbances in the city of Dublin and outside, when Patrick Pearse and the Irish Volunteers commenced their campaign for Irish independence from British control. As a result, it was decided not to hold the Annual Meeting in May, when it would have marked the one-hundredth anniversary of the establishment of the Institution.

Due to the rumours regarding the transport 'strikes' at the end of 1916, some pupils had to leave school early to travel home for their Christmas holidays. During the Civil War in 1922, three pupils, the Brookes brothers from Cork, were unable to travel home for school holidays owing to the unrest in the country. So the Matron kindly took them into her home in Wicklow for the summer, while the Rothwell family (with two deaf brothers, Samuel and William) took the Brookes brothers into their farm at

Clonroche, near Enniscorthy, Co. Wexford, for Christmas. In 1920, for the first time for several years, the potato crop failed, and due to the generosity of Mr Rothwell, the potato supply to the school was restored.

Lack of Compulsory Education for the Deaf in Ireland

In 1915, the Rev. Hemphill said, 'there were a number of Protestant deaf-mutes in different parts of the three provinces of Ireland[8] who were not getting suitable education to prepare them for their future welfare, and he appealed to the parents, in fairness to their children, to send them to that Institution, where they would be well cared for and educated.'[9] In 1917, it was announced at the Annual Meeting that the Government did not make any grant for the education of the Deaf in Ireland. It was 27 years after the Royal Commission of 1889, whose recommendation for compulsory education of the deaf, dumb and blind had been ratified in provision of State aid for England, Scotland and Wales, but not for Ireland. At the Annual Meeting in 1922, it was noted that 'mothers of deaf children usually preferred to keep them in the family, though they would be better looked after in an Institution such as Claremont'.

In 1923, the report in *The Irish Times* titled 'Farce – The State's Duty to the Deaf and Dumb' quoted the Dean of St Patrick's Cathedral, Dublin, as 'it is the business of the State to see children properly educated, and to compel the parents of deaf children to send them to be educated like all other children in the State.' The Chairman said that it would be impossible for the Institution to carry on unless grants were obtained, and the Headmaster stated that the 'absence of a Compulsory Education Act for deaf children in the Free State was disastrous.'[10]

Carpentry Shop at Claremont, c.1924. Instructor: Mr. C. Tivy

In 1928, the Archbishop of Dublin said that it was 'not right to rely on religious enterprise, after over a century of this Christian work progressing at Claremont, and only compulsory education would bring the afflicted (deaf) children out of isolation and gain for them the benefits of an education.'[11]

In 1933, the report in the *Irish Times* was titled '117 Years' Work for the Deaf and Dumb,' and the Rev. J.G.D. Pyper commented that 'if the facilities provided by Claremont were more widely known, they would be utilised to a greater extent.' And in 1935, the Bishop of Kilmore said that 'he welcomed the opportunity of seeing, for the first time, that Institution. He was struck by the fact that in 1814 that had been no such Institution (for the deaf) in Ireland, and that the deaf children had only one occupation – begging.'[12]

At the Annual Meeting in 1937, the Dean of St Patrick's Cathedral, Dublin, said that when he was three years old, he fell into a deep well and was rescued by a deaf mute. He referred to many benevolent men who helped the poor of Dublin, including Dr Orpen, who founded the Claremont Institution. The Dean said that he did not think that the Institution was sufficiently publicised all over the country. In 1939, the Archdeacon of Killala, the Ven. Pike, said that subscriptions seemed to be falling off everywhere, with the landlord class almost disappearing and their lands distributed among smallholders. At the Annual Meeting in 1937 at Claremont, a demonstration of the Multitone Deaf Aid Hearing Set was held to give hearing tests on some of the deaf pupils. A photograph of a girl having her hearing tested appeared in the *Irish Times*.

Outside Claremont after Annual Meeting of 1934
left: Miss Beggs (Matron), behind her – Miss Deacon (Headmistress).
Mr Gick, Secretary, (at centre, with spectacles)

Regarding the prospects of the 87 pupils who had passed through Claremont during the period 1900 to 1925, 44 boys were engaged in farming – 13, tailoring – 6, boot-making – 5, bakery – 2, printing – 1, engraving – 2, carpentry – 15, no occupation – 7, 3 – died. Of 33 girls, dressmaking – 12, house and general work – 15, lace-making – 2, laundress – 2, hairdressing – 1, no occupation – 1. On 2 January 1917, Mr Taylor told the Governors, 'I have received a favourable report of Fred Thompson who is serving an apprenticeship at Sharman D. Neill & Co. watchmakers and jewellers, Belfast. He is working as engraver and is reported doing well and quite content. The Governors secured the services of Mr. C. Tivy as instructor in woodwork and carpentry, and the boys took keen interest in carpentry lessons.

In 1910, a carved oak pulpit, prayer desk, screen for an organ chamber and the hymn board had been designed and erected by the pupils and teachers, and they had done a large part of the carpentry work required in Claremont – repairing the floors, sash windows and doors, as well as making lockers, tables, presses and carved panels for doors, etc. Four panels for a new pulpit in Thornton Church, Leicestershire, was designed by the teachers and executed by the boys.

On rare occasions, one or two male pupils would be sent to St Joseph's School for Deaf Boys in Cabra, to learn boot-making at the training workshops. In 1925, Mr. Taylor commented that it was very difficult to obtain work for pupils as they left school, but he said that 'a vast number of youths, possessed of all their faculties, are unemployed.'

Annual General Meeting at Claremont in 1938
Second left - Miss Beggs, Third at back – Miss Deacon, Mr Gick behind first boy
Seven pupils – four female at left and three male at right

To Sell or Not to Sell Claremont?

For over thirty years from the 1890s to the 1920s, there had been ongoing discussions about the feasibility of selling up Claremont, which was too large to manage with the building itself needing constant repair and maintenance with more than sufficient accommodation while the number of deaf Protestant children in Ireland continued to decline. In March 1922, Mr Casserly, the neighbouring grazing tenant, made a verbal offer of £3,000 for purchase of the house and lands of Claremont. At a special meeting in November, it was decided to approach Mr Casserley about raising the offer. In October, Mr Casserley agreed on the offer of £3,250 and Mr Gick, the Secretary, had to obtain the sanction of the Commissioners of Charitable Donations and Bequests to proceed with selling up Claremont. In the following month, upon recommendation of the Commissioners, a valuation had to be obtained on the lands and premises of Claremont, Glasnevin. In January of the following year, a letter was received from Mr Casserley that owing to the death of his wife, he had decided not to purchase Claremont.

On 23 January 1925, a special meeting of the Board, chaired by the Archbishop of Dublin, was held to discuss the offer of £5,000 for Claremont from a solicitor representing a client. However, it was learnt that the Governors were liable for income tax and rates. After much discussion, the offer was put to vote. Three of the Governors were in favour of the sale, while six, including the Archbishop, were against it. In 1926, the Board of Works approached the Governors, offering £5,500. But it was decided that no offer less than £7,500 was to be considered. After much deliberation, the Governors decided that *'in view of the fact that the Institution had been housed there since its foundation in 1816, it was in the best interests of the Institution to remain at Claremont.'*[13]

In 1928, Mr Stanislius Murphy, Inspector from the Commissioners, commented on the dampness, lack of hot water (even in the Headmaster's apartments), the dull and dreary playground, the matron's room and other rooms needing attention, and the unused portion of the premises becoming dilapidated with much of the plastering of external walls falling off. He furthermore suggested about the disposal of the premises. Four years later, hot water was finally connected to the bathrooms, and in 1937, the telephone was installed. In 1887, when discussing the introduction of gas into the Institution and after studying the estimate from the gas supplier for laying down almost a mile of piping from the mains, it had been agreed not to proceed with this proposal. In 1940, gas-lighting was extended to the wash-house, dormitories, bathroom, etc. which were formerly lit by candles.

In 1942, plans to partition the boys' dormitory and distempering the walls of the sleeping quarters were not undertaken, due to increased costs resulting from the Second World War. In order to comply with the Government's Compulsory Tillage Order, the gardens had to be completely tilled, as well as the fields, and it became necessary to employ an assistant gardener for this purpose. An appeal for more scribers towards the Institution was made, to cover the rising expenses resulting from the prices of commodities due to war conditions. A sum of money intended for a trip to the seaside was, at the voluntary request of the children, sent to the British Red Cross Society for the relief of those affected by the war.[14]

The Closing Years of the Glasnevin Era

Prior to Mr Taylor's retirement in May 1928, the number of pupils in the Institution had declined to seven. After receiving the pension with sanction from the Charitable Donations and Bequest Board, Mr Taylor moved to Winnipeg to join his son, Stanley. In 1932, he died and was buried there. Miss Mary (Lillian) Deacon, who started as pupil teacher in 1921, became the first female Head of the Institution. From 1928 until her death in 1943, she was the only teacher with six to ten pupils of varying ages. A few adults were accepted as day pupils for speech therapy and lip-reading. The Governors continued their policy of advertising for pupils in the daily newspapers from time to time. The Bishops were written to, seeking their assistance in making the objects of the Institution better known throughout their dioceses in the 'Free State' (later Republic of Ireland in 1949).

During the Emergency Years of 1939 to 1945 in Ireland, the constant shortages of basic foodstuffs and fuel, and the stress of wartime conditions, put severe strain on the health of the more vulnerable young people, resulting in tuberculosis. There were 24,000 people with tuberculosis in the twenty-six counties. Although the drug BCG had been used before the war, it was scarce, and there were an insufficient number of dedicated beds. In May 1943, the Secretary of the Department of Public Health and Local Government stated that, under the Emergency Powers Order of 1939, the Minister intended taking over temporarily the main building, owned by the Claremont Institution, as an Emergency hospital. At the time of this order, the number of pupils under the care of the Claremont Institution was eight, four boys and four girls aged from twenty to nine, whereas the building could easily accommodate over one hundred pupils and staff.

A special meeting of the Claremont Board was held to decide on the date the Glasnevin building could be handed over. Alternatively, if the Board wished to sell, an offer would be made to purchase. After the Board obtained the consent of the Commissioners of Charitable Donations and Bequests to sell the building, the Department of Public Health offered £3,700 to cover all removal and other expenses. In October 1943, the Claremont Institution was moved to Monkstown, South County Dublin, to a smaller but more manageable building, situated in a pleasant location, overlooking Dublin Bay once again, like the house of Claremont in Glasnevin did so in the year of 1819.

Claremont House, c. 1914
Private Pupils' bedrooms in the top floor of the Headmasters' House

Claremont with greenhouse at right – c.1932

13

The Monkstown School

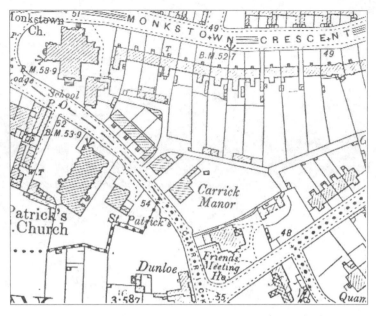

Map of 1921, showing Monkstown with Carrick Manor

The sub-committee, appointed by the Board of Governors to obtain new premises for the Institution, decided upon a house called Carrick Manor in Monkstown, Co. Dublin, which was purchased for £3,050. The previous owner of the house was Mr J. Lyndon, and prior to him, Mr. Burrell, a merchant, who owned a shop in Grafton Street. The 1866 map indicated that there had been a house called 'Mount Ussher' on the site, a fairly large house, which might have been demolished prior to the building of Carrick Manor. The gardens were large, with a small brook, and overlooking was the Friends' Meeting House, where the Boy Scouts assembled, with some pupils from Claremont participating in their activities. Two ladies, Mrs Strain and Miss Pemberton, who conducted drill classes in Glasnevin, continued them in the Knox Memorial Hall, a parochial hall of the parish church, and a few years later in the Friends' Meeting House, next door to Carrick Manor. A successful drill display was given at Claremont, in which outside classes joined.

In fine weather, using some of the sports equipment formerly used at the School in Glasnevin and stored in the garage beside the house, some pupils played cricket, cro-quet, football, lacrosse and pitch-and-putt. One of the boys swung so hard that the ball broke the window of the Friends' Meeting House! Whenever the sun appeared, the class was moved out of the classroom into the garden, stocked with 30 apple-trees, gooseberry bushes and meticulously maintained flower-beds. As part of personal development, the pupils were assigned garden tasks: weeding the flower-beds, raking leaves, cutting the grass and raking the gravel in the driveway.

Carrick Manor, the home of the Claremont School from 1943 to 1978
(collection of Dennis Steenson)

Deaf Links with Monkstown Parish

At the top of the road in the village of Monkstown was the Parish Church of Monkstown where, in the late 1890s, church services for the deaf were held in the Vestry Room, organised by the deaf missionary, Mr Maurice F.G. Hewson. The Rev. Thomas Gallaudet from St Ann's Church for the Deaf in New York, had given a sermon there. In 1899, the Rev. Downings, of Manchester Institute for the Adult Deaf and Dumb, visited Monkstown while on his mission tour of Ireland.

On Sundays, the Claremont pupils and staff congregated in the West Gallery ('seven sittings'), which overlooked the expanse of the interior of the church.[1] One of the pupils had found keeping still and quiet during service, which he could not hear or follow, as sheer agony, not daring to move an inch to avoid Miss Ferris' disapproval.[2] In the 1960s, the Garden Fete in aid of the Knox Hall was held in the gardens of Claremont. At Christmas 1943, the Rev. Kennedy and parishioners kindly supplied books and toys for the pupils. During the first year of the Institution in its new premises, members of Monkstown Parish had taken an interest in its welfare, particularly

Dr. V. McCormick and the Lady Visitors: Mrs Miller, Mrs Forde, Mrs Coyningham and Mrs Pyper. In 1944, Mrs Forde invited the children to a Hallowe'en party and gave tickets for a concert, while Dr McCormick and Mrs Miller organised a Christmas party for the children. Occasionally, the Summer Fetes were held on the grounds of Carrick Manor to raise funds for the upkeep of the Knox Memorial Hall.

Around the corner past the Friends' Meeting House and up Pakenham Road was Monkstown Hospital, now demolished and replaced with apartments, which had treated cases of minor ailments of the pupils. Down the road a couple of houses away, was Hewett's Newsagent and the Post Office, which supplied· most of the needs for the Claremont household, providing much-needed diversion and amusement for the pupils.

At Carrick Manor, in the garden was a little brook, like the old school in Glasnevin. The garden was well-stocked with apple-trees, neat rows of peas, potatoes, cabbage and gooseberry bushes. In the house were seven fireplaces and on the top of the front door was a swinging bell, which would alert the maid. In the village opposite the church was a row of shops, including Lane McCormack's pharmacy. Like many pharmacies in the nineteenth century, this was fitted with tall, oak glass-fronted cabinets for displaying wares, while the walls were lined with racks of drawers for storing compounds and other ingredients for preparing prescriptions. This establishment continues to this day, with the paraphernalia still intact.

Miss Deacon standing in centre, with Miss Beggs (matron) at her right;
Mr Gick standing at right, Pupils seated – three at left and three at right.
Wilfred Neil, Dennis Steenson, Iris Pearson, Maureen Clawson,
Iris Wilson, Bertie Montgomery

Miss Harriet Rose Ferris

From Clogher, near Westport, Co. Mayo, she was appointed as pupil teacher in October 1916 at Claremont in Glasnevin. On 24 June 1921, she resigned to take up a position as teacher at the Exeter Institution for the Deaf, which had 121 pupils on the roll. In December 1923, she left for America. Some years later, she returned and worked as secretary to Lord Sligo, Westport House, for whom her brother-in-law, Mr Henderson, was steward of the estate.

In January 1946, Miss Ferris took up her position as Head. The average roll being five to six, she gave individual tuition to the pupils, whose age ranged from five to eighteen, while creating a homely atmosphere at Carrick Manor. Knowledgeable in flora and fauna, she encouraged the pupils to take an interest in nature and develop creative talents, resulting with two girls obtaining several awards at art competitions. She taught knitting and sewing to boys as well as to girls, which helped them to develop hand-eye co-ordination.

Courtesy, loyalty and deportment were virtues upon which she placed emphasis. She gave instruction in finger-spelling to Boy Scouts and Girl Guides and in lip-reading and speech therapy to some adults, upon request. She sourced vocational training and employment for those about to leave school. Once a week for an hour, the children were given school-work to keep them occupied, so that she would give lessons in lip-reading to a sailor who had become deafened. Her maternal approach led to Carrick Manor as a 'home' for both pupils and former pupils, including those who moved North or to Britain. The children enjoyed story-telling by former pupils about their schooldays in Glasnevin and in Monkstown. In 1968, the Governors raised the minimum school fee to £100 per annum. Parents who could not afford to pay these fees had to apply to their County Council for maintenance grants. During 1970, Miss Ferris managed the school single-handed without a matron since September 1969, and without Mr Gick, secretary of the School, who died in March 1970.

After her retirement in 1971, Miss Ferris returned to her home in Westport and spent time improvising on her life-long interests - painting in watercolours and oils landscapes and seascapes in her home county, Co. Mayo. For many years, she enjoyed playing golf and had excelled in this sport. She died on 27 June 1974 at the age of 81 and was buried in Westport, Co. Mayo.

Miss Ferris with her pupils in May 1948
at back - Wilfred Neil, Iris Wilson, Iris Pearson
at front – Henry Pollard, Maureen Clawson, Dennis Steenson

Now and then, Mrs Henderson, whose husband was agent for Lord Sligo, who owned Westport House and gardens, came over to visit her sister, Miss Ferris. Sometimes, her son would join her, and the children enjoyed having these visitors around, providing much welcome distraction from the lonely existence at Carrick Manor, with the number of pupils so small and themselves far away from home. Nevertheless, Henry and Norman were fortunate to have each other as play-mates, so they would play football and hurling in the garden. Sometimes on Sundays, when in their teenage years, they would sneak away on their bicycles to watch football at Shamrock Rovers' grounds in Milltown. On Saturdays, the children had to carry out household tasks, such as polishing shoes, cleaning the gardens and the driveway, and lay out their Sunday clothes in readiness for the following day.

As well as attending morning service at Monkstown Church, the children would be brought to another church by Miss Ferris, who rapidly transcribed the preacher's 'message' on notes for the children to read, in order to improve their English language. In those days, there was no provision of sign-language interpreters, overhead projectors for hymns and visual aids nowadays taken for granted by deaf people. In order to encourage interaction with the 'outside world', Miss Ferris would bring the children out to visit some of her friends in Co. Wicklow. Occasionally, she would hold conversations with former pupils, such as Willie Rothwell and Tom Ireland, both of whom were excellent speakers.

The garden was well stocked with fruit and vegetables, and the apples – cooking and eating, when picked, were put in storage in the outhouse, placed on shelves lined with brown paper. The pantry in 'Carrick Manor' would be stocked with peas, beans, rhubarb, raspberries, blackcurrants and potatoes, thus ensuring that the children and the staff were well-fed.

In 1971, the Claremont School moved to Monkstown Primary School to form a Unit for the Deaf, where the children attended classes in the afternoons. Mrs Jane Bleakley was employed to teach the deaf pupils in the mornings. Some of the deaf pupils boarded at Carrick Manor under the care of the house-parents, Mr and Mrs Erskine, who offered their help in the outside activities of the children by the generous use of their cars. Officers of the local company of the Boys' Brigade raised funds every year for a few years through their Christmas Bible Class. Some parents from the country had donated some farm produce for the school. The Governors asked the Department of Health for increased maintenance fees for the pupils. Enrolling four or five more children was necessary to break even, and publicity regarding the Claremont School was required. A donation of £1,000 was received from the Variety Club of Ireland, and after negotiations with the Department of Health, maintenance fees were increased from £200 to £300 per annum. The Department of Education at first refunded three-quarters of the teacher's salary, and later on, all of it. In September 1976, Miss Mee Choo Theong, having graduated with a Diploma for Teachers of the Deaf, commenced her position as Teacher in charge of the Deaf Unit in Monkstown National School.[3]

Mrs Henderson with her 'army'
Claire Gilmore, Martha Horan, Ruth O'Reilly, Myrtle Henry,
Norman Rankin, Henry Pollard - 1956

The Demise of Claremont School

Finally after 162 years of providing education to 2,448 deaf children, the Claremont Institution ceased to exist at the end of 1978. The final Annual Report for the year of 1978, the Secretary, Mr Seymour, announced, 'I am sorry to have to record the first signs of the diminishing number of deaf children in residence at Claremont. Miss Theong was married in October 1978, and left for England. We are therefore left without any children in residence in Claremont since July of this year.' Many options were brought before the Board of Governors, such as a hostel, training centre, and Adult Education Centre.   For quite a considerable time, 'Carrick Manor' had been left empty, with the gardens untended and allowed to grow wild, and the grass uncut and waist-high, when a former pupil and her husband came over from England to take a look at her Alma Mater.

Eventually, it was decided to sell the house to Masonic Havens Limited. Carrick Manor provides residential and communal accommodation for the active elderly, with additional self-contained bed-sitting rooms and nine self-contained single and double-terraced dwellings in the grounds.

The cycle of life has made a complete circle in two special places in Dublin. Claremont in Glasnevin, north of Dublin, had provided 'shelter' for deaf children from 1819 to 1943 and now provides day and residential accommodation for elderly people, having been renamed as 'St Clare's Home'. Moving south to Monkstown, Carrick Manor, having taken in deaf children until 1978, provides a 'haven' for elderly people to enjoy the remaining years of their lives in peaceful and secure surroundings.

Part Three

Behind the Doors

14

Teaching the Deaf

To burst the spell that made the mind its prey,
Dispensing charity thy own majestic way.
To teach the Deaf – their fetter'd minds to free –
These are imperial arts, God-like, and worthy thee!

Lucretius

In its infancy, the Institution relied on the knowledge and experience attained by Dr Charles Orpen during his visits to the Deaf Institutions in France, Switzerland and Italy, and through his experiments on his first pupil, Thomas Collins. The mode of instruction was adopted from the Abbé Sicard, but differed in some respects from that pursued in Paris and London.[1] In September 1816, the following books produced by the instructors of the deaf in Britain and in the Continent were ordered for the School: Dr Watson's *Instruction of the Deaf and Dumb,* translation of the Abbé de l'Epée's work, the Abbé Sicard's work *Cours d'Instruction du Sourd et Muet,* and Pestalozzi's System of Education. For teaching religion, the books, Mrs Timmers' *Scripture History* and Kinniburgh's *Life of Christ* were used. In 1821, Dr Orpen sent to Mr Humphreys for his library in Claremont the books relating to deafness by Bebian, Bonilly, Bulwer, Burns, Campbell, de l'Epée, Desloges, Deschamps, Green, Holder, Massieu, Pestalozzi, Sicard, Synge, Wallis and Watson. In 1827, Dr Watson of the London Asylum presented to the Institution three copies of his work, *Education of the Deaf and Dumb,* and twelve copies of his new book, *Vocabulary of Verbs.*

An essential part of the apparatus of instruction in this kind of school was a large collection of classified pictures of natural and artificial objects. Derived from a book published for the use at the London Deaf and Dumb Asylum, the pictures were suspended around the Schoolroom to familiarise the pupils with the objects they represent. The children learnt through the interpretation of signs and gestures, which enlarged their powers of mimic representation, and by improving their common language of 'dumb shew' (mimicry). Five hours in the day were employed at lessons and the boys were divided into five classes. Each of these classes was provided with a different lesson; either in the several parts of language, or in arithmetic or articulation. At the end of each hour, the classes changed their seats, so that all in rotation performed several exercises. Each boy was appointed monitor of the class next below his own, in weekly rotation.

Prior to the Institution's move to Claremont in 1819, the Committee had been unsuccessful in obtaining a trained and competent instructor from the Institutions for the Deaf in Great Britain. In the meantime, the assistant master, Charles Devine, carried out instruction, with assistance from intelligent pupils as monitors, by consulting publications, including Sicard's book, on the subject, and by actual experience in the progress of the school.

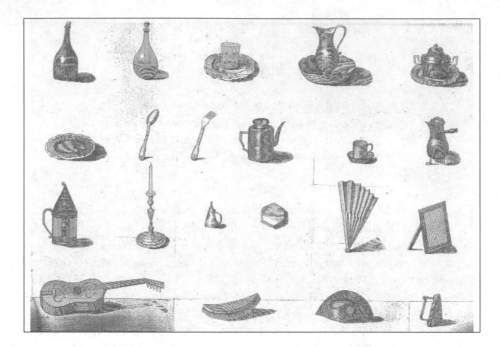

Page of Objects for teaching Vocabulary to the Deaf
from Sicard's Cours d'Instruction du Sourd Muets

In 1819, when Mr Humphreys commenced his training in Scotland, he purchased a variety of books, plates and publications used in the schools, which he visited on his tour of the schools for the deaf in England and Scotland. Dr Charles Orpen maintained correspondence with the Deaf schools in Glasgow, Edinburgh, Paris, Bordeaux, Yverdun, Connecticut, as well as Genoa, Milan, Vienna, Copenhagen, Kiel and Groningen which received the reports on the progress at the Dublin Deaf Institution. In return, the Committee received from some of these foreign schools, particularly those in Bordeaux and in Connecticut, several publications. He had corresponded with the Rev. Gallaudet, who established the first school for the deaf in America, with assistance from Laurent Clerc, deaf assistant from the Parisian Institution under the Abbé Sicard and who accompanied Gallaudet to America in 1817.

Speech or Writing?
In his book published in 1670, Dr Wallis referred to the art of teaching the deaf and dumb to speak:

> 'The person on whom he (Dr Wallis) began the trial was Mr Daniel Whalley, who had once been able to speak, but having lost his hearing at the age of five years. (...) The position of the organs is explained as precisely as possible by signs; and when a particular sound is once attained, the scholar, by frequent repetition, is prevented from forgetting it.'[2]

'I have often asked those who have been taught speech, whether they found it pleasant to speak, and whether it was not painful to them to learn? Always they answered – that they suffered so much in learning, and afterwards found it so unpleasant to speak, that they wished they had been made to depend entirely on *writing, reading and the manual alphabet, as a medium of communication.* It is painful for everybody to hear them attempt utterance; and learning speech spoils their features so much, that I have seen very handsome children so disfigured by it, that in a few years time I hardly knew them.'

Bulwer referred to Sir Edward Gostwick, Baronet of Wellington in Bedfordshire, a gentleman, born deaf and well-educated who had utilised writing as a substitute for speech. The first invention of writing was to make 'Verba Visibilia, missilia, and permanentia,' to remedy the defect of speech.[3] In 1442, Rodolphus Agricola of Groningen alludes, in his work, *Inventione Dialecticae*, to a deaf mute who was able to write in the fifteenth century. In about the year 1560, Joachim Pascha, chaplain to Prince James II of Brandenburg, succeeded in instructing his own mute daughter, by means of a series of pictures, mimic signs and illustrations. Giorolamo Cardono of Milan, who died in 1576, was one of the earliest to believe in the possibility of instructing the deaf and dumb. He was a philosopher of great intellect, as well as a writer of outstanding brilliance and perspicuity, and was the first to promulgate the doctrine, that the deaf mute could be taught to *'hear by reading, and speak by writing.'*[4]

The Jesuits, in their missionary work in other countries, had to familiarise themselves with the languages of those whom they were to Christianise. In 1793, Lorenzo Hervás y Panduro, a Spanish ex-Jesuit and erudite linguist, published his work *Escuela español de sordomudos*, which included a comprehensive study on deaf people and a method of teaching them Spanish by way of writing. He popularised the word *surdomudo* (deaf-mute), which reflected the growing awareness that deafness caused muteness. He realised that signs, like speech, were a manifestation of human language, where they could convey thoughts.[5] For a deaf person to use writing as a means of communication, this is dependent on stimulation strategies used at home and at school, pedagogical techniques used by the teacher of the deaf, the inherent intellect of the deaf person and the amount of language acquired by the deaf learner. In 1880, at the National Deaf and Dumb Convention in Dublin, the subject of debate which was 'animated in the deaf and dumb finger and sign language', related to the fact that:

'A magazine is published recently by the National Society for the Use of the Deaf and Dumb, and it was suggested to have two: one at *one penny* for the *poor and half-educated mutes,* and the superior one at *two pennies* for the *well-educated.'*[6]

The above statement reveals elitist undertones where contents of the publications intended for the deaf would have to be 'simplified' or 'sophisticated' depending on the economic status, the linguistic preference and the literacy level of the prospective deaf subscribers. Wealthy people were equated with culture; poor people with nature, particularly people who were deaf and poor, whose natural sign language was a mark of their uncultured and uncivilised qualities.[7]

Articulation in Ireland

The first instance of teaching articulation, submitted to the public in Ireland, appeared in the *Anthologia Hibernica* in 1793. It is a scheme for a universal alphabet, formed on a suggestion of Sir W. Jones. The original alphabets were formed from an outline of the several organs of speech in the act of articulation, and he gives an engraved sketch of the section of the mouth, lips, teeth, tongue, palate, and nose, being the parts used in modulating the voice as it issues from the *glottis* in articulating the vowel, labial, dental, lingual, palateal, and nasal sounds, which constitute the elements of every oral language. The vowel sounds are formed by the mouth more or less opened, a section of which would form the characters, which nearly resemble the Greek letters. The consonants are no less accurately defined, the letter B, particularly, which has the same figure in most existing languages. Its character is formed of the profile of the lips gently compressed. As a mode of instructing the deaf and dumb, its application is obvious. The author of this essay was Doctor Edward Walsh, Physician to His Majesty's Forces. He left Dublin shortly after, and his suggestion was not acted on.

In 1815, Dr Charles Orpen had spent three months teaching Thomas Collins how to pronounce vowels, syllables and words, and demonstrated his experiments as part of his lectures at the Rotunda, Dublin. In July 1816, Mr Lecky wrote to his daughter:

'I was at a most interesting Lecture on Deaf and Dumb, by Doctor Charles Orpen, where he exhibited a boy of about ten years of age who credibly counted to 100, the boy has been only four or five months under tuition and spoke distinctly and surprised the audience by his cleverness, I believe there were 400 persons present'.

In his book, *Anecdotes and Annals for the Deaf*, was a diagram displaying the organs of speech, engraved by a former pupil, John Johnson.

On 2 December 1829, Dr Orpen asked the Committee that all the children, as far as practicable, should be taught to speak. A week later, Mr Humphreys commenced teaching the upper class articulation, and if he found it too laborious for himself and his assistant, after an experiment of three months, he would be provided with another assistant for this 'special purpose', funds permitting. In 1835, Mr Humphreys was ordered to commence a 'systematic plan of teaching all such of the male and female pupils to articulate as may be found on trial capable of learning to speak'. However, sign language continued to be the main method of communication amongst the officers and the pupils of the Institution under the headmasterships of the Rev. John Martin, and Messrs James Cook, James Foulston and Edward J. Chidley – the last three having had previous knowledge of British Sign Language at their former Institutions in Belfast, Doncaster and London, respectively.

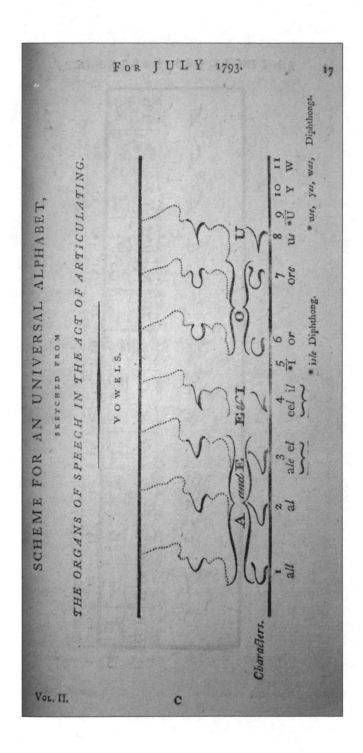

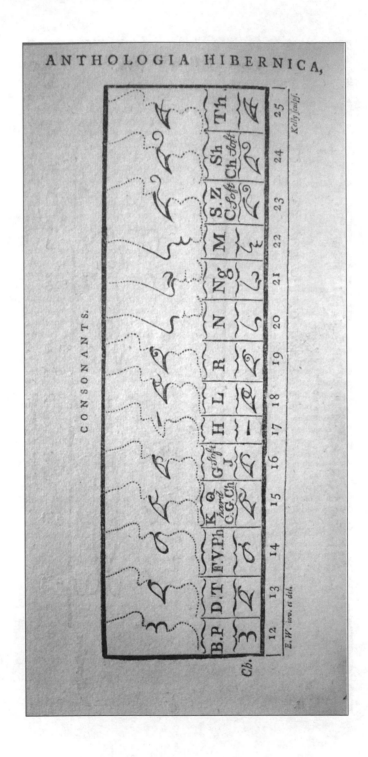

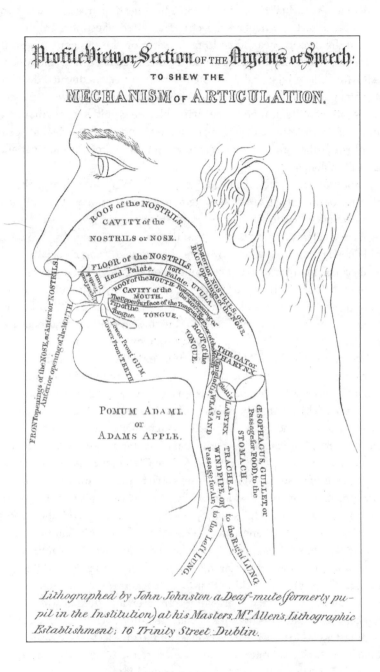

From Dr Orpen's *Anecdotes and Annals of the Deaf*
lithographed by John Johnson, former pupil

The Pure Oral System at Claremont

In an article in a parochial magazine in 1868, the question arose, 'which is the best – the finger speech or the articulate speech? The latter takes more trouble and more time to each the deaf to speak, than to make signs on their fingers; but on the other hand, it restores them almost *completely* to the blessings of society. Not one in 10,000 can use the finger language, and therefore the most perfectly educated deaf and dumb on that system are shut out – they always remain dumb. While we earnestly recommend the Claremont Institution to the charitable, we would suggest that an effort be made in Ireland to introduce the German method,[8] and teach the deaf to speak. Such an attempt is now being made by opening the Jewish Home for the Deaf and Dumb Children in London.'[9]

It was not until 1882 when the headmaster, Mr E. W. Chidley, son of the late Mr E. J. Chidley, introduced the 'Pure Oral System' to Claremont. This meant that sign language was no longer to form one of the methods of educating the deaf. However, difficulties were compounded by the fact that the Pure Oral System had to be taught to the pupils newly admitted, who were to be discouraged from associating with those already at school, in order to avoid contamination with sign language.

On 6 May 1889, Mr G. Taylor, headmaster, wrote, 'I beg to submit to the Committee the enclosed plan of desks, as used for Oral classes in many Institutions, and should be pleased if six of the same design could be obtained for use in our school-room. The advantages derived from desks of this description are: First, by arranging the desks in a semi-circular form, the children obtain full view of each other's lips. Secondly, the teacher's lips can be seen by all the children at the same time and when individual correction is necessary all the children can observe, imitate and practise the actions of the teacher upon any child. Thirdly, desks being narrower than tables, the children who are constantly being handled by the teacher, can be better approached.'

In January 1894, Mr Schoenthiel, principal of the Oral Training College in London, was invited to hold examinations of the pupils in Claremont. Later on, Mr Taylor and Mr Keating, assistant teacher, were called in, at the request of the Governors, to receive Mr Schoentheil's report of his examination. Mr Schoentheil said that two to four weeks was sufficient to teach the vowel sounds. After dealing with the 'Production of Sound', 'Articulation' and 'Language', he read the report of his examination, suggesting certain alterations to the system which had been followed at Claremont. He said that 'articulation' was taught at Claremont on a wrong principle; and 'language' was not taught to the pupils. He added that three teachers were sufficient for 28 pupils, with the fourth teacher to take charge of the children admitted at irregular intervals. Each teacher was to have his own particular class, but to change for special subjects. The Headmaster was to supervise every class and to give lectures to his teachers. One month later, Mr Taylor submitted, at the request of the Governors, a curriculum and arrangement of classes, to be sent to Mr Schoenthiel for his observations.

Oral Class at Claremont, Glasnevin
(reproduced from the Annual Report of the Claremont Institution, 1916)

In April 1894, four applications for post of a female Teacher were received, and none of them were considered by Mr Taylor as properly qualified or experienced, and he suggested that a female pupil teacher of 18 or 19 years of age be engaged and trained for the post. Then Mr Schoenthiel's observations on the Curriculum and Timetable were read, that he did not approve of splitting up the time into divisions of 20 or 30 minutes and suggested that there should be less subjects and more time given to each subject. Mr Taylor said that lip-reading went with every lesson. On 27 June 1896, Mrs Thurson Holland came over from England and she found all classes carefully taught; with the younger children being well instructed in articulation. The advanced class taught by the Headmaster was very good in general knowledge and language. Mrs Holland suggested that a partition be erected in the Schoolroom so as to separate the classes, to block out noise of the neighbouring classes while teaching articulation. It is interesting to note that it must have been quite difficult for deaf people, prior to arrival of electricity for lighting, to learn speech and lip-reading when it was dark in the evenings and in winter-time.

In April 1903, Countess Dudley paid the Vice-regal visit to Claremont. The oral system was explained by the Headmaster, Mr George Taylor. 'The pupils were examined in lip-reading, speech and general conversation. They showed evidence of careful instruction and very marked intelligence as the outcome of Oral Training. Her Excellency conversed with some of the senior pupils, and evinced surprise at the readiness with which they spoke. She asked the Headmaster to convey to the children how much she was gratified by her visit.'[10]

In the early decades of the twentieth century, Mr Taylor provided private tuition in lip-reading to adults. On 10 April 1917, Mr Taylor informed the Committee, 'I wish to draw the Governors' attention to the special work now, being commenced in some of the English institutions, for soldiers and sailors suffering from deafness caused by the war. In the Irish hospitals, there must be a number of men similarly afflicted and also among soldiers and sailors discharged from service. Claremont being the only Institution in Ireland where lip-reading tuition is undertaken, I beg to ask the Governors to approach the Minister of Pensions and offer to undertake some of the work here. I am prepared to give my services free, out of ordinary school hours; on three evenings a week should a class be formed.'

Newburn's System of Articulation

On 11 March 1911, a large number of medical and scientific experts and friends were given the opportunity, by the invitation of Mr Newburn, formerly teacher of Claremont, and now tutor in Castlewood House, Rathmines, Dublin, of attending a demonstration of the oral system of teaching the deaf. In explaining the system of oral instruction, Mr Newburn showed that the principle was founded on vibration or transmission of sound from teacher to pupil by labiation on the production of words. The pupils were first taught by imitation of the movements of the lips and tongue to pronounce the vowel sounds, next the consonants, advancing gradually to the pro-duction of simple words and sentences.[11] One of his pupils was Donal Cameron, nephew of Sir Charles Cameron, Chief Public Health Officer of the City of Dublin. His achievement of creating a large-scale model aeroplane was covered by the *Dublin Evening Telegraph* of 26 February 1910, with a line drawing of Donal Cameron with his project in the garden of Castlewood House, Rathmines.

Sign Languages in Ireland

R.A.S. Maclistair, theorised that the Ogham, the ancient Irish alphabet used in pre-Christian and early-Christian times, was derived from a finger alphabet, and he cited Irish deaf communities as evidence that such alphabets are functional. Ogham is a twenty-character alphabet made up of line strokes of different quantities of lines and different lengths and angles.[12] McManus, an expert on Ogham, points out that the fin-ger alphabet now in use among the Irish deaf is not a descendant of the type that allegedly produced the Ogham. In fact, the modern Irish finger alphabet is an adap-tation of the Franco-Iberian (and now International) Finger Alphabet, imported from the Continent because the British two-handed alphabet was shunned by the Irish.[13]

In order to make one's material needs known, a deaf person would develop a sys-tem of gestures or pantomime. Sir William Wilde observed that 'all intelligent deaf and dumb persons are acquainted with the language of pantomime, and have certain arbitrary signs by which they can express their meaning to those accustomed to them. The adult illiterate mutes among the Irish peasantry – a people remarkable for action and gesticulation – excel in mimic signs'.[14]

As far as it could be known, there is no physical record of existence of sign language or any system of communication used by deaf people in Ireland before the end of the eighteenth century. There had been attempts to develop a Dictionary of Signs and a fund named *The Boyd Fund*, established to raise finance for the development project. This did not materialise, until the year of 1871, when it was commented that 'the lady, Mrs Boyd of Ballycastle, Co. Antrim, understood perfectly the needs of the deaf and dumb, as her husband, a gentleman of property, was unable to hear or speak, and she directed that the money should form the nucleus of a fund, which was to be increased to enable the trustees publish a pictorial Dictionary of Natural Signs. When the lady died, the trustees did not know what to do with the money (which was £153 17s 7d), as it was too small for the purpose for which it was intended. It was then passed to the Claremont Institution instead, interest only, with the principal kept intact.'[15] It is a pity that this initiative had not been brought into fruition, as this would have certainly provided valuable documentary evidence of Irish Sign Language during the nineteenth century.

However, descriptions of some signs used at a public examination were recorded in the annual report of 1825 as follows. 'to describe a *woman*, the pupil generally drew his hand across his forehead, as to allude to the cap worn by the females, and to describe a *man*, they usually placed their hands on the chin, in allusion of the beard'.

Manual Alphabet

Owing to Mr Joseph Humphreys having had spent some time at Edinburgh Institution for the Deaf in 1819, the two-handed Manual Alphabet was used as a mode of communication by Mr Kinniburgh, his deaf assistants and the pupils. Therefore, this particular version of the manual alphabet had been introduced to Claremont and, in turn, to Ireland.

On the reverse of the circulars regarding the Annual Charity Sermon preached by the Rev. Henry Woodward of Fethard, Co. Tipperary, at St. Peter's Church, Dublin in November 1834, was the reproduction of the diagram of the Two-handed Manual Alphabet. The Committee directed that the 'finger alphabet elegantly and tastefully drawn by Mr Humphreys for the purpose of a gothic window, and lithographed by John Johnson, a former pupil, at the establishment of his master, Mr Allen of Trinity Street, Dublin, as a means not only of exciting an interest about the Institution, but in order to afford an opportunity to the public of learning that alphabet, and thereby enabling them to communicate more readily with the Pupils, as this is, of course, the chief mode of communication between the Deaf and Dumb and hearing persons.'[16]

The stone plates, with the diagrams of the English two-handed and of the Spanish one-handed manual alphabets (pages 42 and 43), had survived up to the 1950s, having been seen by one of the pupils. Sadly, they had disappeared and it is very much hoped that they may surface one day, as they are a priceless part of Irish Deaf History.

TWO-HANDED, OR ENGLISH, MANUAL ALPHABET.

The above diagram displaying the English or two-handed Manual Alphabet was produced on the back page of the Annual Reports, as part of facilitating communication between the hearing supporters of the Claremont Institution and their deaf protégées. The manual alphabet was used for spelling personal names, place names, and everyday phrases. There has been mention of 'finger-spelling', 'talking on the fingers' and 'finger alphabet' in newspaper reports and books during the nineteenth century when referring to the deaf.

The diagram was also reproduced in a periodical *The Irish Deaf-Mute and Juvenile Advocate*, publicised by the deaf missionary, Mr Maurice Hewson, in the late decades of the nineteenth century, in order to encourage the readers, particularly the hearing friends of the deaf, to learn the alphabet for facilitating communication. On 16 June 1863, Mr E.J. Chidley mentioned in his Letter-book to the Committee that 'Charles Forgets, Treasurer of the Liverpool Deaf and Dumb Institution has kindly sent me 100 cards of the One-handed Alphabet.' There is no indication if this particular Manual Alphabet was actually used in Claremont at that time, while the Cabra Institution used the French one-handed alphabet since 1845.

It had been noticed that most educated deaf people in the nineteenth century and in the early twentieth century Britain and Ireland used a large amount of finger-spelling, which was owing to the insistence of principals and teachers in the Institutions on usage of finger-spelling in the class-room and in presence of the officers of these Institutions. Naturally, some deaf people preferred to use sign language, out of convenience and to save time, for particular words. There was anecdotal evidence that hearing children of deaf parents were observed by their teachers to excel at spelling, even better than their peers at school.

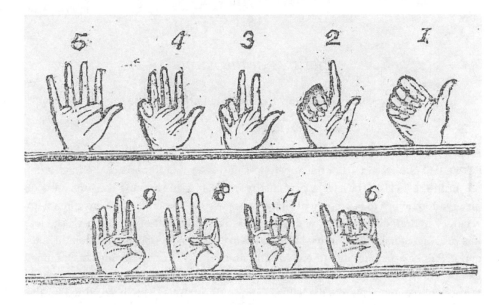

Signs for Numbers

In 1821, Dr Orpen presented to the Committee a plan for 'numeration on the fingers' designed by the Rev. Stansbury, master of the New York Institution for the Deaf and Dumb. Stansbury stated that his plan was 'highly approved on the other side of the water' and was adopted in some of the European establishments. The following diagram depicting the system of numerical signs was reproduced in the Annual Report of 1822. This particular set of signs is still being used among the deaf people in Northern Ireland, and in some districts of Britain.

Signs for numbers of ten to nineteen are used with one hand (in this case, the right-hand), based on the same signs as for one to nine, accompanied with the flicking of fingers. For numbers of 20, 30, 40 and up to 90, the hand is moved outwards from the front. For numbers of hundreds, the hand is quickly moved downwards, and for numbers of thousands, the hand is brought towards the left shoulder.

Speech or Signs?

In 1822, a deaf pupil in the American Asylum for the Deaf, was asked, 'Which do you consider preferable – the language of speech or signs?' His reply was, 'I prefer signs, because the language of signs is capable to give me elucidation and understanding well. I am fond of talking with the deaf and dumb persons by signs, quickly, about the subjects, without having the trouble of voice; therefore the language of signs is more still and calm, than the language of speech which is full of falsehood and troubles.'

15

Pictures in the Mind

'things, not words, are what presented images to the eye'[1]

Letters by Pupils in the early nineteenth century

The letters formed part of the appendices in the Annual Reports of the Institution until the 1840s. They were particularly interesting in showing the quickness of observation, which took account of all that was passing. Descriptions were given with accuracy and amusing *naiveté,* with the phraseology like that of a foreigner. The letters provide valuable descriptive information in regard to the social conditions, events and activities occurring in and outside Dublin during the early decades of the nineteenth century, while some letters describe the daily life at Claremont. Produced here is a selection of extracts from the letters. Some of the extracts have been edited for the purpose of summary and comprehension.

Burglary at Claremont and Daily Life at School

'I have sent you a too long coat by Collogan.[2] Where is the tailor? He will alter my long coat. Will you get a watchdog? There were robbers at Claremont lately; our new shirts were on the hedges to dry in the sun, and some were stolen. I hope two watchdogs will come to Claremont and keep us from robbers. I wish two young swans would come to our river; they are very beautiful. It is very level; you must get a floodgate; the water runs over the little gate. Devine (teacher) asked me to make deaf pupils, who were inattentive, to work. We are tall and stout with shovels and spades.

We will make our meadows and roads beautiful. It is very well when the sun shines. The boys carried the cuttings of the hedges on their backs, and threw them over the wall into the yard; they told me they were tired carrying potatoes in our field. I put my clothes in Brennan's[3] box; mine is broken, his box is very strong. Will you allow me to get his father to make a box for me?'

'Freak-Show' in Sackville Street, Dublin

'We went lately to Sackville-Street; I saw a giant, giantess, and dwarf; they are tall; she was standing near the fire; her arms were very large; she was elegantly dressed; the giant was dressed very well. I think they are ignorant. The dwarf is a very small boy; he was sitting on a small stool. A man called ladies and gentlemen; he took the giantness' wrist; they were surprised to see it. He spoke to the giant, who took the dwarf on his hand; his arms are very strong and long; he is seven feet high. There were musicians in the room playing. The giant and giantess were sitting on the large chairs; they were born in England. I was surprised looking at them. We returned to Claremont.'

Gi-ant-ess.

Public examinations of pupils at the Rotunda, Dublin

'I went to the Rotunda; some gentlemen made speeches for a long time. I liked our examination, because the public will give more money to the deaf and dumb. You appear interested in our progress. The ladies and gentlemen remained for six hours. They wanted to eat their dinner. My father met me there; he told me that my mother, brothers and sisters are very well; he said that he will make a key for my box for me. I like my parents because they support me in food and clothes and have sent me to school. We went to our examinations at the Rotunda, last Saturday. Many gentlemen and ladies were sitting on the forms and looking at us, clapping their hands. I was asked to write on a large slate. William Cunningham was mocking, (mimicking) funny, and queer. The Bishop of Kildare was sitting on a chair. Mr Humphreys and Mr Devine examined us there. The ladies were pleased with our progress. The deaf girls were quiet on the forms there. They were not examined, because they have not been long at school.'

'I will now tell you about the Meeting in the Rotunda, on Monday 15 April 1839. We went there with three teachers. Rev. Harman first read some of the Bible to the gentlemen and ladies. Mr Hopper called Thomas Mailley, a little pupil from among us, he questioned him about the sheep, and Thomas answered him well. He made signs for the sheep, and the gentlemen and ladies laughed. Mr Hopper called me from among the boys, and he examined me about America, Columbus and religion. I saw the Lord Mayor sitting on the chair; several gentlemen addressed the people, and I read their speeches in the newspaper the next day. Mr Hopper chose me and two other pupils to collect the money for the Deaf and Dumb Institution.'

*The Pillar Room in the Rotunda, where public examinations and annual meetings
were held up to the 1860's*

Visitors' Day at Claremont

'I was glad to see you here; you spoke to Mr Devine; your sister and children looked
at us; we were writing on the slates; you were patting my face and smiling; I wanted to look through the microscope. I looked through it at a butterfly which was under
it; it was very beautiful. Collins can speak and draw well, but I can speak little and
write. You laughed much because you like me and because I was funny, mimicking a
barber, hairdresser, shoemaker and cheesemonger. I hope your sister and children are
very well. William Brennan went to Rathgar; his neck is very sore; he was deaf and
dumb, but he can speak now. You told me you saw the giant, and giantess, and dwarf;
they were beautiful. You must write to me; you will not forget.'

Boys playing in the river at Claremont

'My dear Master, Your wife (Mrs Humphreys) got many letters from you; she told me
and some of the boys that a gentleman gave Thomas Collins and Brennan a pound and
umbrella each. I am very much disappointed because you are staying in England (on
deputation tour to raise funds for the building of extensions at Claremont) for so long
time.'

  'You will tell Collins that water is rising in the river (at Claremont) which is more
pretty. The water spoiled part of the island; the water is above part of the island; we
were walking on the wood to make the island; there are some trees in the two islands.
Kelly built a little island with sods, which is much better and stronger than the large

island. Some of the boys were on a door floating in the river; they put stones on it to bring over to the island. Meagher and O'Keeffe fell down into the river when floating on the door; they are all wet. The water is very deep. The water is flowing under the bridge; there was a great flood in the river. The water was very yellow on account of the great rain; there is a great murmuring from the water falling under the bridge; we were obliged to work very quickly. The water was running so fast in the river, we thought that the water was rising up; the river is done. We were very glad that the water was rising before we began to dig the trench. We are now making a ditch, which is nearly finished. Your wife was very much pleased with seeing the river; we were wet without working very hard; she sent (....) away for being a drunkard.'

Sweeping the Chimneys at Claremont

'Yesterday Mr Woods sent some of the big boys to carry the long ladder from Glasnevin to Claremont. Some of the boys brought a long rope with holly at one end. Michael Mailley (pupil) went up the long ladder; some of the boys pulled the rope, and cleaned the flue in the School-room.'

Dream about the Burglar at Claremont

'I was dreaming that the watchdog was barking (at) stranger; his hair was rough; he caught man. Dog heard a noise in the yard; Cunningham, Collins, Collogan and Caulfield got up and dressed themselves. They got sticks and they caught a man who was afraid; he was melancholy. He had gently opened the door. They caught him, and tied him with cord. He was put on the cart, and was sent to town; he will not come again to Claremont.' 'I saw a man who stole hay, and carried it on his shoulder; another beat a horse, which was under cart filled with hay. He heard a noise behind the cart; he pulled hay and carried it home. He ran till a man caught him; he went to gaol and was confined. His hands and feet were bound; watchmen shouted and called mankind in Smithfield; watchman kicked his thigh; the watchman opened the door, man caught him; he spoke to him, he must not steal.'

Excursion to Clontarf Lead-mine and the Beach

'My dear Master – Last Saturday we went to the lead mine at Clontarf; we sat on some stones; then I went to see the steam engine in the house. I was very much astonished. We went to the sea, and then we sought together for shells, and we gave them to you to keep. We took off our shoes and stockings, and tucked up our trowsers (sic), and we walked on the sand. We were happy walking in the cool of the sea. You told us to put on our shoes and stockings and trowsers; we did so and then we went to Baldoyle, and you told a woman to put knives and forks and plates on the table, and then you brought beef and three loaves out of the jaunting-car, and cut some beef, and E.F. cut the bread and gave it to us, and you gave us beef; we ate it; we were very full; you told the woman to bring one loaf and some porter; we drank porter. You examined the fossils of shells, threw away the bad stones, and packed up the good ones.'

Seeking Trades

'I do not like working about the ground. I would wish to learn a trade; I will earn much money. I am growing taller than all the little boys now at school. When will you take me to find a trade in Dublin? I hope God will love you; you are always generous giving money to the poor men and women in Cavan. A gentleman took John Fleming, deaf and dumb boy, to be an engraver in Dublin. Some big boys went away from Claremont long ago; they are apprentices in Dublin. All the boys and girls went to Thomas' Church; the preacher was the Hon. and Rev. Edward Wingfield; he preached a long (charity) sermon. They gave us more money for the deaf and dumb last Sunday. I was with the big boys collecting it from the people. The new school is not finished, but it will be finished this summer. Would you tell me about robbers in Cavan? I want you to tell Mr Humphreys about me to be apprenticed in Dublin.'

'I was looking at some masons who were using hammers to make the stones square this morning; I wished to learn the mason's work; they use many stones for building the four sides of the wall. In Claremont I was bringing with Reilly the big tub of water from the river to the kitchen this morning; it will be for different purposes; the large tub was behind the door; we quickly bestowed the big tub in kitchen.'

'I am very much obliged to you for the cock and hen you sent me by a car man; I will take care of them…I am very sorry not to see my mother and sister. Why will you leave Cavan? My teachers teach me very much, and all the boys and girls about God. Mr Humphreys often goes into Dublin (to the Committee's office in Sackville Street), because he often speaks to the Committee for the deaf in Claremont; he wanted to get more money for the deaf. We are always working in the river.'

Reilly's Letter from London after he left school

'I am bound to a shoemaker about three weeks. I can make new shoes a little; I get up at six o'clock every morning. I am not lazy indeed, you said that I was lazy when at school with you; my master make me work very hard, I am attentive to work. Shoemakers and tailors are Kerry men, and they know Major Orpen, his place is called Ardtully in Kerry. There are a great many Irishmen and women in London, because they get more money than they did in Ireland, but it is dearer than Irish clothes and food. My father's wife is a lady; she is a handsome woman. I have a half-brother and three sisters; I have twin sisters, they died a few weeks ago. My father is very fond of my stepmother, because she is good to him and his children. I know that your dearest Collins is displeased with me for not writing a letter to him, I hope he is not, because I am in a hurry to learn to make a shoe; tell Collins I have seen the Duke of Wellington, who is riding on his fine horse, he has aquiline nose, he is a thin man, his hair is light, his cheeks are half white, he wears a blue sirtout, and white nankeen, his horse has a long tail, soldiers and officers follow him, his lips are small, he has two long teeth like Brennan.'

Collins' Letter about the Visit of King George IV to Ireland in 1821

'Dear Friend – I went to the Park to see the King and the review last Saturday, it was very pretty. The soldiers marched very well, and the artillery very handsome; horsemen pretended to charge on the enemy. Very much amused with them. Saw gentleman with blue scarf and medal, (*people wore blue scarves, ribands, shawls and rosettes on occasion of the visit of King George IV to Dublin*),[4] he was on horseback. I did not see the King, for the crowd was very great, and they pushed me, but I saw the King's coach, which was most handsome. I think I saw him bowing to the people. I am very fond of the King, more than of all the people in this place. The King has a great many horses and soldiers under his command; he is very good, and all the Irish are very fond of him. Last Friday I saw a great many judges and lords in the procession, they were dressed very grand.'

Street Illuminations to celebrate the visit of King George IV to Dublin

'I went to town to see the illuminations. There were three nights of a great deal of illuminations. I saw the people throwing the stones at the windows of the houses in Dublin, and broke some of the glass. I liked the king very much. His dress has very much gold. He went to town to see every place. The people were crowded very much in Dublin. I went to the Park to see many soldiers and officers. I was shocked by the cannons. I saw the lancers. They were keeping away the people. There was a great multitude of gentlemen and ladies, and carriages and horses, and jaunting cars and coaches. I am very sorry that the king has gone to England. He will come to Ireland again in three years, if he lives so long. I will be very glad if the king will come to Ireland, and perhaps he will come to see the deaf and dumb at Claremont. Did you see the king in Drogheda? Do you think about him? God bless you.'

Military Review at the Phoenix Park, Dublin

'I saw many soldiers who were marching, standing and firing in a line; guns were smoking, officers were commanding, soldiers were straight and standing on the grass. Many horsemen were galloping on the grass with swords; men were walking on the grass. Many coachmen were driving coaches in the Park. Many soldiers were in a large ring on the ground. Many boys of the Marine School and of the Hibernian School were marching, and standing in the Park; they were sitting on the grass. Two Officers were commanding the boys of the Hibernian School, who

Re-view.

were marching and beating the drum. Men were climbing trees; and sitting on the trees. I felt a shock, soldiers were firing cannon, horsemen and gun carriages were galloping on the grass, horsemen were with muskets in muzzle-case. Mankind were sitting in the tent, drinking porter on the table. A man was staggering drunk on the grass.'

Knights of the Order of St Patrick's at Dublin Castle

'I walked to the Castle and saw 15 knights (of St Patrick's in Dublin Castle) marching on the streets; which were covered with sand. Many soldiers were keeping mankind away on the streets; dragoons were marching on the streets; I saw many coaches and carriages on the street. Many coachmen and footmen were on the carriages. Mankind were crushing on the street. The footman was opening the coach door. Ladies were coming out of the carriages, and going into the church. They were sitting on a form, and were looking at the knights of St Patrick. I saw men who were dressed in red clothes on the streets marching with poles; I saw officers, who were commanding many Soldiers. A Negro was beating a drum on horseback; many ladies were walking. Gentlemen and Ladies were looking out of the windows at the knights marching on the sand. A dragoon's horse was pushing the crowd back with its legs. He hit a gentleman's horse's mouth which was bleeding. An officer commanded the dragoon to keep away the crowd. A soldier beat my feet with his gun.'

Horse-drawn Road Accident

'I saw a Gentleman driving a Gig in the river; the horse was plunging into the river; The Gentleman's trousers were wet; he was driving through the river, the horse was drowned; the horse's leg was tied with a cord which men were pulling out of the river; men were throwing hot water on the horse's belly; men placed it on a cart, the horse was carried to the bleaching house; they covered the horse with blankets, and were blowing wind into its nostrils with a bellows. The men placed it in a cart to bring to Dublin; the horse's skin was taken off.'

Gentleman robbed and murdered near Santry

'Mr Beels sent a new carter to Claremont; he lives in Glasnevin; the (manual) sign of the carter is a long nose. On last Sabbath night two gentlemen were attacked in this neighbourhood by two robbers; the gentlemen were on horse's back. The robbers shot one of the gentlemen in the body with a great many slugs; the gentleman was killed and robbed by them near Santry; they ran away from being hanged. Another gentleman was riding to Dublin to tell the people about the dead gentleman and robbers. Collogan was cutting the hedge with shears; the hedge is done; it is very straight; it is like the hedge that Thomas Collins cut a long time ago. The boys and girls are very well; they are not impudent to Mr Rayner. I teach him how to sign; he is better now than he was. I think your two pupils are very pleased by travelling in England; you collected one hundred pounds at Manchester.'

Weather and Road Incident in Glasnevin

'It is a warm day. I perspired yesterday; I cannot look at the sun because it dazzles my eyes. The trees were injured and blown down by the wind long ago. The window was broken by the wind; the pigeon-house fell down, and Reilly was nearly hurt by it. The boys put a tree on the wheels of a cart and drew it with ropes'.

'Patrick Caulfield, myself and many people near Glasnevin were on the road when the four horses were drawing carts of hay. One cart-wheel rubbed against the wall, and the cart could not go on. The horses stopped on the side of a little hill near the milestone, under the trees at Glasnevin. The tall horse was trying to pull up the cart, but the cart was upset and the horse was hanging up by the collar. The cart-man had no pen-knife to cut the collar, and he borrowed a knife from a man to cut it'.

Charity Sermon at St Peter's Church on 12 December 1839

'Last Sunday it was 20 minutes to 11 o'clock when Mr Webster minded the twelve boys who went to St Peter's. It was 15 minutes to 12 o'clock when they sat down on the forms in the aisle. People were then assembling and going into the pews; the minister read the prayers and chapters from the Bible to the people. Twelve boys knelt down and rose up as the hearing people did, but the boys could not hear what was said. The Rev. Mr Fleury in a black vestment preached for a long time; a gentleman told six boys to collect the money when the sermon was over. Dr Orpen counted £43 in the Vestry-room. After some time, Mr Hopper gave cakes to the boys and girls to eat. Mr Webster minded the boys back to Claremont, but some boys were tired walking on the road. It was four o'clock in the evening when they came home; they ate the beef and potatoes in the eating-room, and then went to the sitting-room. The twelve boys observed everything in St Peter's Church, and signed to the rest of the boys when they came home. The boys were glad to see them signing.'

Woodcut of Children on See-Saw by a pupil of the Institution for the Deaf and Dumb, Milan, Italy

'The Big Wind of 1839

'On Sunday, 6 January in the night, the house was shaken by the wind; there were many slates on the ground, blown off the roof. I thought that the boys might be killed by the falling slates upon them; there were many fallen trees in the fields. Mr Humphreys went to Dublin on Monday morning, and returned to Claremont, and told us that he saw five houses and a church burning there. When a policeman was passing on the path, a tree in the Botanic Gardens fell upon him.'

Pennsylvanian Institution for the Deaf and Dumb, United States of America

Letter from Levi S. Backus, a pupil in the American Asylum for the Deaf and Dumb[5] *to Thomas Collins*

Hartford, 25 April 1820

'Sir, I am very much pleased with writing this letter to you. My kind and affectionate teacher, T.H. Gallaudet,[6] told me that he has received a letter from Mr (....) Lately; he read it with a great deal of pleasure. I have been in the American Asylum three years; I am almost 17 years old. I was born Deaf and Dumb. Mr. Gallaudet is a minister and also a teacher of the Deaf and Dumb. He has nine pupils. He teaches his pupils about the Bible, and many new words of the dictionary and grammar, and some things. There are 66 Deaf and Dumb in the American Asylum. The number of instructors is five. Mr Samuel Whittelsey is Superintendent. How long have you been in the Irish Asylum? When did the Irish Asylum build? How many Deaf and Dumb in your Asylum? Are your parents living? Mr Laurent Clerc, a (deaf) French teacher of the Deaf and Dumb, came from France to the United States. He lives in Hartford. He teaches his 13 pupils. He has been in the United States for four years and four months. He will embark from the United States to France soon. He will spend in Paris in one year. There are two Congregational churches, and one Episcopal church, and one Baptist church in Hartford. Hartford is a pleasant town – about 7,000 inhabitants. The Hartford Asylum has been built last summer, it is not yet done, will be finished next autumn. There are about 3,000 Deaf and Dumb in the USA. The Deaf and Dumb teachers often explain to the 66 pupils every Saturday morning about the Bible. Tomorrow morning will be the vacation – four weeks. Some of the pupils will go home. I wish you would continue a mutual correspondence for every month to me, and I will also do so. How long shall you stay at the Irish Asylum? What is the name of your teacher? How many teachers in your school? Please tell me how old are you? The pupils in the Asylum have five instructors – Rev. Mr. T.H. Gallaudet, L. Clerc, Rev. W.C. Woodbridge, Mr Isaac Orr and Mr Lewis Weld. I hope you will answer to me very soon, and I shall be very glad to receive a letter from you.

I remain, your most sincere, humble, obedient servant, Levi S. Backus'

Reply from Thomas Collins to Levi Backus
'My dear Levi Backus,

I was very much astonished to get a letter from you and was very happy to read it. I had not heard that there was an Asylum in Hartford. I have been in the Irish Asylum; the house was built long ago, and the Committee gave money for it for the Deaf and Dumb. My parents are both dead. A new school-house will be built in spring. There will be many Deaf and Dumb pupils when the school is done. I have a great deal of pleasure in corresponding for every month to you. I do not know that I will stay in this school for ever. I am 16 years of age, Mr J Humphreys teaches me to read a book. I am an orphan boy. Dr Orpen took me with him from the House of Industry when I was a little boy. He is the founder of the Deaf & Dumb Institution. The deaf and dumb work in the garden and fields, reading and writing. I superintend the big boys and lads to work to do good. There are three large gardens at the Irish Asylum; there is a great deal of fruit in them. Do the Indians in America cut their faces with knives? Have they paint on their faces?'

'We have 18 acres of ground here. We have very fine strong house and we will soon have a large new school for us, and we will be very comfortable. How many men are in the Committee in your place? There are 23 men in the Committee here. Dr Orpen thought himself he will get a great many deaf and dumb to send them to school. Humphreys is a Quaker and the teacher of the deaf and dumb at Claremont in Ireland. He teaches me about God and Jesus Christ, and to love everyone. He is very much clever. Are your masters Quakers or gentlemen?

Thomas Collins'

16

Life at School

Travelling

During the nineteenth century, some children travelled from their homes to school by stage-coach. John Brown, pupil, wrote, 'I came to Dublin, from County Cavan. I did not fall off the coach; if I did, my body would be crushed by the horses which draw the coach, it would be painful. If I walk on the road, it is dangerous, for I cannot hear; I must walk on the foot-path.' In 1822, due to hazardous conditions on the roads, such as highwaymen in Co. Tipperary,[1] a girl, about to be admitted to Claremont, was sent by sea on a steam packet from Cork to Dublin. In December 1846, a female pupil, having completed education, was sent home by the Nenagh 'caravan or coach', to be accompanied by a 'messenger as far as Kildare'. At an Annual Meeting, one of the speakers commented that he had learnt the 'finger alphabet' from a deaf boy accompanying him in a stage-coach on his way home. During the 1820s to 1830s, deaf children resident in the regions of England and Wales were sent to Claremont, as in the case of William Pagen from Cumberland.[2] A deaf child, Henry Cowell, had been sent from the Isle of Man. Whenever the father, serving in either the Army or the Navy, got despatched to Ireland, his deaf child would be transferred to Claremont. One pupil had been born in Ceylon (Sri Lanka) and then sent to Claremont, and another from Malta. At the end of the nineteen century, there was a high number of pupils from North Wales, which was closer to Dublin than to the nearest deaf school in that region. Sometimes, the Committee received requests, very rarely granted, from parents for money to cover the expenses of their deaf child's travelling to Claremont. For that reason, the children were retained at Claremont from the time they were admitted until they either reached the maximum age or completed their term of education.

Daily Life as described by Pupils in their letters

In 1820, William Brennan wrote from Irishtown, where he was sent for recuperation, to Mr Devine, assistant master, 'I was very happy to get your letter, I hope you will understand my letter. (He) lent me a book to read, *Cottage Dialogues* (by Mary Leadbeater), but it was too difficult for me. I shall be glad to see you, but Irishtown is too far from Claremont. Can the boys swim very well? I can leap into the salt water, which is good for my neck. I saw the steam boat went out. Pigeon House is very beautiful, I saw it at a distance. When my neck is well, I shall go to Claremont.'

William Quintin wrote, 'There are three boys washing the potatoes; they get clean water at the pump, and take them in wheel-barrows to the kitchen, to put into the large boiler over the fire. The boys and girls eat stirabout (porridge) and milk, potatoes and milk, and bread and milk for our breakfast, dinner and supper. On Mondays and Thursdays, we get prime mutton or prime beef and potatoes. Ladies and gentlemen come here on Fridays to converse with us on our slates, and leave donations'.

James Gilliland wrote, 'Seven teachers are here; we are learning about religion, geography, arithmetic and the names of animals. New pupils will come here next August. We will be taken to Clontarf by caravan for sea-bathing. We went to the Earl of Charlemont's demesne; the gardens are beautiful and the temple is neat. We were in the Zoo Gardens, and saw a brown bear climb up the pole in the pit and an elephant. We went to the College museum and saw a dead leopard, elk, ostrich, crocodile, serpents and fishes. We often go to the Botanic Gardens, and we were in the Santry church, it is very nice and Rev. Browne preaches about Christ.'

Festivities

During the early and middle of the nineteenth century, on the Easter Monday of each year when the Annual Meeting of the Juvenile Association took place at Claremont, the children were usually treated to a meal of roast meat and plum pudding. During the Great Famine, a starving deaf girl from Achill, Co. Mayo, named Ellen Tullis, her sponsor being the Rev. Edward Nangle,[3] arrived at the school in the year of 1847. The children, seeing her plight, unanimously decided to forego their customary dinner, and donate the sum usually spent on their food to the relief of the starving poor.[4]

In 1870, Mr Chidley asked the Committee for permission 'for the pupils to have their usual Christmas dinner of plum pudding and roast mutton'. He added that the parents of some of the pupils requested to have them for a few days' vacation at Christmas, as they had done on former occasions. It was not until around the end of the nineteenth century, when the practice of discharging all of the pupils for the Christmas holidays was introduced, as it had been difficult to arrange supervision on a full-time basis with the teachers wishing to take their own holidays.

143

In December 1912, Major Poe, one of the Governors, demonstrated his system of 'flash signals' to the teachers and pupils. This would presumably some kind of lamp used by the Navy for communicating with another ship using the Morse code.

Some kindly neighbours brought around a Christmas tree and some fruit and sweets to cheer the children, and occasionally one of the Governors would organise a magician to give a show to the children. In the early 1930s, the Mission to the Adult Deaf and Dumb in Dublin sent over a Christmas tree, and from the 1950s onwards, it became tradition for the Mission to organise the Christmas party for both the adult deaf and the Claremont pupils

Mr Taylor had arranged for the 'Magic Lantern' shows to take place at the School to celebrate the Hallowe'en festivities. Using this particular machinery in the gloomy, dark room in the derelict School would have enhanced the eerie atmosphere for the children. There had been two Jewish pupils in the Institution, Samuel David and Percy Emmanuel Goodman. On 15 September 1909, the latter, born in Birmingham, England, had been given leave to go home in Ballsbridge, Dublin, to keep the Jewish Feast.

Crick-et.

Sports

In May 1888, Mr E.W. Chidley asked the Committee, 'Now that outdoor amusements have commenced, I should like the boys to have their cricketing things replenished. With what they have at present, a sovereign would furnish them completely. A few skipping ropes and soft wind balls would be very acceptable among the girls.' In November of the same year, he requested that 'the boys would be pleased to have a football for the winter months.' In March 1902, Mr Taylor asked the Committee for a cricket bat and two balls for the boys, a few hoops and new ropes for the girls' swing.

In June 1882, the Committee considered the plan to transform the backyard with a ball alley. The next month, they gave the tender to Messrs Dockrell for construction of the Ball Alley at a cost of £30. During the late nineteenth century and the early 1900s, the following sports were played by the Headmaster's family members, the staff, the pupils, the neighbours and the visitors – football, croquet, lacrosse, rugby, tennis and cricket. In September 1914, the Claremont Institution organised a Sports Day, and Colonel H. Gore Lindsay, squire of Glasnevin House and one of the Institution's Governors, did the honour of presenting prizes to the pupils.

Gymnasium

From the 1880s onwards, it was perceived that physical health was necessary for effective breathing which formed an essential element of teaching articulation. Mr Taylor presented the proposals for a Gymnasium before the Board of Governors. In July 1890, the Gymnasium was constructed at the cost of £21. Certainly, the male pupils took part in gymnastic exercises with great enthusiasm, releasing pent-up energies, and so much that injuries were incurred by some of the boys, including Jack Stanton, whose story acted as a curtain-raiser to this book. He recalled his having broken his arm and being sent home in Kingstown, where he enjoyed watching the arrivals and departures of the Royal Navy ships, the mail-boats and the cruise liners at the harbour. Upon return to Claremont after a period of recovery, he created stories around

Swing.

his observations, in animated signs with an element of dramatics, to enthral his fellow-pupils.[5] In May 1891, the Visiting Governors were 'pleased with the great progress' the boys had made in the gymnasium.

One of the pupils, Abraham Hawkins, from Co. Wicklow, was so proficient in gymnastics, that he continued this sport at the Gymnasium at the Dublin Working Boys' Home in Lord Edward Street, Dublin, where he lodged while serving his apprenticeship with J. Walker & Co., Stationers and Printers in Crow Street, Dublin. He was featured in a report, 'The deaf (in Dublin) again scored a great victory over the hearing, this time in gymnastics. At one of the principal gymnasiums here, Mr. A. Hawkins, deaf-mute, who is a member of the club, called all before him, beating his competitors by fifteen marks. He is the proud possessor of a silver medal.'[6]

On 6 July 1896, the Headmaster informed the Governors that 'Mrs Holland, Her Majesty's Inspector, though highly approving of the system of instruction given in callisthenics,[7] suggested that the Swedish Drill be introduced as a supplementary exercise. It is my intention during vacation to gain knowledge of this system and to introduce it when school re-assembles. Twelve pairs of Indian clubs costing about 12/- are required for the Gymnasium, and I ask permission to obtain them.' At the Annual Meetings, exhibitions of callisthenics were usually given by some of the pupils.

Outings

Letters by the pupils during the 1820s mentioned the visits to the Menagerie, Panoramas, fairs and 'freak-shows' (such as the giants, dwarfs, Laplanders and Esquimaux Indians[8]) in the city of Dublin, and to the art exhibitions. 'The pupils, 75 in number, visited Newsome's Grand Circus in the Rotunda Gardens. The mute spectators, testified by their animated gestures, the admiration and delight with which they witnessed the surprising feats of the acrobats, the marvellous docility[9] of the trained horses, the skills of the riders; and their hearty laughter at the grotesque performance of the clowns, proved their thorough appreciation of the comic portions of the entertainment.'[10]

A letter in 1835 read, 'I went to town with the deaf and dumb boys, and we were astonished to see the insects magnified by a microscope in the Arcade in Dublin. The owner of the microscope was polite to us, signing about the insects in a dark room. The deaf and dumb boys

Es-qui-maux.

sat on forms to see the different insects. The proprietor showed us a bright light like the sun in the Arcade. The boys walked two by two, I saw the coaches, cars, gigs, carts, mail-coaches, and the ships in the river near Dublin.'[11]

Pan-o-ram-a.

John Brown wrote to his fellow-pupil, 'I went to Dublin from Claremont to see the two giants and dwarfs in Capel Street and Nassau Street. The dwarf is a little man wearing a frock. He danced and I laughed at him. I thought the little man was taught by a gentleman, wearing a blue cloth coat, and I am not sure whether he be a Quaker, who came from Wales.' In 1840, David Holmes wrote to Dr Orpen, 'we have no subjects to write about, for we have not seen the country this spring. Last year we took a walk to see Lucan, Leixlip and the Salmon Leap.'

In 1842, Mary Anne Dunne, pupil, said, 'After the examination at the Rotunda, Mr Marshall kindly permitted us to see his splendid Panorama; we saw the great Lake Maggiore and the beautiful island, which an Italian nobleman adorned with beautiful buildings, garden walks, pleasure houses and other elegant ornaments. I saw the stable at Bethlehem where Jesus was born, but is now richly adorned with gold and silver lamps. We were greatly delighted with the balloon, in which three gentlemen took an aerial voyage from England to Germany.'

In 1856, as rewards for their diligence and attention, the pupils were allowed to visit the following sights: Mr Fenton's Exhibition of Crimean Photographs, the exhibition of Paintings at the Royal Hibernian Academy and at the Irish Institution, 'The Diorama of India'*, Mr Hampton's *Diorama illustrative of Past and Recent Wars*, the Museum of Irish Industry, St Stephen's Green, the Zoological Gardens, the Phoenix Park and the exhibitions of 'Natural Magic' by Signor Bosco and by Professor Anderson.[12] When the Industrial Exhibition was held in Herbert Park, Dublin, in the year of 1865, pupils were brought there to observe the craftsmanship of various mechanical and artistic objects.

* An advertisement in *Dublin Evening Post* in January 1826 entitled 'Scenography' read, 'The Proprietors of the Dublin DIOMARA, in Great Brunswick Street (Pearse Street), who have, at an expense of £3,000, erected the above building, take leave to announce to the inhabitants of this City and the Kingdom at large that the DIOMARA is now open to exhibit the beautiful picture of the Delightful Valley of Sarnan, in Switzerland, which, from the unbounded imagination and patronage this novel phenomenon of Art has met with throughout England, will give equal pleasure to, and receive equal encouragement in this native country.'[13]

Bathing for Health

During the 1820s and 1830s, the doctor prescribed sea-bathing for the pupils, who were then taken in caravans to Clontarf or Malahide. Lodgings had been organised for them in those locations. In August 1856, one of the pupils had been nearly drowned whilst bathing at the North Wall, Dublin, and that he had been saved by a young man, named Carr, who received a gift of one pound for his bravery. Sick pupils were usually sent out to Ringsend (for salt air), where oysters, clams and cockles could be gathered. During the

Ba-thing.

1880s to 1890s, some pupils, discharged from either the Whitworth Hospital in Drumcondra, or from Dr Steevens' Hospital, were sent to Greystones, a seaside resort in Co. Wicklow, for recuperation.

Royal Events

As already mentioned earlier, the pupils had witnessed the visit of King George IV to Dublin in 1821, having had seen the procession through the Phoenix Park. Even though Queen Victoria had made several visits to Ireland during her reign of sixty years, there was no mention of any special concessions or celebrations organized for the pupils at Claremont. In May 1841, a pupil wrote a letter to the Queen:

'My dear Madam, I am very glad to be a subject to your Majesty. I have been told that your Majesty's gracious husband, Prince Albert, drove with your Majesty when a wicked man shot your Majesty, but you were not killed. God saved your Majesty from being killed. I am very glad that your Majesty sent a gentleman from England to Ireland, to be a Lord Lieutenant. The Deaf and Dumb children of this Institution in Ireland were very glad to see the Lord Lieutenant, because he liked to see Claremont, with the Bishop of Kildare, and captains and gentlemen. This Institution is a very beautiful house; there are many Deaf and Dumb children here. I hope your Majesty will come to see us very soon.

Your Majesty's very much obedient servant,

Edward Musgrave Sullivan,

An Irish Deaf and Dumb Boy'[14]

On 22 June 1911, when King Edward VII was crowned King of Great Britain and Ireland, a kindly lady, who took special interest in the deaf, presented a 'Coronation Cake' to the pupils. On 3 June 1913, the King's Birthday, the pupils were given a holiday, and were taken as a treat to the Military Review in the Phoenix Park. On 15 September 1917, a Fete was held at the Institution to raise funds in aid of the Irish Counties War Hospital.

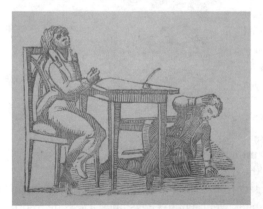

Absconding and Punishment

A insubordinate pupil would be beaten on the back with a hemp 'punish' (sic), after being stretched over the larger boy's back. There were a few occasions of teachers either reproached or dismissed for over-excessive use of punishment or ill-treatment of pupils. Among those teachers were Samuel Gordon, who later obtained a position in the Dublin Day School and then in Belfast Day School in 1831, and George Downing, who left to take charge of the Strabane Institution which had been destroyed by fire in 1857, killing six deaf children. Later on, he became the Missioner for the Adult Deaf and Dumb in Manchester. In 1829, the Secretary informed the Committee that a pupil, Patrick Sullivan, aged thirteen, ran away three times, making his way back to his home-place in Killarney. As he was an ill-conducted boy, it was decided that he should remain there.

In October 1859, letters from the Rev. Sheppard and Mr Chidley, the Headmaster, were read regarding discipline at Claremont. It was decided that the Headmaster and the Matron be advised that female pupils over sixteen years of age, guilty of serious misconduct or insubordination, were to be threatened with being sent home or to the Union Workhouse instead of corporal punishment. Shortly afterwards, a rebellious girl, Mary Gulchenan, was sent to the poorhouse, after her relations could not be traced by the rector of her parish in Co. Cavan.

In 1866, Mr Chidley wrote, 'I am sorry to report an unusually serious case of misconduct of three boys, two of them deputation boys running away and remaining absent from the Institution for several days. The strange fact of two boys so intelligent, engaging in so blameable a freak, is I believe to be described to the discontent at the monotony of school-life, after enjoying for months the pleasure of continually travelling with the deputation. Having to pay the expense of searching for and bringing them back, out of their pocket money, will be one very effective discouragement to a repetition of this dangerous offence, but a few words addressed to them by the Committee will not fail to make a very powerful impression on the more intelligent culprits.'

Public Meetings and Examinations

During the nineteenth century, it was standard procedure for the educational institutions to hold public examinations so that members of the public would observe how

Tru-ant.

subscriptions and donations had been usefully expended on education and maintenance of children of the poor. In the case of the Claremont Institution, these were held in the Rotunda, Dublin. From the 1860s onwards, owing to the decline in numbers of both subscribers and pupils, the Annual meetings and examinations were held at the Schoolroom in Claremont.

In June 1826, in the Round Room of the Rotunda, the female pupils were ranged on each side of the platform, immediately over the audience, and the males were seated at the back of the platform, behind the Chairman's seat. A blackened wood tablet, ten feet long, by five feet wide, was supported high up on triangles, for the pupils to write on with chalk, in front of it was a foot board, reaching its whole length, raised on three high stools, for them to walk on, while writing. By this, almost everyone in the room could see the questions put to them, and the answers given. The Committee informed the meeting that it was 'impossible to make an examination in such a room and before a crowded audience as satisfactory, as it would be in the schoolroom of the Institution. The school was open to the public every Friday between the hours of noon and two o'clock (at which time the pupils went to dinner).'

'Mr Humphreys explained the method taken to instruct the deaf. He said as they were shut out from receiving instruction through the ear, it was necessary to communicate it through the eye. Through this medium it was easy to convey to them the names of objects, by pointing to those objects, and writing the names. With regard to communication between the deaf children, he said, they conducted it by signs, but different children might at first have different signs for the same ideas; so a series of signs was, therefore, absolutely necessary. Mr Humphreys said that deaf pupils in general, although taught to read and write, would still naturally carry on conversation by signs.'

'A child, about eight years of age, appeared before the assembly and Mr Humphreys, having motioned to a gentleman to write with chalk on an elevated tablet, the word 'reaping', the boy immediately expressed, in a style which would not disgrace some of the pantomimic actors, what his ideas were of that process. The words 'mowing' and 'threshing', etc. were next written on the board, which actions he described with success. This boy having written down answers to several questions, and exhibited some admirable specimens of his talent for drawing, was succeeded by another boy, who was further advanced in information.'[15]

In April 1830, at a 'more interesting meeting, the children, male and female, of the Institution, most comfortably clothed and displaying truly intelligent countenances, were placed on the platform and conversed with each other cheerfully, by signs on their fingers. Several ladies and gentlemen, who understood their motions, seemed to give them great delight, by the encouragement they gave them (the pupils), in conversing with them in signs. A large board was placed in the centre of the platform, over metal supporters, and the questions were chalked on it by one of Mr Humphreys' assistants, and one of the boys wrote under each question his answer. Several gentlemen, through Mr Humphreys, gave questions which were answered in a manner which produced universal and prolonged applause. It would be impossible to describe the great astonishment manifested by the meeting, at the rapidity with which answers were given by the monitor (Philip Geary) and boys, to questions, and many voices exclaimed, 'Oh! mark the power and greatness of God!' (…) Mr Guinness said he saw the celebrated Deaf and Dumb Institution at Paris, and he declared Claremont was superior to it.'[16]

In 1838 at the Rotunda attended by several hundred people, a boy named Foley was asked for a sign for 'lawyer', and he described it by putting his hands about his throat representing a man hanging! This caused a great deal of laughter, which was renewed upon his giving the sign for 'soldier' by cocking, loading and levelling the musket.

Hearing Young People challenged by Deaf Pupils[17]

The annual meeting held on 30 April 1861 was the most interesting for many years. The Committee and the Hon. Secretary, the Rev. Hercules Dickenson, made exertions to secure as large an attendance as possible of young persons of both sexes, and to afford them an opportunity of seeking the deaf children under the care of the Society, and of witnessing the progress which, through the mode of instruction adopted at Claremont, they had been enabled to make in various branches of sacred and secular knowledge. The Round Room of the Rotunda was crowded with young persons, and on the platform were a number of clergymen and others who had taken an active part on behalf of the Society, as well as a number of the deaf mutes who were maintained and educated at the Institution.

A large blackboard was placed in the centre of the platform, and a series of questions in Scriptural history and doctrine, geography, English history and other subjects was put to the deaf children, through the medium of the Rev. Sheppard. The answers were written in large characters, by the children, on the blackboard. Some of the questions were severe enough to test the powers of those familiar with Biblical and historic stories, and the quickness and accuracy with which the answers were given, testified at once to the intelligence of the children and to the excellence of the system of instruction pursued. For instance, a little girl was asked, 'Who went to Babylon, but never saw it?' She wrote down 'Zedekiah'. 'Who was Zebedee's wife?' She immediately wrote, 'Salome'. 'What was the last miracle performed by Christ before his death?' The answer was, 'He healed the ear of Malchus, servant of the High Priest'. 'Who was in danger of being killed after he died?' A boy answered, 'Lazarus'. The readiness and intelligence evinced by many of those children in answering the difficult questions put to them brought frequent applause. It may be necessary to observe that it was impossible that they could have been 'rammed' or prepared for the exam, as the questions were dictated not by any of the clergy or managers of the Institution, but were indiscriminately asked by various persons among the audience.

The examination having terminated, much interest was excited by the Sunday school children, in their turn to a similar course of examination, the questions being dictated by the deaf children. Some of the questions were of a very amusing as well as difficult kind. 'What Jewish lady lived in a college?' Answer, 'Hulda, the prophetess.' 'Where is lead first mentioned in the Bible?' Answer, 'In Miriam's song, Exodus 15:10. They sank as lead in the mighty waters.'

Measles Epidemic and Lack of Sanitary Facilities

On 5 October 1866, Mr Chidley wrote 'during the past month more than thirty children have been ill with the Measles. As I was anxious about this epidemic extending to the private pupils and my own children, I provided, at my own expense, a water closet in the house'. In 1879, he wrote, 'I think it desirable for the Vartry waters now brought to Glasnevin could be supplied to the Institution which at some seasons is badly off for water suitable for laundry and lavatory purposes.' In 1883, Mr E.J. Chidley, son of the late Headmaster, said, 'the boys' lavatory is the worst of the two and on severe mornings is quite unfit for young and delicate children. The basins are filled with water collected off the roof and has to be carried in pails to the washroom. A proper supply of water could be obtained from the Vartry pipes which come as far as the Entrance gates. The pressure there is sufficient to fill by a hose the water cart which stands some six feet above the hydrant. If it were satisfactorily ascertained that the Vartry could be brought to the basement storey and the proper authorities were willing to supply it, then a firm could lay the pipes and re-fit the lavatories.' In the following year, he appealed that piped water-supply was necessary for the general health of the Institution, and his request was finally met in 1885.

Governors' Visits to the Institution

Some of the Governors were given, on a rota basis, the responsibility of paying a visit to the Institution in order to carry out inspection with the purpose of ensuring that the Institution was managed in an orderly and economic fashion. In addition to the Governors, there were Lady Visitors, often wives of the clergy or of the Governors, whose duty was to inspect the wellbeing of the children and to take note of the conditions within the Institution. Here is an entry of November 1886 in the Visitors' Book with comments by the visiting Governors:

'I visited the Deaf and Dumb Institution. On arrival I found the Avenue Gate, as I have in every visit I have paid there, open – one of the lodges, inhabited by the Gardener, looks neat and well kept, and the interior tidy and clean. The other lodge, outside, appears neglected and ill kept.'

'The Avenue, as I approached the house, seemed neglected, but certainly not as well kept or neat as I think it might be. I immediately went into the Schoolroom, where I found the two Assistant masters, and the Work-mistress instructing the children, and all seemed satisfactory there. It was near dinner time and I saw the children at their dinner, which consisted of a portion of a round of beef, fresh and boiled. Twenty-three children were at dinner, and the meat provided for them weighed five pounds, including bone, which was not much. No vegetables but potatoes, and I thought there was a marked difference in the potatoes provided for the teachers and pupils.'

'I visited the room inside the Schoolroom, which is appropriated as the Assistant Teacher's sitting room; most of the chairs in this room need repair. I visited Miss Crowley's room (the Work-mistress) which needs papering and painting and the ceiling whitened. It looked gloomy but as far as could be, tidy and neat. The walls, in the back yard, appear to me to require dashing, and in some places, seem in a bad state. The pump within the house was out of order and, when in order, very difficult to use, requiring hard and continued labour to supply the necessary quantity of water. The Gardens were untidy, the walks overgrown with weeds, as also the walks about the house but some allowance should be made for this, considering the time of year, and the hurry of digging and storing the crop of potatoes. Altogether the place, that is the grounds and the house, does not present, in my opinion, a satisfactory appearance. They seem neglected, but not kept as well as might be.'

'For the number of pupils, boys and girls, the house, schoolroom, dormitories, etc. seem much too large, and on a count of their size, comfortless, and requiring, for cleaning, etc. much more labour than is necessary for the number of inmates. The arrangements for the Boys' dormitory seem defective – the two Assistant Teachers sleep in rooms off this dormitory – but it appears to me, they can have but little supervision of the boys during the night, certainly none over those that sleep in that part of the dormitory of which there is no view from the teachers' sleeping rooms.'

Another entry in June 1887 reads as follows:

'I visited Claremont on 27 May and found the children just sitting down to a very good well cooked dinner of Irish stew, potatoes, greens and rice pudding. The table was very neatly laid – the floor of the schoolroom was not clean and Miss Ladbrook says it cannot be washed as often as it should be without more help. The dormitories were very clean and well aired. The lavatories are very much out of repair and cannot be made to look clean. The kitchen also is in a very bad state, the flags are broken and full of holes and the boiler is useless. I should suggest putting a new range in the front kitchen which is now unused. The flags are good and could be kept clean, which cannot possibly be done in the present kitchen.'

Dining Room at Claremont – c.1900

17

Leaving Claremont

'equipped as not to be burden on their family and on society'
- *Annual Report of the Institution, 1819*

From the opening of the Claremont Institution in 1816 to the end of 1850, 1,081 pupils had received education. The period of instruction had been, on average, five years, and the school age was from six to fifteen. It had been acknowledged by the most experienced teachers of the deaf that after a certain age, the majority of persons so afflicted were incapable of receiving literary instruction. Sir William Wilde, the Commissioner for the Irish Census of 1851, stated that the amount of industrial education afforded in all establishments for the deaf should have been more extensive. The Act for the Relief of the Poor in Ireland made some provision for the education of the deaf in special establishments for that purpose; and many of the children in the Catholic Institution were supported by that means.

Regarding industrial education of the deaf, Sir William Wilde believed there were as many born-deaf capable of acquiring a practical knowledge of mechanical and industrial skills as were found among a similar number of hearing persons in the same rank in life. In Appendix 4 is a list of occupations undertaken by deaf people in the late nineteenth century. In regard to the deaf males, the largest number was 493 in the occupation of labourer, the next being 222 as farmer, most certainly working on their family farm. In the skilled occupation class, the highest number was 104 as boot and shoe-maker. As for the deaf females, 263 were servants, some of them having had attained some experience at their schools prior to departure. In the skilled occupation class, 108 deaf females obtained positions as seamstresses and shirt-makers.

Apprenticeship
Once the Committee decided, upon advice of the Headmaster, that the pupil had completed the term of education, some openings in employment had to be found for the pupil prior to removal from the Institution. Some pupils had already obtained training within the Institution – the males in agriculture, horticulture, shoemaking and woodwork, and the females in domestic service, housekeeping, sewing and dressmaking.

Prior to taking on apprentices for a period of a few years, masters of trades required finance to provide accommodation and food for their charges. In 1825, Lady Hutchinson of Merrion Square, donated £25 towards a Deaf and Dumb Apprentice

Fund, established by the Committee, and was granted two votes for the election of applicants for admission to the Institution. The Rev. Robert Jessop also donated £25 towards the fund. Thomas Collins' friends established a fund to apprentice him to a printer, with Dr Orpen's brother contributing £10. In 1824, the Committee applied to the Linen Board seeking donation of six spinning wheels for purpose of training the female pupils in spinning.

In addition to sourcing masters and mistresses to take on pupils as apprentices, the Institution organised training on the premises at Claremont. Lodges in the Claremont demesne were erected to provide accommodation and workshops for the resident gardener, shoemaker and tailor, in order to provide vocational training for the deaf boys.'[1]

Deaf Apprentices sponsored by Guardians
John Fleming, an orphan from the Foundling Hospital, was among the first group of deaf boys admitted into the Institution in the year of 1816. On 30 September 1822, he was bound apprentice to an engraver, who having been himself educated in London in an engraver's office, where there were some deaf and dumb workmen (who were found peculiarly adapted to a business such as engraving, requiring fixed attention), applied at Claremont for an apprentice. Another boy, Thomas Collogan, from Collon, Co. Louth, was apprenticed to a cabinet-maker in Dublin. For Collogan's apprentice fund, a private subscription had been made up by the executors, legatees and friends of the late Rev. Alexander Bradford, who had first recommended the boy to the Institution.

Letter to the Committee from a gentleman enclosing a letter from T.Collogan
'Sir, I take leave to enclose of T. Collogan, a pupil in the Deaf & Dumb Institution, addressed to me, and written in my office. It both surprised and gratified me, as being a specimen of the advancement of the individual, and of the benefits of the Establishment.

'Dear Sir,
I am a friend of the late Rev. Bradford, and would be glad to go to Collon (Co. Louth) to see him interred, if you would have the goodness to take me in your coach. The Rev. Mr Bradford put me to school, and I would like to pay him any respect I could. I am Deaf and Dumb, and my family lives at Collon. I am living at Claremont, at the Deaf & Dumb School. I will be for ever obliged if you can make room for me. Yours, Thomas Collogan'

At an annual meeting in 1834, it was stated that it was difficult to obtain masters and mistresses, particularly Protestant, for pupils about to leave school. Many masters had an 'aversion to take deaf-mutes, because they allege that to teach them the rudiments of a trade requires knowledge of the mode of communicating with them, which it is troublesome to acquire'.

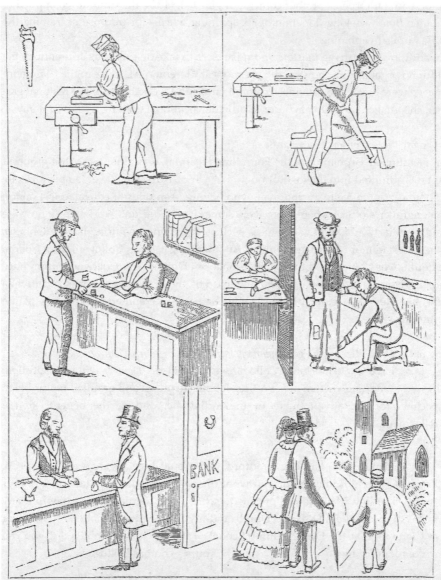

Drawn by G. C. M. G.   Engraved by Young Ladies in Dublin.

"THE HAND OF THE DILIGENT MAKETH RICH."—Proverbs i. 4.

Work-shop.

In their Letter books to the Committee, the Headmasters made references to organising apprenticeships, some of them initiated by parents of some pupils. On 18 February 1863, Mr Chidley wrote, 'The father of Elizabeth Covey, a pupil, requests me to state that Mrs Alexander of Rathmines is willing to take his daughter as an apprentice to the dressmaker. The Rev. Loftus Shine will answer any inquiries as to Mrs Alexander, who is also known to Mrs Sheppard (one of the Lady Visitors to Claremont)'. He went on to say, 'I beg also to report concerning another pupil, Ann Willis, admitted nine years ago and now nearly seventeen years of age, that it is time she should be removed from the Institution and apprenticed. She came from the Workhouse of Skull (sic), Co. Cork. As to Timothy and Michael Crowley, there should be no difficulty in apprenticing them to shoemaking trade in Dublin.'

In the following month, he wrote, 'I have succeeded in finding a shoemaker, William Holme, of Aungier Street, who will take the younger of the Crowley brothers as apprentice.' In the same letter, he referred to a girl, Isabella Whelan, in the school 'whose parents should be required to remove her, she having been ten years at Claremont.' One year later, he wrote, 'The sureties of Whelan should be called on to remove her. She has been allowed to remain eleven years at eighteen years of age. She is discontented at her long stay here and difficult to manage.' In the following month, 'nothing having been done since the last meeting about Isabella Whelan, she should be removed if the Committee agree to pay her third-class railway fare to Limerick.'

Meanwhile, the Committee made some enquiries as to the possibility of the pupils obtaining employment in 'America and other colonies' where there was much demand for agricultural labour, a sphere of work for which 'deaf mutes were in no respect disqualified by their infirmity, and for which their training at Claremont might be regarded as some preparation.'[2]

Having disabilities in addition to deafness presented difficulties for the deaf while they sought employment. Mr Chidley informed the Committee on 15 December 1864 that:

'I can no longer defer reporting to the Committee the impossibility of retaining the young man, Alfred Groves, at Claremont. Owing to his defective sight, he is incapable of learning a trade and he has neither parents nor friends who can take charge of him. He is now 23 years of age and is altogether beyond the control of

the Teachers who are indeed afraid to thwart him. He has lately shown a disposition to be mischievous. He has wrenched the holdfasts of the fireguards out of the
wall and burst open the door of a room which he found locked. On one occasion
he threw the heavy padlock of the farm-yard gate at Killeen (handy-man) when he
insisted upon him doing some work. I know of no place but the Workhouse when
he could be received if dismissed from Claremont.'

Not only positions in employment and apprenticeships were sought within and
outside Dublin, but also in Britain. In 1864, Mr Chidley sourced a heraldic painter in
London to take Ralph Tector, 17 years old and showing much talent for drawing, as an
apprentice provided that £12 be offered as apprentice fee. Some months later, Chidley
said, 'A shoemaker named James Woods is recommended by Rev. Patton as able to
teach an apprentice. I think therefore he might have Ralph Tector bound to him'. In
June 1865, Mr Chidley wrote, 'It is necessary to transfer Ralph Tector from James
Woods, his present master, who neither feeds him properly nor employs him at his
trade, to another shoemaker, John Lennon, to whom a former pupil, George Stafford,
is already apprenticed and with whose treatment we have good reason to be satisfied.
Lennon is willing to take the boy for £7, so that the Institution will only have to pay
£1, in addition to the balance of the apprentice fee still unpaid.' And on 1 June 1866,
the Committee were informed by Mr Chidley, 'Ralph Tector, apprenticed to a shoemaker in Stafford Street, was suddenly attacked with English cholera and died in the
hospital. His master having no means of paying for his interment came to me for
assistance. The office being closed it being a general holiday, and so not being able to
consult with you, I was obliged to act on my own responsibility, and therefore paid the
undertakers' account and by the kindness of the Rev. Mr Carroll, the interment took
place at Glasnevin.'

Chidley wrote, 'I am very desirous that George Holden should be well apprenticed,
as his good conduct and intelligence as a Deputation pupil have been a credit to the
Institution. Mr William Fisher, Boot and Shoemaker, 26 Thomas Street, would take
this boy, but he asks for £12. If he can be induced to accept £10 would the Committee
grant that sum. I may remark that the low fee of £8 is the cause of our great difficulties in satisfactorily apprenticing the boys.'

In 1887, the Committee provided a pupil, James Callow,[3] about to depart for
London to join his widowed mother and learn the trade of carpentry there, with a set
of tools. Upon leaving the Institution, the deaf were not only able to earn a livelihood
but were generally well spoken of in their neighbourhoods. Sometimes they continued to improve themselves after leaving school. The Rev. H.H. Dickenson, addressing the annual meeting, said that he had met one young man who learnt French and
Latin after leaving Claremont, in addition to English acquired at school.[4]

Sadly, some parents had been unwilling to take back their deaf children, once they
completed their term of education, effectively abandoning them. In May 1865, Mr

Chidley wrote, 'I succeeded in discovering the parents of Francis Clarke, whose father is a railway porter and residing at Phibsborough near Broadstone. When the parents called here (at Claremont) and saw the scrofulous condition of their child, they were unwilling to be burdened with him, and I do not believe they will do so unless legally compelled. The boy has been on the books of the Institution for nine years, more than half of which have been at Greystones.' One month later, he wrote, 'The matter is an urgent one. If his parents are not at once compelled to take him, they are very likely to leave Dublin and the boy remains a burden for life on the Institution. Should I do right in having the boy left at his parents' house in Phibsborough?'

There were few instances of some deaf apprentices changing trades, masters or mistresses. Among reasons for change were that the master had to reduce or close down his business and let go his apprentices, the apprentice had been so ill-treated by his master that he had to leave, or that the trade chosen for the apprentice was either unsuitable or too difficult. On 13 June 1884, a letter from the Rev. O'Brien, Adare, Co. Limerick, said that a young carpenter named Henry Baker, in his parish, was willing to take Christopher Switzer as apprentice. The Committee agreed on the apprentice fee of £8 to Baker in two instalments. More than one year later, another letter from the Rev. O'Brien was received regarding apprenticing Christopher Switzer to George Logan, shoemaker, of Blarney Street, Cork, that the instalment of four pounds, together with two pounds refunded by Mr Baker, his former master, be paid as fee to George Logan.

Charles Adams

He was one of the compositors employed by James Charles, printers at 61 Middle Abbey Street, Dublin, which had been commissioned by several religious societies under the Church of Ireland for pamphlets, annual reports, periodicals. The organ of the Established Church and then the Church of Ireland – *Irish Ecclesiastical Gazette* and later *Church of Ireland Gazette*, was printed at that establishment. In an issue of that periodical, the Editor expressed high praise for the 'deaf and dumb compositor', commenting that Adams had been visiting the deaf at their homes. In some periodicals for the deaf, his

Print-er.

warm welcome and zeal in his voluntary work for the deaf were commented on.

From Rathcormack, Co. Limerick, his father working as land steward, Charles Adams was admitted to the Institution on 2 August 1840, at the age of ten years, and left the Institution in December 1849. Extremely well educated and of remarkably good conduct, he was apprenticed to Mr James Charles, an 'eminent printer.' In November 1851, he asked the Committee for assistance towards his maintenance, and was granted 2/6 per week. At the annual meeting in 1857, the Committee 'were happy to record that Charles Adams, having finished his apprenticeship to Mr Charles, received from that gentleman, on completion of his apprenticeship, a most excellent testimony to the diligence, truthfulness and obedient attention to orders exhibited by the lad during his servitude, and that he acquired such a mastery over his trade as would enable him to secure constant remunerative employment'.[5] To show their esteem for Charles Adams' excellent references from his employer, the Committee presented him with a gift of a Polygrot Bible with a clasp.

Henry Molyneux Twamley's mother as Ladies' Debtor Keeper[6]

His mother, Elizabeth, left a widow by her first husband, Mr Barker, became account-able for the debts of her family and was sent to Carlow prison, while her home was sold to pay off the creditors. Through her influential friends, she was given a job as Ladies' Debtor Keeper in Carlow Jail, for nearly 40 years. She married again, to Thomas Twamley. Her fourth child, Henry, was found to be deaf, and was admitted to Claremont in October 1837, at age of nine, on condition that her mother was to pay £10 a year and to clothe her son. In 1896, Mr W.J. McCormick, Cork missionary to the Deaf, reported, 'Carlow has one mute, with a very grand name – Henry Molyneux Twamley; he is a gardener, and has a profound veneration for the Dean of Leighlin (Very Rev. John Finlay), who was chaplain to the Workhouse.' In the following year, he reported that the Dean organised a public meeting in the Y.M.C.A. hall in Carlow, which was well filled, and Henry Twamley was present, 'beaming upon everybody.'[7]

The Deaf Blacksmith and Bee-keeper

In Fiddown, a few miles from Piltown, Co. Kilkenny, Henry Ruck was 'The Village Blacksmith'. In 1897, Mr McCormick, visiting him, wrote, 'the sparks were flying thick and fast from his anvil when I arrived, and Henry is very industrious and a mighty man.' Two years later. the missionary returned to the parish for a public meeting and said, 'Mr Henry Ruck finds time to work his hobby – Bees. They have odd ways sometimes, but the honey is ample compensation.'

Mr W.S. Love – Cabinet-making Business in Cork

In 1897, a former pupil, James Blennerhasset, was apprenticed to Messrs Love & Co., cabinet-makers in Cork. His master, Mr W.S. Love, was deaf, having lost his hearing at the age of 28, through cold caught while on a voyage on the Arctic Ocean in 1872. He commenced his business of cabinet-making, after he became deaf. He personally superintended the business, which gave employment to 50 male and female workers. Skilled work of all description was sent out daily to leading establishments in Cork and South of Ireland. Mr Love was a firm but kind master, a good friend, and a practical sympathizer with the work done amongst the deaf.

Court Cases involving former Claremont Pupils
A deaf boy, named John Fleming, on his way through Fishamble Street, Dublin, was attacked by three young villains, who took from his pocket a seal and a tin canister. Fleming grappled with them, and succeeded not only in regaining possession of the goods, but also in detaining two of the robbers. The third ran away. Some watchmen (police) came to his assistance and secured the two delinquents. The other was pursued and also taken. They were brought to the Head Police-Office, where the boy, partly by writing and partly by signs, gave information of the robbery. The question, 'What were you robbed of?' was written on a slip of paper. He wrote, 'The lads wanted my money, and they beat me. I told them that I am poor, they struck my neck and stole from my pocket some things.' 'Did they take the seal out of your pocket?' 'Yes'. Then the prisoners were committed to Newgate for trial.[8]

Inquest – A Deaf and Dumb Juror![9]
A farmer sent his son, aged about twelve years, to a forge of a blacksmith on business. About half an hour after arrival there, he collapsed, went into a fit and died. He was in good health at that time. The next day, an inquest was held on the body before James Dillon, coroner, who arrived at that part of Lusmagh, King's County, which was thinly populated. The police had tried to get a quorum to constitute a jury, the minimum which, by law, was seven. The coroner, after a delay, noticed amongst the assembly an intelligent-looking young man, who happened to be deaf and a former pupil of Claremont. He beckoned to the young man and wrote, 'Can you either read or write?' The young man replied, 'Yes, both'. 'What is your name?' – 'John Pearson.' 'Then I am about to swear you , as a juror, on this inquest, to assist me in investigating the cause of death'. Then the coroner wrote for him the form of obligation, and Pearson took off his hat, raised the Gospels in his right hand, surveyed the obligation attentively, kissed the book, and quietly left to view the body. On his return, he took up his position in the rear of the coroner, watching the progress of the proceedings. When the verdict was about to be recorded, he took up the finding, as noted by the coroner from evidence, compared it with the minutes, and, when satisfied, he signed his name at the foot thereof. Upon inquiry, Pearson's parents originally held some responsible situation under the O'Moores of Cloghan Castle, where they acquired means to enable them to send him to Claremont, where he was educated and bound an apprentice to a cabinet-maker in Dublin, and he is now a tradesman of respectable means'.[10]

Deaf Man's Citizen Arrest of Potato-Stealer and Interpreter at Court
A former pupil, Kirwan, apprenticed in Abbeyleix, Queen's County (Laois), arose at four o'clock in the morning, to find a man robbing a potato-pit nearby. He instantly made him as his prisoner, and was bound over by the magistrates to prosecute at the Sessions in Maryborough (Portlaoise). The Rev. Francis King was requested to inter-

pret for him. The oath was put to him and he was questioned by the Grand Jury, all of whom were much impressed with his intelligent appearance and manner. Those not acquainted with the Claremont Institution seemed greatly amazed at the mode of correspondence (by signs); the result was, the robber was transported for seven years. Kirwan's evidence had helped to get rid of a very bad character from Abbeyleix and its vicinity.[11]

Murder Trial in 1851 involving a Deaf person held in Downpatrick, Co. Down

Ad-vo-cate.

'In Kilmore, Co. Down, a man named Francis Dunlop, got into a dispute with his deaf brother, Thomas Dunlop, who seized a large knife and stabbed his brother in the abdomen. Once arrested, he was immediately transmitted to Downpatrick Gaol.'[12] The prisoner, when asked was he guilty or not, did not appear he understood the proceedings, and a jury was compelled to try whether he was mute of malice, or by the visitation of God. The counsel said that as he could not expect to reduce the charge below manslaughter, it would shorten the case if the prisoner would plead 'guilty', and leave the matter in the judge's hands. A man, named James Mateer, who knew a way of communicating with the prisoner by signs, was sworn in as interpreter. The prisoner signed that his brother had beat him first and that his brother brought down the knife, but he could not be got to say that he stabbed his brother. The counsel addressed the Jury, on behalf of the prisoner, arguing from the evidence that from the injuries inflicted by the deceased on the prisoner, he might have been led to commit the act to prevent a repetition of the assaults, thereby rendering the deed justifiable homicide. The judge recapitulated the evidence at much length, and the jury, without leaving the box, returned a verdict of Guilty.[13]

Deaf Youth absconding from Downpatrick Workhouse

James Blow,[14] a deaf and dumb boy, was indicted for stealing a suit of clothes, the property of the Governors of Downpatrick Union. The trial was singular, as the prisoner had to be made aware, by writing on a slate, of the whole proceedings. The prisoner, in reply to the question, 'Are you guilty or not?' He wrote; 'I am; must go away to workhouse; will give them up well next Saturday'. On being removed, the prisoner made a laughable bow to the Court.[15]

Educated Deaf and Dumb Witness at Mullingar Workhouse

In 1858, Mr Julian, Crown solicitor, in a report to Lord Naas, Chief Secretary to Ireland, described Mullingar Workhouse as a 'nursery of crime'. His report arose out of a case before the local assizes when six of the inmates were charged with attempting to set fire to the Workhouse buildings. They varied in age from 16 to 20 years but all of them, including other inmates who were witnesses in the case, had spent from seven to twelve years in the Workhouse. None of the inmates in the workhouse knew how to write and read, except a deaf and dumb boy who was a witness. Another charge against the six inmates was that they had crossed the wall at night, stolen and killed a ram, brought it back to the Workhouse and boiled it openly in the day-room; it was shared with the other paupers. When the crime was discovered, none of the inmates, except the deaf and dumb boy, was prepared to give evidence against the culprits. After the witnesses had been lodged for eight days in the local gaol, they were induced to make statements incriminating the six youths. The boys were found guilty of the charges and sent to gaol.[16]

Will of Deaf Millionaire Contested

This was an exceedingly sad case, though it ended fairly well in a justified way. Frederick Edward Blunden, born deaf in 1860 and using the 'Dumb alphabet' for communication, was walking along the pier in Dun Laoghaire. Since he had an odd appearance with red hair and quaint dress, he was teased by a group of children, and he threw a girl into the sea, resulting with his committal to the Stewart's Institution for Lunatics, Palmerstown, Co. Dublin in 1888. It was not until 1924 when he was released, and taken into care by Abraham Blunden, his first cousin once removed, at his home in Cork. He died on 3 June 1937, aged 77, having made a will on 27 August 1935, leaving the assets worth £7,500, which was a large fortune in those days, to Abraham Blunden, his executor. This will was contested by two distant cousins – both ladies, one of them being a rector's wife, stating that Frederick was unstable and therefore the will should be declared invalid.

This case took around five days, and was reported by the national newspapers. Several witnesses were called, including the Rev. Harbord, rector of Macroom, Co. Cork, who had been in contact with deaf children and adults, to give evidence of Frederick's sanity, that he was intelligent, with capacity of writing, holding political views and spelling the words using the manual alphabet. To contest the will, Dr Keene, Chief Medical Officer of the Stewart's Institution, said that Frederick was found to be insane, but when cross-examined, he admitted that he was at Stewart's Institution for 18 months with insufficient opportunity to assess the mental capacity of Frederick Blunden properly.

'Mr Justice Hanna, in summing up, said that, before there were any means of educating deaf-mutes, the law was that they were deemed to be insane, and incapable of making a will, but they had moved a long way from that now, and the usual question in such cases was whether the court was satisfied that, at the time a deaf mute made his will, he was *capable of understanding* what he was doing. Dealing with evidence, Mr Hanna said that Abraham Blunden and his mother, under whose care Frederick Blunden had been from 1924 when he left the Stewart's Institution, seemed to be honourable and kind people. They gave him a home and they jury would have to consider whether they would be the natural objects of Frederick's bounty.'

'A man was not bereft of all his faculties if he could teach the Deaf and Dumb Alphabet to another, as had been done by Frederick. Letters and notes which had been written by Frederick were 'dumb witness of this man's capacity'. It was for the jury to say if they could accept the evidence of Dr Keene, who had described Frederick as having had 'mentality of a child'. Professor Stokeley, a man of great judgement, said there was nothing about Frederick suggesting mental weakness, that Frederick had capacity to express strong political views, and that the idea of anyone changing them was ridiculous. District Justice Connor, who knew Frederick, had never seen anything abnormal about him. The evidence of several witnesses rejected the suggestion that Frederick was 'an object of terror to children.'[17] It was mentioned that Frederick took keen interest in the Royal Family, having had asked his relatives to listen to and sign the radio broadcasts on the illness of King George V, and enjoyed reading 'Dublin Opinion', a satirical magazine covering the social and political topics in Ireland, as well taking interest in mechanical workings of aviation. In conclusion, the jury found that the will was valid, with the assets to go to Abraham Blunden, and the contestants to pay costs of the case.

Research on the genealogical details of Frederick Blunden revealed that one of his descendants was Sir John Blunden, Member of Parliament for Co. Kilkenny, born around 1717. The estates – Blunden Castle, Co. Kilkenny – were granted by patent in 1667 during the reign of Charles II. His father, William Pitt Blunden, J.P. and High Sheriff, of Castle Blunden, Bonnettstown, Co. Kilkenny, was appointed President of the Association to the Adult Deaf and Dumb, with his mother as one of the Patronesses.[18]

Respectability attained by Former Pupils

At the annual meeting in 1848, the audience was informed, 'that the Committee have derived much pleasure, not only from very satisfactory reports of the former pupils' masters and mistresses during their apprenticeships, but from the statements communicated to them of the respectability to which many of the former pupils have afterwards attained. One of the former pupils, Samuel Sadlier, who was some years since apprenticed to a tailor, is now following his trade in Dublin on his own account with very considerable success.'

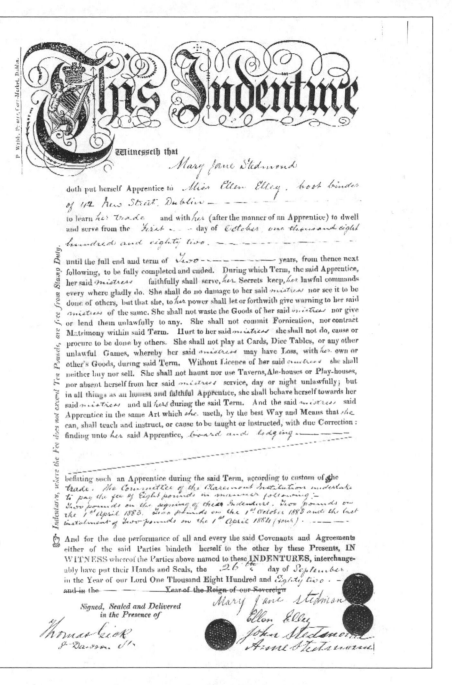

Indenture Form dated 26 September 1882
to apprentice a pupil, Mary Jane Steadman, to Miss Ellen Elley, boot-binder

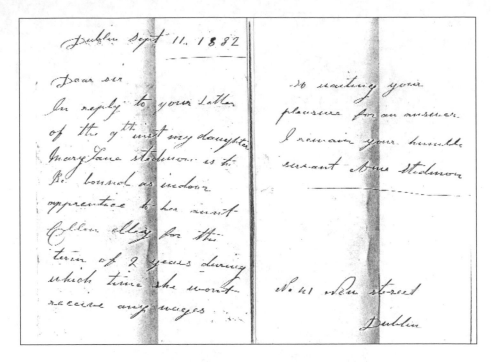

*Letter from Mary Steadman's mother giving her consent for her daughter
to be apprenticed to Miss Ellen Elley, Mary's aunt*

During the nineteenth century, the usual practice of apprenticing was to have an indenture form filled in and signed by the pupil about to be apprenticed, by the Secretary of the Institution, and by the master or mistress to whom the pupil was to be apprenticed, together with the details of the terms such as the fees. Displayed herein is the application form. The pupil in this case is Mary Jane Steadman, whose parents resided in New Street, Dublin. The father's occupation was shoemaker, and his character as 'industrious'. Before her admission to the Institution, the girl had lost her hearing totally owing to scarlatina. When she completed her education, it was time for her to be apprenticed out. Her aunt, Miss Ellen Ellery, boot-binder, offered to take her on for the term of two years. However, as it was usual practice for all prospective masters/mistresses, her character had to be assessed by the clergy of her parish, in order to assure the Committee that she would be in a position to treat her apprentice well. The letter received from the Rev. D. Holden, rector of St. Luke's, confirmed that 'Miss Ellen Elley, of 41 New Street, is a parishioner of this Parish; I have a good (...) of her and her parents. I consider her a suitable person to have charge of an apprentice.' The Committee undertook to pay the fee of eight pounds: two pounds on the signing of the indenture, two pounds on 1 April 1883, two pounds on 1 October 1883 and the last instalment of two pounds on 1 April 1884.

St Luke's Vestry
9th August 1882

Miss Ellen Elley, of 41
New Street, is a parishioner
of this Parish. I have a good
of her & her parents. I
consider her a suitable
person to have charge of
an apprentice—
D Holden
Minister in charge
of St Luke's

In September 1865, Mr Chidley wrote: 'A sewing machine would be a great acquisition for the Institution. Without such assistance, great difficulty is experienced in making up the clothing of so many children and instruction in the use of such a machine will be advantageous to the girls. From enquiries made by Mrs Chidley at the *(Dublin Industrial)* Exhibition, the cost would not exceed £10'.

In May 1887, giving evidence in London to the Royal Commissioners for the Blind, Deaf and Dumb and Imbeciles, the Rev. Hercules Dickenson, representing Claremont, stated that the pupils, upon leaving Claremont, had very little difficulty in obtaining their livelihoods, the girls going into domestic service, and the boys mostly as tailors and shoemakers, and sometimes as compositors, lithographers and printers. He added that industrial training had to be discontinued owing to its interference with academic education, but that the girls were taught needle-work and the boys taught farming and gardening in the farm at Claremont. At that interview, the Rev. Dickenson said that in 1881, there were 3,993 deaf in Ireland, and out of the number, the 3,037 deaf were uneducated. He informed the Commissioners that in the year of 1886, only 481 deaf children were maintained out of the poor rates, and that it had been extremely difficult to persuade the Board of Guardians to contribute towards the education of the deaf. When asked whether many deaf inter-marry in Ireland, the Rev. Dickenson stated that they did not do so, and, even though he had performed a few times the marriage ceremony between the deaf, he believed that deafness was not in general inherited. He informed the Commissioners that he thought that extreme poverty in some parts of Ireland was the cause of deafness, owing to squalid, crowded houses and the resultant transmission of scrofula.[19]

Role of the Missioners in Employment for the Deaf

Mr Francis Maginn, Missioner for the Adult Deaf in Belfast, reported that 'he had been most fortunate, in early 1899, in procuring employment for the deaf who came to him for help. A deaf couple named Russell, with six children, walked all the way from Dublin. They were in rags and penniless. He succeeded in getting work for the father, who is a stonemason, at the new City Hall. He is now able to earn 38 shillings a week. Subsequently he got work on the recommendation of his late foreman at Messrs. Courtney's, whose foreman tells him he is a good tradesman. He also succeeded in getting a job for Russell's son at the harbour, and afterwards at Harland & Wolff's, where he earns 18s. 6d. a week. Work has been provided for Russell's daughter at the Franklin Steam Laundry. Maginn also got them a house and furniture.'

'Owing to the book-binding trade going into the hands of women, James Savage found it difficult to work in Belfast. He crossed over to England, but failed to get work in Liverpool, Manchester, Wigan and other towns. Mr Muir, Missioner of Blackburn, got him started as a weaver in a large cotton mill. As Savage had to protect his eyesight, he decided against taking up weaving, and returned to Belfast. However, Maginn secured for him a good situation as an engine painter at Workman & Clark's. The foreman was so pleased with Savage that he had given him charge of the store room.'[20]

Deaf and Dumb Traders.

CABINETMAKER would be glad to get jobs, can put up shelves, library, shop-counters, and work neatly. References to Rev. J. Striven, curate of St. Matthias' Church, or Maurice F. G. Hewson, Missionary, Christian Union Buildings, Lower Abbey-street.

GARDENER.—A good worker, understands gardening would be found satisfactory. Apply to M. F. G. Hewson, C. U. B., Lower Abbey-street.

TAILOR can turn and clean gentleman's clothes, at a moderate charge. Apply to M. F. Hewson, Lower Abbey-street.

BOOTMAKER.—Good worker would be glad of jobs for the winter. Apply to M. F. G. Hewson, Lower Abbey-street.

CHARWOMAN.—A active woman would be found a good worker strictly honest. Highest references. Apply to Maurice F. G. Hewson, Lower Abbey-street, Dublin.

A RESPECTABLE WOMAN would be glad to get some light needlework can be well recommended. Apply to Maurice F. G. Hewson, Lower Abbey-street.

The above advertisement from *The Irish Deaf-Mute and Juvenile Advocate* in 1886 reveals that the 'Rev.' Maurice Hewson took on the role of seeking employment for the deaf resident in Dublin, and displays the variety of trades undertaken at that time – carpentry, gardening, tailoring, boot-making, cleaning and needlework.

18

'Six shillings and six pence'

'… (hearing children) feeling compassion for their (deaf) fellows of an equal age,
though of severe poverty, to whom Providence had not been so bountiful …'
- Dr Charles Orpen, 1836

Donations

On the list of donations for the year of 1818 was a sum of six shillings and six pence, for which a little girl sold her doll and gave personally to Dr Orpen for the 'poor deaf children'. At a parish school in Dublin, the children had a collection for the deaf of the poor, to which the above quotation refers. In the late 1870s, at annual meetings of the Institution, young children were invited to observe the examinations of the deaf pupils and to address questions to these children, most of whom had outfoxed the hearing children with their informed answers.

Doll.

Those who donated ten guineas or more became 'Life Members', and among them were the Earl of Whitworth, the Earl of Annesley, the Earl of Cork, the Bishop of Kildare, the Archbishop of Cashel, Arthur Guinness, Benjamin Guinness, and Dr. Orpen's brother, Richard J.T. Orpen, who was later knighted for his services to law.

In May 1823, Lord Powerscourt sent a donation of £20. Upon receiving Dr Orpen's thanks, he sent £100 more, and it was found that the funds were insufficient for the admission of more than six out of the seventy applicants. The names of the seventy were sent to Lord Powerscourt, that he might make a selection of the six. He wrote to Dr Orpen, saying that he found that a greater number of poor deaf children were applying for admission to the benefits of education than the funds of the institution were adequate to afford. He added, 'As God has been pleased to give me the means of helping you, I request £1,000 to be given to you.' His letter read as follows:

6 Grafton Street, 22 May 1823

'My dear Mr Orpen,

As I find that there are 37 deaf and dumb boys in indigence, who seem to have no possible prospect of being brought to the Gospel of Christ, I considered it my bounden duty, as the Lord has given me the wherewithal to provide for the maintenance of their bodies, and I trust also for the conversion of their souls, which are of eternal value to which are made the great object in the Institution of which you are the Head. By giving the enclosed note as there is no use in getting a stamp, I have no doubt my friends at LaTouche's Bank will pay you a thousand pounds, believe me.

Very faithfully and sincerely yours, Powerscourt'

In January 1833 a letter was received from Lady Bandon, Cork, which read:

'Lady Bandon begs to say that she will undertake the nine pounds for Mary Burchill's admission and education at the Deaf and Dumb Institution. She will communicate with Mr Knox on her return to Castle Bernard. She wishes to take the liberty of asking Dr Orpen's advice respecting a young man named George Stanley Scott who was educated at the Deaf and Dumb Institution and who is a native of and a resident in Bandon. He has a very decided talent for drawing and is anxious to receive instruction. The Dublin Society was mentioned as offering a channel of instruction but the difficulty of funding a place for this afflicted person to board and lodge is one that Lady Bandon knows not how to make arrangements.'

Legacies

On 31 August 1821, the Committee was informed that Archdeacon Digby had lodged £300 of Sir Gilbert King's legacy to the credit of the Institution, and it was resolved that the Archdeacon be entitled to six votes at every half-yearly election of pupils. On 19 September 1822, Archdeacon Digby had applied for the admission of a deaf boy, James Lyons, who will be clothed by Archdeacon Digby. It was resolved that in gratitude to him for his liberal donation of £360 out of Sir Gilbert King's legacy, the boy be admitted on the first day of the next month. In January 1825, a bequest of £2,000 for the Claremont Institution was received from the executors of the late Dr Barrett, Fellow of Trinity College Dublin, and the Dean of St Patrick's, the Rev. Wingfield, rector of Powerscourt, Co. Wicklow and Mr James Digges La Touche were appointed as trustees. On another occasion, £200 had been allocated from Bishop Sterne's Charities for the benefit of the Institution at Claremont.

Letter from Mr Harris of Stroud dated 9 August 1858:

'Sir, I beg to inform you that the late Miss Margaret Dunne of 4 Spa Buildings, Cheltenham, has by her will left a legacy of £200 to the Deaf and Dumb Institution

at Claremont near Dublin payable at the death of an old and faithful servant to whom she has left an annuity for life out of the principal of which this and other charitable legacies are to be paid, free of legacy duty when the annuity ceases.
                                        Henry Harris'

Letter from Harris of Cairness near Stroud dated 19 August 1858
        'In reply to your letter, the name of the late Miss Dunne's servant (to whom an annuity for life is left) is Mary Calaghan. I do not have her exact age but I should say she was over 60. She resides in Cheltenham having removed to a lodging there after Miss Dunne's death but I have not yet heard where it is, and I have not been over very lately to enable me to make the inquiry which I shall do when I am next there.   Henry Harris'

Benevolence of the Quakers towards the Deaf
Due to Mr Humphreys' connections with the Religious Society of Friends, several adherents, some of them from his wife's family, the Chandlees, and Mary Leadbeater, had contributed over several years towards the funds of the Institution. Miss Mary Lecky of Kilnock, Carlow, donated £50 towards the Building Fund. In November 1824, Mr Humphreys had arranged for his friends to raise sufficient funds to purchase bedsteads for the girls' dormitory which had been by his exertions procured without any expense to the Institution.

Among the Quakers was Jane Sarah Russell, of 25 Eustace Street, who offered private tuition for deaf and dumb children. An advertisement in the *Dublin Evening Mail* in November 1829 read: 'A respectable Female, residing at one of the healthful outlets of this City, who has learned the system of Instruction from the Principal Master of the Institution at Claremont, and has also had several years experience, having one Female pupil at present, would receive two more into her Family. Terms: 50 guineas per annum, paid quarterly in advance'.

Cork Day School for the Deaf
In Cork, among the Quakers was John Humphreys, brother of Mr Joseph Humphreys, headmaster of Claremont. One of the best known Quaker educators in Cork, John Humphreys had a boarding and day school at North Main Street. As librarian of the Royal Cork Institution, he gave scientific lectures and operated 'Pestalozzi's System of Mental Arithmetic'. In 1822, Dr Kehoe, a Roman Catholic, established the Day School for the deaf at 53 Georges Street in Cork. Out of its ecumenically based Committee of 15 members, William Lecky, Reuben Harvey and Joseph Harris were the Quaker members.[1] By 1828, the Cork School had admitted 28 children, some of whom had been apprenticed, one to a printer.[2] In a report of September 1825 to the Committee of the Claremont Institution, Mr Joseph Humphreys, on his deputation tour to Clonmel, Waterford and Cork, referred to the Deaf School in Cork, saying that 'it was very imperfect and the children have little more than a parrot-like knowledge of language,

and that they appear thoroughly grounded in the dogma of the Romish Church'.[3]   In 1846, this school was located in Douglas Street, with William Carroll as teacher, and then in 1856, was re-located in Mary Street, with Jane O'Sullivan as teacher.[4] Once the Catholic Institution for the Deaf and Dumb was established in Dublin in 1846, the Cork School finally closed its doors.[5]

Alfred Payne, in England, quotes the example of the 'Cork Asylum' as one which all 'exile' (boarding and segregated) institutions should follow. The Committee of the Cork school, wanting to improve the mental condition of the pupils, arranged for them to attend lectures and classes in other schools, along with the 'five-sensed' pupils. This is equivalent to the mainstreaming environment in operation today. It had been noted that 'very few deaf-mutes who had been educated in 'semi-monastic' institutions had risen to distinction, whilst a formidable number of deaf persons owed their success to the blessings of the social system.'[6]

Auxiliary Societies

In schools for the upper classes of both sexes, auxiliary societies were established to practise the principle of benevolence in providing financial support for education and maintenance of the children of the poor. In the year 1819, auxiliary societies were formed in various parts of Ireland to aid the Institution at Claremont. The duty of these societies was to collect subscriptions and support the pupils sent from their districts. The Cork Society, after being established for one year, remitted £179 to Claremont. They sent up one pupil for whose maintenance and education they engaged to pay 20 guineas annually. The Committee agreed with Cork that for every sum of 200 guineas remitted by them, they shall have a permanent right to keep one indigent pupil, elected by themselves, in the Institution. Among the Cork pupils was Anne McCormick, South Main Street, admitted on 16 April 1820, aged 12, with sufficient education in writing and needlework, being 'remarkably intelligent'. On 22 March 1824 she was appointed assistant mistress, and therefore she became the first Deaf teacher in Ireland.

In 1824 a Juvenile Association was formed where the young hearing people were encouraged to collect funds for educating and supporting deaf children which they elected every six months for admission to Claremont. In the Annual Reports published by the Juvenile Association is the list of Pupils, a useful source of information on pupils. In 1831, a request by the Committee of the Juvenile Association was sent to the Ordnance Office for loan of two tents to accommodate 100 'youthful members who annually meet on Easter Monday to breakfast at Claremont and elect indigent pupils. Owing to illness of the Headmaster preventing the members from occupying the School-room, the alternative was to assemble on the Lawn if tents could be procured.' This request was turned down as it was not the practice of the Ordnance Office to lend tents. A Ladies' Juvenile Auxiliary was also formed in 1829. In 1845 the sum of £2,066 was raised, and at least 90 pupils at Claremont were supported by these Juveniles at one time.

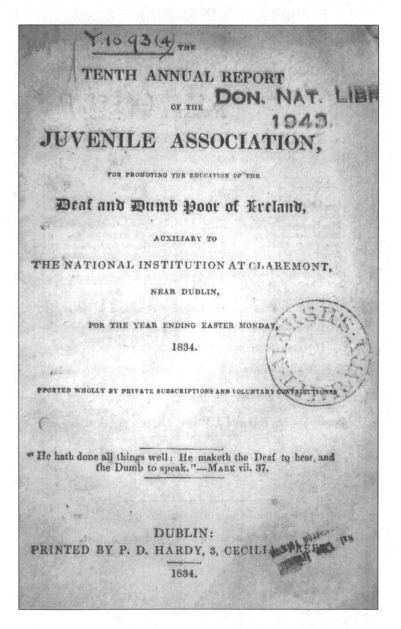

THE

TENTH ANNUAL REPORT

OF THE

JUVENILE ASSOCIATION,

FOR PROMOTING THE EDUCATION OF THE

Deaf and Dumb Poor of Ireland,

AUXILIARY TO

THE NATIONAL INSTITUTION AT CLAREMONT,

NEAR DUBLIN,

FOR THE YEAR ENDING EASTER MONDAY,

1834.

SUPPORTED WHOLLY BY PRIVATE SUBSCRIPTIONS AND VOLUNTARY CONTRIBUTIONS.

" He hath done all things well: He maketh the Deaf to hear, and
the Dumb to speak."—MARK vii. 37.

DUBLIN:

PRINTED BY P. D. HARDY, 3, CECILIA STREET.

1834.

PUPILS PLACED IN THE INSTITUTION

BY THE

JUVENILE ASSOCIATION, SINCE ITS FORMATION

IN 1824.

Thus marked (*) died in the Institution.
Thus marked (†) were removed to the Belfast Institution.

Present Number.	Pupils' Names.	Age when elected.	When elected.	Where from.	Number removed.
	John Donovan	8	July, 1824	Newry	1
	James Cassidy	11	July, 1825	Bray	2
	James Harper	10	July, 1826	Letterkenny	3
	Thomas Dixon	8	May, 1827	Dublin	4
	*Henry Payne	8	do	Stranorlar	5
	James Madders	10	April, 1828	Leitrim	6
	Eliza Murphy	12	do	Athy	7
	Martha Clinton	8	April, 1829	Maryborough	8
	Thomas Scott	10	do	Kingstown	9
	Sarah Mary Mann	12	do	Markethill	10
	*Bridget Condron	12	do	Rathangan	11
	William Mitchell	12	do	Larne	12
	Robert Tuite	12	do	Tullamore	13
	Margaret Moore	9	do	Mountmellick	14
	John M'Carthy	11	April, 1830	Castlepollard	15
	*Matilda Harris	11	do	Cootehill	16
	Catherine Carey	16	do	Navan	17
	Mary Kavanagh	16	do	Ferns	18
	John Howard	10	do	Lismore	19
	Joseph Darby	8	do	Rathowen	20
	David Wright	10	do	Newry	21
	Joseph Browne	11	do	Tullamore	22
	David Arthur	11	do	Kells	23
	Johanna Morony	8	do	Clonmel	24
	William H. Martin	8	do	Banbridge	25
	James Beatty	10	do	Cootehill	26
	James Deviney	8	do	Lisburn	27
	Loughlin Gillerin	11	do	Roscommon	28
	William Allen	11	do	Markethill	29
	Patrick Magee	11	do	Castlewellan	30
	Joseph Farrell	10	do	Longford	31
	Francis Merritt	10	do	Cloughjordan	32
	Eliza Cuddahy	11	do	Castlecomer	33
	Andrew Tallon	11	do	Dalkey	34
	Catherine Gallagher	11	do	Ruskey	35
	Henry Fea	9	do	Armagh	36
	Margaret Gilleran	8	do	Roscommon	37
	Mary A. Broughall	10	do	Athlone	38
	Catherine Quail	9	do	Glasslough	39
	Johanna Walshe	10	do	Killarney	40
	Ellen Maguire	9	do	Navan	41
	Mary Allen	8	do	Markethill	42
	Mary A. Rogers	10	do	Do.	43
	Isaiah Rogers	10	do	Cootehill	44
	Daniel Quigley	10	do	Clonegal	45
	James Craig	11	do	Ballymena	46
	James Murrane	9	do	Tuam	47
	Michael Mulloy	14	April, 1831	Westport	48

Among the former members of the Juvenile Association was the Rev. Hercules H. Dickenson, chairman of the Claremont Institution in the late 1880s. In 1887, he said that he had been 42 years, 'ever since he was a little boy, connected with Claremont, first on the committee of the Juvenile Association, and when that was amalgamated with the Parent Society in 1851, as one of the Honorary Secretaries of the Institution.' He recalled that in 1844, when Claremont was in serious danger of financial difficulties, the Juvenile members met in each other's house and sent out thousands of appeals to every part of the country, and got several thousand pounds as a result. He went on to say that Claremont was still supported by the young people, and looking over their collection cards, he observed that a great deal of originality and imagination was used. Not only did the children record subscriptions from 'Papa', 'Mama', 'Uncle John', 'Aunt Jane', but from 'Snooks' (a nickname for a favourite toy). The Rev. Dickenson remarked that 'Snooks' had contributed a great deal to Claremont, having turned up all over Ireland.[7]

In 1854, the Committee heard 'with great pleasure' that the turnpikes on the northern side of the city had been abolished, as the tolls on the road leading to Claremont in Glasnevin had seriously affected the finance, by preventing the attendance of visitors to the School and by entailing a large annual expense on the managers and friends of the Institution.[8]

Preach-er.

Charity Sermons

In June 1819, the first sermon on behalf of the deaf and dumb was preached in St Peter's Church by the Rev. Robert Daly, and the collection was £253. In June 1821, the Charity Sermon was preached at the Chapel of the Molyneaux Asylum for the Blind by the Rev. B.W. Mathias, and the collections produced a total of £229, which was augmented by a private subscription for the admission of Cecilia White, the deaf orphan girl, whose sad case the Rev. Mathias announced on that occasion. In 1823, a Charity Sermon was held at St Thomas' Church, Marlborough Street, Dublin by the Rev. Edward Wingfield; the collection was £145. The deaf pupils were usually brought to the church on those occasions in order to invoke sympathy amongst the congregation, and the male pupils were allocated collection plates to pass around the church. The pupils were, depending on the location of the church, to walk from Claremont and back. In 1829, they were brought in furniture caravans, courtesy of some gentlemen proprietors.

The Century-long Campaign for State Aid

In August 1825, Dr Orpen wrote to the Right Hon. Henry Goulbourn, M.P., Chief Secretary for Ireland, for a grant of £5,000 to buy up the rent of Claremont, informing him that the Institution had never received any aid from Government since its establishment. Six months later, Goulbourn replied that 'private benevolence' would be the better option for obtaining financial assistance for the Institution. Dr Orpen said in his response that the following charitable institutions had received grants for purpose of maintaining and educating its inmates: the Foundling Hospital, the Hibernian Military School, the Marine School, the Charter Schools, the Education Society in Kildare Place, Dr Steeven's Hospital, Cork Street Fever Hospital and the House of Industry. Dr Orpen added that 'in the Report of the Education Enquiry Commissioners, it appears that the Deaf and Dumb Institution was refused any aid from this fund to erect a school room, and the reason is simply, thus – *Deaf and Dumb.*' He concluded his letter with the comment, 'I have several times seen the *uneducated* deaf and dumb, *sick and dying* in hospitals and without any means of explaining to the medical attendants their sufferings, or any medium of receiving consolation. Their arms were too weak to use their natural gestural language, their fingers ignorant of writing, and their tongue not loosed in speech.' On his return from London, Goulbourn informed the Committee that their application was not successful, but understanding the Institution to be in severe financial difficulties, he managed to obtain from the Lord Lieutenant a donation of £200 to pay the overdue rent.[9]

In 1835, the Committee noticed from the audited accounts of all the Deaf Institutions in Great Britain and America that large fees were sought for the maintenance and education of the pupils, for instance, the Liverpool Day School charged £50 a year. The Claremont Institution had to pay rent, tithes, parish cess, county cess, washing expenses of pupils while sick and at hospital, rent of office and Committee room in Sackville Street and fires, printing of election lists, expenses of annual meetings in town, salaries of assistant secretary and collector, interest on debts, and clothing for all pupils. It was noticed that in the Institutions outside Ireland, there was a larger number of teachers than at Claremont, and a higher average of salaries of teachers. The Juvenile Association was charged at £17 per annum for each pupil they elected for admission to Claremont.

In 1836, an appeal to the clergy of Ireland was inserted in the newspapers, *Evening Mail, Packet, Warder* and *Record*, seeking their assistance to raise funds for the Institution by making their pulpits available for the visiting preachers to deliver their charity sermons, to arrange the public meetings in their parishes for the deputation visits by the Clerical Secretary and the pupils, with the purpose of increasing publicity about the work of the Institution and about the need to source any uneducated deaf children in the localities to be visited by the deputations.

In 1839, Dr Orpen reported that the Foundling Hospital in Cork was to send two deaf children at twenty guineas per annum, and later on, a letter was received from the Secretary of the Hospital stating that the Poor Law Commissioners would not allow the deaf and dumb children to be sent up on its funds.

Engraving of Claremont by Lawrence Feagan, former pupil and drawing master (used for cover of Annual Reports)

Deputation Tours in Ireland and England

As mentioned elsewhere, Dr Orpen and Mr Joseph Humphreys had travelled across the country in Ireland and in England, taking with them a couple of the best pupils for demonstration purposes, with the dual object of raising funds for the Institution at Claremont and of increasing awareness of the deaf needing education. In October 1822, Mr Humphreys gave lectures on the Deaf and Dumb 'who could be taught to read and write and also partially to speak' in Liverpool. During the examination of two deputation pupils, one of the audience asked what games they played at Claremont, and one boy replied, 'Leaping frogs'. Another asked whether he preferred to be deaf or blind. The answer was, 'It is dangerous to be blind, but deaf is very quiet.' When asked, 'What is sound?', the reply was 'A noise' 'What is noise?' One of the boys illustrated it by a blow on the table, with his hand.[10]

During the middle and the late nineteenth century, the clergymen throughout the country had been contacted by the clergyman, appointed by the Institution as Clerical Deputation Secretary, to organise public meetings in their parishes. Some were favourable while others were not, due to the fierce competition amongst numerous religious societies, such as the Protestant Orphan Society, Society for Converting the

Jews to Christians, Hibernian Bible Society, etc. for contributions towards their funds. A clergyman in Limerick in 1877 wrote in reply, 'The people here are very apathetic about missions in general. You will not get more than average, but if you (the Deputation Secretary) do not come, you will get *nothing* at all.' Another letter from Carlow said, 'The D&D meeting will be in the Young Men's Hall. We shall be happy to see you and the boy (Claremont pupil) here at dinner, but regret we have no beds to offer.'[11]

Charles Joynt, from Belmullet, Co. Mayo, admitted in 1839, was mentioned as 'a very superior boy, and a deputation pupil in every county of Ireland'. In 1843 at the public meeting in the Rotunda, which was crowded to excess, all the pupils, 119 in number, were seated upon the platform. One of them was Charles Joynt, who was called forward to sign the Scripture verses. Then he was examined as to different signs to express their feelings without any reference to the 'finger alphabet', in which he illustrated the several trades to the great entertainment of the meeting.

In 1844, at a meeting in Ballinasloe, Co. Galway, the Rev. Green exhibited the efficiency of the system, as 'proved by the intelligence of the pupil. Young friends from several Parochial schools were highly gratified with the mute language.' It seems that meetings of that type drew crowds of young people out of curiosity to watch the deaf pupil using sign language. In Mohill, Co. Leitrim, at the meeting in the Methodist Meeting-house, a large number assembled, including several Roman Catholics. A former pupil of Claremont and resident in the area, Dobson, was present and gave satisfactory answers to questions put to him. The Committee was pleased to hear 'that he was most industrious and was of good conduct'.[12]

Nearly every year at the Annual Meeting of the Institution, there had been reference to the lack of action on the part of the Government, often quoted in the newspapers up to the 1960s. The Institution struggled on, depending on the goodwill of the Church of Ireland members, despite the dwindling numbers, and on prudent budgetary and investment strategies. Finally, in 1972, the Department of Education agreed to fund the salary of the one and only teacher at the Claremont School at Monkstown at £828 – more than 150 years after Dr Orpen appealed to the Chief Secretary for statutory assistance towards the education of the deaf.

Administration Office of the Claremont Institution
In the city of Dublin, the Committee rented the office at the Committee House at 15 and 16 Sackville Street (O'Connell Street), the building which provided office accommodation for several charities and religious societies. In 1866 the Institution moved to Dame Street, where they shared the building with the Young Men's Christian Association. Then in the late 1880s, they moved to 8 Dawson Street. In the late 1920s, they moved around the corner to 28 Molesworth Street, where they remained until the late 1960s.

ONE HUNDRED & SEVENTEENTH ANNUAL REPORT

FOR THE YEAR ENDED 31st DECEMBER,

1932.

Claremont Institution

FOR

THE EDUCATION OF THE

DEAF AND DUMB.

FOUNDED 1816.   INCORPORATED 1887.

[Supported by Voluntary Contributions].

WITH AN

ABSTRACT OF CASH ACCOUNT, LIST OF
SUBSCRIBERS AND DONORS, &c.

Office—28 MOLESWORTH STREET, DUBLIN.

Dublin :
The Church of Ireland Printing and Publishing Co., Ltd.,
61, Middle Abbey Street.

The Gick Dynasty at Claremont

At least three generations of the Gick family gave a total of 94 years to the service of the Claremont Institution by taking on the duties of the Secretary. In 1876, Dr. Thomas Gick, B.Mus., started working for the Institution. He had made the distinction of possessing musical talents in being the organist for St. Patrick's Cathedral, in Dublin. After his father passed away in 1908, his son, Mr. Charles Helmesey Gick, insurance clerk at the time of his father's death, took over the administration of the Institution. In the year of 1928, when Mr Taylor, headmaster, left the Institution on retirement for Canada, Mr. C.H. Gick took on an additional role as House Warden at Claremont. He maintained that role during the time when Miss Deacon was Headmistress. In 1932, Mr. Charles Gick passed away, and his son, Mr Thomas Gick, whose occupation was railway official and resident in Sandycove, near Dun Laoghaire, Co. Dublin, took over administration of the Institution until March 1971. The Secretary in the final years of the Claremont Institution was Mr E.N. Seymour, Monkstown, Co. Dublin.

The La Touche Dynasty at Claremont

Among the Huguenot refugees to Ireland in the seventeenth century was the LaTouche family. David Digges (was 'Digues') LaTouche was one of the most intensive Huguenot property developers, and he launched a successful banking enterprise, as well as acquiring an interest in weaving/cloth manufacturing industry in the Liberties, Dublin. His success in banking was due to his connections with Huguenot veteran war officers, who entrusted their wages and savings to him and with the Anglo-Irish nobility. In 1816, James Digges LaTouche was appointed as auditor for the Committee which established the National Institution for Educating the Deaf and Dumb Poor of Ireland, having had given a speech at the public meeting at the Rotunda. In 1825, he was one of the trustees for the bequest of £2,000 for Claremont received from the executors of Dr Barrett, Fellow of Trinity College Dublin. The Committee continued to use LaTouche's Bank as their bankers until it was taken over by the Munster Bank in 1870.

In 1876, William Digges LaTouche was one of the members of the Committee which established Dublin Working Boys' Home, a hostel for boys undertaking apprenticeship or starting employment in Dublin City. This Home had admitted some male pupils from Claremont.

Among the Huguenots with involvement in the Claremont Institution are the Singer brothers, including the Rev. Singer, and Mr LeFanu, whose wife, Emma, was the biographer of Dr Charles Orpen. Her book, published in 1860, the year of her death, received favourable comment in the *Dublin University Magazine*.

19

Faith Cometh by Seeing

Let Christian feelings then your souls inspire,
To touch his silent lips with living fire;
Teach him to know Religion's happy road,
And grateful bless his Saviour, and his God!
                                    - Richard J.T. Orpen

In 1820, the Committee resolved that the masters be required to devote at least four hours every Sunday to religious instruction, choosing such times of the day as would 'least interfere with the pupils' own public and private devotional duties.'[1] On 3 March, the Committee instructed Mr Humphreys to send the pupils on Sundays to their respective places of worship. On the Sabbath, the pupils were to rise at six o'clock in the morning, wash and prepare for worship in Church (Protestant) and Chapel (Roman Catholic) until half-past one in the afternoon.

On 24 August 1821, one of the Committee members tendered his resignation, as a protest against the suitability of Mr Humphreys and his wife, being Quakers, as Master and Matron of the Institution for providing religious instruction to the pupils on Sundays, considering that the Humphreys seemed to focus more of their time on management of the 'private' establishment for the 'rich' than on the education of the deaf of the poor. When the subject of dismissing Mr Humphreys was raised, Dr Charles Orpen threatened to tender his resignation as Secretary. On his motion, owing to inconvenience arising from the pupils being out at various places of worship on Sundays without any benefit as they could not hear, understand or join in the services, they were to be kept at Claremont in a Sunday School as was the case in the Edinburgh Institution.

At an annual meeting of the Juvenile Association for Education of the Deaf and Dumb, one of the clergymen advocated the need for the deaf to gain knowledge of Jesus Christ, as seen in the following speech:

'In Ireland, nearly 5,000 mutes are ignorant of God. That of this number, 500 is qualified by age for admission to Claremont, the instrument of bringing the bright lamp of God's eternal truth to their dark minds and eyes. It is your duty to make Him known to the poor deaf and dumb; I leave the cause of Ireland's deaf and dumb to God and to your own consciences, beseeching you to follow the example of the Saviour, who felt for such objects, and by his miraculous work – *maketh the deaf to hear and the dumb to speak.'*[2]

Seal of the Claremont Institution with the design similar to
'Ephphatha' by Thomas Davidson (1842-1910), British deaf artist

In 1825, the Inquiry Report by the Commissioners for Irish Education stated that out of 45 pupils at the Institution. 33 were Roman Catholics, 11 Established Church and 1 Presbyterian while the headmaster was a Quaker, and that the Authorised Version of the Scriptures was read at the Institution.

In November 1829, the Committee discussed the practicability of establishing at Claremont public worship for the deaf. It was resolved that the Rev. Denis Browne, a convert from Roman Catholicism, be requested to preach a sermon on a week day in Claremont School, as to ascertain how far it was practicable to repeat to the pupils, and that Mr Henry Overend, one of the assistant teachers, was to interpret as much of the sermon as he could on 'his fingers'.

Some letters penned by pupils and former pupils, and accounts by the deputation clergymen displayed a great sense of devotion and desire to love and worship God on their part. Requests for bibles had been received by the Committee from former pupils after they had returned home, some having been convinced of their need for salvation by putting faith in Jesus Christ. In 1859, the year when Ulster was touched by the Revival, a deaf and dumb man, aged thirty, who had been educated at

Claremont, was working in the bog, preparing fuel for the winter. He was alone when 'the Lord touched his heart'. He felt the pangs of sin and was anxious to have it removed. He went to his sister's house, where he lived. He was so paralysed that he had to lie down. After a sleepless night, he was not relieved until till the following morning, he jumped some height from the ground, clasping an imaginary person to his chest, his face beaming with joy, and his body language indicating gratitude and love. The Rev. Robert Park, pastor in Ballymoney, Co. Antrim, wrote:

> 'In my conversation with him afterwards by fingers, he made me to understand that the first text of Scripture that impressed his mind and awakened comfort was Luke 15:7, 'Joy shall be in heaven over one sinner that repenteth'.

On 2 August 1843, a letter was received from Lord Eliot, Chief Secretary,[3] regarding a clause introduced into the new Poor Law Amendment Bill, giving powers to Boards of Guardians to send Deaf and Dumb children on payment of cost of their maintenance to the National Institution for the Education of the Deaf and Dumb Poor of Ireland. He said that he understood that an objection on the part of Roman Catholics was likely to be raised to this clause on the grounds that no provision made in that Institution for education of Roman Catholic children in the doctrines of their own church; and that conversions to Protestantism would be the probable consequence. He asked the Committee to confirm that Roman Catholic deaf would receive the ben-

efits of an education in their own church. The reply was that the Institution at Claremont had been founded and maintained by voluntary contributions of private individuals on the understanding that the education given to the objects of their care should be based upon the Scriptures, and that over the past 27 years, very few Roman Catholics had refused to avail themselves of the advantages which the Institution provided.

Left: Woodcut engraved by a pupil of the Institution for the Deaf and Dumb at Milan, c.1820, given to Dr Orpen during his visit to that Institution

Religious Knowledge

There were several references in newspaper reports covering the annual meetings of the Claremont Institution to the intelligence on Scripture demonstrated by the pupils. The Rev. Thomas Tomlinson outlined some accounts of the deputation tours he undertook with one or two of the boys of that Institution. He travelled around the counties of Kerry and Limerick with a boy named Patrick Clarke, one of the most intelligent boys that he had ever known. In 1850 while travelling with Clarke through Cork and Waterford, a public examination was held at Portlaw, Co. Waterford, where the boy answered every question put to him. At the request of a lady, the Rev. Tomlinson allowed Patrick Clarke to put some questions to him. The first question which the boy asked was, 'what did Pharaoh change Joseph's name into?' The clergyman had read the Book of Genesis with great care, but he was obliged to make a motion that he did not know. He knew half of the name, but not the rest. The boy was quite satisfied that he had him 'stuck' and immediately, on a sign, completed the word. The next question was, 'In what year was Solomon born?' The clergyman did not understand chronology; he knew that it was sometime about 1,000 years before Christ, but he was unable to give the exact date, and he had to appeal to the meeting to supply his deficiency. They were as bad as himself! The next question was, 'What was the name of the Queen of Madagascar?' He signed to him that he did not know, and when the boy wrote it, he could not pronounce it. In every department he was admirably taught, and as to a thorough knowledge of the Scriptures, he never met a boy of his age who surpassed him in their understanding.'[4]

At an annual meeting in 1854, the Rev. Walshe said that he remembered travelling in a coach from the North of Ireland to Dublin, and he had for a fellow-passenger a young man who was deaf and dumb. By means of the manual alphabet he was able, for 50 miles, to carry on an interesting conversation with him. The young man was well read in history and the Scriptures, and told him a great deal of the marvels of chemistry, of which he was totally ignorant. He added that he was once greatly struck with the answering of a boy from Claremont. It was in the town of Arklow, where he happened to be one of a deputation. A lady wrote a slip of paper, on which was the question – 'Whom do you like best in the world?' He asked the question from the boy on his fingers, and the reply was – 'God.' The lady meant, 'in the world,' and the boy, being appraised of it, took up his Bible, and put his finger on averse from Psalm 73 – 'Whom have I in Heaven but Thee, and there is none on earth that I desire in comparison with Thee.'

Religion at Home and at Work

Before apprenticing pupils out to trades, the Committee enquired, by contacting the clergy of the parishes, into the religion and characters of their masters and mistresses. It was stated at an Annual Meeting that it was becoming difficult to source Protestant employers for the pupils about to leave Claremont. Some of them, after removal from

Claremont, wrote letters to Claremont, giving accounts of ill-treatment they received from their relations, because they refused to give up their Bibles and go to mass.

In June 1862, the Headmaster, Mr Chidley wrote to the Committee, 'It may be interesting to remark that I have just ascertained in answer to an enquiry from Dr Wilde, that at present there are only 11 children of Romanist parents in the Institution and that, including private pupils, there are 61 deaf-mute inmates, the children of Protestant parents'. There were some instances in 1868, in 1869 and in 1874, of some Roman Catholic deaf children, who having been admitted to the Claremont Institution, were then removed for transfer to the Cabra Institution for the Deaf and Dumb.

On 15 October 1862, Mr E.J.Chidley, Headmaster, wrote to the Committee:

'Dear Sir, I enclose a letter from a Roman Catholic priest respecting *John Casey* who had been 18 months a pupil. Last Thursday, two ladies called to see this boy; one of them who gave her name as Miss Mary Boyce, expressed surprise that 'his father should allow him to receive a Protestant education. The priest, she said, would have sent him to Cabra, but for the father's inability to pay £12 a year'. On the following Saturday the letter from the priest arrived. Since the boy's admission, the father has at different times written to enquire about him and was always satisfied with my replies.'

Religious Bribery and Blackmail

There were some instances of bribery in order to induce the deaf pupils to transfer to the Institution in Cabra. A pupil, John Spencer, from Parsonstown, King's County (Offaly), had been visited by his mother at Claremont, who told him that he could get £40 a year if he would go to the Cabra Institution and instruct the deaf there, but he refused.[5] Having lost his hearing at the age of nine years and with his speech declining, he had been admitted to Claremont in August 1844. Having left Claremont on 22 November 1852, he was apprenticed in 1866 to a japanner in London, and became a designer in glass.

In June 1849, a letter to the Committee stated that 'Romish priests will not allow James Noon to be sent to Claremont'. In October of the same year, the Rev. Chester, Kilrush, Co. Clare, said that 'he was afraid that Michael Walsh will not be sent to the Institution. The priests have taken him out of the Poor House, and will not let his mother send him'. Two months later, he wrote that 'Roman Catholic priests have succeeded in getting Michael Walsh into their Institution in Dublin'.[6]

A letter was received by the Committee from the Rev. J. Walker of Ballinasloe as to how the deaf boy, George Anderson, was not permitted to enter the Institution, the local priest having threatened to drive his parents out of town and to deny them the rites of their church if they should dare to disobey him, by sending their son to Claremont. The cost of sending deaf children to the Catholic Institution in Cabra was

£12 per annum, which some parents could not afford, and in consequence, they had to send their child to Claremont. In the late 1880s when the oral system was in operation in Claremont, the Catholic parents, anxious for their deaf child to learn to speak, chose Claremont over Cabra. Alternatively, Catholic parents had to send the deaf child to the Catholic Institution in Boston Spa, Yorkshire, which adopted the oral system.

In July 1873, the Committee discussed the removal of a deaf pupil, Bridget Kelly, on the grounds that her father was supposed to be at the point of death, and was refused the rites of his church by his priest unless he withdrew his

Ti-a-ra.

daughter from the Institution. Since it appeared from the poverty of the father that it would be useless taking legal proceedings for recovery of the sum due under bond for the child's maintenance, it was agreed that no further steps be taken.

Religious Intimidation

In the 1850s, when the Catholic Archbishopric of Dublin was taken up by Cardinal Paul Cullen, who had spent several years in Rome prior to his appointment to Ireland, religious intimidation was gathering pace. On 4 August 1852, Mrs Fisher, Charleville, Co. Cork, informed the Committee of the Institution that Maurice Herbert had been prevented from coming to Claremont through the interference of the priest. The records indicated that Herbert was actually admitted on 25 September 1852. He remained until 2 October 1857, when he was found employment as a gardener in Clonmel, Co. Tipperary.

On 25 August 1852, the Rev. Hugh Gelston requested that 'Mary Kahany of Sligo should be admitted, at once, into Claremont, as the Romanists were using great exertions, to get her into the Romish Institution.'[7] Aged ten years of age, she was admitted on 17 September and was sent home five years later, having completed her term of education.

In 1843, a former pupil, Thomas Neill, of Kilkeel, Co. Donegal, was forced to leave his family, due to intimidation from the neighbours in his home location. On 8 December 1852, a letter from a former pupil, Michael Gready, was read. He had been punished and ill-treated by his father for refusing to go to mass and he begged the Committee to give him a trade. Shortly afterwards, the Rev. Roe wrote that Michael's father would not consent to his son being bound as apprentice by the Committee. In January of the following year, Michael asked for ten shillings to enable him to run away from his father and pleaded with the Committee to obtain an apprenticeship for him. His request was turned down. Two weeks later, Miss Bridge informed that

Committee that Michael Gready intended to leave Roscrea without the knowledge of his parents and requested that the Committee have him bound to a trade at once. Another letter came from her expressing her surprise at finding Gready back in Roscrea, after having been refused admission by Mr Clarke, the Providore, into Claremont on a Sunday night. Michael Gready had to walk the streets of Dublin all night and Miss Bridge requested that this matter be investigated. The Committee replied that Mr Clarke had acted under a rule of the Committee to refuse admission to any pupil who had left the Institution.

At a deputation meeting, a former pupil told the following story. After leaving Claremont, he returned to his friends in his home area. He attended church regularly and read the Bible constantly. It was in 1858 when religious persecution became prevalent and his Roman Catholic friends used violence to prevent him going to church and deprive him of his Bible. They beat and abused him until he became ill for several weeks. He was sent to the Infirmary in Galway, where the nuns came to visit him. When they took out their rosaries, he brought out his Bible which he kept under his pillow, and, opening it, held it up before them. The nuns retreated and left him to recover in peace. When he regained his health, he was rejected by his friends, until the Bishop of Tuam, Lord Plunkett, took him into his employment, and since then, he continued to work for his eminent master.[8]

At the Annual Meeting in 1860, it was stated that seven pupils were elected, but two of them had been prevented through 'interference of Romanist priests from coming to the Institution'. The number at that time, including three grown-up girls who were employed as domestic servants, was 57 while there was accommodation for 150. There was mention of the 'struggles which the deaf mutes have often to undergo in maintaining against opposition and enticement, the faith in which they have been taught at Claremont.'

Nun.

Kidnappings and Deaf Girls sent to Nunnery
The Rev. Sheppard said that 'the Roman Catholic Institution was vigorously at work, more anxious to get *Protestants* than Roman Catholics.' He knew of the kidnapping cases that were going on over the country, 'where men and women were prowling about endeavouring to pounce on some poor Protestant orphans.' In January 1849, a letter from John Mulloy of Castlerea, Co. Galway, was read, 'Regarding Sarah Plunket, Co. Roscommon, who has been elected for admission to Claremont, I regret to state

that she has been kidnapped by the Roman Catholics and sent to their Institution in Dublin.'[9] Her name appeared on the pupil list of the Annual Report of the Catholic Institution. In the year 1852, there were two attempts by the Catholic parents and friends to 'kidnap' their deaf children from the Institution.

In February 1853, a letter was received from the Rev. E.A. Lucas stating that a girl, Mary Morrison, who had been educated at Claremont, had been sent to a nunnery in Sligo where she was forcibly detained and requesting the Committee to admit her into Claremont if she could be rescued or to procure an asylum elsewhere for her. The Committee replied that they would give a suitable fee for Mary Morrison, if the Rev. Lucas could procure a mistress for her and that Dr Ringland, one of the Committee members, would apply to the Matron of the Providence Home for Females to see if she could be admitted there.[10] On 13 April, the Rev. Lucas wrote that Mary Morrison would be in town on a Thursday evening and requested that the Committee arrange for someone to meet her at the Railway Terminus and take her to the Providence Home, whose matron promised to admit her until a suitable mistress could be found.

In May 1849 the parents of a deaf girl, Mary Scanlan, sent her to a nunnery in Harold's Cross, Dublin. When her father attempted to take her out, the nuns and priests persuaded him to leave her there.[11] On 6 February 1867, the father of a pupil, William Geary, from Tallow, Co. Waterford, who had been at Claremont since April 1863, forcibly removed his son from Meath Hospital, Dublin. This boy had suffered serious opthalmia since admission to school.

Violent Assault on the Roman Catholic Priests by a Deaf and Dumb Lunatic [12]
On 5 May 1850, it was Sunday morning at half-past nine, when the two Roman Catholic clergymen were saying mass in Whitefriars Street Chapel, Dublin. A young deaf and dumb man, named Francis McMahon, advanced towards them and struck each of them on the head with a very heavy whitethorn stick. One of the priests was knocked down, the other was staggered. The attacker was at once seized by a civilian and two policemen who were present. The indignation and excitement of the congregation was such that the policemen conveyed him away by a side door of the chapel. A police inspector deceived the angry crowd by placing a car in Aungier Street and another in York Row. In the Inspector's room, at the station house in Chancery Lane, some questions were put to the deaf and dumb man in writing, which were answered in a similar manner.

> Inspector - Why did you strike the clergymen in the chapel?
> Prisoner - Because my head is confused and half mad.
> The pain goes from my thumb to my head.
> How long have you been subject to this pain?
> About three years and two months.
> Were you educated at the Deaf and Dumb Institution at Claremont? - Yes.
> How long is it since you were at Claremont? - About ten years.

After this examination, the prisoner was removed to a cell. He was a tall, thin, respectable-looking young man. Even though dressed in a frock-coat, his appearance indicated his poverty.

In the following morning, Francis McMahon was brought from Chancery Lane Station before Mr Porter and Mr Magee, magistrates, on a charge of having violently assaulted the Rev. E. O'Rourke and Rev. R..J. Colgan, in Whitefriars Street Chapel.

Mr Thomas Mulhall attended as solicitor for Mr McMahon, father of the prisoner. Mr J.A. Curran acted as counsel for the prosecution. The board room was crowded, and hundreds gathered in the street adjoining Exchange Court. The case excited great curiosity.

Mr T.Mulhall said that he appeared on behalf of the family of the prisoner to express their deep regret at the incident that had taken place, and then sympathy for the injured clergymen. There was no doubt as to the insanity of the prisoner - the only course would be to commit the prisoner as a lunatic.

Mr Porter - Can the prisoner hear what is said? Mr Mulhall - No, your worship, he cannot. Are any of his relatives present? Yes, his father and brother. He has been deaf and dumb for 20 years. On Sunday morning, he stole away from the house in Cabinteely, procured the stick, and committed the assaults. Dr Ireland had examined him before the assault but he did not think Mr McMahon was a dangerous lunatic; however, no doubt can now exist that he is so.

Mr McMahon, brother of the prisoner, was then examined. He stated that his brother, Francis, left Cabinteely for town on Sunday morning before the family were up. He was born deaf and dumb, but can write very well. He tried to get employment in London, but did not succeed, and a medical friend expressed his opinion that if employment were not found for him, he would become insane.

Mr J.A. Curran said that the only course for the magistrates to adopt was to send the case for trial, and if then the prisoner was acquitted on the plea of insanity, he would be left to the Lord Lieutenant to make such arrangements for his comforts and security as would be necessary.

Mr Porter - I think it advisable that we should have some evidence of what occurred yesterday. It is well that the public should be satisfied and appeased upon that point.

The next witness examined was Mr Gogarty. He said that he was in the sanctuary when the Rev. O'Rourke was saying mass at the side altar and the Rev. Colgan was saying mass at the front altar. The prisoner walked into the sanctuary and approached Fr Colgan. He raised the stick with all his might and struck him across the back of the head. The sound of the blow and the screams of the people were heard by Fr O'Rourke, who came to save Fr Colgan. The prisoner met him, and struck him with the stick on the front of the head. The two policemen, who were in chapel, seized the prisoner.

Mr Curran asked the magistrates to put some questions to the prisoner. Dr Ireland remarked that if it were the intention of counsel to treat the prisoner as a lunatic, that might be the proper course, but if as a criminal, perhaps it would be better to reserve such an examination till the time of the trial. Mr Curran said that cutting and maiming with intent to murder was a capital offence. It was quite plain that if the prisoner was permitted to go at large, he might commit a more fatal act; whereas if he was acquitted upon a plea of insanity, he would remain in the hands of the Executive for life. Dr Ireland, in answer to questions put by Mr Mulhall, said that he had been acquainted with the prisoner for some years, but it was only lately that he heard he was deaf and dumb. The following examination of the prisoner then took place.

Mr Porter, magistrate, wrote the questions with pen and ink, and the prisoner made his replies in the same manner.

What's your name? Francis McMahon. Do you know what you were brought for? For telling you that my head goes pain from my thumb, and that I have beaten the Papist with a blow yesterday morning and that the people beat me before. Where did you get the stick? In Cabinteely, I live with the children of my brother. Did you cut the stick yourself? Very true. Did any person go with you to the chapel yesterday? No. For what did you go? For I wanted to beat him. I was sure I was not hypocrite to be a Roman Catholic, and that the people should know. I am honest to be a true priest. Are you a priest? Yes, but I read the Bible in faith. The examination of the prisoner was then terminated.

The next witness examined was Sergeant Dowling. He was in the chapel when he heard a person screaming. He looked around and saw the prisoner standing at the altar holding a stick over the head of the clergyman, and striking the clergyman.

At close of the examination, Mr Porter said he would send the case for trial on 19 June. The charge was: inflicted wounds upon Rev. Colgan and Rev. O'Rourke, with intent to murder, or grievous bodily harm. He would not admit the prisoner to bail, but his family and relatives should have access to him. The prisoner was then removed to the cell.

On 19 June 1850, Francis McMahon was indicted for having, committed on 5 May, a malicious assault upon the Rev. O'Rourke in the Chapel, Whitefriars Street, with a large stick, with intent to kill. Mr O'Hea defended the prisoner.

Mr Baldwin, QC, for the prosecution, said that as the prisoner was deaf and dumb, it was necessary that the first issue to be sent to the jury should be whether he was mute of his malice or by the visitation of God.

Mr Arthur McMahon, brother of the prisoner, stated he was deaf and dumb from birth. The jury accordingly found that he was mute by the visitation of God.

Mr Baldwin - Next question for the jury was to the prisoner's insanity, so that he could not be tried under the indictment charged against him. The same jury was again empanelled on the issue.

Dr Harty, examined by Mr Baldwin, said that he was in the habit of attending a lunatic asylum, and had considerable experience in that department, saw the prisoner at the time of his committal for the offence and frequently since then. He had formed an opinion as to the state of the prisoner's mind, considering him to be under the influence of religious 'monamanis', with the impression that if he did not manifest his decided Protestantism and that he was not a Roman Catholic, he would be taken for a hypocrite; this state was increased by a tendency to epilepsy.

After hearing evidence from Drs. Ireland and Millard, the jury found that the prisoner was insane and not responsible for the act. The court intimated that he would be dealt with as is usual in such cases.

Religious Confusion

In February 1905, there was an unusual case where a deaf boy, Frederick Sharp, born in Battersea, England, and his stepfather, Reuben Thomas Sharp, being a gunner, was transferred to the military barracks in Clogheen, Cahir, Co.Tipperary. Even though the Sharp family were members of the Church of England, the Board of Governors of Clogheen Union ordered that the boy Sharp be sent to the Catholic Institution for the Deaf in Cabra. Having heard of this proposal, the Rev. Leslie, rector of Clogheen, wrote to Mr Gick, secretary of Claremont as follows:

'Dear Sir, At our adjourned meeting today the Governors refused to send this child to Claremont. At the meeting four weeks ago, when the Roman Catholic priest applied to have him sent to Cabra as a Roman Catholic, they unanimously agreed to do so. It is a sad state of things but only a sample of what happens in the south of Ireland. I enclose a cutting from the *Clonmel Chronicle* which gives a fairly accurate idea of what occurred when I applied to have the boy sent to Claremont. I sincerely hope the Governors can help me in the matter if only in taking the boy as long as parents reside here. I enclose the application form which I had filled up for the Board. I am compelled now to do something for the child, as I fear his parents will hand him over to the priest if I cannot send him away.

Yours, J. H .Leslie'

Clogheen Union - The Recent Application on Behalf of a Deaf and Dumb Child[13]

At the meeting of the Clogheen Governors, was the application by the Rev. R. Phelan, P.P., to have the child of a Protestant soldier named Sharp sent to the Catholic Institution for the Deaf and Dumb at Cabra, Dublin, both clergymen were present.

Mr Galvin moved that the resolution regarding the boy to be sent to Cabra be rescinded, on the grounds that the Governors were misinformed when the resolution was passed. The Parish Priest of Clogheen, Father Phelan, had also been misinformed.

Fr Phelan explained that he took no action whatever in the matter until the parents of the child waited on him, and even then he did not move until they had given their full consent in writing to having the child sent to Cabra. He would now ask the Board to carry out their original intention of sending the child way. The Chairman said he could not assume the responsibility of sending the child away to any Institution whether Catholic or Protestant, as the parents had absolutely no claim on the ratepayers of the Union.

Fr Phelan added that he had been on most friendly terms with Rev. Leslie since the latter came to reside in Clogheen, and he would be very sorry that anything should crop up to disturb these friendly relations. The Rev. Leslie endorsed the remarks of Fr Phelan as to the friendly relations always subsisting between them, but he thought there was no way out of the matter but for the Governors to send the child to the Claremont Deaf and Dumb Institution, which was an Institution connected with the Church of Ireland, to which the child belonged.

Very Rev. Hercules H. Dickenson

Son of Bishop Charles Dickenson, Hercules was born on 14 September 1827 in Dublin. Educated at the Academic Institution in 62 Harcourt Street, Dublin, under the Rev D.Flynn, he had received prestigious awards at that school. After entering Trinity College Dublin in 1845, he was ordained in 1851. He became curate of St Ann's in Dawson Street, Dublin and in 1855 was Vicar of that church until his retirement in 1902. Three years later, he was appointed as Dean of the Chapel Royal, in Dublin Castle. He made his mark in the General Synod as a debater and a wit.

He was involved with the Claremont Institution since as a young boy in the Juvenile Association for the Deaf and Dumb. He served the Institution for nearly 60 years, at one time as Honorary Secretary for several years. In 1887, at the Royal Commission on the Education for the Deaf, Dumb, Blind and Imbeciles in London, he gave evidence on the need for State aid for the education of the deaf.

He said that in Ireland Poor Law Guardians were unwilling to give maintenance for education of deaf children, effectively condemning them to remain in ignorance and therefore a life burden on public resources. He referred to a case of a farmer in very reduced circumstances, with several children, who was reluctant to apply to the local guardians, who, he thought, would not grant it, so the deaf child could instead be taken into Claremont, at the Committee's expense.

He interpreted some meetings for Maurice Hewson, the deaf Missioner, and other deaf, and had performed some marriage services for the deaf. As Governor for the Dublin Working Boys' Home and for St Ann's Lodging Home, he assisted some of the former male pupils of Claremont, while taking up apprenticeship in Dublin, in obtaining accommodation at these hostels.

In 1902, he retired from active duties of the ministry. He died on 17 May 1905 and was buried in Mount Jerome Cemetery, Dublin. His memory was honoured by the reredos in St Ann's, Dawson Street, which also contains the Memorial Stone to his father, Charles Dickenson, private secretary and chaplain to Whately, Archbishop of Dublin. In Whately's treatise in 1847, *Elements of Logic*, he stated that the mental state of the deaf was that of a 'brute', only to be rebuked by Charles Baker, Headmaster of the Yorkshire Deaf and Dumb Institution in Doncaster.[14]

Rev. Henry George Carroll

Son of Anthony Carroll, solicitor, he was born in Dublin, and entered. Trinity College Dublin in 1837, at the age of 17. Ordained in 1844, he became assistant chaplain in Dr Steevens' Hospital, then curate of Drumcondra; and in 1847, moved to Glasnevin and was Vicar of this parish until 1895. Member of the Old Evangelical School, he was a constant student in the Library, Trinity College. He died on 29 November 1897, aged 78.

He was on the Claremont Committee for several years. He had buried some pupils in St Mobhi's, having been catechist to the Institution. His burial place is also at St Mobhi's, close to that of Edward James Chidley, headmaster of Claremont.

The Rev. Carroll spoke at an annual meeting that through his position in the parish, he had opportunities from time to time of seeing something of the workings of the Institution. It had been his responsibility to conduct the examination of the female pupils who had received the rite of confirmation. He conducted it for several days by means of writing, and he was then enabled to judge by a test of the Scriptural knowledge of the pupils. The examination of which he spoke demonstrated to him that here was a high degree of intelligence in the properly trained and educated deaf mind. He found amongst them, after a most careful investigation, an amount of Scriptural knowledge which would really put to shame some young persons who enjoyed the blessings of speech and far more advantages than the deaf were commonly supposed to have.

In 1852 he had an opportunity of seeing the Deaf and Dumb Institution in Paris. He went through it with considerable interest, and as regards internal economy and arrangements, the Claremont Institution was by no means inferior. But one thing struck him particularly, which was, that on being conducted to the lecture room in which the pupils received their instruction, he saw a large black board, and the first question that was written on it in French was; 'What do you think of the Emperor Napoleon?' 'Well', I thought to myself, 'We do things better than that at Claremont, by keeping before the minds of the inmates the glory of God that passeth not away, and by telling them not only of their duty as citizens, but by also impressing on them that their citizenship was in heaven'.[15]

Letter from a Pupil of the Edinburgh Institution
'Before I came to school, I thought that the stars were placed in the firmament, like grates of fire, and that the moon at night was like a great furnace of fire. I did not know, how the stars, the moon, and heavens, were made; but I did not know, whether the heaven was made by art or not. I had no proper idea of the extent of the world; but I thought it was little, and I was always intending going to the end, but it was too far. I thought it was round, like a round table. I knew nothing about God or Jesus Christ; I did not know, what became of the soul after death; but I thought the dead bodies were crumbled into dust, like dead beasts; and I did not know, that the bodies of the dead would be raised; neither that there was a place of punishment, nor a place of happiness, after death. My heart made me unhappy, when I could not understand what was said. There are many untaught deaf and dumb, and I feel very sorry for them.'

Letter from Collins about Angels
'When I die, I shall ask angels, where is Addington (one of the pupils, who had recently died) in heaven? Angels are pretty, angels are always happy; they are ever. The light is ever in heaven. Angels have wings in heaven, floating on the air; angels are wise; they see not breaking friendships in heaven. Are they always friends in heaven? Yes. Angels do not eat bread. They are ever happy; they with harps are ever in heaven. Angels do not die.'

Extract from An Investigation into the Principles, Management, and Deficiencies of the National Institution at Claremont- by an Observer, 1822
'We, who if we have wants, can disclose them, if we have sorrows can alleviate them, if we have thoughts can impart them, - can hear the soothing accents of consolation, and pour into the bosoms of others all the overflowings of our own; let us open to these afflicted beings too a communication with their fellow creatures, and give them a knowledge of their God. Oh, let us instruct them, in His name, and for His sake who died for us – who will hold us responsible for their ignorance of Him; and will demand their instruction, perhaps their very salvation at our hands.'

Part Four

Out into the World

20

Working for Themselves

Samuel Hawkins

He was born on 5 September 1868, in Castlesallagh, Stratford-on-Slaney, Co. Wicklow. His parents, Christopher and Martha (nee Hobson), had eight children, four of whom were deaf. On 4 August 1874, he was admitted to the Claremont Institution. A report covering the Annual meeting in 1876 referred to two of the smallest pupils in the school, little Sarah Wheatley and Samuel Hawkins, stood side by side on the platform, and exhibited their accomplishments. They spelled and signed the words which had been taught to them.

In 1884, he began his apprenticeship as a harness-maker under Mr Miller, saddler in Kevin Street, Dublin. In 1889, Hawkins emigrated to Winnipeg, Canada, where he found work at the Great West Saddlery. In 1890, he opened his harness-making shop in the village of Roundthwaite, Manitoba. In 1901, he married a deaf Austrian-born woman, Anna Mary Lennius (Lennon). They had seven deaf children. Samuel Hawkins featured in the following story about the 'Saskatchewan Deaf Homesteaders'. In early 1903, a small group of deaf people living around Manitoba, met to discuss ways of obtaining free homesteads being offered under the Dominion Lands Act. Those in attendance included

Har-ness-ma-ker.

an Irish immigrant, Samuel Hawkins, and several former pupils of the Ontario Institution for the Education of the Deaf and Dumb. By the summer of 1903, they began their trek westward, led by John Alexander Braithwaite, graduate of Gallaudet College, Washington D.C. Because there were no railways or paved roads to their destination, these early settlers and their families travelled for several days in covered ox-wagons.

Thus began an influx of deaf pioneers to the 'promised land' near the Qu'Appelle Valley in the North-West Territories (now South Saskatchewan). The deaf homesteaders settled on farms scattered around the towns of Lipton, Cupar and Dysart. They were isolated from each other during the winter months but came together for a picnic every summer from 1905 to 1912. Those settlers living farther away often arrived at the picnics in a wagon or buggy drawn by a team of horses. The annual picnics provided the deaf homesteaders with an opportunity to catch up on the events that had occurred during the long winter months. They also helped maintain the identity of this rural Deaf community. After 1912, however, several of the families moved from the area, and the picnics were no longer held.

During the autumn harvest each year, the number of deaf people in the area would increase when some 50 deaf harvesters arrived by train from Toronto to help the farmers of Lipton thresh their wheat. Each harvester was guaranteed a $10 return fare under the Harvest Special Excursion Plan. The merchants, doctors, lawyers, farmers and even the 'red-coated' policemen learned to converse with these labourers by using the manual alphabet and some signs. The influx of these harvesters brought news of Ontario to the homesteaders, several of whom had attended school in that province.

Letter from Mr Gick, Secretary of the Institution to Mr Hawkins,
father of Abraham, regarding contributing towards his son's apprentice fee

On 2 July 1904, Hawkins obtained a homestead about 16 kilometres northwest of Lipton. Harness shops were profitable as long as horses were the main motive power. Between early November and late March every year, Hawkins operated a harness-making shop on Railway Street in Lipton. The other months of the year was devoted to cultivating his homestead. Hawkins' harness-making business flourished until the advent of self-propelled tractors in the 1920s. The rest of the Hawkins family scattered to such cities as Vancouver, Regina, Winnipeg and Toronto during the economic hardships of the Great Depression of the 1930s. He died in 1934 at the age of 66.[1]

George Samuel Orr

He was born on 11 January 1861 in Bray, Co. Wicklow. At the age of two years, he lost his hearing. His mother, Ellen, was a widow and supported herself and the family as a laundress. In 1866 the Rev. George Scott referred the boy for election to Claremont and George was admitted in May of that year. He showed such an intellect that he had been selected as deputation boy. The Annual Report of 1875 stated that George Orr was to be taught tailoring, the trade of his stepfather, who contemplated emigrating to Canada with his family. However, he was apprenticed to a shoemaker, Heathers & Co., Lower Bridge Street. On 3 February 1878, he was given lodgings in the Dublin Working Boys' Home in Denzille Street, Dublin. In the Register Book of that Home, it was stated that Orr, aged 17, received 14 shillings per week while on apprenticeship. On 3 August 1878, having reached the maximum age of 19, he moved to St Ann's Lodging Home, with assistance from the Rev. Hercules Dickenson.

On Easter Monday, 29 March 1880, he married Mary Anne Regan, also from Claremont, who was in the same factory as himself. The ceremony was performed at St Matthias' Church, Adelaide Road, Dublin, by the Rev. John Robinson in the presence of two former pupils, Thomas Russell and Ruth Griffin.[2] They had two children, Annie and Samuel George. Mr Orr went into business as a boot maker, having opened a shop in Woodstock Gardens, Ranelagh, Dublin, and employing two deaf men. Annie, his hearing daughter, assisted in the shop, and when George retired to Limerick, his son, Samuel, took over his father's business.

As Mr Orr frequently travelled to England to purchase leather for boot-making, he visited the deaf in Liverpool, Sheffield and Nottingham. In the 1890s, he formed a Gospel Group in Leicester and he assisted with organising conventions for the deaf in the Midlands of England.

On 13 April 1929, Mr Orr's wife, Mary Anne, died and was buried in Mount Jerome Cemetery. On 6 November 1929, at the Methodist Church at Ballingrane, Co. Limerick, he married Charlotte Arabella Switzer, who also was a Claremont pupil. Her parents, Jacob and Fanny Switzer of Courtmatrix, Rathkeale, Co. Limerick, had eleven children, four of whom were deaf. They set up home in her parents' cottage in Courtmatrix. George Samuel Orr died on 3 January 1932, after suffering from spinal tumour for twelve months. His widow, Charlotte, died in 1942.

George Orr and his wife, Charlotte (née Switzer) at Courtmatrix, Rathkeale, Co. Limerick
This house was built by Christopher Switzer in 1701 after emigrating from Germany

The Switzers
In Rathkeale and Adare, Co. Limerick, there were numerous members of the Switzer family, descendants of the immigrants from the Palatine district in Germany. They were part of the contingent who fled in the 17th century for various reasons – religious persecution, heavy taxation and poor farming conditions in their place of origin - to the Netherlands, England and then Ireland. In Courtmatrix, three miles south of Rathkeale, was a family headed by Jacob and Fanny (Frances), who had eleven children. Amongst the children were four deaf children - Mary Ann, Henry, Susan and Charlotte. This family was residing in a cottage constructed in 1709 by Christopher

Switzer, one of the immigrants. The house is still standing and undergoing renovations by one of the descendants of the Switzers, having moved from England in 2003. It used to form part of a community with a chapel and 26 houses erected by the Palatine immigrants.[3] Facing the cottage is an apple tree, planted by the patriarch of the Switzer family, Christopher.

On 22 December 1860, both Mary Ann and Henry were admitted into the Claremont Institution, and were removed on 1 July 1872, upon completion of their education. In February 1878, Susan was admitted, and removed in July 1886. On 14 September 1880, Charlotte, the youngest of the family, was admitted, but in the summer of 1887, she did not return to Claremont, as she was needed by her father at the farm. Some years later, she established a small business in dress-making in Limerick, until her marriage to George Orr, when she returned to her home in Court Matrix. Her brother, Henry, was living with her after George Orr's death. Marie Reid, hearing daughter of Susan Switzer who moved to Liverpool after marrying Mr Reid, returned to Court Matrix to look after Henry and Charlotte. After her death, the house was bequeathed to the Teskey family, also descendants of the Palatine immigrants. The cottage is now back into the ownership of Gary Switzer, the present descendant of the Switzer family.

Following are the entries in the Minute Book, the Letter book from the Headmaster and correspondence referring to the Switzer children:

'Dr Eustace is afraid that Mary Ann Switzer, one of the younger female pupils, has a tendency to curvature of the spine and he recommends that she should be placed as a patient paying 2/- weekly at the Whitworth Hospital.'

Mr Chidley wrote to the Committee that:

'October 1862 - the Protestant parents of Mary Ann Switzer lately discharged from the Whitworth Hospital are desirous of having her home for change of air. A clergyman who called at Claremont today will take her down with him to Rathkeale, Co. Limerick, if the Committee will pay her railway expenses which will not exceed twelve shillings.'

'14 June 1872 - he father of Mary Ann and Henry Switzer should be asked to remove his two children, they having been retained in the Institution beyond the usual term.'

'Jacob and Fanny Switzer had a small farm, and having eleven children, were unable to contribute towards the maintenance fees for their deaf daughter, Susan'.

Letter from the Clerk of the Rathkeale Union on 10 July 1880:

'We made enquiries on Jacob Switzer, the father, and found that he is not as destitute as he had been represented to be. However, the Board made him an offer to pay for the maintenance of the child, Charlotte, in your Institution by his agreeing to pay £5 and he has declined to accept the offer.'

Charles Conrad Williams

Born on 17 February 1871, 'CCW' was ninth in a Quaker family of eleven children. His father, Benjamin Joshua Williams, spent much of his life in commercial pursuits in Edenderry, Co. Offaly. Conrad's oldest deaf brother, John, and himself entered the Claremont Institution as private pupils, and they were highly intelligent and fluent with the manual alphabet. Due to their status as private pupils under Mr George Taylor, there was no mention of their progress at school.

In 1898, Conrad obtained a position with Marcus Ward & Co, Royal Ulster Works in Belfast. Later on, he left to return to Edenderry and set himself up as an electrical and automobile engineer, as well as acting as an agent for Michelin and India Tyres. Then he went into partnership with his brother, Arthur, to run a garage, and became an authorised dealer in Ford motor-cars. He married Alice Mary Moore, a hearing lady, from Co. Clare. His brother, John, married Ellen Marcella Hilliard, also pupil of Claremont, from Castlegregory, Co. Kerry. She became deaf at the age five from a dose of scarlet fever. They moved to London, where John worked for a firm installing ovens. The highlight of his career was helping to install one at the Paris Exhibition of 1900.

In the 1890s to 1900s, C.C. Williams had made a reputation of being one of the best cyclists in Ireland. According to the local newspaper, *The Midland Tribune*, August 1895, he was member of the Cycling Club in Edenderry. The *British Deaf Mute*, June 1893, said that 'C.C. Williams, the well-known Irish cycling racer, is busy getting himself into good trim for the coming 100-miles record and championship of Ireland.

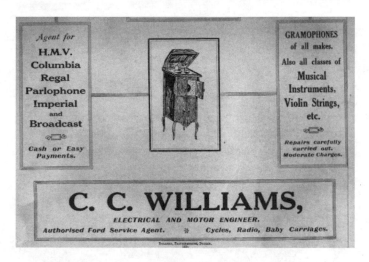

Extract from Record Sleeve supplied by C.C.Williams
(it is strange that he, being deaf, would advertise musical instruments!)

On 23 November, he, at that time the 50-miles bicycle champion in Ireland, was challenged to a mile-long flat race by Mr R. Gywnne, a member of the Covecliffe Harriers of Dublin. Great interest was taken in this match, which was run on the best racing and running track in Dublin, commonly called 'Jones Road Ground'. Bets were taken on C.C. Williams. When the race started, Mr Gywnne quickly showed business and ran off like a rocket, with Mr Williams dragging his burly but athletic figure along. Mr Gwynne finished the race in 4 minutes 50 seconds.[4] In the following year, the 'honour of deaf cyclists had been well upheld' in Dublin, when C.C. Williams succeeded in winning two gold medals, and a gold badge for covering his distance under the club's standard time, and breaking the record for the day's racing.[5]

'Mr C.C. Williams, Edenderry, made a very plucky ride in the 100-mile cycle race of the Irish cycling club, the competition was very keen and Mr Williams contended most successfully. The time was 5 hours 27 minutes and 10 seconds for the 100 miles, in favour of Mr C.C. Williams of the Edenderry Club. His success is the source of much satisfaction to the people of Edenderry as he is very popular.'[6]

During the 'Big Freeze' of 1947, when the canal froze over, C.C. Williams and his son, Freddie, decided to skate to Dublin, starting from the Grand Canal Harbour in Edenderry. It took them a couple of hours to skate the whole way to Dublin and then back. The ice was so thick that there was no problem at any stage.[7] He was regularly visited by the Rev. V.J. Walker, the Missioner to the Adult Deaf and Dumb, and up to the time of his death he was a very active man. He died on 4 June 1963, aged 92 years, and was interred in the burial place of the Religious Society of Friends, in Edenderry, Co. Offaly.

The newspaper, *Dublin Evening Telegraph* of 26 February 1910, read as follows:

'*A DUBLIN-BUILT AEROPLANE*'

'This aeroplane has been built at Castlewood College, Rathmines, Dublin, by a remarkable boy Master Donal Cameron aged 16 years who is a pupil of Mr Newburn for some time and he was born deaf and has been educated on the pure oral system at the above college.   He is a nephew of Sir Charles Cameron, C.B., and throughout his school career displayed a decided tendency for engineering and is very happy when explaining the possibilities of his new machine. He certainly reflects the greatest possible credit to Mr Newburn, and one is inclined to ask if the age of miracles has passed when we hear the dumb speak and particularly in the case of Master Cameron who articulated fluently and whose intellectual powers, working under difficulties, have been so remarkably demonstrated.'

Donal's uncle, Sir Charles Cameron, son of a veteran of the Peninsular War, was well-known in Dublin, with a memorial assigned to him for improving public health in Dublin, in his role as Public Analyst for the city since 1862 and as Chief Medical Officer since 1879, and was the Grand Master of the Irish Freemasons in his time. He was knighted in 1855, and it was said of Sir Charles Cameron that he appeared to be a permanent feature of Dublin life.[8]   He recorded his observations of life in Dublin in a book called *Reminiscences*, printed in 1913, and he published scientific works and poems, including the history of the Royal College of Surgeons in Ireland in 1866.[9]

Naturally it could be wondered if the aeroplane built by Donal Cameron was ever tried in the air, not necessarily by him but by anyone else. It was certainly a large model and building it was an achievement for Donal because it required skilled carpentry and knowledge in the latest aero technology in those days. Donal Cameron was probably the first British deaf person (Ireland was part of the United Kingdom until 1922) to build an aeroplane.

Jack Stanton outside his father's shop in Dun Laoghaire

David John (Jack) Stanton

Born on 13 September 1899, Jack was the fourth in a family of seven. His father, William, was a greengrocer and the family lived above the shop at No. 67 Lower Georges' Street, Kingstown (Dun Laoghaire), almost opposite the famous Findlater's Store. Jack lost his hearing at the age of 21 months due to meningitis, and on 25 September 1906, he was admitted to Claremont as an intermediate pupil at £26 per annum.

However, his father had fallen behind with the payments, and on 6 October 1911, the Institution Secretary, Mr Gick, wrote to him, 'you owe for maintenance and education of your son the sum of £56 5s, no payment having been received from you since January 1908. We shall be reluctantly compelled to send the boy home. If you are not in a position to pay, you should apply to the Board of Guardians who are empowered under 6 and 7 Vic. Cap 92 (the Poor Law) to make a maintenance grant'. So the father started in small payments of £1 per month, under threat of legal action from the Committee.

Findlater's Shop in Kingstown (Dun Laoghaire)

In December 1915, Jack left school to follow in his father's footsteps, working as a shop assistant and collecting fruit and vegetables from the nursery gardens in Monkstown, and from the fruit and vegetable market in Smithfield early in the morning.

Jack had assisted with deliveries of fresh provisions to the mail-boat steamers and yachts mooring in the harbour nearby. Whenever the Royal Yacht paid the visit to Kingstown, he took opportunity to go out to watch the Royal Procession down the street, decorated with Union Jacks, buntings and ivy-twined triumphal arches, where the Royal carriage and the horsemen passed his family shop.

Jack loved walking down the pier to watch the passengers boarding for Holyhead on the steamer, and the mail-bags loaded into the vessel, awaiting sorting by the postal staff, who travelled by train from Westland Row, Dublin City. Whenever the mail-boat arrived from England, Jack would ask the sailors for tips on the running racehorses, and he passed on the information to punters prior to placing their bets.

During the 'Troubles' in 1916, curfew was in place in the streets of Kingstown. One night, Jack had some 'jars' in a public-house in the town. He decided to depart for home, and was passing the Royal St George Yacht Club, when a British soldier shouted a warning to him. Jack walked on, without hearing, so the solider approached him from behind and stuck the gun into his back, until Jack felt a prick in his back and froze. He turned around, and was startled to face the soldier holding the bayonet out at him. He was then ordered to march to the barracks, where he was told he had ten minutes to get out, so he ran for his life!

Jack developed a relationship with a school-friend called Alice Liddy. She was living in Wales when the Great War broke out. He had hoped to take the mail boat to see her, but war intervened, making it dangerous for the ships to travel across the Irish Sea, owing to the German U-boats prowling about and looking for prey. Among the vessels which fell into the German traps was the *R.M.S. Leinster,* which was torpedoed on 11 October 1918 near the Kish seabed, a short distance from the harbour of Kingstown. Among the 530 passengers, crew and postal sorters, was Jack's school friend, James Gibson, on leave from the army and returning to England. When the war was over and it was safe to travel, Jack travelled to Wales only to find that his girlfriend had married a Mr Leece from Liverpool, whose occupation was 'collector for the Deaf and Dumb Benevolent Society'. Ironically, Alice's son, Cyril Leece, was sent in 1941 to Claremont for education. However, with the Second World War intervening with sea travel, her son had to be removed from Claremont and was sent instead to a deaf school in England.

After the family shop was sold up, Jack obtained a position as a shop assistant, carrying out deliveries of food provisions to the houses in the township of Kingstown. Upon his retirement, he continued his active life, by taking walks along the West and East Piers in Dun Laoghaire, and by doing some gardening and odd jobs for his former customers and others who admired his capacity for hard work and honesty. He had developed a close rapport with those who knew him. He had been an immense help to a former Claremont pupil, living in Dun Laoghaire and working full-time and unable to take time off work, by carrying out messages on his behalf. He was a true example of a gentleman, with genteel and old-fashioned manners, doffing his hat to passers-by and greeting them with a beaming smile. After a road traffic accident in Dun Laoghaire, he died on 24 November 1979, aged 80 years, and was buried in the unmarked grave of his parents in Deansgrange Cemetery, Dublin.[10]

Reginald Ferguson Peacocke - First Deaf Pilot in the United Kingdom[11]
Irish-born, with a strong clerical background, he was second son of the Venerable Archdeacon of Kildare (Gerald William Peacocke) and Kathleen, nee Crozier, Kill Rectory, Co. Kildare. His grandfather (Joseph Ferguson Peacocke)[12] was the Primate

of Ireland until 1915. Fergus, as he was called, received his education as private pupil at Claremont Institution, and was transferred to Spring Hill School for the Deaf, Northampton. In 1925, he gained successes in Oxford Junior Local examinations and returned to Ireland.

There followed the years of depression and recession in the United Kingdom and, anxious to set Fergus off on the road to support himself, his father told him to go on his own and gave him £20. Outside Leixlip, Co. Kildare, Fergus obtained a position as foreman of a woodworking company, which manufactured house and garden furniture. He designed a folding tea-trolley, and found the work in the factory very interested. In his spare time, he took up flying, and an article appeared in the *Spring Hill Magazine*, December 1935 issue:

'It was a foggy evening and the sun was nearing the horizon when my instructor and I landed after practising landings in a Moth plane. The last landing was my doing without any interference by the instructor. After it, we taxied back to the take-off position for another round. The instructor got out of his cockpit and stepped to my side. To my surprise, he said, 'Do not fly too high as the fog is coming down'. Then he stooped into his cockpit and drew out the joystick. SOLO! I could not believe my eyes. I was declared fit to go up myself after only three and a half hours' instruction.

Ferguson Peacocke, second right, at his business premises in Denzille Lane, Dublin (photograph from Norman Rankin and restored by David Breslin)

'I looked at the instructor standing at the wing tip. I stammered, 'All right'. Summoning my courage, I opened the throttle fully and pushed the stick forward. The plan sped along the grass until I felt it taking to the air. Then I gently pulled back the stick and I was in the air. What a joy to be flying under my own control! I was happy. My ambition has been realised at last. Circling the aerodrome, I gazed at the clubhouse below. There was a good crowd watching me. My instructor was in the middle of the field standing nervously and praying that I would land safely. Gliding down, I reached the edge of the field and landed well in the middle. Phew! As I struggled out of my cockpit, pilots and pupils with amazement in their faces appeared across the field. The instructor with a beaming face ran to my side and proposed a drink out of a Solo Cup. I had broken the Club's record and also the record for the whole of Ireland. The previous best pupil had four and a half hours' instruction before going solo. It was a perfect day and the greatest moment of my life.'

After the experience, Fergus Peacocke studied Aeronautical Engineering and Design at the Institute of Technology, Bolton Street, Dublin, in order to get into an air-craft factory and passed. Unfortunately, his old factory was destroyed by fire, and he left for England. In 1937, Fergus was employed to make spare parts for aeroplanes in a Manchester factory. Then he moved on to various places, such as Reading and Witney, for the same purpose, and soon he returned to Ireland. When the Second World War came, Fergus was engaged at a new factory making cabins and petrol tanks for the new RAF training planes. When this firm was closed, he moved on to another firm in April 1940 and was in charge of hands looking after the windscreen assembly. In the 1950s, he worked for Herman Welding Engineers, in Denzille Lane, Dublin, from whom in 1960 he bought out the business, renaming it as 'R. Ferguson Peacocke Ltd'. As the premises faced the back of the offices of Dublin's most prominent architect, Michael Scott, Fergus received valuable commissions for some of Dublin's landmarks, such as Busaras (National Bus Station) and the Abbey Theatre.

In 1960, Henry Pollard and Norman Rankin, having completed education first at the Claremont Institution in Monkstown and then in Blackrock Technical School, were taken on to undertake seven years as apprentices at Fergus Peacocke's factory dealing in metalwork and precision engineering. Henry recalled of his manager, Fergus, telling stories of himself flying solo and carrying out aerobatics at the Flying Club in Co. Sligo. Fergus Peacocke was in demand, taking commissions from the Embassy of the United States of America, Radio Television Éireann and the developers of Stillorgan Shopping Centre, which made the reputation of being Ireland's first shopping centre which opened in 1966. Fergus was married twice, with his first wife dying shortly after their marriage. When Fergus retired, he was resident in Monkstown, Co. Dublin, and often spent time out at sea with the Silver Knights Deepsea Angling Club, and was member of the British Legion Club in Dun Laoghaire. He and his wife moved to Malaga, Spain where he died in 1990.

21

Messengers of the Gospel

'though their tongues were still, their faces so shone that they became
effective messengers of the gospel' - *Rev. John Shearer*, Old Time Revivals[1]

Religious Instruction for the Adult Deaf

At the Annual Meeting in 1858, Edward Whitfield,[2] deaf gentleman, said that
'Daniel Pennefather, deaf and dumb gentleman, having ascertained that there
were deaf and dumb adults in the city (Dublin) who did not attend any place of worship, or had no instruction on the Sabbath Day, set a Sunday school going some weeks
since. A meeting of around thirty deaf and dumb adults, chiefly tradesmen, is held
every Sunday at the Dorset Institution, Upper Sackville Street.'[3]

In 1834, the Committee considered that the Sunday School in the city of Dublin was
necessary for those who left the Institution in order to carry on their religious instruction and to keep up a moral influence over them during apprenticeship through life
as well to preserve a friendly connection on moral grounds themselves and the friends
of the Institution. Dr Adams, of the Committee, reported that as the uneducated deaf,
after leaving Claremont, were tempted to turn to alcohol, he wished to form
Temperance Societies among the male and female pupils based on the plan adopted
in the New York Deaf and Dumb Institution. It was resolved that a Sabbath School be
opened for affording religious instruction to all the *educated* deaf and dumb; that
Edward Whitfield (deaf) be Superintendent; that the following gentlemen shall be the
Committee and Teachers: Dr. C. Orpen, Dr Adams, Isaac Butt, William B. Overend
(deaf), William W. Woods (teacher from Claremont), Arthur Hopper (teacher from
Claremont) and William Hopper; that the school shall be opened on 11 May 1834; that
the time of instruction be from three to four o'clock on each Sunday and that the business shall open and close with prayer.[4] The Sunday School Society for Ireland presented a number of testaments, and a girls' Sunday school was opened when a sufficient
number of female pupils was discovered and some ladies came forward to superintend and instruct the girls.

William Burke Overend (1808-1862)

Son of the Rev. John Overend, curate of Castlemacadam, near Glendalough, Co.
Wicklow, the application for admission of William, aged thirteen, to the Institution
was lodged, but there was no indication of his actual admission to Claremont.
Partially deaf, he was highly intelligent and possessed good signing and writing skills,
having had received education beforehand. His brother, Henry Overend, had been
teacher at Claremont until he was induced by Mr Pennefather to become private tutor
to his deaf son, Daniel. Then he moved to Strabane Institute for the Deaf and Dumb.

THE DEAF AND DUMB AT CHURCH.

In 1826, William Overend commenced Bible classes on Sundays for the instruction of the deaf and dumb, with assistance from a former pupil of Claremont, John T. Morris.[5] He appointed Anne McCormick, former assistant teacher in the Female School, Claremont, as his assistant for the female deaf adults in the Sunday School. The Dorset Institution, with Viscountess Lorton as patroness, provided employment for destitute women in the city and schooling for their children, and within it was the Day School for the Deaf and Dumb, a preparatory school for deaf children before transferring to Claremont. However, there had been 'difference' between Overend and Miss McCormick over the management of the Day School, incriminating J.T. Morris and Mrs Hare, committee member of the Day School. William Overend, Castle Street, Dublin, died from bronchitis on 9 February 1862, at the age of 59.

John T. Morris

From Stackallen, Navan, Co. Meath, John Morris was admitted to Claremont at the age of ten on 1 April 1825. He was found to be intelligent, has had education and was remarkably obedient, whereas his parents, though poor, were able to pay £20 per annum for his maintenance and education. His talents were drawing and mechanics. After leaving Claremont on 31 December 1829, he became an assistant Biblical instructor at the Sunday School managed by William Overend. According to Maurice

Hewson (Biblical Teacher and Secretary to the Dublin Deaf and Dumb Adults' Association), 'Mr John T. Morris had entirely devoted himself to the ministry of the deaf-mutes, at our Society's lecture-room, 13 York Street, Dublin'.[6]

'The first recorded death of a Deaf person on any British railway line occurred in June 1875. A 60-year-old man from Dublin decided to take a short cut along railway tracks whilst visiting Cardiff, and failed to notice the approach of a goods train. He was struck by the wagon, and was run over before railwaymen could bring the train to a halt. In hospital, he managed to write his name - John Thomas Morris - and that he was deaf and dumb. He had three limbs amputated, but his injuries were so severe that he lost consciousness, and afterwards died. The jury at the inquest donated all their fees to the Llandaff School for the Deaf and Dumb. John Morris was said to have cycled all around Britain and supposedly visited every school for the deaf during his cycling tour. He was the senior Biblical instructor at the Dublin Protestant Deaf and Dumb Association, having worked among the Dublin Deaf and Dumb for 35 years. He had left Dublin for a holiday in South Wales and only a few days prior to his death, he had visited the Llandaff School. He was buried in Mount Jerome Cemetery, Dublin, on 30 June 1875.'[7]

'Rev.' Maurice Fitzgerald Hewson

Following William Overend's death in 1862, the mission work was taken up by his pupil, Maurice Fitzgerald Hewson. He was the eldest son of Falkiner Minchin Hewson, of an old Kerry family who, in 1840, settled in Dublin to establish a business as merchant, and who married Miss Mary Brownrigg, the only daughter of Captain Brownrigg of Wexford. Maurice Hewson was brought up by his grandmother, Mrs Brownrigg. He was a familiar figure at most conferences of the Mission workers among the deaf in Britain and Ireland. He organised the meetings in various places of Ireland, inviting the deaf and hearing Missioners to speak at these occasions. One of the deaf speakers was the Rev. Edward Rowland of the Glamorgan Mission to the Deaf and Dumb. On 26 June 1882, he was ordained in Cardiff, the first British Deaf person to be ordained to the priesthood. His devotion to the deaf won him much respect from all the deaf and he was also respected by many hearing people who were aware of his relentless work among the deaf.[8] His account of his tour to Dublin in July 1876 follows:

'Upon receiving an invitation from Dublin, to preach again, and knowing the condition of the brethren in that Irish Metropolis, I fixed my heart and soul on the Emerald Isle. On Saturday, 15 July, at 6 a.m., the *Argo,* having left Bristol the night before, glided into the Dublin harbour. Mr Allen, a kind-hearted gentleman, met me and we went to Mr Adams' home where I received a hearty welcome, with a nice breakfast of eggs and beefsteaks; both husband and wife, being deaf and dumb, with a laughing baby. Mr Hewson, the indefatigable Secretary of the Deaf and Dumb Society came in at 10 o'clock to arrange with me respecting the Sunday services and the forthcoming picnic. We then went to William Street to see the mission room. At 6 o'clock, Mr Hewson took me to his home to dinner, his good mother, a very pleasant lady, received us kindly. The next day; despite the hot weather, I had three services, one at 12 noon, the second at 4 p.m., and the third at 7.30 p.m. Being asked to remain for another Sunday, I consented to do so, and offered to speak on the following Wednesday evening.'

'Monday, July 17, will probably be remembered by the Dublin mutes as their first picnic, set up by Mr Hewson. The weather was very fine, and 40 deaf and dumb and their hearing friends had an enjoyable time in Killiney. At the station Mr Hewson elected brawny mutes to carry the large baskets full of bottles and food. On the top of the hill, sandwiches and bottles of ginger beer, lemonade and claret were freely dispensed, followed with rice and plum puddings. The afternoon was spent in chats and games, and taking a view of the surrounding scene – the sea in its majestic beauty on one side, and mountains and plains, woods and hills on the other side. At 5 o'clock, Mr and Miss Hewson took care to 'tea' the company; after which we held a short meeting on the grass. After prayer, we went down the 'softly carpeted path' out of the castle ground to the station, for home. Every day, Mr Hewson took me to some places of interest, including Howth, where Mr Mottan kindly treated us with a substantial dinner in a hotel, and took us through the castle grounds of the Earl of Howth.'

'Sunday, July 23 – full attendance at the services. Dining at a deaf and dumb party that day, the repast was first-class – mutton, beef, pork, cabbage, potatoes and pudding. The following day, a farewell tea party previous to my departure from Dublin was provided, and I was then pressed to come again next year'.[9]

On 7 June 1877, Maurice Hewson had been formally 'set aside' for ministry work with the deaf by the Archbishop of Dublin, Chenevix Trench, at St Ann's Church, Dawson Street, Dublin.

Mr Hewson, with assistance from his brother, Thomas, solicitor by profession, and his sister, Miss Hewson, established the Dublin Protestant Deaf and Dumb Association, with its office in the Christian Union Buildings (later Metropolitan Hall), Lower Abbey Street, Dublin, owned by the Dublin Young Men's Christian Association, where services were held in the 'deaf and dumb' language on Sunday mornings and evenings, with meetings and lectures (including the Literary Debating Society) on Wednesday evenings. The funds were derived from collections, subscriptions and donations, with some help from bazaars, to which some deaf and hearing ladies contributed their handiworks. The work was confined to the city of Dublin, where there were in the year of 1894 about fifty Protestant deaf mutes. Mr Maurice Hewson visited the sick at their homes and assisted the 'deaf and dumb of all denominations to obtain suitable employment.'[10] At the services held for the deaf in Cork,

MR. MAURICE F. G. HEWSON.

Donegal, Dublin and other places, he 'spoke on his fingers and by signs to the deaf and dumb.'

In 1886, the Hewsons published a magazine, *The Irish Deaf-Mute Advocate and Juvenile Instructor*, with some scriptural texts, sermons and news received from the Missions for the Adult Deaf in England, Scotland, Wales and Northern Ireland. Regular contact was made with Wilhelmina Tredennick (1837-1891), who established the Mission to the Adult Deaf and Dumb in Belfast, having started her work among the deaf in her native town, Ballyshannon, Co. Donegal, after coming across a deaf young man who could not communicate with his aging parents. She was a grand-daughter of the Archbishop of Dublin, Dr Magee, and was beloved by the mutes of all denominations.[11]

Maurice's brother, Thomas, assisted with the interpreting of church services for the deaf and some engagements. In September 1894, Maurice Hewson had been appointed by the Lord Lieutenant as School inspector under the Educational Endowments (Ireland) Act 1885 for the Claremont Institution, but this appointment was challenged by the headmaster, Mr Taylor, who refused to allow his brother to accompany his deaf brother to Claremont. After the Institution sent to Dublin Castle a letter of protest submitting two names for Inspector of the following year, a response from the Undersecretary stated that Mr Hewson had discharged his duties efficiently and that he was to make a further inspection.

In 1885, he assisted with the organisation of the Congress in Dublin for the British Deaf and Dumb Association in the Metropolitan Hall, Lower Abbey Street, Dublin. On 26 March 1888, he assisted the officiating clergyman, the Rev. Fletcher, at the 'deaf and dumb wedding' in St James' Church, Dublin. 'The deaf-mute missionary for Dublin translated every word into the finger language with grave emphasis and much gesticulation for the benefit of the attentive congregation. To 'Wilt thou, Simon?' and 'Wilt thou, Sarah?' etc, the answer was made by bowing of the heads. The church was filled by friends of the couple and members of the public.[12] The happy couple was Simon Connor, labourer, of Ellis Street, and Sarah Wheatley, spinster, of Rialto Place, South Circular Road, Dublin. The best man was James Robertson, and all of the three named deaf were former pupils of Claremont.

Even though he had never been officially ordained, he was acknowledged by the deaf as 'the Rev. Hewson'. This unofficial title was disputed in 1904 by an anonymous correspondent to the *Church of Ireland Gazette*, as follows:

Sir – Not noticing the name of 'Rev.', Maurice F.G. Hewson amongst the licensed clergy of the Diocese of Dublin given in the *Irish Church Directory*, I should feel obliged if Dr Clarke would inform your readers of the date of Mr Hewson's ordination as Deacon and Priest; and the name of the Bishop by whom he was ordained. Further, would Dr Clarke be so good as to say how far Mr Hewson's work is controlled or guided by any committee representing the Church of Ireland, or how far he himself is subject to the discipline and rule of the Church of Ireland? – Yours, etc. Enquirer'

Dr William J. Clarke, rector of St Thomas, Marlborough Street, Dublin, sent a reply to the same periodical as follows:

'The anonymous correspondent must be aware that thousands receive the title of 'Reverend' by common consent, who have never received Episcopal ordination. He must know, moreover, that hundreds of women receive this title. In the case of the Rev. Maurice F.G. Hewson, 27 years ago on 7 June 1877, he was solemnly set apart by the late Archbishop Trench, at a special service in St Ann's Church, Dublin, to 'minister to the Deaf and Dumb of the city'. He had been already engaged several years at this work, and the Archbishop was desirous to admit him to Holy Orders, but Mr Hewson, afflicted as he was, could not make the necessary preparations for the Bishop's examination, and so the dedication mentioned above was made to take the place of regular Ordination and Admission to Holy Orders. Ever since his dedication he has received the title 'Reverend'; he has borne it well and worthily, and having acted in his position as minister to the Deaf and Dumb in Dublin for nearly 40 years, you will hardly succeed in depriving him of it'.
'You asked – 'How far Mr Hewson's work is controlled by the Church of Ireland?' The patrons of the Dublin Protestant Deaf and Dumb Association consist of the Lord Primate, the Archbishop of Dublin, and the Bishops of the Church of Ireland. The Vice-Patron is the Earl of Bandon. The Committee is composed of members of that Church, including two clergymen. This, I think, ought to satisfy you, and I cannot conceive how anyone could try to criticise such good work conducted by Hewson. Should 'Enquirer' wish to ask me any more questions, he must do so over his name. Yours, etc. – William J. Clarke'[13]

In August 1880, at the National Deaf and Dumb Convention in Dublin, the subject of the 'ordination of deaf mutes' arose for discussion, and it was unanimously resolved that when qualified deaf men were found, they should be ordained. At that time, there were three ordained deaf men in America (Austin Mann, Henry Syle and Koehlr). The Rev. Mann used a pad of paper, like the ordinary deaf, but he wrote upside-down, so that the words could be read by the other as they were written rapidly.[14] In Britain, there were two deaf clergymen – Edward Rowlands (Glamorgan, ordained 1882) and Richard Pearce (Winchester, ordained 1885).

The 'Reverend' Maurice FitzGerald Hewson, of 2 Leeson Park, Dublin, died on 2 April 1919 from diabetes at the age 77, and the work of the Dublin Deaf and Dumb Association was continued by his sister, Miss Hewson, on a temporary basis.

Deaf Links with Monkstown, Co. Dublin

On 30 June 1882, a meeting for the purpose of advocating the Mission work amongst the Deaf and Dumb was held in the large Vestry Room, Monkstown, the Rev. Canon Peacocke, presiding. Representatives of the two associations which carry on the work in Ireland, including several deaf and dumb persons, were present. Mr J. Scott Hutton of Halifax Institution for the Deaf and Dumb, Nova Scotia, attended. Mr Maurice Hewson signed the hymn *Rock of Ages*, and explained the difficulty of teaching the Deaf and Dumb and the necessity of Missions to reach out to the deaf. While Mr Hutton was speaking to the hearing people, Mr Hewson and Mr Robert Lyons addressed the Deaf and Dumb alternately in the finger and sign language. The meeting concluded with the doxology, and the ladies presented bunches of flowers to each of the Deaf and Dumb, having had treated them to strawberries and cakes before the meeting.

DONATION FORM.

To the Hon. Treasurer,
MISSION TO THE ADULT DEAF AND DUMB
OF EIRE (DUBLIN AREA).

Dear Sir,

I enclose herewith my donation of £....................
for the ELLIOTT INSTITUTE FOR PROTESTANT DEAF AND DUMB.

Signed ....

Address ....

....

....

Date.....................................

FORM OF BEQUEST.

MISSION TO THE ADULT DEAF AND DUMB
OF EIRE (DUBLIN AREA)

I bequeath to the Treasurer for the time being the sum of...............................
pounds, free of all duty, including Estate Duty on such part of legacy as is payable out
of the proceeds of the sale of real estate, to be applied to the general uses and
purposes of the PROTESTANT MISSION TO ADULT DEAF AND DUMB OF EIRE
(DUBLIN AREA), and I declare that the receipt of the Treasurer for the time being
of the said Association be a sufficient discharge for the same.

AN APPEAL FOR £3,000

To establish in Dublin an Institute for
PROTESTANT DEAF AND DUMB
IN EIRE.

CASTLES IN THE AIR ARE TOO OFTEN THE MISFORTUNE OF THE DEAF AND DUMB.

DREAMS WILL NOT **BUILD**
WE NEED REAL **BRICKS**
WE NEED REAL **MORTAR**
TO ESTABLISH AN INSTITUTE
SOMETHING LIKE THIS

WILL YOU HELP?

THE IRISH
DEAF-MUTE ADVOCATE,
AND
JUVENILE INSTRUCTOR.

EDITED BY MISS HEWSON.

No. 2. FEBRUARY, 1886. Vol. I.

Christ Church Cathedral, Dublin.

Printed for Dublin Protestant Deaf and Dumb Association.

METROPOLITAN HALL.

DUBLIN.

Price One Penny, or One Shilling and Sixpence per Annum, including Postage.

Periodical produced for circulation amongst the deaf in Ireland and in Britain

DUBLIN PROTESTANT DEAF AND DUMB ASSOCIATION.

Lecture Hall, Reading Room, and Office,

Metropolitan Hall, Lower Abbey Street, Dnblin.

SERVICES FOR THE DEAF AND DUMB,

IN THE FINGER AND SIGN LANGUAGE.

ARE HELD ON

Sunday Mornings, at Eleven o'clock, a. m.

Sunday Evenings, at Half-past Seven o'clock, p. m.

LECTURES AND READING ROOM.

Lectures on instructive and amusing subjects are delivered on Wednesday Evenings at half-past Eight o'clock. The Reading-room is open free to all deaf and dumb.

The Committee would be thankful to receive grants of such publications as the *Sunday at Home, Leisure Hour, Good Words, Illustrated London News, Graphic, British Workman, Band of Hope Review*, the local or other papers.

MAURICE F. G. HEWSON,
Missionary and Secretary.

Notice from *The Irish Deaf-Mute Advocate and Juvenile Instructor*

In 1920, upon the recommendation of the Archbishop of Dublin, the Dublin District of the Mission for the Adult Deaf and Dumb was amalgamated with the Cork District. The Missionary was the **Rev. Frederick A. Elliott** *(see picture)*, himself deaf, but retaining some speech. His range of tasks was wide, visiting the isolated deaf in their country homes, organising Bible classes, church services and annual reunions in Cork and in Dublin, sourcing employment and lodgings for the deaf, organising Sales of Work and bazaars to raise funds for the Mission, as well as holding down the curacy in St Audeon's, Dublin. He died in 1930 after an illness brought on by overwork, having travelled all over the country, taking on both Dublin and Southern Districts of the Mission. Upon his

wishes, he was buried in St. Luke's Churchyard, Douglas, Cork, with his first wife, Edith Anna Kathleen (neé Lyntham) who died in 1917 at the age of 24. He was the last deaf person to have been appointed as a licensed clergyman of the Church of Ireland.

Born in Dublin, younger son of the Rev. Alexander Elliott, Methodist minister by profession, Frederick Elliott became deafened by fever. At the age of 28, he entered Trinity College Dublin in 1891 and graduated with a B.A. degree in 1895. After undertaking Divinity Testimonium in 1896, and graduating with a M.A. in 1904; he was ordained priest in 1905. He was licensed to be preacher in the Diocese of Cork as part of the missionary work among the Deaf 1903. From 1911 onwards, he was curate of St Peters, Cork; and in 1920 he was transferred to Dublin and his residence was in Rathgar until his death in 1930.

He was so highly regarded by both deaf and hearing, that the Committee of the Mission to the Adult Deaf and Dumb in Dublin proposed to raise funds to source a building to house the Mission to be named, in his memory, as 'The Elliott Institute'. Unfortunately though inevitably, this proposal had not taken effect, primarily due to the gradual decline in the number of Protestant deaf people in south of Ireland.

Sale of Work at Rathmines, Dublin, c.1924
Rev. F. Elliott (centre), with former and present pupils of the Claremont Institution

On 1 July 1884, the Bazaar and Sale of Work was opened at the Metropolitan Hall, Lower Abbey Street, Dublin, by the Countess of Aberdeen, accompanied by Princess Edward of Saxe-Weimer and Lady Ridley. *The Irish Times* reported that 'the bazaar looked very picturesque with the gaily decorated stalls, laden with a great variety of fancy wares, including Mountmellick lace. A large quantity of handsome work was displayed, and attracted a good many purchasers.' There were a number of raffles, and Miss Hewson of 26 Upper Fitzwilliam Street was in charge of the general arrangements, assisted by ladies. In the evening, there was a good attendance, and recitations in sign language were given by some deaf men, with the 'whole scene being animated and gay'. The proceeds of the Sale of Work went towards the aid of the Dublin Deaf and Dumb Association, which, during the winter, gave a 'great deal of timely relief to a number of deaf mutes who were out of employment owing to the depression of trade'.

Some of the deaf who could not obtain employment had no option but to move either to Belfast or to England. In the columns of some periodicals such as *The Messenger* or *The British Deaf and Dumb Monthly*, names of former pupils of Claremont were listed, indicating their new locations outside Ireland.

Gospel Services for the Deaf and Dumb

Mr George Orr of Dublin and Mr Evans of London organised the Gospel meetings, where the 'messages' were to be based on the authority of the Bible itself, and not accountable to the Protestant denominations. It had some features of the 'Plymouth Brethren', a splinter group which separated from the Church of Ireland under the leadership of John Nelson Darby.[15] On 20 November 1893, at the Dublin Protestant Deaf and Dumb Association's rooms in Lower Abbey Street, there was 'fair attendance, though not so large as at first expected', at the meeting of the Debating Society, just formed, owing to a 'new mission under the Plymouth Brethren being got up by Mr Evans of London, which had unfortunately thrown the deaf and dumb into confusion.'

While maintaining a boot-repairing business in Dublin, Mr Orr and his wife provided an 'open house' for deaf adults, most of them former pupils of Claremont. While in England, he provided Bible teaching and was one of the speakers at the Conferences for the deaf in Sheffield. In Leicester, he established a Deaf Christian group which continued after his death in 1931.

At the Gospel Conference for the Deaf in Sheffield, England
Mr George Orr, Dublin, seated at left
and Mr Evans, London, seated at right.

Tom Ireland

Born on 7 March 1880 in Inistioge, Co. Kilkenny, Tom was one of eight children and his father was a caretaker, and he had a deaf sister, Elizabeth. Thomastown Union paid for their maintenance at Claremont. After leaving Claremont, he became apprentice to the French-polishing trade at Suir Valley Saw Mills. Some time later, he moved to Dublin and obtained employment in Varian Brush Works, Dublin. Having a keen interest in the Bible, he regularly attended the Bible meetings for the deaf, and occasionally arranged for a clergyman with proficiency in sign language to interpret the 'hearing' meetings at various locations. He travelled around the country in Ireland, and to England, to interact with the deaf sharing similar interests.

In 1930, the Rev. Frederick Elliott, deaf Missioner in the Dublin district, died, and his replacement was a hearing clergyman, the Rev. V.J. Walker. This did not go down well for Tom Ireland. Over several years, he wrote to the committee of the Mission, seeking permission to speak at the services for the deaf and each time the reply was that 'this matter was under consideration.' In December 1942, Tom Ireland had again written challenging the Scriptural authority for an ordained ministry. The Chaplain, the Rev. Walker, replied stating that 'no good would come of entering into a controversy and telling him that he would be welcome at the Mission at any time.'[16]

Deaf Service under Merrion Hall, Dublin

According to Jack Stanton, around 200 deaf and their friends congregated in the basement hall under Merrion Hall, which used to be the largest Gospel Hall established in the 1860s by the Plymouth Brethern. Close to No. 1 Merrion Square, which used to be the home of Sir William Wilde, aurist and oculist, this Hall had since then been converted into a hotel, having been renamed the Davenport Hotel. In the 1950s, the deaf Christians, including Tom Ireland, and some from Northern Ireland, attended meetings at Parkgate Hall, formerly the Soldiers' Institute, in Parkgate Street, close to the main entrance of Phoenix Park.

Mission to the Adult Deaf and Dumb in Cork

In 1882, Francis Maginn was asked by Mrs Kingstone, whose husband was Governor of Cork Gaol, if he could conduct bible classes for the deaf adults in the schoolroom of Christ Church, Cork. Her interest in the spiritual welfare for the deaf was due to her sister, Wilhelmina Tredennick, who established the Institute for the Adult Deaf in Belfast, superintending the residential facilities for the deaf women in the same city. In the following year, several gentlemen from England and America were in Cork while en route to attend the International Conference of Teachers of the Deaf in Brussels and also the Convention of the Society of Adult Deaf Mutes in Great Britain and Ireland. Among the visitors were the two deaf gentlemen: Mr Benjamin Payne (Swansea) and Mr G.F. Healey (Liverpool), and from America were the Rev. Thomas Gallaudet, minister of St Ann's Church for the Deaf, New York, and the Rev. A. Mann, himself deaf. During their stay a special service was held at St Finbarr's Cathedral, and in the evening, a public meeting was held, where it was decided to establish the Mission for the Adult Deaf in Cork, with the Rev. Dr. R. Gregg as President, and Robert Stewart Lyons, deaf, as Missionary.

Robert Stewart Lyons

From Newtownstewart, Co. Tyrone, Robert S. Lyons was admitted to Claremont in 1861. His father wrote to Mr Chidley, headmaster, thanking him for the progress his son made at Claremont, enclosing £5 sterling to assist in the 'support of the very valuable Institution.' Robert decided to go into missionary work for the deaf, and later became the catechist of the northern district of the Mission. At the church service at Ballyshannon, Co. Donegal, he signed the sermon for 27 deaf persons.

In September 1882 Robert Lyons commenced studies at the National Deaf-Mute College, Washington D.C. Francis Maginn joined him for studies at the College from 1884 onwards. Three years later, the diary of the Rev. T. Gallaudet read: 'May 1, 1885: I saw Mr Lyons and Mr Maginn, students, on board a steamer for Belfast. Mr Lyons had been forced to leave the college on account of serious illness.' His father wrote to Gallaudet that Robert died at home on 5 June, and that 'he was loved and respected by all who knew him, his funeral being one of the largest in the country for years'.[17]

Mr W. J. McCormick, missionary, reported as follows. At a well-attended meeting at Rathkeale, Co. Limerick, in October 1896, the Rev. Wills, rector, was 'in grand form and performed the duties of chairman and interpreter with an ease and grace that would astonish some of the clever interpreters of Belfast.' The meeting in Tralee was a 'great success, the schoolroom being completely filled. Archdeacon Orpen, nephew of Dr Orpen, takes a keen interest in this mission.' At Adare, the Rev. Canon O'Brien is a 'real friend of the mutes'. He visited Mr and Mrs Maunsell, Patrick's Well, whose two boys, both deaf and dumb, were 'being instructed in the pure oral method. They read my lips fairly well.'

Francis Maginn (*see picture*), son of the Rev. Charles Maginn, rector of Killanully, Co. Cork, was born on 21 April 1861 in Mallow, Co. Cork. He became deaf at the age of five from scarlet fever, and he was nine years old when he was sent to the Bermondsey Asylum for the Deaf, south London, as a parlour boarder, with Mr Richard Elliott, as headmaster. Displaying a high level of intelligence, he became a pupil teacher at the Asylum. Keen to improve his own education, he applied for admission into the National Deaf Mute College and travelled there in September 1884, in company of Robert Lyons. After bringing the ill Lyons home to Ireland in 1885, Maginn undertook the mission tour of the country, having witnessed the appalling conditions undertaken by the deaf, such as lack of employment, religious and social support, and the general apathy in the neighbouring communities.

In 1887, upon the death of his father, Maginn left America, before completing his course, and was appointed Missionary, working under the sanction of the Primate of all Ireland and the Bishops of the Church of Ireland. He was to spend six months in Cork and then six months in Belfast. At the close of that year, it was decided that 'during 1888 Mr Maginn shall spend three months in Cork and nine months in the Northern district, and shall visit the country deaf mutes in their homes during the summer months'. While Maginn was absent from Cork, several ladies looked after the deaf. Miss Austen took charge of the Sunday and weekly Bible classes. Miss Fleming wrote a letter to each of the deaf every month, and Miss Warren taught the women and girls needlework. Owing to the expansion of the Belfast branch of the Mission, Maginn found it difficult to give time to the deaf in the southern part of the country.

Maginn's work involved a substantial amount of sourcing employment and lodgings for the deaf, a few of whom travelled from Dublin and south of Ireland. He represented Ireland at Conferences for the Missioners for the Deaf, the International Congress for Educators of the Deaf in Paris and the annual meetings of the British Deaf and Dumb Association, which was formed in 1890 after his proposal for 'an Association of the deaf, powerful in its members and unity', commenting that 'in the Kingdom there are about 20,000 mutes and here is no organised association for their educational, moral and social interests'.[18]

Giving evidence at the Conference of the Headmasters of Institutions for the Deaf and Dumb in 1881, Maginn said that there were 'teachers signed to my fellow pupils interesting and instructive stories and these enlightened our minds and delighted us as well. (…) Hundreds of deaf mutes, like myself, had received a good education in the French (sign) and Combined (sign and lip-reading) System schools. I do not believe in avoiding what is commonly called the natural language of the deaf-mute. In the lower classes, I think signs should be encouraged for the sake of development of intelligence, but in the higher classes, a free use of them should be deplored, and the pupils should converse more in the finger language.'[19]

In 1911, Francis Maginn was conferred with the honorary degree of Bachelor of Divinity by Gallaudet College on account of his work among the deaf in Ireland. At that meeting, Maginn retorted that the maxim, 'all men are born free and equal', was nonsense, and insisted that the deaf had a still greater claim on the State for education, being, through no fault of their own, shut out from ordinary schools. He further pointed out that the deaf must be educated before they could be helped, and that language, most needed by the deaf, was neglected. He said that, upon inquiries about the type of jobs obtained by the deaf after leaving school, it was mostly as tailors, shoe-makers and french-polishers, and he thought that the deaf should branch out for better and more skilled jobs. For several years, he had campaigned for better education for the deaf, after having seen for himself, while in America, the better standards of education and employment experienced by the deaf there. Maginn informed the meeting that the deaf suffered hardship through the Workmen's Compensation Act. Before the Act was passed, Maginn was able to get work for many deaf men in Belfast as iron-moulders, dressers, etc. but now he could not do that, with the insurance companies 'closing the door against the deaf'. He referred to the difficulty which men and women who lost hearing late in life had in obtaining employment, saying that the 'door was closed to the deaf in the colonies' (Australia and Canada).[20]

In January 1898, Francis Maginn married a hearing lady, daughter of Mr R.C. McCleane of Rathgar, Dublin, and a social function was held at the Mission Hall for the Adult Deaf and Dumb, at Fisherwick Place, Belfast, to welcome them from their wedding trip. After the presentation of gifts and tributes in recognition of his work for the deaf, Maginn replied, 'Whatever work God has enabled me to do during my residence in Belfast has been made easy by your co-operation and by the help most unselfishly by other workers. If my deafness has drawn me closer to you, then I bless God for the affliction which has become my strength'. Then Mrs Maginn expressed her own thanks in a 'few well-chosen words spelled on the fingers'.[21] In December 1918, Francis Maginn died after a short illness and was buried in City Cemetery, Belfast. His grave was unmarked until in the year of 1990, the deaf in Belfast raised funds to erect a headstone in black marble with an inscription in gold letters – 'A friend to the Deaf'.

In the year of 1890, Mr Bence was appointed catechist for the Southern district (Cork), and in 1895, he was replaced by **W.J. McCormick** *(see picture)* of Belfast. Born 25 January 1862, McCormick showed talent in music and was studying for a degree in 1893 when he became totally deaf. In the following year, he decided to become missionary to the deaf. His work consisted of holding a Sunday afternoon service in the Christ Church School, Cork, visiting the deaf in the more distant parts of his district, and addressing public meetings in Cork and elsewhere, making appeals on behalf of the Mission to the Adult Deaf and Dumb. He wrote most detailed reports on his work for *The Silent Messenger*, which provided valuable information on former pupils of Claremont and other deaf people in Ireland. By 1898, he had 124 voluntary collectors, and a Mission hall was opened in Marlborough Street, Cork.

Annual reunions were organised for the deaf from the distant parts of the Southern district, preceded by a special service in St Mary Shandon Church, and concluding with tours by train or car to interesting places, such as Youghal, Fota Park, and Cobh. In December 1899, McCormick left Cork to take up a post as Missionary to the Deaf in Oldham, England. In January 1900, he married Miss B.J. Williams of Cork, who had been assisting with the work of the Mission in Cork since 1892. The departure of Mr and Mrs McCormick from Cork had been a heavy loss for the Mission.[22] He was replaced by the **Rev. Frederick A. Elliott**, who had been deaf at a young age. From 1900 to 1920, he ministered to the deaf in Southern District. In 1919, after the death of Maurice Hewson, the deaf Missionary, the Archbishop of Dublin asked the committee of the Southern District to permit the Rev. Elliott to take on responsibility for the Adult deaf in the Dublin area as well as for Cork. In 1930, the Rev. Elliott died in Dublin.

From 1930 to 1939, the mission work in Cork was taken up by Miss Gladys Williams, and after her, Miss Campbell from 1939 to 1974. By then the work for the Southern district was amalgamated with that covering the Dublin district. As well as organising church services and annual reunions for the Adult Deaf, the Missionaries looked after the needs of the young deaf members of the Church of Ireland. Some of them were usually referred to Claremont for education, and occasionally the Secretary of the Institution asked the Missionary regarding the ability of parents of prospective pupils to pay the school fees. Upon request, the Missionary sent progress reports on the pupils and school-leavers, and sourced employment and accommodation for some of the former pupils. Occasionally, the Missionary would meet the deaf passengers disembarking off the steamers at Cobh en route from England, Europe and America.

ANNUAL GATHERING OF THE DEAF AT CORK.

The above picture was taken outside the School-house of St Mary's Shandon, Cork, on 20 July 1906. According to the report in *The Messenger*, it was a 'most successful and enjoyable function.' These reunions had been organised for sixteen years, and the deaf, numbering 36, came from thirteen counties of Ireland. They arrived by the evening trains the day before the reunion, and were 'hospitably entertained until the following day, the Mission bearing the expense'. A substantial breakfast was held in the School-room, followed with Divine Service in the nearby church. Mr Bright-Lucas, a deaf gentleman who moved to Cork from England, interpreted the first part, Mr McCormick the sermon, and Mr Francis Maginn, the remainder of the service.

At the conclusion, the group gathered outside for the photo shoot, and then to the School-room for dinner. Afterwards, a hired electric tram conveyed the party to Passage Railway Station for the train to Monkstown, where the steamer awaited passengers for the journey to Crosshaven and back. Returning to St Mary's Shandon for tea, after which followed the speeches and then games which went on till ten o'clock in the evening. All the country deaf had left for their homes on Saturday afternoon. Mr McCormick conducted the service at the Mission Hall in Marlboro Street in the city of Cork, on the following Sunday, 22 July. He had left Cork in 1899 to take the position of Missioner in Oldham, England.

Samuel Bright Lucas (1840-1919)

Deaf himself, and an acclaimed water-colour artist with exhibitions at the Royal Academy, he was Secretary of the Royal Association in Aid of the Deaf and Dumb and also of the Charitable and Provident Society for granting pensions to the aged and infirm Deaf and Dumb. In 1900, he married a lady, Mrs Parker, from Passage West, Cork, and moved there. Elected onto the Committee of the Mission to the Adult Deaf and Dumb, he assisted with interpreting for the deaf at the services at St Mary Shandon and other churches in Cork. He died there in 1919 after a short illness.[23]

Charles Radcliff

Son of the Rev. Stephen Radcliff, rector of Lisnadill, Co. Armagh, Charles Radcliff was admitted in October 1867 to Claremont as Intermediate pupil, his father, to pay £20 per annum. Having talents for art, he trained in the 'Art of Design'. For over 25 years, he worked as an Art Designer for the linen and damask manufacturers, McCrum, Watson & Mercer at Milford, Co. Armagh. He was involved in mission work in Northern Ireland, assisting with meetings in Banbridge, Portadown and Armagh. He had received support and encouragement from the Primate of All Ireland. In 1903, he married a deaf lady, Jeanie Dickson. After contacting typhoid fever, Charles died on 19 February 1905, at the age of 44, leaving a widow and an infant son. The funeral at Lisnadill was largely attended by some members from the Ulster Society for the Adult Deaf and Dumb.[24]

Visits of the Rev. Thomas Gallaudet to Ireland

In 1883, the Rev. Thomas Gallaudet, New York, visited Cork while en route from Brussels, where he attended the International Congress for Educators of the Deaf and Dumb. In 1888, he made a return visit to Ireland and again in the following year. In July 1895, accompanied by the Rev. Austin Mann, deaf himself, he went to Dublin for the Congress of the British Deaf and Dumb Association at the Metropolitan Hall, Lower Abbey Street. By invitation of the Archbishop, Lord Coyningham Plunkett, members of the Congress went to the garden party in Connaught House, Bray, Co. Wicklow. In September, the Rev. Gallaudet enjoyed hospitality in Belfast and then in Bundoran as guest of Mrs Johnston, sister of Miss Tredennick. On Sunday, 22 September, he was staying with the Rev. Dowse, rector of Monkstown, Co. Dublin. At the service there, the Rev. Gallaudet spoke about the work of the Mission to the Deaf and Dumb in Dublin. In October, he was at the annual reunion of the Deaf and Dumb from the south of Ireland, held in St Mary Shandon, Cork. He interpreted the sermon of the Rev. Dr Meade, Bishop of Cork. The social gathering took place in the nearby school-house. After preaching at Queenstown (Cobh), Co. Cork, the Rev. Gallaudet left Ireland for Wales.

22

'Talent for Drawing'

'drawing may be made an important agent in communication'
Dr John Ringland and Mr John Gelston[1]

History has instances of instructed deaf people in art. Pliny tells us that Quintus Pedius, a relative of Caesar Augustus and deaf from birth, was proficient in painting. In the middle of the sixteenth century, a deaf artist, Juan Fernando Navaretti, surnamed El Mudo, established a reputation in Spain because of the works of his pencil, with which he could 'speak'. Many deaf people, in compensation for the lack of hearing, are exceptionally observant and, therefore, pay more attention to detail when executing works of art. They utilise the skill of drawing when describing the events while conversing with hearing people.

Two women at work in the Waterford area, by Sampson Towgood Roch, c.1824

Before the establishment in 1816 of the Deaf and Dumb School at Smithfield, Dublin, there had been some Irish Deaf artists who put their talents and creative skills to good use. **Samuel Close** (c.1740-1807) maintained a business as an engraver and jeweller, and some of his illustrations are in the custody of the National Gallery of Ireland, Dublin. **Sampson Towgood Roch** (1759-1847), born deaf near Youghal, Co. Cork, established himself as a miniature painter in Capel Street and then Grafton Street in Dublin. He left in 1792 to take residence in Bath, England, where his business as a miniaturist flourished. Among his works were the miniatures of several members of the Royal Family and aristocrats. Several of his miniatures are in the National Gallery of Ireland and in the Holbourne Museum in Bath. Born in Dublin, **Thomas Cooley** (1795-1872) attended the Braidwood Academy for the Deaf and Dumb in Hackney, London and painted portraits of Irish eminent persons including John Cash, the Lord Mayor of Dublin (1813).[2] His father, Mr Cooley, was on the Committee of the Claremont Institution, and having a talented deaf son provided good publicity for the Institution in their campaign to press home the message to the public for the need of educating the deaf.

In the Deaf school just opened at the House of Industry, some deaf pupils had been noticed to possess considerable talents for drawing and had begun to learn that useful art, partly on Pestalozzi's system, and partly in the ordinary manner, under the direction of Mr Pearce, who had given his assistance free of charge. The pupils appreciated this gesture, as well as the kindness of a lady, who made a collection among her friends to enable Mr Pearce, drawing master, to purchase drawing paper for the boys. The Committee expressed their gratitude to Mr Allen of Dame Street, Dublin, an eminent lithographer (who later took on John Johnson as apprentice) for a generous present of maps and drawing books for the use of the pupils.

At the Annual Meetings during the first half of the nineteenth century, some pupils were asked to demonstrate their skills by drawing pictures on the blackboard. Sometimes, visitors to the Claremont Institution at Glasnevin would purchase specimens of drawings. In the late nineteenth century, some pupils had participated in the Art Exhibitions organised by the Royal Dublin Society, while some pupils had been awarded premiums for excelling at the examinations organised by the South Kensington Branch of the College of Art. In the twentieth century, the Department of Education awarded certificates to the pupils of the Glasnevin School, such as Betty Bateman. Some of the pupils of the Monkstown School had participated in the Texaco Art Competitions, and many prizes had been awarded.

John Johnson

Deaf from birth, John Johnson, aged six, was admitted to the newly-opened Deaf and Dumb School in Smithfield in June 1816. His father was in the police and his residence was in Barrack Street, Dublin. On 31 December 1827, Mr Allen of Dame Street had offered to take Johnson and another pupil as apprentices to lithographic printing if fees to cover lodging and board were provided for. The apprentice fee sought by the masters in the lithographic and printing business was usually £20, which was expensive in those times.

A letter sent by Dr Charles Orpen and published in *Saunders Newsletter* of 7 October 1829 warned the public about an impostor, pretending to be deaf, who called himself by various names, often changing them to prevent detection. He had been travelling about Ireland for the last two or three years, and has been conning considerable sums from the public, by impositions upon their benevolence. At the bottom of this letter was the acknowledgement that this letter was lithographed by John Johnson at Allen's.

John Johnson's illustration of the Banquet at Hillsborough Fort

In 1836, John Johnson had been commissioned to engrave the plates depicting the two 'Gothic Windows' with the English and the Spanish manual alphabets which had been designed by Mr Joseph Humphreys. These illustrations and a picture titled *Profile View or Section of the Organs of Speech to shew the Mechanism of Articulation* were included in Dr Charles Orpen's book, *Anecdotes and Annals of the Deaf and Dumb*.

On 4 October 1837, the marriage of the Earl of Hillsborough, Co. Down, was celebrated with a banquet for the tenants of the Downshire estates at Hillsborough. John Johnson recorded the scene of the banquet in an intricately-detailed illustration showing lines of tables across the lawn surrounded by walls with an arch at the left side and a church steeple in the background. Hand-coloured lithographs were made from these illustrations and copies given to members of the tenantry.[3]

Francis McDonnell (1822-c.1885)

According to *A Dictionary of Irish Artists*, a deaf and dumb artist named Francis McDonnell studied at the Royal Academy School of Sculpture under Constantine Panorma (1805-1852), Sculptor, A.R.H.A. and in 1843 he obtained a prize there. Francis, son of a poor shoemaker, was born at 29 Francis Street, Dublin, in 1822, and was admitted to Claremont in 1830. At the age of sixteen, he was removed from the Institution in 1838. His headmaster, being Mr Humphreys, he had excelled in art, and while young and at home, he must have observed stonemasons carving headstone sculptures in the monumental mason yards that operated in Francis Street, and this may have led him to decide to apply to the School of Modelling, Royal Dublin Society, to study sculpture and drawing. In 1839, he was accepted as a pupil of Panorma and studied under him for a number of years. After completing his studies, he moved to 134 Francis Street and later on, he sent three marble sculptures to the Royal Hibernian Academy of Arts for exhibition.

In 1846, Francis left Dublin and settled at 5 Howland Street, off Fitzroy Square in London. He continued to send paintings and sculptures to the Royal Hibernian Academy for exhibition. One of his paintings, *The First Born*, was exhibited at the Dublin Exhibition of 1853. He contributed another two sculptures to the Royal Academy of Arts in London in 1846 and 1852. Most of his surviving works might have been in private collections as no trace of his work could be found in the National Gallery of Ireland or the National Museum of Ireland. He is presumed to have died in London around 1885.[4]

Lawrence Feagan (1825-1898)

He was born in Drogheda, Co. Louth, in 1825, in the parish of Moore, Listoman, and was deaf from birth. His parents, Sylvester and Mary Feagan, had seven children, and two of them were deaf. Sylvester was a poor labourer. Laurence was admitted to Claremont on 28 July 1836 at the age of eleven. He was there for over six years, and was instructed in art, geography, English, Scripture, and arithmetic. Mr Joseph Humphreys, headmaster, was an excellent artist and draughtsman, and he taught the pupils to draw and etch the pictures.

When Feagan completed education in 1842, he was sent home at the age of 17 years. However, he had run away due to religious persecution and was henceforth maintained by the Juvenile Society. In 1843 employment in the office of the Ordnance Survey was sought for Feagan. In July 1848, he wrote to Mr Foulston, headmaster, seeking employment as drawing master at the Institution. Two months later, Mr Foulston informed the Committee that Feagan was 'capable of executing Scripture illustrations which were required for the use of the School, and also of instructing the teachers and pupils in drawing'. Feagan was appointed for six months and paid £5 for that period. However, Mr Foulston reported that the conduct of Feagan in making sale of his drawings had not been approved, and would have an 'injurious effect on other pupils', and the Headmaster was ordered not to allow the pupils sell samples of their work. In November, the Juvenile Committee reported that Feagan had been bound by the Countess of Clarendon and Lady Domville to an engraver without their knowledge, and requested Mr Foulston to verify that fact. Mr Foulston replied, enclosing some specimens of Feagan's progress in wood engraving, which were considered as 'highly creditable to his artistic skills'.[5] In June 1849, it was agreed that a sum of £5 be paid to Feagan, and in December, he was placed on a regular salary of £10 per annum, his duties to instruct the pupils in etchings and drawings. In January 1850, on Feagan's insistence, his salary was paid on a monthly basis, in line with the assistants.

Sketch of Magdalen Tower, Drogheda, Co. Louth
by L.Feagan (with permission of David Breslin)

In March 1851, Feagan asked for and was granted permission to attend the Drawing Schools of the Dublin Society. In May 1853, Feagan was directed to prepare a lithographic engraving of the Institution to be inserted as a frontispiece for the Annual Reports. In June 1854, he engraved a circular vignette of the Institution for the title page of the Annual Report. In the same year, a letter was received by the Committee from a Mrs Still whether her daughters were learning the art of drawing, and Feagan was directed to commence teaching the two Still girls. Some time later, Feagan objected to teaching Eliza Still in the Girls' Schoolroom, and he was ordered to commence at once to 'teach the little Still'. Two weeks later, the Committee had heard 'with great surprise that Feagan refused to assist in the instruction of the pupils in Mr Edward Clarke's absence', and Feagan was informed that he would be dismissed if he refused to obey the Headmaster's instructions.

In June 1856, Feagan was informed that he was not to go out of Claremont without the permission of Mr Chidley, the headmaster at that time. In the following month, the Committee ordered that Feagan, Feeney (deaf assistant teacher) and Dixon (deaf messenger) be allowed butter and tea for breakfast for the future. In March 1857, Mr Chidley complained of the 'insubordinate conduct' of Feagan, who was then informed that his services would no longer be required in two months' time. In the following year, the Rev. Eccles asked for 'testimonials regarding Laurence Feagan, retired pupil.'

Sketch of Mellifont Abbey, Co. Meath by L. Feagan
(reproduced with permission of David Breslin)

He was fond of travelling and visiting archaeological sites around the country, carrying with him some paper, pens and ink to sketch drawings of ruins, monuments and architectural features. He travelled by horse-drawn carriage and disembarked whenever he noticed an interesting location or feature for sketching. He had red hair and a massive red beard and possessed sharp observation skills for detail and accuracy. He occasionally contributed his pictures to exhibitions, and had produced several pictures featuring prominent buildings and ruins including of St Patrick's Cathedral in Dublin, Mellifont Abbey in Co. Meath, St Lawrence's Gate and Magadalen Tower in Drogheda. In addition to drawings in pen and ink, he produced sketches in pastel, including a portrait of an Arab Boy in his costume, which was presented to the Committee of the Juvenile Association for the Education of the Deaf and Dumb. In 1864 he had sent some sketches of local scenes to the Exhibition of Manufactures, Machinery and Fine Arts organised by the Royal Dublin Society at the New Hall, Kildare Street, Dublin. He died a bachelor in 1898 at the age of 73 years.[6]

George McNaught

Son of William, a Protestant servant, and of Bridget, a Roman Catholic, George McNaught was admitted at the age of seven on 18 February 1853. The observation on the register book was that George was 'a pretty, sprightly and very clever little boy'. In March 1856, his mother was under pressure to move her son to the Cabra Institution by feigning of planning to emigrate to Australia and applying to the Committee to remove her son. However, she was asked to produce tickets for herself and George for their passage before she would be allowed to take her son. The only record of his artistic work was the engraving of the Claremont Institution for use as frontispiece or back cover for the Annual Reports of the Institution.

The following extracts from the Committee Minute Book refer to attempts at obtaining employment for George Naught, spanning over two and half years.

19 November 1861 - An offer was made by Mr Goggin, printer in Limerick, to take McNaught as apprentice with fee and payment for his board and lodging, the sum of £20 which the Committee could not afford.

13 May 1862 – George McNaught has not yet been apprenticed and that there seems no prospect of getting this accomplished. He is 15 years of age and has been in the Institution for nine years.

21 August 1862 - Re George McNaught, with very great artistic taste and remarkable talent for drawing, it would be well to have him bound to an engraver. To see some of the engravers, and Mr Russell to speak to the Archdeacon of Dublin about applying for grant from 'Gardiner's Charity'. (This was Loves and Gardner's Charity which provides financial assistance for children's education in the diocese of Dublin.)

2 April 1863 – Messrs Forsters, Engravers and Chromolithographers at. 2 Crow Street, Dublin, had offered to take George McNaught and teach him the trade of ornamental writing in their establishment, for seven years for the fee of £20. No salary to be paid in the first year, with annual increases up to the seventh year at ten shillings per week.

19 February 1864 – Re removal of G. McNaught from Claremont he being now under weekly salary of Messrs Forster's Engravers, and receiving five shillings per

week and having been kept at the Institution (since 20 May 1863) that a lodging be found for him in Dublin.

18 March 1864 – Chidley made arrangements for McNaught to obtain lodgings outside the Institution.

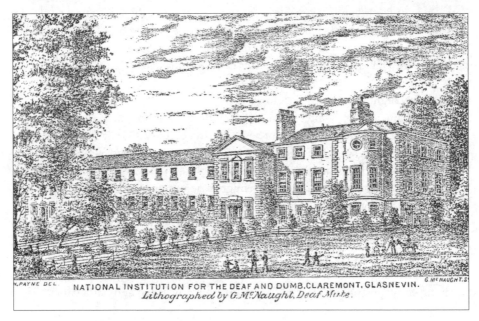

H.PAYNE DEL   NATIONAL INSTITUTION FOR THE DEAF AND DUMB, CLAREMONT, GLASNEVIN.   G. MCNAUGHT.S
Lithographed by G. McNaught, Deaf Mute.

Benjamin Payne

After completing education at Claremont, he remained as Pupil Teacher, and was a most efficient and diligent teacher, and was highly respected by the Headmaster and the staff.   He was one of the Select Vestry of St. Mobhi's Church, Glasnevin. He taught drawing to the pupils at the Institution, and he created a line drawing of the Institution as a frontispiece for the Annual Reports (see above picture). He left Claremont to take up the position of Principal of the Cambrian Institution for the Deaf and Dumb in Swansea, Wales.

Betty Bateman

Born in Queenstown (now Cobh), Co. Cork, Betty Bateman was admitted to Claremont at the age of six years on 5 January 1926. Her father, George, a gardener at Fota Park, was in a position to pay £15 to £20 to the Institution for Betty's maintenance and clothing. However, financial circumstances were reduced at home, and in August 1928, an application on behalf of Mr Bateman was made to the United Services Fund (Irish Area) in Harcourt Street, Dublin, which resulted with a grant of £7 10s as a contribution towards the maintenance of Betty for one year. In October 1928, Betty who had been a paying pupil since 1926, was transferred to the Free Pupil Roll.

Left: Betty with her brothers, William and Abner

In January 1933, Miss Deacon, Head-mistress, suggested that Betty Bateman be allowed to attend the drawing lessons at the School of Art for five months with two lessons per week at a fee 17/6 each. This was agreed on condition that the Headmistress accompanies her for the first week or two, and after that as often as possible. On 30 June 1933, a set of drawings done by Betty Bateman was inspected by the Governors who considered that these drawings might be exhibited at the Royal Dublin Society Art Exhibition. On 12 January 1934, it was agreed to authorise the Headmistress to allow Betty to take a further term's drawing at the School of Art. The next year, Betty was allowed to take a further course of instruction, and in 1937, she was awarded several Art Certificates by the Department of Education Technical Instruction Branch. On 9 September 1937, the Committee was notified that Betty had left the Institution after the summer holidays, and was with her relatives in London.

She met her future husband, Stephen Taylor, at a club for the deaf in Kentish Town, London. Partially deaf at the age of eight years after contacting scarlet fever, Stephen attended a school in Birkenhead, and then Royal School for the Deaf in Margate, before transferring to a school for the deaf in Plaistow, London. They had four daughters. A few years before her death in October 2000, Betty Taylor (née Bateman) had paid a visit to her old school in Glasnevin. A sample of her artwork is depicted below.

23

Deaf Women

This chapter focuses on another 'hidden' sector of the Deaf community - the Deaf women, unsung heroines in the eyes of those who valued their company, empathy and compassion. It is sad that very little information had been recorded on the experiences and achievements of deaf women who had been at the Claremont Institution. Indeed, it was in the early decades of the nineteenth century when the deaf female teachers at Claremont came into being, before they eventually disappeared by the 1850s. In the Female Branch of the Catholic Institution for the Deaf and Dumb, deaf girls who excelled in education and, in some cases, with no-one to take them back upon completion of education, were retained as teachers at Cabra. There has already been a substantial amount of information recorded by academic researchers and historians on hearing females making their contribution for the welfare of the deaf in many roles – teaching, missionary work, collecting funds and home-visiting, and it is timely to redress the balance by writing this chapter on the deaf women in Ireland themselves.

Charlotte Elizabeth Tonna

Charlotte Elizabeth Tonna[1] was one of the most prolific writers of her day, having produced at least 100 books, poems, articles and magazines. She was born in Norwich on 1 October 1790. Her father was the rector of St Giles' Church, and she had comfortable childhood. She became severely ill at the age of eight and was blind for a short time. She was given doses of mercury, and this caused her deafness at the age of ten. She was a very bright child, listening to adult conversation and reading books. Her deafness cutting her off from social interaction, she spent more time reading and writing. She

Charlotte Elizabeth Tonna

used finger-spelling for communication. At the age of seventeen, she married a soldier, Captain George Phelan. His regiment was sent to Ireland and they lived in Kilkenny. The marriage broke down, and she left her husband.

It was in Ireland that Charlotte took interest in social reform, and was an evangelical Protestant, opposed to Catholicism and its teachings and practices. During her time in Ireland during the early 1820s, the Rockite movement was at its height, where some bands of Catholic young men travelled in some parts of the country, launching attacks on Protestant property and individuals, particularly the landed gentry. In Kilkenny, she started a small school for deaf children. She wrote many tracts and articles, many against popery. Some of her poetry was considered to be amongst the best songs of the Protestant Orange cause, and were listed in anthologies of Irish poetry. She had made a pilgrimage to Vinegar Hill in Co. Wexford, which she regarded as a site of Protestant martyrdom during the 1798 Rising.

Charlotte first became interested in the education of deaf children through meeting Dr Orpen of Dublin. She maintained her friendship with Dr Orpen and an interest in Claremont. She wrote of a meeting with Thomas Collins, formerly a monitor, and then a journeyman printer. She described the deaf as 'shut out from communicating their ideas, except by such signs as they can devise to express themselves (...) until they are brought under instruction'. In her book, *Irish Recollections*, she referred to Major Sirr, Dr Orpen's father-in-law. She described him as 'that loyal Protestant soldier, Major Sirr, who maintained a collection of antiquities, natural curiosities and specimens of the rocks in Achill.' She referred to the Rev. Edward Nangle's mission in Achill, where some of the converts from Catholicism spent their time in a specially designed, self-supporting community, with its own local newspaper, *The Achill Herald*. A couple of deaf children, from Achill, had been sent to Claremont with financial support from the Rev. Edward Nangle.

In the Schoolroom were the classes of children of varying ages and abilities. Some of the classes had monitors and monitresses, who were generally senior pupils with reasonable capacity of intelligence and discipline. In the early years of the Institution, the male monitors were Thomas Collins and William Brennan, while in the Female School, the monitresses were Anne McCormick, Charlotte Riddall and Cecilia White. In due time, their roles were upgraded to assistant teachers. There was mention of a bedstead with the word 'Monitress' inscribed on it, so it appeared that the monitors and monitresses had to sleep in the dormitories, to supervise the children, since both sexes were accommodated in the same building, requiring vigilant supervision. There was mention of the windows in the girls' rooms and in the boys' yard fitted with bars, to prevent unsupervised interaction between the male and female pupils.

Mon-i-tress.

Deaf Servants

It was usual practice for young girls from poor families to obtain employment in domestic service, and deaf girls were no exception. Some of the sponsors obtained positions in the 'Big House' in their locality for their protégées. These were usually the wives of the landed gentry, the nobility and the clerical and professional classes.

On 26 February 1829, Miss Briscoe had applied on behalf of Mrs Perry for a deaf girl, Barbara Doyne, as a housemaid on trial for a time with liberty to send her back. In the following month, Dr Charles Orpen reported that Mrs Perry had declined to take Barbara as her servants objected to having a deaf and dumb girl in the house. The unfortunate girl, with

Maid-ser-vant.

no friends willing to receive her, was finally apprenticed on 24 March 1830 to a dress-maker in the country, a benevolent lady having contributed £10 as fee for indoor apprenticeship of three years.

In 1843, according to the timetable at school for the week, girls were assigned tasks of mending, housework and, on Saturday evenings, washing. Some girls, particularly those without family or friends, remained at Claremont, after completing their education, either as servants, laundresses or assistant cooks. Some of the girls were apprenticed to Mrs Saurin's Training Institution for Servants, 101 St Stephen's Green, Dublin. In the year of 1856, it was stated that all washing of the Establishment was done by the girls, under conduct of one of the former pupils, an excellent trained laundress, who, being a destitute orphan, was engaged by the Committee, two years since, at the salary of £2 per annum, to direct the laundry. 'The snowy whiteness of the counterpanes and other clothes shows how thoroughly the (female pupils) have learned to wash. The account book kept at the Laundry showed 28,484 articles had been cleaned – sheets, blankets, quilts, bedticks, heavy articles.'[2]

Most headmasters at Claremont employed former pupils as their servants. Mr James Foulston asked the Committee for permission to employ Mary Frahill when she completed her term of education. When the Foulstons left Claremont in 1856, she went with them to England. A few years later, the Committee received a letter from Mrs Foulston that Mary Frahill had decided to emigrate to Australia.

A Faithful Servant

Some of the deaf servants had been highly valued by their mistresses and their families, including those connected with Claremont, including Dr Orpen. Most of the headmasters during the nineteenth century took on former pupils as part of the household. On 21 July 1838, Catherine Connolly, aged twelve years, had been sent to Claremont by Mrs Molloy and the Viscountess Lorton, patroness of the Dorset Institution in Sackville Street, Dublin. On 20 June 1844, she was removed from the Institution, having completed her term of education. At an annual meeting in April 1861, a letter was read from Miss Molloy of Oakport Cottage, Boyle, Co. Roscommon, referring to the intelligence, usefulness and exemplary behaviour of Catherine Connolly, at that time in her service. Roman Catholic by birth, she had adopted the Protestant faith, after some time at Claremont. She believed in working diligently and hard, often rising at four o'clock in the morning on Mondays and get the whole week's washing done by nine o'clock. She took on the usual tasks with enthusiasm, and loved to give attention to the family and their friends. She took great pleas-

CATHERINE.

ure in her mistress' children, and she had always some cakes for them. At one time, the nurse was ill, a boy aged two years woke up in the morning and climbed into Catherine's bed and put his little fingers on her eyelids in order to wake her up. He was able to understand the sign language, and this delighted Catherine.

When the family lived abroad, Catherine learnt to understand the value of the different kinds of foreign money. She liked going to the market, and was able to bargain with the Germans. The people in the market were amused at her sharp ways, and her knowledge of the price and quality of butter, eggs, vegetables, fowls, etc. They often gave her presents of fruit and sweets, which she brought home and divided amongst the other servants. When the family left Germany for France, she took interest in everything that passed around her, and was quick at finding out all the news of the place. She liked to be present at Morning Prayers, and followed the reading in her own Bible. She was most generous, and thought nothing of giving away money. She always sent money to her poor relations in Ireland.

Owing to disturbances in Europe, the family had to move to England and stayed at a friend's house which had a number of servants. Catherine criticised these English servants: 'Eat much, work little'. She remarked about the 'grand dinners and suppers the servants had in the kitchen'. She read everyone's character that came into the house. At one time she was called 'dummy', which was a great offence in her eyes.

In France the people spoke of her as 'madame'. Whenever she wanted to speak to her mistress, she was so enthusiastic that she forgot about other people speaking to the lady of the house at the same time. Catherine was one of the most attentive sick-nurses. She could almost guess what was wanted. If any anyone was ill, she would walk on tip-toe and look to see what could be done for the invalid. She would bring a cup of tea, just at the right time. At one time, when her mistress was ill, she sat beside her bed all night. The mistress used to speak on Catherine's hand in the dark if she wanted anything, and the deaf servant would understand at once. She had been in faithful service for 40 years.[3]

Sarah Russell Darby[4]

Sarah Russell was born at Spitalfields, Dublin, on 21 August 1821. Her father, Alexander Russell, was a silk-weaver. She had several brothers and sisters, and she found that she was not like them, as they could hear and speak and so could enjoy themselves talking and laughing together, while she was deaf. She was sent to the Dublin Day School for the deaf and dumb in Sackville Street, Dublin, and there Sarah went regularly every morning for some time. She was afterwards sent to the Claremont Institution at Glasnevin where she remained for several years. Miss Simpson, senior teacher of deaf girls at Claremont, wrote, 'she was always a steady, well-principled, good girl. She often came to me in after years, and I had always a very high opinion of her, being convinced that she was influenced by the Holy Spirit, and endeavouring to lead a life pleasing to the Lord'.

On leaving Claremont, she went to live with her widowed mother, brother and sister. But after some time, they went to Australia, and she was left alone. She was not strong enough to become a servant and she did not know where to look for employment as a needlewoman. She was alone in Dublin, without money, and no friend to whom she could look for support. She prayed more earnestly to God, and a gentleman, in whose employment her brother had been, gave her a cottage containing one room, rent free. Some ladies gave her needlework to do.

She was kind and affectionate, and was willing to help others. Indeed she had been known to pawn her things to get money to give away to persons poorer than herself. It made her happy to help others, so her neighbours loved her. Her employers also respected her on account of her upright and truthful character. She was very clever and industrious, but she would not always get enough work to do. In winter, when food and fuel were dear, she was frail and the cold often made her ill. Many times, kind friends, visiting her in her little room, found her ill in bed, with no fire in the grate, or food in the cupboard. She never complained. There was one lady who regarded Sarah so highly, that whenever she heard she was ill, she would arrange for her brought to her own house, and nurse her herself till she was better. Sometimes, she was sent to the hospital and she went back to her own home to work as soon as she was able, as she did not like to live on charity. In July 1871, she married Joseph

Darby, but their married life was cut short, and she was again living alone in her little cottage, trying to support herself, as in her early years, by needlework.

Deaf Nurses

In June 1888, Dr Francis Xavier McCabe, Medical Commissioners of Local Government Board for Ireland, informed the Royal Commissioners that 'because my experience is that in all the workhouses where I have met with a few adult deaf and dumb; they were generally employed in the sick wards as nurses. They make very good nurses; they are very quiet, and they can see what they are doing, and they get the extra allowances, so that they are slightly better off'.[5]

On 20 February 1833, Dr Orpen reported to the Committee that Catherine Carey (pupil), who had been in Whitworth Hospital, had while there stolen half a crown from one of the patients and had also gone with two other patients and one of the deaf girls also in hospital into the men's ward, and had also, since her return to Claremont, written a 'nonsensical love letter' to some person at the hospital. It was resolved that since she was so advanced in years that she could not be subject to discipline, her friends (sponsors) be advised to remove her from Claremont.

Deaf Female Assistant Teachers

In 1837, in the London Asylum for the Deaf, the 'first female deaf teacher was appointed, and a second one was appointed one year later'.[6] In fact, it was 1824 when a former pupil was appointed at Claremont, whose story follows.

Anne McCormick

Her parents were Henry, a harness-maker, who emigrated to America, and Mary, residing in South Main Street in the parish of Christ Church, Cork. On 16 April 1820, she was admitted to the Institution at age of twelve, supported by the Cork Auxiliary Society and by her mother, who pledged to pay ten pounds and clothing. She was intelligent, having received education at school and at home before admission to Claremont. In March 1824, Mr Humphreys was authorized by the Committee to employ her as an assistant teacher in the Girls' School. She was to take meals with the Matron, and Mr Humphreys was granted £20 a year for her board, and £8 for her salary.

Mr Wyon, one of the Committee members, said in his letter dated February 1833,

'I visited the Deaf and Dumb Institution at Claremont on Friday ... I was highly satisfied with the clean appearance and regular order of the schoolrooms. I had a long conversation on the slate with the Schoolmistress (Anne McCormick) who gave me considerable information respecting the education of the children, and I assure you (the Committee) fully impressed with the conviction that everything was done that our means could afford.'

She had been teaching until 1852, when her services and also Charlotte Riddall's were no longer required. She taught privately for a number of years, as well as spending some time in teaching at the Dublin Day School. On retirement, she returned to Cork, where she took part in the religious and social meetings organised by the Mission to the Adult Deaf and Dumb. After ten years until her death, she resided at the Incurables' Home, in the parish of St Luke, Cork. The possessor of a marvellous memory, she would tell for hours entertaining stories about her work at Claremont, the names, characters and careers of her pupils. Many of her pupils were in Cork, to whom she was much attached. Anne McCormick died on 26 June 1900, at the age of 97; and was laid to rest in St Luke's Cemetery at Douglas, Cork.[7]

Charlotte Riddall

An application for Charlotte's admission was received on 8 March 1831, and it was not until December 1832, when she was admitted at the age of eleven, after a vacancy occurred with a boy leaving the Institution. In December 1843, her term of education having expired, she was retained as assistant teacher in the Female School, having been a diligent person around the Institution. In August 1851, Anne McCormick and Charlotte Riddall were informed that their services at Claremont were no longer required, and that their future welfare would be looked after by the Institution.

As Charlotte, herself from Belfast, had no friend who would provide for her or any asylum to receive her, she was boarded out with a lady in Kiltegan, Co. Wicklow, on a trial of three months. In 1852, she wrote to the Institution asking to be taken back. In November 1854, her landlady, Mrs Gillespie, informed the Committee that she would no longer keep Charlotte. In March 1855, she was removed to the Dublin Providence Home, the Institution paying for her maintenance. In 1857, the Matron wrote that 'the doctor recommended change of air for Riddall, who had been in poor health', and she was sent to Greystones for that purpose. In 1861, Charlotte wrote to the Committee about her clothes having been stolen at the Home. In October 1862, the Secretary of the Providence Home informed the Committee of the Claremont Institution that Charlotte Riddall, a resident there for some years, had left to go into private lodgings, where she was working for her living, though in much reduced circumstances. She then received a small pension from the Institution, and died in 1885.

Cecilia White

A deaf orphan, Mary Anne Horan, whose father was shot in war and her mother killed by horse and cart in Parsontown, King's County (Co. Offaly), died from fever at Claremont in June 1821. Her place was taken up by another deaf orphan, Cecilia White, aged eight years, having also lost her father through the Napoleonic Wars, and then becoming destitute after the sudden death of her widowed mother. Her sad case was mentioned at the Annual Charity Sermon by the Rev. B.W. Mathias, rector of the Bethesda Chapel, Dublin. Adherent of the Evangelical Movement, he was one of the most prominent preachers of the time, drawing large crowds. His appeal at the Molyneaux Chapel regarding the plight of the young orphan girl stirred so much excitement that the collection produced a sum of £229, augmented by a private sub-scription specially opened for immediate admission of Cecilia White.

In June 1826, at the public examination in the Rotunda, one of the speakers, the Rev. Hastings, in response to accusations of the Institution not using the Bible, recollected a lady and her son visiting Claremont. In his presence, she put an exceedingly diffi-cult question to the youngest of the girls, Cecilia White. The little girl made a sign to the Rev. Hastings that she could not answer the question. The lady said that she would then withdraw her support from the Institution. The clergyman asked the lady to put the same question to her son, who was five years older than Cecilia, and he could not answer. The lady then continued her support and subscription to the Institution.

On recommendation of Mr Humphreys, she was retained after completing her edu-cation for training as assistant teacher in the Female School. On 11 April 1848, James Cook, headmaster of the Edinburgh Institution, wrote to the Committee asking to allow Cecilia White to join him in Edinburgh for two years. This request was granted with the condition that they could not promise of taking her back at the end of two years. When James Cook emigrated to Australia, she transferred to the Ulster Institution for the Deaf, Dumb and Blind in Belfast. In 1877, Maurice Hewson, deaf missionary from Dublin, wrote that during his visit to Belfast, he had met 'Miss Whyte, former pupil of Claremont, assistant teacher at the Ulster Institution'.

Frances Lorrigan

Frances Lorrigan emigrated to Australia, and in 1864 she was appointed as assistant teacher by Frederick John Rose, from Oxford, England. Mr Rose had received educa-tion at the Old Kent Road School for the Deaf in London. In 1852 he sailed to Australia with his young brother to seek his fortune at the height of the Gold Rush. In 1860, after replying to an appeal for a school for the deaf in Australia, he established a school in his home in Peel Street, Windsor in Melbourne. He financed the school at a loss, until in 1861 he met the Rev. William Moss who formed a committee to estab-lish the Victorian Deaf and Dumb Institution in Melbourne. Frances Lorrigan shared the teaching of 75 pupils with Rose until 1871. She later married Rose's brother-in-law, Frederick Telfer.[8] Her brother, Michael Lorrigan, also pupil of Claremont, had emigrated to America.

Martha Overend-Wilson

She was admitted to Claremont on 9 October 1879, and she left on 9 December 1879. Her parents, Matthew and Annie, lived in Portadown and then Rostrevor, Co. Down, and her father was an ex-police officer. Even though she was deaf, she had retained so much speech that association with deaf mutes was inadvisable for her. She then received education at home and at a private school, and in 1888 she and her family emigrated to Queensland, Australia. Later on, she became a Missioner to the Deaf in Queensland, organizing religious services for the Adult Deaf at the Victorian Institute for the Adult Deaf and Dumb.

Elizabeth Whelan (Platts) (see picture)

On 5 March 1895, Elizabeth Whelan and her brother, John, were admitted to the Institution, her parents residing at 24 Clarendon Street, Dublin. Her father, a bicycle mechanic, became an alcoholic and he moved the rest of his family to Birmingham, abandoning his two deaf children at Claremont. In 1901, the parents were found to be residing in Birmingham, and John left school to be apprenticed to tailoring there.

In February 1903, Elizabeth (Lizzie) was apprenticed to Mrs Cobb, a dressmaker, off North Circular Road, Dublin. She had been treated harshly by her mistress, forcing her to wash the floors in the workshop and around the house, where she had been lodging. After suffering lacerations on her hands resulting from splinters while washing the wooden floors, she decided she had enough and left Dublin for England. Mr George Orr, former pupil of Claremont, and running a boot-repairing business, gave Lizzie some money for travelling to England to obtain employment. She was about to board the ferry-boat to Liverpool, but as she was deaf, the captain refused to take her on. Fortunately, a hearing lady persuaded the captain to allow her onto the ship, and in due time, Lizzie arrived at Sheffield. Through contacts provided by George Orr, who travelled there for business and to attend Gospel conferences for the deaf, she obtained lodgings and a position in a dressmaker's shop owned by a Jew. Two years later, George Orr assisted her to establish a business in dress-making by giving her a 'Singer' sewing-machine. In due time, she made contact with her family, and discovered that she had five brothers and three sisters, all hearing, and that she and her deaf brother had been 'abandoned' in Ireland.

She married Harival Platts, and set up home in Nottingham. They kept regular contact with her brother John, and her sister, Celia, also deaf, in Sheffield. She had a deaf son, David, and a hearing son, John. She died in 1948, aged 60.[9]

Lizzie Platts (nee Whelan), John Whelan, Celia Rymill (nee Whelan), 1901
(collection of David Platts)

Mary Gillespie

Mary Gillespie, from Ballina, Co. Mayo, came to the attention of a local benefactor, who sent her to Claremont to be educated. When she reached the age of twelve in November 1853, she was ordered to be bound to Mrs Soden, Co. Sligo, as a servant. On 30 November 1853, Mrs Gillespie wrote to the Committee, refusing to allow her daughter to be bound to Mrs Soden, and have her sent home. She then was sent to the Female Branch (St Mary's) of the Catholic Institution for the Deaf and Dumb, in the Dominican Convent, Cabra, Dublin. She married Thomas Devine, a former pupil of the Male Branch (St Joseph's) also in Cabra. She kept in contact with the Claremont Institution, and was visited at home by the staff from Claremont. She also attended social events organized by the Claremont Institution in Molesworth Hall, Dublin.[10] The picture shows Mary with her husband, Thomas Devine, and her daughter, Julia.

The Unwanted Females

During the nineteenth century Dublin had its societies for the blind, the deaf and dumb, the aged, the young, the penitent female, and latterly the Servants' Homes. However, a class, and a numerous one, that had not yet met with sympathy: the class of females of correct morals, from 14 to 35 years of age, who, having lost one or both parents, or from limited circumstances, were without employment and without support. Under this conviction, a Society had been formed on 11 August 1838, and was called 'The Dublin Providence Home' for the purpose of providing a temporary home, with support and employment, for such females until some permanent situation could be found for them. In September 1866, a representative from the Committee of the Providence Home called at Claremont, offering to receive any of the girls who had nowhere to go after leaving Claremont. Miss Brooke, sponsoring a pupil named Susan Porteous, accepted the offer.

In May 1885, Miss Wynne, superintendent of the Providence Home, in Peter Street, Dublin, asked the Claremont Committee to remove a former pupil, Margaret Farrell, as nothing could be done with her. The Committee was then to ask the Master of South Dublin Union, which maintained the Workhouse in Brunswick Street, if Margaret Farrell could be put under their charge. The Relieving Officer of the Union would then enquire if she was from the district covered by North Dublin Union and had any other means of support (such as her family) before she could be admitted. A letter of 7 April 1849 from Derry to the Juvenile Association mentioned of a 'deaf and dumb girl named Anne Jane Robinson committed to Derry Gaol for begging; she says she ran away from Claremont'.[11]

The Rev. Robinson, after mentioning 'his pleasant experience of uniting in the bonds of matrimony a deaf and dumb man to a deaf and dumb woman on Easter Monday at St Matthias' Church, Adelaide Road, Dublin', said that 'he had one other experience of encountering the deaf, though a much more painful one'. There was a place in Harcourt Road – the House of Refuge for women discharged from prison, where it was his duty to minister to the inmates. Among those who sought refuge, one was deaf and dumb. Her history was sad, and the cause of it was her being deaf and therefore ignorant of the ways of the world, and so 'she fell prey to designing and wicked people.'[12]

On 14 July 1864, Mr Chidley informed the Committee, 'I regret to report that Isabella Whelan still remains here unapprenticed. Mrs Hunt last November promised if she was allowed to remain here until Spring, she would provide a mistress for her at Kingstown but this she has failed to do. The poor girl who is an excellent needle-woman is very unhappy under the apprehension that a situation will not be obtained for her.'

Some of the former female pupils of Claremont occasionally sought assistance from Mr Maurice F.G. Hewson, deaf missionary and secretary of the Dublin Protestant Association for the Deaf and Dumb. His sister, Miss Hewson, organised bazaars for which the deaf females supplied their work in dressmaking, embroidery and knitting, to raise funds for the welfare of the needy deaf. By the late 1880s, women were instrumental for establishing the Missions for the Adult Deaf and Dumb - in Cork (Mrs Kingstone) and in Belfast (Wilhelmina Tredennick, sister of Mrs Kingstone); where employment and lodgings were sourced for some of the deaf females.

The Rejected Child

In his book, *Anecdotes and Annals of the Deaf and Dumb,* Dr Orpen wrote frequently about the dangers of deaf people neglected without education, especially deaf females. A lady living in Dublin told the following anecdote of a deaf young lady, to a friend, and urged that friend to make it as public as possible.

A wealthy gentleman's eldest child and only daughter was deaf. He considered she would be a heavy burden on him, calling her his curse. She sought comfort and company from the servants in the kitchen. Each servant was under strict orders to prevent her being seen, by any person who visited at the house, and also not to tell anyone that there was a deaf person in the house. She was aged seventeen, when her father discovered that she was with child. He summoned up the butler, footman, coachman and gardener, and he compelled each of them to take an oath, declaring their innocence, regarding the young lady's situation. She was more strictly concealed than ever when she became very large. One morning, on her finding herself extremely ill, she went to her father. He took her by the hand, led her up to his room, and left her, and locking the door, seated himself outside it. The lady hammered on the door and screamed so violently to get out, that all the servants rushed upstairs. At length her cries became fainter till they ceased. Her father then arose, and admitting the servants, gave them the key and went downstairs. On unlocking the door of her room, they found the young woman lying on the floor, dead, and a baby boy lying beside her, also dead. This event happened many years before there was any school in Ireland for the deaf and dumb. There were, however, other schools,[13] within the reach of the father's fortune.

The Deaf lose the protection of the Laws, by being left uninstructed[14]

'City Court, Cork - Saturday, 8 August 1829. Michael Hennessy, a sergeant in the 21st Fusiliers, was put upon trial for a brutal assault upon Mary Brien. The prosecutor is deaf and dumb, and the trial was put off last assizes, in order to have her sent to Dublin, to receive instruction, respecting the nature of an oath. It appeared now, by the testimony of her mother, that she had not been sent to Dublin, nor received any instruction here; and as the prosecution could not succeed without her testimony, it was given up, and the prisoner was accordingly acquitted.'

24

Going Away for Good

Lack of employment prospects in Ireland, financial difficulties and the Great Famine forced families with deaf children and deaf adults to take the option of emigration. The Committee had received several requests from parents seeking permission to take out their deaf child from school prior to emigration. However, some requests were feigned as a disguise, usually under threat from the Roman Catholic priests, in order to move the child to the Catholic Institution for the Deaf in Cabra. Inevitably, the most popular country to emigrate to was Great Britain, which had better social services for the adult deaf such as the Institutes and Missions to the Adult Deaf and Dumb

Ship.

located in major industrial cities and towns. Beyond Europe, pupils and former pupils relocated to the United States, Canada and Australia.

William Pagen

On 14 January 1829, the friends of William Pagen, from England, had agreed to pay £19 a year for his maintenance and education, and thus he was admitted into the Institution at the age of ten years. On 5 April 1833, he was discharged and returned to his parents in Cumberland. After his death, the obituary follows:

'William Pagen was a native of Cumberland. When he was born in 1818, there was no Institution for the Deaf and Dumb in the North of England. The nearest schools by land were those at Edinburgh and at Birmingham; but travelling was erratic and very costly in those days. The readiest and the cheapest route from a sea-bounded county like Cumberland was by sea; and so William Pagen was sent for education to Claremont, near Dublin.'

'After leaving school, William Pagen went on several voyages to the east with his brother, who was captain of a trading vessel. On leaving the sea, he settled in Liverpool, and was very industrious and prosperous in the business of a sail-maker. About two years before his death, he retired from active employment. In 1852, he married, and he leaves behind a most devoted wife and family. Mother and children all hear. Mr Pagen was an excellent husband and father. He was shy and reserved, and was little known about the deaf and dumb. He had been invited to join them in their religious services, but he shrank from doing so. However, last Christmas, the Rev. and Mrs Stowell invited the adult Deaf and Dumb of Liverpool to a social gathering; he was encouraged to attend, and after that he regularly attended Sunday services. Mr G. F. Healey (deaf Secretary of Liverpool Institute for Adult Deaf) and other friends visited him in his last illness. He died on 27 August 1875, and was buried at Smithdown Road Cemetery, Liverpool.'[1]

John Donovan

The following extract from the *New York Tribune* in 1862 refers to a former pupil at Claremont:

'Connected with the Springfield City Guard, Captain Lombard, 10th Regiment Massachusett's Volunteers, now stationed at Camp Brightwood, Virginia, is a deaf mute, named John Donovan, who is regularly enlisted as a soldier, and retained as the regimental tailor. He learned the trade of tailor in Brooklyn. About eight years ago he went to Springfield, from which city he enlisted at the commencement of the rebellion. His infirmity, of course, precludes him from performing the ordinary duties of a soldier, and being employed as the regimental tailor, he has many leisure moments, which he has improved by the practice of a natural gift of drawing. In this art he is a self-taught man, and the efficiency he has attained is truly astonishing. An accurate draft of Camp Brightwood made by him is in the hands of lithographers, and will be shortly issued. He is spoken of in the highest terms of praise by the officers of his regiment, and despite his infirmity, is fully equal mentally and bodily to the rank and file of the grand army'.[2]

The Lorrigans

At least six deaf children from the Lorrigan family of seven were admitted to Claremont. Their parents were Francis, a farmer in Kilfidane, Co. Clare, and Margaret, a labourer. The first one to enter the school was **Margaret (Frances) Lorrigan**, aged eight years, on 13 July 1842, and left in 1850, after eight years of education. After emigrating to Australia, Frances became assistant teacher to Frederick John Rose, a deaf emigrant from Oxford, England. Educated at the Old Kent Road School for the Deaf in London, Frederick Rose sailed to Australia with his young brother to seek his fortune. In 1859, after replying to an appeal for a school for the deaf in Australia, he established a school in his own home on Peel Street, Windsor in Melbourne. Miss Lorrigan shared the teaching with Rose from 1862 until 1871.[3] She later married Rose's brother-in-law, Frederick Telfer.

Michael Lorrigan entered Claremont in 1843 at the age of nine and left in June 1848. His brother, **Thomas**, aged ten years, was admitted in May 1852 and left in June

1857, to be apprenticed at home. Later on, he was apprenticed to a shoemaker in Kinnitty, King's County (Co. Offaly). In April 1861, he wrote to the Committee, applying for a Bible, he having collected a sum of one pound and eleven shillings for the Institution.

In 1866, at an Annual Meeting, it was said that, 'One man (Thomas Lorrigan) of whom the Committee had heard nothing for the last four years, wrote recently from America, where he is in steady employment at £12 per month. This man is one of a family of seven, six of them deaf and dumb, all educated at Claremont and all doing well in life. His brother (Michael) had lived with one master ever since he left Claremont eighteen years ago and a sister (Frances) who emigrated to Australia is now a teacher in the Melbourne Deaf and Dumb Institution.'[4]

Martha Overend-Wilson

Born in Portadown, Co. Armagh, she was admitted to Claremont on 9 October 1879, and left on 9 December of the same year. She was deaf but she retained so much speech that association with deaf mutes was inadvisable for her. She received education at home and at a private school. In 1888, she emigrated with her family to Queensland, Australia. She obtained a position as Missioner of the Deaf, organising religious services for the Deaf.

The MacDonald Brothers[5] *(four photographs on following page)*

Their father, Henry James MacDonald, a civil servant, married Hannah Jane Beville, a headmistress with a M.A. degree (a rarity for a woman at that time) who was living on a farm in Co. Cork. In Dublin, they lived at 9 Mespil Road. They had six children, the first four born in Dublin and, coincidentally, deaf, namely, Alec, Harry, Ethel and Muriel. The last two children were born hearing and in England, after their father, who took holy orders, moved his family to Barrow-in-Furness, Cumbria. Henry was the curate for over five years before moving to Islington in London. He communicated with his deaf children using finger spelling and some signs.

Born 29 August 1882, Thomas Alexander (Alec), the eldest of the family, was admitted to Claremont on 11 January 1889. Among the witnesses who applied their signatures to the application form were Canon Wynne and Mr William Watson, J.P., of Fitzwilliam Place, Dublin. The latter pledged £5 per annum in addition to Mr MacDonald's promise to pay £2 per annum towards the maintenance of his son. Canon Wynne wrote to the Dean of the Chapel Royal, the Rev. Hercules Dickenson, one of the Governors of the Institution,

'Mr MacDonald is a man for which I have a very high regard and esteem. He is applying to have his little boy received into Claremont free, except for clothing which he will supply. He, though very respectable, is unable to pay for the boy.' Mr MacDonald's income was limited due to expenses attached to the Divinity course he undertook at Trinity College at that time.'

Hurry, Ethel and Alec MacDonald

Harry MacDonald
as Missioner

Alec MacDonald

Harry as ARP firewatcher at
Truro Cathedral

On 21 September 1892, Alec's younger brother, Henry Beville (Harry) aged six years, was admitted. Two years later, Mr MacDonald left Dublin to take up parochial work in London. On 5 April 1895, Mr MacDonald asked, by letter, the Governors to allow Alec and Harry to spend the Easter holidays at his home in Barrow-in-Furness. On 10 May 1895, Mr MacDonald wrote to the Governors that as his deaf daughter (Ethel) was of school age, and being anxious she should be as near home as possible, he intended sending her to a neighbouring Institution (Royal Cross School for the Deaf at Preston, Lancashire). Alec and Harry were taken out of Claremont to join their sister.

After school, Alec worked as a tailor in London. He married Isabel Drake, Alec later became a Missioner for the Deaf in London before moving north to Stockport where he and his wife lived until his retirement. Alec died at the age of 84, the longest living of his siblings, in January 1965.

His brother, Harry, was born on 29 June 1886 in Dublin. He worked as a silver engraver in London but owing to poor health with stomach problems incurred through fumes, he had to give up his job. During the First World War, he worked in a poultry farm in Cranbrook, Kent. Then he moved to Coventry working in the BSA motorcycle factory. On 1 August 1918, he was married to Edith Hudson by his own father, and they had three daughters, all deaf.

His wife, Edith, died on 3 June 1929, after giving birth to their third child. He became Missioner in Bath for two years. He moved to Truro in Cornwall, replacing Rev Gilby. Harry remained there for 16 years until his retirement. During the Second World War, he was appointed as an Air-raid Policeman (ARP), his main responsibility being to fire-watch Truro Cathedral. He had to learn how to climb down the rope from the roof to the ground at his late age of 53 years. In February 1963, he died at the age of 77.

Ethel, oldest deaf sister of Alec and Harry, was born in Dublin in May 1888. Because her father moved the family to Cumbria, she was sent to a school for the deaf in Preston, and her two deaf brothers were moved there from the Claremont Institution. After she left school, she worked as a milliner after obtaining a certificate in hat-making. She married Francis D'Alton Rye, a wealthy deaf gentleman. He used to spend his time with servants in the kitchen rather than being 'upstairs' with his parents. His stepfather asked the Rev. MacDonald if he could help his deaf son, so both Alec and Harry had to teach him manners and etiquette.

Ernest Simpson
Ernest Simpson was born 26 October 1892 in Thredkeldt, Cumberland, and was admitted at the age of eight to Claremont on 12 January 1901. Even though he was not deaf, he suffered from 'one serious impediment, amounting to dumbness'. He was not dumb until his third year when he was attacked by whooping cough and measles, accompanied by hydrocephalus (meningitis). His parents were members of the

Church of England before moving to Galway. In a booklet produced by the Irish Church Missions, Townsend Street, Dublin, it was stated that 'a priest wanted to get him into a home for mutes (the Cabra Institution), without his father's permission.' He remained at Claremont until December 1906, and obtained a position in Dublin as boot-maker. On 10 January 1907 his family moved to Canada and in the year of 1910, he joined them, living in Ontario. According to his letters to Mr Taylor, headmaster, he obtained work on the railways, shoemaking, biscuit manufacturing, tinsmith and even as a seaman. He had served his time in the Canadian Army during the First World War, having been despatched to Kent, England in 1917, 'expecting to go to the Western Front soon, to fight the murderous and brutal Germans'.[6]

James Gibson (mistaken as a German spy)

James Gibson was born on 3 December 1892 at the Cootehill Union Workhouse, Co. Cavan. His mother, Sarah Gibson was a domestic servant, and his father was Charles Fisher of Cootehill. Having paralysis of the limbs, he was sent by a lady in Cootehill to the Cripples' Home, Bray, Co. Wicklow. Having recovered the use of his legs, he was admitted, at the age of five, to Claremont on 1 December 1897. In 1910, he started training in the Carpentry workshop in the Institution with two other pupils. In 1911, James Gibson started work at Spruce Hill Farm, Roscrea, Co. Tipperary, and three days later, he unexpectedly returned to the Institution. He said that the work was too dirty and he refused to do it. The boy was then staying at Claremont, assisting the gardener there. In April 1912 the Rev. J. McConnell, rector of Desert Serges, Cork, and brother of the Institution's matron, kindly offered to employ James Gibson as gardener and general man.

In January 1917, Mr Taylor informed the Committee that 'James Gibson, late pupil, joined the Royal Scot Fusiliers and is now in France. His degree of hearing combined with his ability to lip-read enabled him to pass his medical examination. This lad speaks well but with a peculiarly foreign accent and before joining the army, he had the misfortune to be twice arrested (in Dublin and Belfast) as a German spy. He proved his connection with Claremont, and in both places he was able to call on his friends to speak for him.'[7] On 11 October 1918, he boarded the mail boat, the *R.M.S. Leinster*. When the ship approached the Kish Bank outside Kingstown (Dun Laoghaire), a German submarine surfaced and fired torpedoes on the mail boat, and the ship was destroyed. The death toll on the *Leinster* was 530 including James Gibson, out of a total of 771 on board. Twenty-two Irish postal workers died along with 14 crew members who lived in Kingstown and 20 from Holyhead were drowned. Also among those who perished were troops from Britain, America, Canada, New Zealand, Australia and South Africa. The ship carried three Royal Navy personnel and a 12-pounder gun for self-defence, in case a submarine surfaced.[8]

James Roxburgh

Born in Glasnevin, he was day scholar at Claremont, together with his sister, Dorothy. In 1918, he left the Institution and took up employment in London as a photo-engraver in Boots.   He enjoyed his job and made many deaf and dumb and hearing friends out there.   He became an Assistant Scoutmaster at St. Barnabas' Boy Scouts Group. He said that there were several former pupils of Claremont.   At an Annual Meeting in 1926, Mr Taylor, headmaster, said that James Roxburgh, former pupil and aged 24, was awarded a Testimonial on Vellum by the Royal Humane Society for saving a six-year-old from drowning in the River Thames on 25 August 1923.[9]

Former Pupils apprenticed out of Ireland

In his Letter-book to the Committee, Mr Chidley wrote in regard to having pupils apprenticed out of Ireland. In 1874, Samuel David whose father was a Sergeant Major in the Royal Artillery, was to be apprenticed by his parents to a Printer in London. In 1873, David Jones was apprenticed at Holyhead to Mr Thomas Roberts, tailor. who, in 1882, took on John Williams, pupil, as an apprentice.   Admitted to Claremont in November 1878, Williams was mentioned as a 'speaking boy from Wales'. His father was employed on one of the mail-boats. In 1883, Mr Roberts, Tailor of Holyhead agreed to take James Hawkins, one of the pupils, as indoor apprentice for 4 years if £15 was paid down.   The boy's father was to pay £7, with the Committee to pay £8.

Left: Ms Deacon, Right: Betty Bateman
Taken at Glasnevin in June 1931
Most of the pupils in the photograph moved to England.

25

History of the Dublin Working Boys' Home

'...to help them to help themselves...'
- F.B. Ormsby

In July 1876, a preliminary meeting was held at St Ann's Vicarage, Dawson Street, and a committee formed for the purpose of establishing in Dublin a Home for Working Boys similar to those in various parts of London. Among the members of the Committee were the Rev. Hercules Henry Dickenson, Dean of the Chapel Royal and Vicar of St Ann's Church; William Digges La Touche, and J.B. Pim. The object of the Home was to 'afford comfortable, healthy and attractive lodgings at cheap rates for boys who were earning their bread'. At that time, the boys had no home to which they would go after work, and they frequented lodging homes, which could not provide comfort or security, and where they were exposed to many temptations and dangers. The establishment of such a Home proved useful to country clergymen, when their young male parishioners came to Dublin for employment.[1]

On 14 March 1878, at the Conference of the Lay Help Association, held in Dublin, Mr Francis Ormsby, honorary secretary of the Dublin Working Boys' Home, presented his paper on 'Homes for Working Boys'. He said that homeless boys who were in employment in Dublin fell into three classes – (1) orphan boys, (2) country boys, who had come up to the city for employment, and (3) those who had 'dissolute or criminal parents' who were 'not a help to their children's advancement'.

In September 1876, the Committee had taken Nos. 34 and 35 Denzille Street to establish their first Home. On 5 February 1877 three boys were admitted. They were two brothers, Edward and William Hadden, the former born in Colchester and the latter in Aldershot; and the third boy was Stephen Lyons from Dublin. Some applicants did not remain for long owing to their reaching the maximum age of 19, where they had to relocate to other lodging homes, such as St Ann's Lodging Home in Molesworth Place. Some were so wild that they were either expelled or departed to join the Army or the Navy. Others left to emigrate to America, Canada, England and South Africa. The amount of £140 was raised, after an appeal, whereas a sum of £400 was required to defray the preliminary expenses. By the end of 1878, already upwards of 130 boys had availed of the Home's facilities, among whom were many who had been under the care of the following charities: Protestant Orphan Society, Protestant Orphan Refuge Society, the Grand Canal Home, the Coombe Boys' Home, the General Orphan Home, etc. as well as several boys admitted from various parts of Ireland, who came to Dublin to learn trades.

Move to Lord Edward Street

Owing to the increase in the number of residents, it was decided to advertise for a site in order to construct a larger building. On 16 April 1888, the Committee signed the contract for the site at the top of Lord Edward Street, facing Christ Church Cathedral. On 21 June 1888, a sum of £800 was paid for the site. Completed in 1891, the building was of brick, faced with Dennis' Ruabon red brick and buff terracotta. It had a frontage of 162 feet in Lord Edward Street, and was built in the Elizabethan style. It contained an entrance-porch and hall, dining-hall, kitchen, pantries, and superintendent's office, recreation-room, and large lecture-hall, with platform, etc. for entertainments. On the first floor, the superintendent had his private apartments, and over this was sleeping accommodation for about 75 boys, with sanitary arrangements, baths, etc. There was a considerable space at the rear, to be used as a recreation ground and gymnasium. The contractors were H. and J. Martin of Belfast, for general work, and Mr H. MacGarvey, of Lombard Street, Dublin, for the plumbing and gas-fitting, and the whole was from the designs and under the superintendence of Mr Albert E.Murray, F.R.I.B.A., architect, 37 Dawson Street, Dublin.   On 22 February 1892, the Lord Lieutenant officially opened the new building.

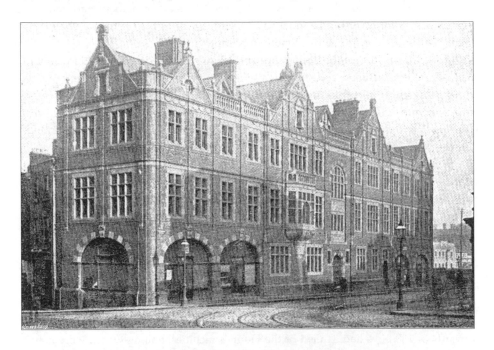

The Dublin Working Boys' Home and Harding Technical School,
Lord Edward Street, Dublin

Gymnasium at the Dublin Working Boys' Home

Harding Technical School

In the late 1880s, the Misses Harding, two sisters who had run a school in Dublin, took an interest in the educational welfare of the boys. In 1889, Miss Anna Middleton Harding died and left a bequest to the Committee for establishing a technical school for the residents of the Working Boys' Home. This bequest enabled the Governors to purchase the site at Lord Edward Street and construct a larger building to provide residential accommodation for the boys and the staff, and classrooms for the Technical School. Instruction continued to be provided there until a Technical College in Bolton Street, Dublin, opened in the 1920s which met the requirements of the bequest.

By 1904, the Governors had been constantly approached by employers seeking boys, and by boys seeking employment, and for that reason, the Governors decided to open a free registry office for 'respectable Protestant lads' seeking employment as apprentices to trades or otherwise in Dublin.

Recreation

Shortly after the establishment of the Home, funds were raised to construct the Gymnasium, which provided healthy exercise for the residents. During the period of 1933 to 1959, the Gymnasium Club had been successful, the team having won the Irish Junior Challenge Shield in 1933. The competition was open to all of Ireland, and teams representing Northern Ireland clubs regularly competed. In the realm of sport, the boys had their cricket, badminton soccer, rugby, table-tennis and swimming. The

Cricket Club played their matches at Londonbridge Road, Sandymount, Dublin. In the early and mid twentieth century, a soccer team was formed, which then participated in matches in the United Churches' League. The Harding Old Boys' Union still fields a soccer team. In the recreation-room of the Home, the residents could play billiards and board-games, while in the sitting-room; they would catch up with the news or reading. In the dining-room was the Cherry Memorial plaque with a list of Boys who received the Good Conduct prize. According to a report in 1934, the spiritual welfare was not forgotten, and each boy, in addition to receiving religious tuition, attended the parish church of St Werburgh at least once every Sunday. The church was around the corner from the Home, less than eighty yards away, so the boys had no way of avoiding going to church! Before its closure in March 1901, the Rutland Club, at No. 42 Rutland Square (Parnell Square), had 30 members from the Working Boys' Home, who attended there for socialising, evening classes and access to the Reading Room. At one time, some residents formed a 'string band' to maintain and develop their musical talents. For those leaning towards 'clangers', a Bell-ringing club was set up. There was a Literary and Debating Society for the residents of the Working Boys Home, and in December 1933, William 'Bill' Lockhart presented a paper on *'Dublin – A Sketch'*, outlining the history of that city.

In Mount Jerome Cemetery, the Dublin Working Boys' Home had a plot for the residents, purchased by one of the Governors, Thomas Spunner, in 1885. Those interred in this grave were: John McConnell, died on 27 December 1885, aged 18 years, from tuberculosis, Peter Luke, on 25 August 1886, aged 19 years, from consumption, Joseph Clarke, on 13 June 1894, aged 21 years, from consumption, Thomas Hickey, on 28 September 1891, aged 14 years, from peritonitis, William Walsh, on 17 January 1905, aged 19 years, from hip disease, Edgar Pankhurst, on 21 October 1918, aged 17 years, from influenza, Duncan McCullum, on 28 December 1931, aged 16 years from pneumonia, and William Lockhart, aged 80, on 7 December 1948, from strangulated hernia. According to the minutes, Lockhart was the librarian at the Home.

Since the foundation of the Home in 1876 to October 1959, more than 2,483 boys had passed through, many of whom filled important positions in the city and elsewhere. In the year of 1906, the number of boys in the Home was 70, and their ages varied from 13 to 19. Their occupations were as follows: eight carpenters, four mechanics, two watchmakers, two electricians, one jeweller, one wire-worker, one upholsterer, one motor mechanic, ten plumbers, two ships' platers, one telegraphist, two tailors, one printer, two gasfitters, six shop assistants, 14 clerks, and 12 messengers.[2]

Table Tennis Group from the Harding Boys' Home
Sitting in the centre is Mr Dudley Dolan, Superintendent of the Home

In 2006, nearly twenty years after the closure of the Home, some former residents have their own businesses, such as hotels, restaurant, construction, while others are employed in accountancy, insurance underwriting, stock-broking, retailing, etc. Two of the former Boys were ordained in the Church of Ireland – Dean Victor Griffin and Kevin Dalton, at present a rector of Monkstown Parish Church, Co. Dublin. His story has been recorded in a book titled *That could never be*. This book includes a chapter on his time at the Harding Home. Many men now influential in business life have testified to the debt they owed to the Home. In 1964, a large donation came from Canada from the widow of an Old Boy who said that throughout their married life her husband had spoken of what the Harding had meant to him in his early days. Another Old Boy, J.D. Robinson, had been in the Home in 1890, when it was in Denzille Street. He later emigrated to South Africa, but returned to Ireland several times and presented the Home with the pictures of African wild life. He never forgot the Home, was a constant subscriber under the name of 'Old Denzille Street Boy', and his generous legacy was one of many signs of his life-long support and interest.

In the Great War (1914-1918), over 300 old boys served in the forces, while of these over 30 gave their lives, and a large number sustained wounds in the 'service of King and country'. During the Second World War, 1939 to 1945, some of the 'Old Boys', numbering 76, served with the British forces. Out of that number, eleven were killed in action. Another ten enlisted in the regular and auxiliary forces of the Irish Free State.

Managing Committee

When Frank B. Ormsby (*pictured at right*) became Honorary Secretary in June 1876, he resided at 9 Northbrook Road, Leeson Park, Dublin. He was also on the committee of the Coombe Boys' Home. He had served some time as Chairman of the Protestant Orphan Society, and was instrumental in directing some of the orphans to the Dublin Working Boys' Home. He was a Governor of the Erasmus Smith's Board, the Church of Ireland Training College, the Irish Clergy Sons' Society, the Widows' and Orphans' Society, the Bluecoat School Hospital, the Incorporated Society, Dr Steevens' Hospital, St Patrick's Hospital, Love's and Gardiner's Charity, and a member of

the Diocesan Board of Education and of the Committees of St John's Ambulance Association and the Rest for the Dying. He was a man who had endeared himself to many by the charm of his personality. He was remembered for his generous and kindly views of men and affairs, and his interest in whatever he undertook. He died on 28 June 1917, and was buried in Deansgrange Cemetery.

Each year, until 1978, the Annual Meetings were held to review the finances and progress of the services afforded by the Dublin Working Boys' Home. The Harding Home had managed to survive so long with very little in the way of endowments. The bulk of the original bequest from Miss Harding was invested in railway stock which in 1964 was worth little or nothing. Most of the Home's income came from boarding fees and private donations, and from the proceeds of the Annual Sale of Work organised by the Friends of the Harding's' Home.

Harding Residents from Edenderry, Co. Offaly

Among the boys who entered the Harding from Edenderry, a town of the 'Faithful County', were John Kelly, Richard Pollard and Jim Pollard. Kelly became a member of the Harding Gymnastic Club, and in 1933, the team won the All-Ireland Junior Challenge Shield of the Irish Amateur Gymnastic Association. (See photograph at the end of this chapter). Undoubtedly, this was partly due to a 'certain military strictness and discipline about the Home'. Jim Pollard, who played cricket at his old school, King's Hospital, joined the Harding Cricket team. Edenderry Cricket Club paid for his travelling expenses to Edenderry. He was selected as part of the Leinster Cricket team.

Superintendents of the Home

J. Sides (1876-78)

Thomas Spunner (1879-1896)

James Harris (1897-1901 and 1910-1929), (pictured at left)

Henry S. Meredith (1901-1910)

James 'Nobby' Clarke (1930-1960), himself an ex-soldier with a fine record, having like so many other young Dubliners, joined the 'Pals' Battalion' of the immortal Dubliners in the ranks in August 1914. He was later transferred with a commission to the Suffolk Regiment, leaving the Army with the rank of captain. His military service and experience had been of great assistance to him in the running of the Home. His wife acted as Matron of the establishment.

Dudley Dolan (1960-1970). When he took charge in 1960, there were 39 boys in the Home, and at his retirement ten years later, there were 85. He started a fund to improve the structure of the building and provide amenities for the boys, such as carpets on the dormitory floors, installation of wardrobes and lockers, improved washing facilities and modernisation of the kitchen.

Jim Condell (1971-1978)

The End of 'The Ranch'
By the 1980s, the Dublin Working Boys' Home had served out its purpose. The quality of life, education and employment had improved, resulting with young males preferring to lead independent lives outside their family homes. In 1987, the Home (fondly known as 'The Ranch' by the Old Boys) finally closed its doors. The building was sold to USIT Ireland, the student and youth travel agency, and was subsequently converted into a hostel for students and budget travellers.

Harding Old Boys Union

In 1930, this was set up in order to maintain contact amongst former 'Boys', and to support the work of the Harding Trust. The committee organises social functions and sports outings for members. Annual Dinners are held, giving the Old Boys, their partners and friends an opportunity to meet and renew contact. In November 2005, at Finnstown Hotel near Lucan, Co. Dublin, there was a large turn-out of Old Boys and their partners and friends, to celebrate the 75th anniversary of the Old Boys' Union. The President's chain of office has a badge which displays the picture of a young apprentice wearing an apron and carrying his tools.

Harding Boys from Claremont

In 1889, at a meeting of the Governors, a letter was read from Dr Gick, Secretary of the Claremont Institution, asking for admission of a deaf and dumb boy, and it was decided to admit the boy on trial. And in 1893, they were again asked to take a couple of boys from Claremont. However, they decided to admit only one on trial, on the Claremont Institution agreeing to remove him hereafter if he should prove unsatisfactory. The following Harding residents were the former pupils of Claremont. (When the boys reached the age of 19, they had to move to other lodgings.)

Thomas Russell. Admitted 9 February 1878, age 19. Born in Dublin. Apprenticed to William Curtis & Sons, Brass founder, Gas-fitter & Plumber, at 96-99 Abbey Street. Lived with mother. Observed as 'very good boy.' Departed 3 August 1878. Left for St Ann's Lodging Home. (This was located behind St Ann's Church, Dawson Street. The Rev. H.H. Dickenson, vicar of St Ann's, was Governor there, as well as for the Dublin Working Boys' Home and the Claremont Institution for the Deaf and Dumb).

George Samuel Orr. Admitted 3 February 1878, age 17. Commented on as 'very good boy'; apprenticed at 14/-; lived with his father. Also left on 3 August 1878 for St Ann's Lodging Home. Worked for Mr Heather Bros & Co, Wholesale Boot & Shoes Warehouse, 22 Lower Bridge Street. Factory: Usher's Court near St Audeon's Quay.

Abraham Hawkins. Admitted on 18 December 1890, age 17. Lived at Claremont. From Co. Wicklow. Apprenticed with J.Walker, Lithographer, Jones Road, Dublin. Excelling in gymnastics, he won some medals at competitions, representing the Dublin Working Boys' Home.

William Henry Hickie. Admitted on 4 September 1893, age 17. Lived at Claremont. Parents both born in Dublin. Apprenticed as stone carver to Mr Sharp, Brunswick Street (later Pearse Street).

Thomas Henry Pollard. Admitted on 13 July 1960, age 17. Lived at the Claremont School, Monkstown. From Edenderry, Co. Offaly. Prior to admission, he spent the final year of his formal education at Blackrock Technical School. He undertook seven years' apprenticeship in metalwork at Ferguson Peacocke Ltd, in Denzille Lane – about fifty yards from where the Dublin Working Boys' Home was established. His manager, 'Fergus', deaf himself, had sent him out to work on the projects commissioned by the famed architect, Michael Scott, such as the Embassy of the United States of America in Ballsbridge. He had an input in producing the original logo of the Stillorgan Shopping Centre, which had the distinction of being Ireland's first shopping centre, opened in 1966. When business declined at Denzille Lane, Pollard obtained employment as a fitter and welder at Upright Ireland Ltd, a manufacturing factory from the United States, producing aluminium scaffoldings, span decks, work platforms and alloy tower systems. Henry is the husband of Rachel, the author of 'The Avenue', and he provided an enormous amount of assistance with research for the story.

William Norman Rankin. Age 15, from Clonmel, Co. Tipperary. He was a close friend of Henry Pollard, as they were the only two boys from the school at Claremont in Monkstown. He went with Pollard in 1960 to the Harding Home, and also apprenticed to Ferguson Peacocke Ltd. After some years, he left to work with his father in Clonmel, maintaining a business in metalwork.

John Hobson. Age 16, from Avoca, Co. Wicklow, where his father maintained a large farm. After leaving Claremont, he spent some time at the Harding Home, while studying agricultural mechanics. Then he continued his training at Teagasc, and afterwards spent some years working on his father's farm, along with his deaf younger brother, Cyril. Later on, he established a business in hiring out agricultural machinery in Arklow, Co. Wicklow.

The Harding Football Team c.1964.
At back, from right (in togs): Henry Pollard and Norman Rankin
former pupils of the Claremont Institution

Photo by]   **HARDING GYMNASTIC CLUB**   [Ernest, Fairview.
Showing All Ireland Junior Challenge Shield won by Team.

Female Pupils at Glasnevin, August 1935
Left: Betty Bateman, Right: Ann Fager

Appendices

Appendix 1

Principals of the Claremont Institution

1819	Joseph Humphreys
1840	Rev. John Martin
1843	James Cook
1847	James Foulston
1856	Edward J. Chidley
1882	Edward W. Chidley
1888	George Taylor

From the year of 1928 onwards, due to the small number of pupils, only one teacher was required for the Claremont Institution.

1928	Mary L. Deacon (Headmistress)
1945	Harriet R. Ferris (Headmistress)
1971	Jane Bleakley
1976	Mee Choo Thoeng Kelly

In 1840 the Rev. Charles Stanford was appointed Manager of the Institution, dealing with correspondence and domestic management. After his resignation in 1843, his successor was Mr George Clarke, who took on the title of 'Providore' (Steward), and his duties were to keep the Institution and the demesne in good condition, employing the gardeners and labourers for the farm, and the resident shoemaker and tailor for training the deaf boys. He organised the domestic arrangements, in partnership with his wife as Matron of the Institution, with access to medicines, linen and clothing for the children, and assigning household tasks to the servants and officers of the Institution.

Matrons and Year of Appointment

Mary Anne Cullen, 1820	Miss Elizabeth Bates, 1829
Mrs Martin, 1841	Mrs Chidley, 1856
Mrs Cudmore, 1882	Mrs Sutcliffe, 1891
Miss Prendiville, 1894	Miss Miller, 1895
Miss Jameson	Miss Laura Jacob, 1901
Miss Maude Adams, 1906	Miss Elizabeth Marion McConnell, 1912
Miss Coates, 1920	Miss Beggs, 1934
Miss Judge, 1953	Miss Hill, 1953
Miss Odell, 1956	Mrs Robinson, 1960
Mrs Boxham, 1964	Miss Nuala Pollard, 1966
Mrs U. Thomson, 1969	Mr & Mrs Erskine, 1971 (House-parents)

Appendix 2

Records on the Pupils of the Institution for the Education of the Deaf and Dumb of the Poor in Ireland (1816-1978)

The total number of pupils admitted to the Claremont Institution for the Deaf and Dumb from its establishment in 1816 to the closure of the Claremont School in Monkstown, Co. Dublin is 2,448. It must be pointed out that this number did not include deaf children who were taken under the entire charge of the Principals of the Institution as 'private pupils' or 'paying pupils', and therefore not recorded on the Register Books. Those whose parents or friends had no means of paying the annual fees, on average £20 per annum, were placed on the 'Free List'. This was to preserve the distinction between the 'rich' and the 'poor' classes within the Institution at Claremont, Glasnevin. This practice had been discontinued in the 1920s. It was through scrutinising the Minutes, Annual Reports, Audits, Letter books of the headmasters, newspaper reports and periodicals when names could be put to some of those 'private pupils'. *Note for genealogists: As we have maintained lists of pupils' names since 1816, we can be contacted for further details.*

Application Book (from 1816 to 1842)

There are two books with the records of the pupils since 1816; the first one being the 'Application Book', which contains the applications received for pupils since the establishment of the Institution in May 1816. Not all children named on the Application Book were admitted; that was dependent on the outcome of the elections held by the subscribers, on the monies available to support the education and maintenance of pupils, and on the willingness of the successful applicant's family to allow the deaf child to be taken to the Institution. In some cases, consent to transfer the responsibility for care of the child to the Committee of the Institution was withdrawn under duress owing to pressure and intimidation from Roman Catholic priests and neighbours.

The Application Book has black leather covers, and is 24 inches long when closed. Some written details are legible, though in some instances, very tiny handwriting makes it difficult to decipher the particulars of the applicants. The book contains 38 pages with 749 names of applicants. The first name is, of course, Thomas Collins, admitted on 17 May 1816. The last name is Rose McEntegart, whose application was received in 1842. The headings at the top of each set of two pages are contained in the following table.

First page

Date of application	Any other bodily defect	Moral conduct
Applicant number	Previous health	Disposition
Applicant's name	Smallpox	Talents
Age of applicant	Cowpock	Parents' names
Residence	Measles	Parents living
How long deaf	Whooping cough	Friends' names
Cause of deafness	Any other disease	County
Total or partial deaf	Present health	Parish
How long dumb	Education	Residence
Cause of dumbness	Writing	Post Town
Intellect	Occupation / trade	Characters
Can sign	Begging Occupation (of parents)	

Second page

Circumstances of parents, Number of children, No. of deaf and dumb
Ability to pay for maintenance or education, To clothe
Signature to Attestation, Signature to Medical Attestation
Signature to Witness to Engagement (usually three are required)
Eligible or not, Reason for ineligibility, No. of elections, No. of votes
Date when admitted, Supernannuation, Date of leaving school, Observations

Listed below are some of the particulars taken from the first page.

Applicant Name	Date applied	Age	Residence and Cause of deafness
Thomas Collins	17 May 1816	11	Bedford Asylum, deaf from birth
James Murphy	16 May 1816	11	63 Manor Street, Dublin, ditto
William Brennan	17 May 1816	9	Rathgar, Dublin, ditto
John Johnson		6	4 Barrack Street, Dublin, ditto
William Cunningham		13	Little Temple Street, Dublin, at Mr Dumb's Glazier, partially deaf
John Stinton		15	Broadstone, partial deaf from birth
Daniel Price		9	Phenia Street, Dublin, partial deaf
John Fleming	20 May 1816	11	Foundling Hospital, totally deaf
John Millwright		11	Ditto, ditto
Thomas Collogan	5 August 1816	15	Collon, Co. Louth, ditto
Philip Reilly	20 August 1816	11	Co. Wicklow, ditto
Francis Addington	24 August 1816	9	Foundling Hospital, ditto
Edward Collins	22 October 1816	11	Carlow, deaf from birth

James Leonard	31 Dec. 1816	10	83 Townsend Street, ditto
James Mansfield	5 January 1817	14	1 Francis Street, Dublin
George Browne	10 Feb. 1817	15	High Street
Luke McNally		11	Dean Hill, Navan, Co. Meath
			Deaf for 7 years from sickness
Philip Geary		6	12 Barn's Yard, Rainsford Street
John Hickey		16	
Patrick Cusack		6	88 Coombe, Dublin
James Jordan	August 1816	11	Clontarf Charter School
			Sent back in December 1816
			for inattention

Some applicants were ineligible due to being under the age of eight, as in the case of Philip Geary and Patrick Cusack, not admitted to them being six years old and therefore too young. When they reached the eligible age, they were then admitted.

Register Book (from 1837 to 1978)

On recommendation of Mr James Cook, headmaster from 1843 to 1847, the Register Book, in form of a large volume, was obtained. This volume is in good condition, and contains useful information as to what happened to some of the pupils after they left the Institution. The headings at top of each set of the two pages are as follows:

Name of Pupil, Age at admission, Date of Admission, Date when pupil left the Institution, Trade of pupil at time of admission, (for example, William Whiteside was admitted in 1840 at the age of twelve, and his trade was weaver), Details of dates when pupil was out of the Institution and reason (Sick or on Leave), Parents' Names, Trade of parents, Residence, Family (number of children in family, including number of deaf and dumb), Born Deaf, Miscellaneous Remarks (observations by the Committee regarding pupil – intelligence, talents, health, disposition, cause of deafness, progress in education)

Overleaf are samples of the two pages from the Register Book. The pupil, number 39, John Feeney, was retained, after completion of education, as an assistant teacher from July 1845 until his resignation in May 1857.

Nº	Name of Pupil	Age	Admitted	Left	Trade	Sick or on Leave
			1840	1845		42 Jan. 25 to 5 April; Jun. 3 to 24; 43 June 30 to 2 Sep; 44 Jan 2 to 24; March 1st to 13 March
35	James Barry	11	Augt 1st	Aug. 1st	Sawyer	
36	Patrick McCafferty	12	,, 1st	Sep. 19th 1845		
37	Eleanor Kennedy	12	,, 1st	August 20 1845		
38	John Coleman	12	,, 3rd	June 30th 1846		43 July 1st to 11 July
39	John Feeney	10	,, 3rd			[illegible]
40	Ellen Downes	11½	,, 3rd	45/ July 4th		
41	Ellen Howell	10½	,, 5th	Dec. 8th 1846		42 Nov. 19 to Dec 4; 43/10 July to Aug 23
42	Richard Cosby	12	,, 19	Decemr 10th 1845		45 July 5 to 11 July
1.43	Elizabeth Green	11	Sept 3rd	Novemr 1st 1847		[illegible]
44	William J. Whiteside	12	,, 9th	March 31 1847	Weaver	
L45	Judy Brachan	12	Oct. 5th	April 2d 1848	Dressmaker	43/10 Feb to 13 Mar. May 9 to 28
P.46	Margaret Seaman	11	1841 Jany 5th	June 20th 1848		45/14 Mar to 29 April 26
P.47	Anne Rowe	11	,, 7th	June 4th 1847		45 Mar 21 to 25
P.48	Hugh Dowling	9	Feby 27th	June 13th 1846	Dead	45 July 4 to 29 July
P.49	Christopher C. Allen	9	March 26	May 25th 1847		[illegible]
50	James Norman	12½	May 17th	May 5th 1846		[illegible]
51	Anne Dalton	13½	April 16	Feb. 18th		[illegible]

Parents' Names	Trade	Residence	Family	Born Deaf	Miscellaneous Remarks
Richard & Mary	Sawyer	Fermoy	3 sons 1 daughter	Yes	Very delicate lungs. After leaving school became very stout & a good workman
John & Margaret	Labourer	Pettigo	2 sons 1 daughter	Yes	By no means hard-working &c. has advanced beyond the second class
Thomas & Eleanor	Weaver	Granard	8 children		A very dull heavy girl. Has not beyond the progress of an ordinary pupil of two years standing
Margaret		Cashel	2 sons 1 daughter	Yes	Apparently healthy & free from trouble... stouter...
Michael & Honoria	Labourer	Kilconnell	2 sons 2 daughters	Yes	A very inferior little boy... Habitation healthy though not strong
Thomas & Mary	Labourer	Waterford	1 daughter & &c	No	Consumptive removed on account of her health not likely to recover
John & Ellen P	Pensioner	Newtown-Barry	5 sons & 2 daughters	No	Scrofulous. Small dull inactive girl
Richard & Margaret	Bleacher	Bannbridge	2 sons 4 daughters	No	Scrofulous affected in his eyes & with a nervous affection
John & Amelia P	silk & cotton draper	Goldenbridge	3 children	Yes	Mother an Italian. A heavy scrofulous unhealthy girl
Theophilus & Mary P	Weaver	Bannbridge	1 son 5 daughters	Yes	About average
Patrick & Rose	Mason	Athboy	5 children	Yes	
George & Sarah P	Labourer	Killeshandra	5 children	Yes	
Bartholomew & Eliza P	Hatter	Mespil	4 children	No	
Patrick & Mary	Slater	Goresbridge	4 children	Yes	A small healthy little boy but different in language (British) when talking to children
Eleanora P	Professor of Music	Dublin	9 children	No	Plains deaf... bold child in school... healthy & talented... &c speaks many words &c would learn to speak well
Thomas & Anne P	Soldier	32nd Regt	3 children	Yes	Very healthy & great whistler
John & Sarah	Carpenter	Cork	4 children	Yes	Nearly blind from scrofula

Appendix 3

Occupations of Parents and Guardians of Deaf Children

The main source for obtaining information on occupations of parents and guardians who applied for admission of their deaf children into the Claremont Institution was the application form for admission. The range of occupations was widespread and diverse. For instance, in the Application Book dated from 1816 to 1842, the occupations are as follows:

Pauper	Boatman	Weaver	Charwoman
Baker	Miller	Messenger	Servant
Watchmaker	Soldier	Flax Dresser	Broker
Housemaid	Stucco Plasterer	Farmer	Corn merchant
Chandler	Sells herrings	Shoemaker	Clergyman
Labourer	Grocer	Shopkeeper	Steward
Brogue maker	Postman	Blacksmith	Schoolmaster
Herdsman	Gamekeeper	Chimney Sweeper	Washerwoman
Brass Founder	Drummer	Postmaster	Millwright
Clerk to Jury	Hackney Maker	Tailor	Confectioner
Woollen Draper	Journeyman	Hustler	Sawyer
Papermaker	Tide Waiter	Seaman	Sailmaker
Pensioner	Cooper	Tradesman	Bootman
Painter	Gunner	Earthen Dealer	Spinner
Excise Officer	Car Driver	Saddler	Mendicant
Policeman	Vintner	Fisherman	Slater
Fish Dealer	Mason	Dressmaker	Keeps lodgings
Linen Weaver	Publican	Stone Cleaner	Gardener
Pedlar	Sergeant	Bleacher	Householder
Dancing Master	Ploughman	Governess	Wood Ranger
Nailer	Innkeeper	Watchman	Brazier

Commissioner in Navy who died, mother receiving pension

Based on the information provided by the applicants on their ability of paying the fees for maintenance and boarding of their children, the amount of fees varied. Children from poor families were admitted without charge, having been placed on the 'free list' or 'free foundation', while for others, the fees were on a sliding scale - from £1 per annum to £25 per annum, depending on the ability of the parents to pay. The Secretary often asked the Board of Guardians of the district (or 'Union') in which the applicant resided, to contribute up to £18 per annum towards maintenance fees. Upon receipt of the application for grant towards fees, the Clerk of the Union arranged for the Relieving Officer to assess the means of the applicant's father - such as the amount of acreage of land farmed, the nature of occupation and the wages brought into the applicant's household. In some instances, the parish raised funds by means of church collections for the maintenance of the pupils whose parents were members of the congregation.

Appendix 4

Occupations of Male and Female Deaf and Dumb
reprinted from the Census Reports of England, Scotland and Ireland
from the Report of the Royal Commission
for the Deaf, Dumb, Blind and Imbecile, 1889

In Ireland, 1,542 deaf males were occupied, and 1,332 deaf females were engaged in work.   The list of occupations follows:

Occupation	Deaf Male	Occupation	Deaf Females
Artist	19	Charwoman	14
Architect	3	Coal Merchant	1
Blacksmith	10	Factory	23
Boot/Shoemaker	104	Farmer	62
Bricklayer/Mason	9	Furniture Broker	1
Cabinetmaker	9	Fruit Stall-keeper	1
Carpenter	29	Gentlewomen	9
Factory worker	12	Fruiterer	1
Farmer	222	Housekeeper	53
Fisherman	9	Labourer	8
Gardener	12	Laundress	16
Gentleman	4	Machinist	4
Painter/Paper Hanger	9	Milliner/Dressmaker	92
Labourer	493	Servant	263
Lithographer	4	Shirtmaker/Seamstress	108
Printer	18	Teacher	1
Saddler	14	Unspecified	638
Servants	192		
Tailor	70		
Weaver	27		
Jeweller/Goldsmith	1		
Unspecified	200		

Appendix 5

Table of Business for Girls and Boys Schools
for the year of 1845
Boys and Girls are divided into five classes
(1st, 2nd, 3rd, 4th, 5th)

Sunday

7-7.15am	All at Prayers
7.15-8am	None
8-10am	Breakfast, Housework and Exercise
10-11am	Scripture, Reading, Prayer
11-12	Church catechism (1st to 4th), Religion (5th)
12-12.15pm	Exercise in Playground
12.15 – 2pm	Lesson on Collection (1st and 2nd),
	Scripture Doctrines (3rd & 4th), Scripture History (5th)
2 to 5pm	Dinner, Copying lessons and exercise
5 to 6.30pm	Questions on Sermon (1st and 2nd),
	Church Catechism (3rd to 5th)
6.30 to 7pm	Scripture reading and prayer

Monday

7.15-8am	Arithmetic
10 to 11am	History (1st), Natural History
11 to 12pm	Language
12.15-1pm	ditto
1 to 2pm	Composition (1st and 2nd), Lessons on Man, writing
5 to 6.30pm	Vocabulary

Subjects taught to Boys

Arithmetic, Composition, Language, Grammar, Lessons on objects, Natural History, Geography, Scripture History, Lessons on Man, Religion, Scripture Doctrines

Subjects to Girls

Same as boys, though at different times – depending on teachers availability

Tasks on Saturday evening
Girls – Mending, Housework and Washing
Boys – Brushing shoes and clothes for Sunday, cleaning and washing privies

Housework performed by Pupils (Girls) - for the year of 1903

Dormitory	Make beds, sweep floors, dust &c.
Stairs	Sweep and dust
Day-room	Sweep and dust
Lavatory	Leave in order after use
Dining-Room	Sweep, dust, prepare tables for meals, clear away and wash up
Infirmary	Sweep and dust. Wait upon matron when attending morning cases
Kitchen	Prepare vegetables for dinner, scour pots, sweep floors
Laundry	Assist with folding and mangling
	Prepare underclothes for Sunday
	Sewing – 9 hours per week
Boys	Sweep, dust and keep in order
	School, Gymnasium, Lavatory, Dormitory, Outdoor office

Appendix 6

Pupils buried in St. Mobhi's Churchyard, Glasnevin

Name of Pupil / Former Pupil	Date of Burial	Age in years
Mary Kinsella	22/9/1836	10
Anna Jane Melton	23/5/1843	12
Margaret Fizzell	19/11/1843	14
Eliza Maguire	20/3/1844	14
John Neil	20/5/1844	13
Francis Twanbe	9/5/1846	12
Hugh Dowling	16/6/1846	15
Michael Hartnett	20/3/1847	15
Catherine McPick	5/6/1847	16
Richard Bridget	27/6/1847	15
*Margaret Giblin	24/9/1847	13
Judith Mahony	25/9/1847	15
Lawrence O'Donnell	29/1/1849	11
Margaret Pearson	16/10/1849	16
Thomas Collins (former pupil)	25/9/1850	45
Thomas Payne	23/11/1850	7
Richard Barry	9/5/1851	14
William Birmingham	21/6/1851	9
*Jeremiah Fitzgerald	26/3/1853	10
John Neill	1/7/1853	13
Bridget Giblin	3/12/1853	15
Jane Still	31/5/1855	10
Thomas Carson	30/7/1857	14
John Shaughnessy	14/11/57	17
Ellen Crowley	25/7/1859	9
Mary Reynolds (former pupil)	25/11/1859	28
Maria Henderson	22/1/1860	10
Eliza Ryan	7/5/1860	14
Mary Dolan	9/6/1860	11
John Tiernan	20/5/1861	13
Anne McCusker	27/6/1861	12
John Hennessy	27/1/1865	11
Ralph Tector (former pupil)	May 1866	20?
Ellen Power	18/10/1866	17
Martha C. Wyatt	3/10/1870	15

Margaret Wigmore	22/5/1873	14
Thomas Dixon (former pupil)	4/5/1877	58 (Claremont messenger)
Elizabeth Wood	31/3/1880	14
Charlotte Davis	17/4/1880	13
**Edward James Chidley	21/2/1881	62
Isabella Esmonde	12/5/1881	15
John Wheeler	14/9/1881	16
**John Chidley (E.J. Chidley's son)	30/11/1882	22
**Emma M. Chidley (E.J.C.'s wife)	12/4/1884	54
*David Growcock	3/10/1888	18
Janet Marshall	11/3/1896	11

* whose death was mentioned in the Annual Report which was then reproduced in daily newspapers

** their graves were marked with a large headstone, with the inscription 'Headmaster of the Claremont Institution'

Sources: Burial Records of the Parish of St. Mobhi's, Glasnevin, at the Representative Church Body Library

Appendix 7

Pupils from the Army Regiments, the Navy and Police

Name / From	Admitted	Age	Details
'Deaf and Dumb Orphan'	May 1819		Found in Royal Barracks
Henry Browning	April 1833	8	50th Regiment
Henrietta Lawson	April 1835	9	25th Regiment
Edward Stanhope Worsley Burnett's Cottage, Ballsbridge, Dublin	Oct. 1835	8	Father: Commissioner in Navy, decd.
Mary Anne Porter	April 1841	11	85th Regiment
James Norman, Dublin	May 1841	11	Colour Sgt, 32nd Regt.
Roderick Mackenzie			Father in Navy
Jane Mulhall			Father, ex-serviceman
Henry Pengelly			Father in Navy
Charles Way			Father in Navy
Mary Prescott Driscoll	Jan 1855	6	Father - soldier
Mary Ann Hean, Aldershot Camp	April 1865	10	Father - 21st Regt
Samuel David, Portbello Barracks	Feb. 1867		10 Sgt Major, R.A.
James Robertson, Islandbridge Bcks Father to pay £1-10-0 p.a. and General Griffith to do same	April 1870	7	Royal Scot Greys 2nd Dragoons
James Callow, Portbello Barracks	June 1877	8	Father - soldier, decd.
Ellen Cuthbert, Dingle, Co. Kerry	July 1882	7	Father – coastguard
Charles W. Clarke, Aldershot, UK	Sept. 1889	15	Parents – Army teachers
Daisy Llewellyn Hayden, Curragh	Nov. 1889	5	Father - Staff Sergeant, Medical Staff Corps, dispatched to Ceylon
Mary Tough, born in Malta Richmond Barracks, Dublin	June 1898		11 Father, Army teacher
John Fletcher, born in Bermuda	Oct. 1899	7	Father – Royal Barracks
Mary Gargan, day pupil for lip-reading	no date	14	Father – Sgt Major
Frederick Sharp, Salisbury	March 1905	9	Father - gunner, Cahir
Kathleen Corrigan, Dublin	Nov. 1906	9	Father - policeman
Arthur Gibbs, day pupil for lip-reading	1914		24 Father – Army Major, decd
Jane Peasland, born in Manchester	April 1914	9	Father in Curragh Camp
Betty Bateman, Queenstown, Cork	Sept. 1926	6	Father, formerly a soldier

Appendix 8

Extract from 'The Freeman's Journal', 14 April 1840

National Deaf and Dumb Institution at Claremont

The annual meeting and public examination of the pupils of this very useful Institution was held yesterday, at the Round Room of the Rotundo (sic). The meeting was very well attended, a large portion of the assembly consisting, as usual, of fashionably dressed ladies and of boys. The latter, however, behaved throughout the proceedings in so rude and boisterous manner that great numbers of persons were obliged to leave the room, and every one of the speakers were under the necessity of making repeated, though unsuccessful appeals to them to remain quiet. The Lord Mayor, who was to preside, did not arrive for more than an hour after that time, and in the interim the company were amused by an examination of the junior boys of the Institution, who all answered the simple questions put to them by the elder boys in the correctest manner.

The Lord Mayor having taken the chair, and prayers being said, the Secretary proceeded to read the report for the year 1839, which stated that the Institution was then in a very prosperous condition, there being at present 112 children in the school. They had, however, to regret the loss of Dr Charles Orpen, their secretary since the foundation of the Institution in 1818, and who was lately gone to the sister country, where, however, he still lent them his valuable assistance. They were also deprived of the labours of Mr Joseph Humphreys, their head superintendent, whose reviews were peculiarly valuable. There were 29 new inmates admitted since their last annual meeting, and their improvement, especially in Scriptural education, was most gratifying. The Institution had been visited during last year with a much greater amount of sickness than in any preceding year, there being no less than 30 children attacked with scarletina, and several with fever. There were, however, but three deaths, and of these two were from consumption, which had existed in its incipient stages before their admission into the house. There were 16 of the pupils gone out of the Institution in the same period, of whom 13 were sent home to their friends, and the others absconded; one of the latter, however, they were in hopes would be induced to return. The Juvenile Society, which was in conjunction with theirs, was most useful, and supported no less than 87 of the inmates. The subs, donations, collections, etc, for the year amounted to 894 pounds, and the money received form the parents and friends of the pupils to 1,809 pounds, making in all 2,703 13s 8d, or with the balance on hands at their last meeting, 2,776 9s 9d. The disbursements for the year amounted to 2,533 2s 7d, leaving a balance in the hands of the treasurer of 222pds 7s 2d.

The examination of the pupils was resumed after the reading of the report, and afforded considerable satisfaction to all present. After the junior pupils were examined by their seniors in writing down to names of substantives and adjectives, they proceeded with examples in the conjugation of verbs, and the answers in every instance were perfectly correct. A number of questions were then sent up form the body of the meeting on slips of paper, and the nature of the answers to them may be conceived from the following examples, the replies being given by the more advanced boys:- "In what state was man created?" "In a state of happiness". "What is sin?" "Sin is the transgression of the law of God". "What is doctrine?" "Learning about religion". Etc.

The proprietor of the Panorama of the Eglintoun Tournament, at present exhibiting at the Rotundo, having kindly offered a free admission to the pupils of both sexes, they were then allowed to withdraw, and the other business of the meeting was proceeded with.

The Rev William Bushe moved the first resolution, recommending the adoption of the report, and addressed the meeting on the very flattering exhibition which they had just witnessed. In other charitable institutions the inmates were, when necessary, able to plead their own cause with the public; but here the poor deaf children of misfortune were obliged to look altogether to others for those appeals in their behalf, which were rendered necessary from their situation. He was on this account the more ready to call on the meeting to assist them, and he was confident that the call made upon the universally large meeting which he then addressed would be attended with lasting benefits to the Institution. The report which he had just heard read showed, by its feeling appeal to their humanity, that there was a class of persons who were still more miserable and deserving of commiseration than the blind themselves. They were doomed, without the benefit of that Institution, to remain for ever in the state of gross ignorance and helplessness in which they were born. They could know nothing of their own natures of the existence of a soul, or even of the Almighty himself. They were not aware that the world had ever been created, or that it would be again destroyed, and followed by an awful eternity, and thus contented themselves with having a bare idea that day and night would succeed each other for ever. It was from this fearful and melancholy state that the Institution was endeavouring to release them; and he trusted that, from the support which it would meet with from a charitable public, that this delightful object they had in view would be fully accomplished.

The Rev Joseph Bailey moved the next resolution, and said he rejoiced at being able to state that the Institution was at length placed on a truly religious and scriptural basis; and he trusted the time would come when he would find every public and charitable society in the kingdom similarly blessed. He had made calculations, from which he knew that the average annual cost of each pupil was 18 pounds; and as, according to the best authorities, there are 4,000 deaf and dumb persons in Ireland, the cost of educating them all would amount to about 70,000 pounds. That might appear a very large sum; but if each family in the kingdom gave only one shilling in the year for so laudable a purpose, they would be able to collect the entire sum, and the beneficial results which would arise from it could scarcely be believed.

The Rev Francis Sanderson seconded the resolution, which was agreed to. The Rev Lambert Hepenstal moved the next resolution, to the effect that, when they took into consideration the great importance of the Institution, and the necessity of educating the Deaf and Dumb poor of Ireland, they felt themselves called upon to make renewed exertions in its behalf. Dr Nugent Dunkan seconded the resolution, which was carried. The Rev Edward Markey was then called to the chair, when the thanks of the meeting were voted to the Lord Mayor for his kindness in coming among them on that occasion. The meeting then separated.

Appendix 9

Weddings of former Pupils

Wedding of Eva Weily and former teacher, Joseph Keating

On 29 July 1896, Eva Charlotte Weily, aged twenty, married Joseph Keating, aged around 33, at a tiny church of St Michael's, located in a hamlet of Rathcore, near Enfield, Co. Meath. Her father, Charles, a gentleman farmer, with a large demesne called Cullentra, three miles from Rathcore, gave her daughter away, to Mr Keating, whose occupation was secretary of an insurance company and whose father, William Keating, worked in the Civil Service. Mr Weily was delighted to see his deaf daughter having found happi-

ness in her new husband, whom she had known for some time while at Claremont.

On 10 December 1880, Joseph Keating commenced as Pupil Teacher, his salary at £10 per annum plus board. In 1884, Mr Chidley, headmaster, recommended that Keating's salary be increased from £20 to £30 as 'his present salary as principal assistant and drawing master was very small compared with those given to teachers in England'. In late 1894, he had taken ill and took some time off to recuperate from 'debility and weak heart'. On 8 March 1895, he tendered his resignation from his position of Assistant Teacher, having secured a position of secretary in the Ocean Accident and Guarantee Corporation, Dublin.

On 10 July 1885, an application was received for admission of Eva Charlotte Weily, her father to pay £24 per annum for her education and maintenance. She had seven sisters and a deaf brother, George, six years younger than herself. On 10 January 1890, the Rev. James Murphy, rector of Rathcore, wrote on behalf of her father, Mr Charles Weily, that 'owing to financial difficulties, Mr Weily could not send his daughter, Eva, back to Claremont, unless the Governors would reduce the payment from £24 to £20, as he has a deaf son to educate as well'. In the following year, her brother, George, was admitted, Mr Weily to pay £18 per annum, 'due to his large family'. In June 1896 George left Claremont to return home to assist his father with running the farm. He died on 2 November 1924, at the age of 42, and was buried in Rathcore, Co. Meath. His father died in 1901, aged 73 years, and his mother died in 1922, aged 80 years.

Wedding between former Pupils as described by a Clergyman

On 3 March 1880, at an Annual Meeting, the Rev. Robinson said that although he had been in Dublin a year, he had never been to Claremont. His information on the subject of the deaf and dumb dated from the day before the Annual Meeting, when it was his lot at St Matthias Church, of which he was curate, to unite in the bonds of matrimony a deaf and dumb man to a deaf and dumb woman. As he was unable to speak to the couple himself, he got their scripture reader to act as interpreter. The Scripture reader interviewed the man for him and made inquiries as to whether he fully realised the solemn step he was about to take, and the result of that interview was that he (Mr Robinson) was thoroughly satisfied that the bridegroom, a most respectable young man, knew what he was about.

At half past 11 o'clock he repaired to the church, where a good many people had assembled, and there were the bride and bridegroom and the best man and the bridesmaids, the whole party being deaf. One point it was found absolutely necessary to alter in the service, where it said that the bridegroom was to keep his hand on the bride's finger holding the ring there while he repeated the words "with this ring I thee wed".

He had had some experience of Easter Monday marriages of a very different character indeed, for when he was curate in East London, where Easter Monday was a great day amongst the lower classes for getting married, he was sorry to say the weddings he had seen take place had often been scores of great disorder, and they frequently required to call in the assistance of the police to compel the people to behave themselves. With that recollection in his mind, the contrast presented by the Easter Monday marriage in St Matthias Church yesterday, was most striking. Nothing could surpass the reverent demeanour of that couple, and the earnest glance with which he looked at her when he made that solemn promise, or the earnest glance upward of the bride when they received the blessing in the name of the Father, the Son, and the Holy Ghost, he had never seen surpassed.

He told them afterwards through the interpreter how much he was struck by the intelligence and reverence they had displayed, and how he thanked them for having assisted him in a duty about which he knew so little. So they shook hands and parted very good friends, and it was not a surprise to learn that that young man and young woman had been educated at that most invaluable institution (Claremont). He was particularly struck by the earnestness of the newly married pair when the time came for the repetition of the Lord's Prayer, which, in the Marriage Service, was too often a mere form, and the thought came to his mind, what patience and trouble must have been taken to train them up to understand these things. *(Daily Express, 3 March 1880)* *(The married couple was George Orr and Mary Anne Regan.)*

ANNUAL REPORT

FOR THE TWENTY-FIFTH YEAR ENDING DECEMBER, 31st, 1850.

OF THE

Dublin Day School for Deaf and Dumb,

Held at the Dorset Institution, 54, Upper Sackville-street.

PATRONESS:

COUNTESS OF RODEN, LADY FLORENCE BALFOUR, MRS. BUXTON,

COMMITTEE FOR 1850.

DOWAGER VISCOUNT-TESS HABBERTON,	MRS. H. DIGBY,	MISS EXSHAW,	MISS BRASLEY,
MRS. BARRETT,	MRS. WARREN,	MISS BROOKE,	REV. DR. SINGER,
MRS. MOLLAN,	MRS. BELFORD,	MISS MASON,	ARCHDEACON MAGEE,
MISS ELLIS,	MISS FRY,	MISS LOUGHLIN,	REV. JOHN HARE.

TREASURER AND SECRETARY:

MRS. HARE.

This interesting School having arrived at its 25th year, the Committee desire to return thanks to the great Giver of all Good for his protection and guidance.

The following extract of a letter from Sligo, shews the satisfactory condition of the two girls apprenticed there. "I am much pleased with them both, never had their Mistress to find fault with either of them, and my own opinion is, that they are actuated by the highest principal LOVE TO GOD. These girls were received into the School, one at the age of fourteen, the other nineteen, a pleasing proof of the advantage to be derived from Education, even at that advanced period of life.

The Committee wish to renew the statement given last year, that this School is intended as a day School for Deaf and Dumb Children, residing in Dublin, of both sexes, at the small expense of one penny per week, to the poorer one's of whom they are enabled to give food daily; that it also boards and lodges, taking a parental care of such children from the Country as being unable to obtain admission into Claremount, are intrusted to their charge by parents or friends contributing £5 annually, quarterly in advance, towards their support.

The Children are also apprenticed, when the Committee having faithfully used the appointed means to make known the name of Jesus, "that only name given among men whereby sinners can be saved," think that their state of mind and capabilities, render them fit for this advantage.

The Committee hope that the sum of £5 annually, to be paid quarterly in advance by country friends will not be deemed too much, when they consider the moral and spiritual darkness, to which without peculiar care, this suffering class is confined.

Subscriptions and donations paid at the Dorset Institution 54, Upper Sackville-street, or any communications directed to the Secretary, will be duly received and acknowledged.

Annual Report of Dublin Day School for the Deaf and Dumb, 1850

NATIONAL ASSOCIATION

FOR PROMOTING THE EDUCATION OF THE

DEAF AND DUMB, CLAREMONT, GLASNEVIN.

⊰ RULES. ⊱

Head Master.

I. The Head Master shall be responsible to the Governors for the performance of his duties : he shall have the entire direction of the business of the school ; and shall not absent himself from the Institution for more than 12 hours at one time nor during School hours without leave. He shall report to the Governors any irregularity which he may observe in the conduct of the several departments, and shall take care that the outer doors of the Institution are locked and the keys given into his possession at 10 o'clock every night, after which no person shall be allowed to enter or leave the Institution without his permission.

II. Prayers shall be read by the Master before the members of the Institution morning and evening. He shall attend the parish church with the pupils and teachers at least once each Sunday.

Welsh terrier, Airdale terrier, Yorkshire terrier, King Charles, Pekinese, bull terrier, bull-dog & buff are different breeds of dogs.

My Christmas Holidays.

I went home with my Aunt and Uncle on Friday the 20th December 1935 by motor-car.

There was a frosty fog in the morning as we left Dublin but when we arrived home it was fine.

We delayed in Cashel and ~~warted~~ warmed ourselves by the fire and had tea.

We arrived home at 4 o'clock.

We went down to the party in the Parochial Hall at 6 oc.

My two brothers and cousin Sybil got prizes.

Jack Phibbs came up to see us on Sunday evening.

I helped my mother to clean up the room.

We went to Middleton for the market to buy a turkey and a goose.

My two brothers and I decorated the rooms with holly

Page from Betty Bateman's Copybook

List of Illustrations and Picture Credits

Front Cover: *Dr C.E.H. Orpen (1791-1856), founder of the Claremont Institution,* courtesy of the National Library of Ireland
Miss Harriet R. Ferris, Headmistress, courtesy of Frank Ferris
Carpentry workshop in Claremont, courtesy of Martha Horan
Group of male pupils at Claremont, c. 1915, courtesy of Alice Rothwell

Back Cover: *Map of Glasnevin, 1821,* courtesy of the National Library of Ireland
Claremont House, c.1915, courtesy of Alice Rothwell and Martha Horan
William and Samuel Rothwell, courtesy of Alice Rothwell

Frontispiece: *National Institution for the Education of the Deaf and Dumb of Poor in Ireland at Claremont, near Glasnevin.* Lithographed at Allen's, Dublin from a Sketch by Mr Joseph Humphreys, Headmaster at Claremont (c.1825), courtesy of Dublin City Archives

Title Page: *'Av-e-nue',* from *An Illustrated Vocabulary for the Use of the Deaf and Dumb,* London 1857, engraved by Mr J.W. Whymper. The words under the pictures, some of which are displayed throughout the book, are specially structured in phonics, for teaching pronunciation to the deaf.

Prologue: *Henry Pollard with his Da,* courtesy of Michael Pollard

1 – A Letter to the King
George IV, from 'George the Fourth', by R.Fulford, 1932

2 – My First Day at Claremont
David John 'Jack' Stanton. collection of Henry Pollard
Thomas Henry Pollard, courtesy of Iris Pearson

3 – Children of Silence
Sir William Wilde, from 'Brief Lives of Irish Doctors', by J.B. Lyons
Statue of Juan Pablo Ponce in Madrid, author's photograph
London Asylum for the Deaf and Dumb, courtesy of National Archives of Ireland
Institution for the Deaf and Dumb, Birmingham, courtesy of National Archives of Ireland

4 – The Doctor who loved the Deaf
Dr Charles Edward Herbert Orpen, courtesy of the National Library of Ireland
The Abbé Roch-Ambroise Sicard, Institution for the Deaf and Dumb, Paris

Johann Heinrich Pestalozzi, from 'Pestalozzi', by Sibler, 1960

Signature of Dr Orpen inside a book, dated 1836, National Archives of Ireland

Crest of the Orpen Family at Ardtully Castle, Co. Kerry, author's photograph

Major Sirr, father-in-law of Dr Orpen, courtesy of National Library of Ireland

Alicia Orpen, wife of Dr C. Orpen, from 'The Microcosm', by T.Gutsche, 1960

Sir Richard John Theodore Orpen, from 'The Orpen Family' by Goddard H. Orpen
(1932)

Ardtully Castle, Kilgarvan, Co. Kerry – the home of Sir R.Orpen, author's photograph

5 - The Clergyman who served his people

Colesberg painted by Thomas Baines in 1850, from 'The Microcosm' by T.Gutsche,
1960

Christ Church, Colesberg, of which the Rev. C. Orpen was the first rector in 1857, author's
photograph.

Ox-wagon, in which the Orpen family travelled from Colesberg to Port Elizabeth,
from The Microcosm, by T.Gutsche

*Monument and the inscription on Orpen's burial-place at St Mary's Cemetery, Port
Elizabeth*, author's photographs

Rev. C. Orpen's sons in South Africa. Francis Henry, Charles Sirr, Arthur Richard,
Joseph Millerd, Richard John Newenham, Henry Martyn Herbert, Theodore
Robert Morrison. Their sister, Alicia, married John Murray of Grahamstown,
where their mother, Alicia, was buried in the Anglican Cemetery. From 'The
Microcosm' by T.Gutsche

6 – The Quaker who taught the Deaf

Statue of Mary Leadbeater at Ballitore, Co. Kildare, author's photograph

Institution for the Deaf and Dumb, Edinburgh, courtesy of National Archives of Ireland

Collection of Tobacco Pipes by T. Crofton Croker, Antiquarian, Dublin Penny Journal, July
1835

The English Two-Handed Manual Alphabet, designed by Mr Joseph Humphreys.
Engraved on stone by John Johnson (Deaf and Dumb), a former pupil of the
Institution and printed at the Lithographic Establishment of his Master, Mr J.W.
Allen, Trinity Street, 1836, courtesy of National Library of Ireland

The Spanish One-Handed Manual Alphabet, designed by Mr Joseph Humphreys.
Engraved on stone by John Johnson (Deaf and Dumb), a former pupil of the
Institution and printed at the Lithographic Establishment of his Master, Mr J.W.
Allen, Trinity Street, 1836, courtesy of National Library of Ireland

7 – The First Pupil of Claremont

Rotunda Assembly Rooms where Dr Open conducted lectures and exhibited Collins. Picture
by J. Malton, 1797, courtesy of Friends of the Rotunda

Nicholas Street, Dublin – where Thomas Collins lived before his death, author's
photograph

8 – Claremont, Glasnevin

Glasnevin House, courtesy of Patrick Wolohan

Colonel H. Gore Lindsay, from 'The British Deaf Times', Vol. 2, 1904, Royal National
   Institute for the Deaf (RNID) Library, London

Glasnevin, showing 'Claremount', Map by William Durcan, 1821, courtesy of National
   Library of Ireland

Claremont, with extensions, as at 1826, from 'Visits to Claremont', courtesy of Dublin
   City Archives

St. Mobhi's Church, Glasnevin, author's photograph

Pulpit crafted by Claremont pupils, author's photograph

9 – The Early Years of the Institution

Penitentiary in Smithfield, courtesy of Dublin City Archives

Engraving of the Institution at Claremont by Clayton, from Dublin Penny Journal, 2
   April 1836, courtesy of David Breslin

Boys' Section and Girls' Section of Classroom in the Birmingham Institution, National
   Archives of Ireland

10 – Claremont: The 1840s

Ulster Institution for the Deaf, Dumb and Blind, Belfast, courtesy of Linen Hall Library,
   Belfast

The Rev. Charles Stuart Stanford, Superintendent at Claremont (1840-1842), courtesy of
   Representative Church Body Library, Dublin

Yorkshire Institution for the Deaf and Dumb, Doncaster, from 'The History of the
   Yorkshire Residential School for the Deaf, 1829-1979', by Anthony J. Boyce

Sackville Street, Dublin (Barker, 1835). The Institution's office was located at No.16;
   courtesy of National Library of Ireland

*First and second pages of the Application form for admission of Mary Jane Steadman into the
   Institution*, courtesy of National Archives of Ireland

11 – Claremont: The 1850s to 1880s

Thirty-eighth Annual Report of the Institution for the year of 1854, with vignette of
   Claremont designed by Lawrence Feagan, former pupil and drawing master at
   Claremont, courtesy of National Archives of Ireland

Notice of Annual Meeting at Claremont on 2 April 1877, found at St Andrew's Church,
   Suffolk Street, Dublin, courtesy of Brian Lawson

Edward J. Chidley, Headmaster from 1856 to 1881. The Deaf and Dumb Magazine, Vol.
   9, May 1881, RNID Library

Benjamin H. Payne, teacher at Claremont, The Deaf and Dumb Magazine

Samuel Johnson, teacher at Claremont, The Silent Worker, New Jersey, 1892

12 – Claremont: The 1890s to 1940s

Mr George Taylor, Headmaster (1888-1928), The British Deaf Times, Vol. 8, July 1889,
    RNID Library

1842 Map showing the Claremont demesne with the Avenue and the farm behind, courtesy
    of Royal Irish Academy

*Teaching Staff at Claremont, 1904. Mr Wootton, Miss McConnell, Mr G. Taylor, Miss
    Jacobs, Mr Rowan.* The British Deaf Times, Vol. 1, September 1904, RNID Library

Male Pupils at Claremont, c.1915, courtesy of Alice Rothwell and James Horan

Pupils with Miss Ferris at right, c. 1916, courtesy of Maureen Wood

Female staff, c.1916. Miss Ferris, Miss Taylor and Miss E.McConnell, courtesy of Alice
    Rothwell and James Horan

Pupils with Mr. C. Tivy, instructor, in Carpentry Shop at Claremont, c.1924, courtesy of
    Martha Smith

*Annual Meeting at Claremont in 1937. Left: Miss Beggs (Matron), behind her, Miss
    Deacon (headmistress), Mr Gick (secretary) – in centre with spectacles.* National
    Archives.

Annual Meeting in 1938 - courtesy of David Platts

Claremont, c.1914. Private pupils' bedroom in top floor of Headmaster's House - courtesy of
    Alice Rothwell and Martha Smith

Claremont in derelict condition, c.1932, courtesy of Martha Smith

13 – The Monkstown School

1921 Map of Monkstown, showing Carrick Manor, from Dun Laoghaire Historical
    Society

Carrick Manor as at 1945, the home of the Claremont School from 1943 to 1978, courtesy of
    Dennis Steenson

Annual Meeting at Monkstown, c.1944, courtesy of Dennis Steenson

Miss Ferris, Headmistress, courtesy of Frank Ferris

Pupils with Miss Ferris in May 1948, from the Irish Independent

Mrs Henderson with her 'Army', in 1956, courtesy of Martha Smith

Norman Rankin, starting school in January 1950, courtesy of Norman Rankin

14 – Teaching the Deaf

Page of Objects for teaching language to the deaf from Sicard's 'Cours d'Instruction du
    Sourd Muets', Institution for the Deaf, Paris

*Scheme for an Universal Alphabet, sketched from the Organs of Speech in the act of
    Articulation*, two pages, from 'Anthologia Hibernica', July 1793, courtesy of
    Marsh's Library

Section of the Organs of Speech to shew the Mechanism of Articulation, lithographed by
    John Johnston, a Deaf mute (formerly pupil in the Institution) at his Masters, Mr
    Allen's, Lithographic Establishment, 16 Trinity Street, from Dr Orpen's book,

Anecdotes and Annals of the Deaf and Dumb, courtesy of Dublin City Archives
Oral Class at Claremont, from the British Deaf Times, September 1904, RNID Library
Two-handed, or English, Manual Alphabet, from Dublin Penny Journal, April 1836,
     courtesy of David Breslin
Signs for Numbers, from Annual Report, 1822. courtesy of National Library of Ireland

15 – Pictures in the Mind

'Dog and Kennel' – woodcut by a deaf pupil of the Institution for the Deaf at Milan,
     c.1820, courtesy of National Archives of Ireland
*The Pillar Room in the Rotunda, where public examinations and meetings were held up to
     the 1860s* - courtesy of Friends of the Rotunda
'Two men with wheel' – woodcut by a deaf pupil of the Institution for the Deaf at
     Milan, c.1820, courtesy of National Archives of Ireland
'Children on see-saw' - woodcut by a deaf pupil of the Institution for the Deaf at
     Milan, c.1820, courtesy of National Archives of Ireland
Pennsylvanian Asylum for the Deaf and Dumb, courtesy of National Archives of Ireland

16 – Life at School

'Crying Girl' - woodcut by deaf pupil from Milan, courtesy of National Archives of
     Ireland
'Two boys fighting' – woodcut by deaf pupil from Milan, courtesy of National
     Archives
Dining Room in Claremont, c.1900, from the British Deaf Times, Vol. 1, September
     1904, RNID Library

17 – Leaving Claremont

Chart showing various trades, engraved by G.M.G. The Deaf and Dumb Magazine,
     1874, RNID Library
Indenture Form, apprenticing Mary Jane Steadman to Miss Ellen Ellery, boot-binder,
     courtesy of National Archives of Ireland
*Letter from mother of Mary Jane Steadman, giving her consent for her daughter to be
     apprenticed*, courtesy of National Archives of Ireland
Letter from Rev. Holden, testifying on Miss Elley's good character as employer, courtesy of
     National Archives of Ireland

18 – Six Shillings and Six Pence

Annual Report of the Juvenile Association, 1834, courtesy of Marsh's Library, Dublin
List of Pupils placed in the Institution by the Juvenile Association, courtesy of National
     Archives of Ireland
Sketch of Claremont by Lawrence Feagan, courtesy of National Archives of Ireland
Annual Report of the Institution, 1932, courtesy of National Archives of Ireland

Tom Ireland, from Co. Kilkenny, courtesy of David Platts
Francis Maginn, missionary to Cork and then Belfast, The Deaf and Dumb Times,
    May 1890, RNID Library
W.J. McCormick, missionary to Cork, The Messenger, November 1899, RNID Library
Reunion of the Cork Mission for the Adult Deaf and Dumb in July 1906, The Messenger,
    September 1906, RNID Library

22 – 'Talent for Drawing'
'Two women at work in the Waterford area' by Sampson Towgood Roch, c.1824,
    courtesy of Ulster Folk and Transport Museum
John Johnson's illustration of the Banquet at Hillsborough Fort, collection of Trevor Neill
Magdalen Tower at Drogheda, by Lawrence Feagan, courtesy of David Breslin
Mellifont Abbey, Co. Louth, by Lawrence Feagan, courtesy of David Breslin
Picture of Claremont, designed by Benjamin Payne and lithographed by George McNaught,
    courtesy of National Archives of Ireland
Betty Bateman with her brothers, William and Abner, courtesy of Penny Turner
Sample of artwork by Betty Bateman, c.1936, courtesy of Penny Turner

23 – Deaf Women
Portrait of Charlotte Elizabeth Tonna, courtesy of Doreen Woodford and British Deaf
    History Society
'Catherine' from 'The Silent Worker', Trenton, New Jersey
Elizabeth 'Lizzie' Whelan, courtesy of David Platts
Lizzie with her brother, John, and her sister, Cecilia, courtesy of David Platts
Thomas and Mary Devine (née Gillespie), with their daughter, Julia, courtesy of Sean
    Magee

24 – Going Away for Good
Harry, Ethel and Alec MacDonald as young children;   Harry as missioner;   Harry as ARP
    fire-warden at Truro Cathedral;   Alec as missioner, courtesy of Davina Merricks
Miss Deacon, left, and Betty Bateman, right. Most of the pupils in the photograph moved to
    England for good. Taken in June 1931 - courtesy of Penny Turner

25 – History of the Dublin Working Boys' Home
The Dublin Working Boys' Home and Harding Technical School, Lord Edward Street,
    Dublin, courtesy of National Archives of Ireland
Gymnasium at Harding Home, courtesy of National Archives of Ireland
Mr Dolan, Superintendent, with Table Tennis Group, courtesy of National Archives of
    Ireland
Mr Frank B. Ormsby, Secretary, courtesy of National Archives of Ireland
Mr James Harris, Superintendent, courtesy of National Archives of Ireland

Select Bibliography

Akenson, Donald H., 1970 – *The Irish Education Experiment: The National System of Education in the 19th Century*, Routledge & Kegan Paul, London

Atkinson, Alexander, 1865 (reprinted 2001): *Memoirs of My Youth*, British Deaf History Publications, Middlesex

Atkinson, Norman, 1969 – *Irish Education: A History of Educational Institutions*, Allen Figgis, Dublin

Banyon, Douglas C., 1996 - *Forbidden Signs: American Culture and the Campaign against Sign Language*, University of Chicago Press, Chicago

Berg, Otto B., 1984 – *A Missionary Chronicle: being a history of the ministry to the deaf in the Episcopal Church (1850-1980)*, St Mary's Press, Maryland, U.S.A.

Best, George, 1992 – *Mid-Victorian Britain: 1851-75*, Fontana Press, London

Bowen, Desmond, 1978 – *The Protestant Crusade in Ireland, 1800-70*, Gill and Macmillian

Boyce, Anthony J. et al, 2004 – 'Flying High!', *Deaf History Journal*, Vol. 8, Issue 2, British Deaf History Society

_____, 1996 - *The History of the Yorkshire Residential School for the Deaf, 1829-1979*, Doncaster M.B.C. Arts and Museums Services, Doncaster

_____, 1996 – *The Leeds Beacon*

_____, 1999 – 'A Little Boy from Hull', *Deaf History Journal*, Vol. 2, Issue 3, British Deaf History Society

_____, 1999 – 'The Claremont Stone Windows', *Deaf History Journal*, Vol. 3, Issue 2, British Deaf History Society

_____, 2001 – 'British Links with Claremont', *Paper presented at the Claremont Reunion in Dublin*

Boyd, Gary A., 2006 - *Dublin 1745-1922: The Making of Dublin City - Hospital, Spectacle and Vice*, Four Courts Press

Branson, Jan and Miller, Don, 2002 – *Damned for Their Difference: The Cultural Construction of Deaf People as Disabled*, Gallaudet University Press, Washington DC

Bremmer, Jan & Roodenburg, Herman, 1991 - *A Cultural History of Gesture: From Antiquity to the Present Day*, Polity Press, London

Breslin, David, 2001 – 'The Deaf O'Brien's of Ireland', *Deaf History Journal*, Vol. 5, Issue 1, British Deaf History Society

Broderick, Terri & Duggan, Regina, 1996 – *Origins & Developments of St Mary's School for Deaf Girls, Cabra*, St Mary's School for Deaf Girls, Dublin

Bulwer, John, 1644 - *Chirologia or the Natural Language of the Hand, composed of the speaking motions and discoursing gestures*, London

_____, 1654 - *Philocophus: or, the deafe and dumbe man's friend*

Burke, 1912 – *Dictionary of the Landed Gentry of Ireland*

Connolly, S.J., 1982 – *Priests and People in Pre-Famine Ireland, 1780-1845*, Gill and Macmillan, Dublin

Copleston, J., 1866 – *How to Educate the Deaf and Dumb- a short exposition of the Proposed Plan for the Establishment of Day Schools for teaching the Deaf to Speak by means of articulation and lip-reading on Mr Mary's System*, London

Crean, Edward J., 1997 – *Breaking the Silence: History of Deaf Education in Ireland*, Irish Deaf Society Publications

Crowe, John S., 1928 – A Concise Dictionary of Irish Biography

Daniels, Marilyn, 2003 – *Benedictine Roots in the Development of Deaf Education*

D'Alton, John, 1838 - *The History of County Dublin* - 3rd edition, Tower Books (1976)

Dalton, Kevin, 2003 – *That could never be: A Memoir*, Columba Press, Dublin

Dowling, P.J., 1971 – *A History of Irish Education: A study in conflicting loyalties*, Mercier Press, Cork

Fisher, H, and Lane, H. (eds), 1993 – *Looking Back: A Reader on the History of Deaf Communities and their Sign languages*, Signum Press, Hamburg

Fisher, H. and Vollhaber, Tomas (eds), 1993 – *Collage: Works on International Deaf History*, Signum Press, Hamburg

Foulston, James, 1856 – *Education of the Deaf and Dumb*

Fulford, Roger, 1932 – *George the Fourth*, Duckworth, London

Gilbert, J.T. – *History of the City of Dublin*, (Dublin, 1854-9; 2nd ed. With index, 1978)

Goodbody, Olive C., 1967 – *Guide toIrish Quaker Records*, Irish Manuscripts Commission

Grubbs, Isobel, 1927 – *History of the Quakers in Ireland*

Gutsche, Thelma, 1968 – *The Microcosm*, Howard Timmins, Cape Town

Hall, Catherine, '*Missionary Stories*' – Grossberg, Lawrence et al, 1992 – *Cultural Studies*, Routledge, New York

Harrison, Richard S., 1991 – *Cork City Quakers: A Brief History 1655-1939*, Dublin
_____, 1997 – *Biographical Dictionary of Irish Quakers*, Four Courts Press Ltd, Dublin

Hayden, Mary - *Charity Children in 18th Century Dublin*, Dublin Historical Record, Vol. V, 1942-43

Hull, Susannah, 1889 – *Education of the Deaf*, London

Jackson, Peter W, 1990 – *Britain's Deaf Heritage*, The Pentland Press Ltd, Edinburgh

Jackson, Peter W. and Lee, Raymond, 2001 – *Deaf Lives: Deaf People in History*, British Deaf History Publications, Middlesex

Jones, H.Z., 1990 – *The Palatine Families of Ireland*, Picton Press, Rockfort, Maine

Jones, M.G., 1938 – *The Charity School Movement in the 18th Century*, Cambridge University Press

Keenan, Desmond J., 1983 – *The Catholic Church in the 19th Century Ireland*, Gill and Macmillan, Dublin

Lapp, Eula C., 2000 – *To Their Heirs Forever*

Lane, Harlan (ed.), 1984 – *The Deaf Experience: Classics in Language & Education*, University of Harvard, Massachusetts

_____, 1984 – *When the Mind Hears: A History of the Deaf*, Random House, New York

_____, 1994 – *The Mask of Benevolence*, Random House, New York

Leadbeater, Mary, edited by John MacKenna, 1986, *The Annals of Ballitore, 1766-1824*, Stephen Scroop Press

LeFanu, Emma, 1860 – *The Life of the Rev. Charles Edward Herbert Orpen, M.D.*, Dublin

Leslie, J.B., 1912 – *Succession List of Dublin Clergy (Volumes 1 and 2)*

Lewis, Samuel, 1837 - *A Topographical Dictionary of the Parishes, Towns and villages of Dublin City and County*, edited as *Lewis' Dublin* by Christopher Ryan, 2001

Luddy, Maria, 1995 – *Women in Ireland:1800-1918*, Cork University Press

Lyons, J.B, 1978 – *Brief Lives of Irish Doctors*, Blackwater Press, Dublin

Machan, Tim W. & Scott, Charles, T. 1992 – *English in its Social Contexts: Essays in Historical Sociolinguistics*, Oxford University Press, New York

MacLeod, Manson A., 1950 – *The Work of the Protestant Churches for the Deaf in North America (1815-1949)*, American Annals for the Deaf

Matthews, Patrick A., 1996 – *The Irish Deaf Community, Volume 1* – The Irish Linguistics Institute of Ireland, Dublin

Maxwell, Constantia, 1946 – *Dublin under the Georges*, George Harrap, London

McCarthy, Muriel, 1992 – *Marsh's Library: All Graduates and Gentlemen*, Dublin

McDonnell, Patrick J., 1979 – *The Establishment and Operation of Institutions for the Education of the Deaf in Ireland, 1816-1889*, An unpublished thesis in part fulfilment for the degree of Master in Education, University College Dublin

McLoughlin, M.G., 1987 – *A History of the Education of the Deaf in England*, G.M. McLoughlin

McManus, Joe, 2002 – *Milford, A Village History*

N.Z.R. Molyneux, 1904 - *Genealogical and Biographical History of the Molyneux Families*, C.W.Bardeen, Syracuse, New York

Murphy, Étain, 2003 – *A Glorious Extravaganza: A history of Monkstown Parish Church*, Wordwell Press, Dublin

National Gazetteer, 1868 – *A Topographical Dictionary of the British Islands*, Vol. III, Virtue & Co., London

O'Cléirigh, Nellie, 2003 – *Hardship & High Living: Irish women's lives 1808-1923*, Portobello Press

O'Dowd, Michael, 1955 – *The History of the Catholic Schools for the Deaf, Cabra, Dublin*, An unpublished thesis for M.A., University College Dublin

Olden, Thomas, 1895 – *The Church of Ireland*, Wells Gardner Darton, London

Orpen, Charles E.H, 1828 – *The Contrast between Atheism, Paganism and Christianity of the Uneducated Deaf and Dumb, as Heathens, as compared with those who have been instructed in language and revelation and taught by the Holy Spirit as Christians,*

Goodwin, Dublin

_____, 1826 – *Address regarding the Poor of Ireland*, Dublin

_____, 1828 – *Pestalozzi and his Plans*, The Christian Examiner and Church of Ireland Magazine, Vol. VII

_____, 1833 – *Errors of the Irish Bible*, Dublin

_____, 1836 – *Anecdotes and Annuals of the Deaf and Dumb*, Tims Dublin

Orpen, Goddart H., 1930 – *The Orpen Family*

Plann, Susan, 1997 - *A Silent Minority – Deaf Education in Spain, 1550-1835*, University of California Press, Los Angeles, California

Ringland, John and Gelston, John, 1856 - *Report of a Deputation from the National Association for the Education of the Deaf and Dumb Poor of Ireland*, Dublin

Robins, Joseph, 1980 – *The Lost Children: A study of Charity Children in Ireland, 1700-1900*, Institute of Public Administration, Dublin

_____, 1999 – *The Workhouses of Ireland*, Anvil Press Ltd, Dublin

Sibler, X, 1960 – *Pestalozzi: The Man and his Work*, Routledge and Kegan Paul, London

Simpson, Edward, 1863 – *Poems on the Deaf & Dumb*

Strickland, Walter, 1913 – *Dictionary of Irish Artists (two volumes)*

Taylor, George (undated) – *History of the Claremont Institution for the Deaf*

The National Gazetteer – A Topographical Dictionary of the British Islands, Vol. III, Virtue & Co. London, 1868

Tonna, Charlotte, 1850 – *The Happy Mute*

_____, 1841 – *Personal Recollections*, reprinted and edited as *Irish Recollections* by P.Maune in 2004, University College Press, Dublin

Van Cleve, John V., 1999 – *Deaf History Unveiled*, Gallaudet University Press, Washington DC

Warburton, Whitelaw and Walsh , 1818 - *History of the City of Dublin (two volumes)*, London

Watson, Joseph, 1857 – *Illustrated Vocabulary for the Deaf*

Whelan, Irene, 2005 – *The Bible War in Ireland*, Lilliput Press, Dublin

Widdes, J.D.H, 1972 - *The Richmond, Whitworth & Hardwicke Hospitals, St. Laurence's Dublin, 1772-1972*

Wilde, William, 1854 – *On the Condition of the Deaf & Dumb*, John Churchill Press, London

Woodford, Doreen, 2001 – 'Charlotte Elizabeth Tonna', *Deaf History Journal*, Vol. 4, Issue 3, British Deaf History Society

Archival, Primary and Secondary Sources

Church of Ireland College of Education Archives: Administrative Papers of the Kildare Place Society

Cork Archives: Minutes of the Board of Guardians of Cork

Cork City Public Library: Street Directories; Newspapers and Pamphlets

Dublin City Library and Archives: Newspapers and periodicals – hardcopy and microfiches; *Thom's Directory,* various; Maps of Dublin City from the 1800s onwards

Gallaudet University Archives, Washington D.C.: Annual Reports of the Claremont
Institution; Journals of the Rev. Dr. T.H. Gallaudet; Biographical details on the
Deaf Clergy of the U.S.A.

General Register Office, Dublin: Certificates of Births, Marriages and Deaths

Irish Architectural Archives: Newspaper Files on Various Buildings in Dublin

John Rylands Library, University of Manchester: The Farrar Collection (Deaf Education)

Kildare County Council Library – Ballitore: Books on the Quakers in Ireland

Linen Hall Library, Belfast: Newspapers and periodicals; Genealogical Directories;
Street Directories and Almanacs

Marsh's Library, Dublin: Annual Reports of the Juvenile Association for the Deaf and
Dumb; Bulwer's *Chirologia or the National Language of the Hand;* Holder, Dr
William (1668) – *Philosophical Transactions.*

Mercer Library, Dublin: Minutes of the House of Industry; Biographies of Medical
Practitioners

National Library of Ireland, Dublin: Almanacs; Annual Reports of the Claremont
Institution; Atlases and Ordnance Survey Maps; Biographies; Newspapers and
periodicals – hardcopy, microfiches and the Internet; Parliamentary Papers

National Archives, Dublin; Administrative and legal documents of the Claremont
Institution; Annual Reports; Application Papers of Pupils; Chief Secretary's
Office Papers (1816-1850); Minutes of the Claremont Institution; Minutes of the
Dublin Working Boys' Home; Wills and Testamentary Papers; Thom's Directories

Offaly County Council Libraries – Banagher, Clara and Tullamore: Local History Files

Public Records Office of Northern Ireland, Belfast: Belfast Street Directories; Church of
Ireland Records; Minutes of the Ulster Society for the Education of the Deaf,
Dumb and Blind (incomplete); School/Educational Records; Wills /
Testamentary Papers

Religious Society of Friends' Historical Library, Dublin: Biographies of Irish Quakers;
Records of Births, Marriages and Deaths; Shackleton Papers and other documents

Representative Church Body Library, Dublin: Crockford's Directories of Clergy;
Church of Ireland Directories; Minutes of the Mission to the Adult Deaf and
Dumb (Dublin District); Minutes of the Mission to the Adult Deaf and Dumb
(Southern District); Records of Baptisms, Marriages and Burials; Succession Lists
of Clergy in Ireland; Vestry Minute Books of various Parishes of Ireland

Royal Irish Academy Library, Dublin: Journals of Historical Societies of Cork, Dublin, Kerry and Sligo; Pamphlets from the Halliday Collection; Genealogical Books by Goddard Herbert Orpen

Royal National Institute for the Deaf Library, London: Periodicals covering items in relation to education of the deaf and related issues

Trinity College Dublin Library: Censuses of Ireland; Reports of the Royal Commission for the Education of the Deaf, Dumb and Blind (1889); Various books and periodicals covering education of the deaf, charities and religious societies; Journals of various Archaeological and Historical Societies

Trinity College Dublin – Manuscript Room: Records of Alumni and Graduates of Trinity College Dublin

Newspapers, Journals and Periodicals Consulted:

British Deaf History Journal, Christian Examiner, Church of Ireland Gazette, Cork Constitution, Daily Express, Dublin Builder, Dublin University Magazine, Dublin Historical Records, Freeman's Journal, Halliday Pamphlets, History Ireland, Irish Ecclesiastical Gazette, Irish Independent,

Websites:

Australian Deaf History (www.aslia.com.au/vic.history and www.vicdeaf.com.au)
British Deaf History (www.dcmon.co.uk/deafhistory)
Irish Deaf History (www.geocities.com/Mythyka29/DeafHeritage)
Dublin History (www.indigo.ie/kinlay)
Lisburn Local History (www.lisburn.com)
Orpen Family History (http://members.rogers.com/dnmunroe/orpen)
Ulster Religious History (www.revival-library.org)

End-Notes

1 – A Letter to the King

[1] This story was written by Sean Griffin and recited on the radio programme, *Sunday Miscellany*, broadcast by RTÉ, in May 2003.

2 – My First Day at Claremont

[1] Nineteenth-century term for 'meningtis' – inflammation of membranes enveloping brain and spinal cord, which is often the cause of deafness.

[2] *A Glorious Extravaganza, A History of Monkstown Parish Church* - Étain Murphy (2003)

3 – Children of Silence

[1] *Damned for their Difference* – J. Branson and D.Miller (2002)

[2] *Forbidden Signs: American Culture* – D.C. Banyton (1996)

[3] *Belfast Newsletter*, 1 June 1832, p.4

[4] *On the Physical, Moral and Social Condition of the Deaf & Dumb* - W.Wilde (1854)

[5] *Concise Dictionary of Irish Biography* – John S. Crowe (1928)

[6] *Brief Lives of Irish Doctors* – J.B. Lyons (1978)

[7] *On the Physical, Moral and Social Condition of the Deaf & Dumb* - W.Wilde (1854)

[8] Ulster Institution for the Deaf, Dumb and Blind in Belfast, established in 1831

[9] *On the Physical, Moral and Social Condition of the Deaf & Dumb* - W.Wilde (1854)

[10] *Benedictine Roots in the Development of Deaf Education* - Marilyn Daniels (2003)

[11] *A Silent Minority: Deaf Education in Spain 1550-1835* – Susan Plann, 1997

[12] *Oxford Dictionary of National Biography* (2004)

[13] *History of the City of Dublin* – Warburton, Whitelaw and Walsh (1818), Vol. II

[14] *Deaf Lives* – David Breslin, British Deaf History Publications (2001)

[15] Register Books of the Royal School for the Deaf, Margate, with assistance from A.J. Boyce

[16] Minutes of the Claremont Institution, May 1847

[17] *The National Gazetteer – A Topographical Dictionary of the British Islands*, Vol. III, Virtue & Co. London, 1868

[18] *The Deaf O'Brien's of Ireland* – David Breslin, Journal of the British Deaf History Society, August 2001

[19] *Saunders Newsletter*, 7 June 1854

[20] *Britain's Deaf Heritage* – Peter W. Jackson (1990)

4 – The Doctor who loved the Deaf

[1] *The Life of the Rev Charles Edward Herbert Orpen, M.D.* – E. LeFanu (1860)

[2] *The Church of Ireland* – Thomas Olden (1895)

[3] *The Life of the Rev. C.E.H. Orpen, M.D.* – E.Le Fanu (1860)

[4] *Pestalozzi and his Plans* – Dr C.E.H. Orpen, *The Christian Examiner and Church of Ireland Magazine,* November 1828, Vol. VII

[5] *Dublin Evening Post,* 10 April 1832

[6] Chief Secretary's Office Registered Papers (CSO 1831/3568)

[7] *East London Daily Dispatch,* 20 November 1920

[8] *The Life of the Rev Charles Edward Herbert Orpen, M.D.* – E. LeFanu (1860)

[9] Dublin Historical Record, Vol. 4, No.1 – September/November 1941

[10] His Dublin residence was at 41 North Georges' Street, where Dr Charles Orpen also had his family home at number 11, after some time at 40 St Stephen's Green.

[11] *East London Daily Dispatch,* 20 November 1920

[12] *The Silent Worker,* Vol. 6, No.6 - February 1894 - New Jersey School for the Deaf, Trenton, USA

[13] This was Cove until named as Queenstown in honour of Queen Victoria on her visit to Ireland in the year of 1849, and after the War of Independence in 1921 as Cobh, which was the gateway for transatlantic ship travel to the United States, the United Kingdom and some European sea-ports. The Mission of the Adult Deaf and Dumb in Cork occasionally welcomed deaf passengers disembarking from the transatlantic and European sailings up to the 1950s, including the Rev. T.H. Gallaudet, son of the founder of the American Asylum for the Deaf in Hartford, United States of America in 1817.

5 – The Clergyman who served the people

[1] *Reminiscences of Life in South Africa from 1846 to the present day* - Joseph Millerd Orpen (1964)

[2] *The Life of the Rev. C.E.H. Orpen, M.D.* – E. LeFanu (1860)

[3] *The Microcosm* – T. Gutsche (1968)

[4] Annual Report of the Institution, 1857

[5] *The South African Church Magazine & Ecclesiastical Review,* May 1856

6 – The Quaker who taught the Deaf

[1] *The Life of the Rev. C.E.H. Orpen* – E. LeFanu (1860)

[2] Term usually applied by the members of the Religious Society of Friends when addressing each other.

[3] The house was at 11 Brunswick Street, Dublin.

[4] Administrative Correspondence of the Kildare Place Society, Church of Ireland College of Education Archives

[5] *Memoirs of My Youth* - Alexander Atkinson (former pupil of the Edinburgh Deaf & Dumb Institution)

[6] *The Dublin Penny Journal,* 25 July 1835, Vol. IV

[7] The Selina Fennell Collection, Historical Library of the Religious Society of Friends, Dublin

[8] Annual Report of the Institution, 1841

7 – The First Pupil of Claremont
[1] *The Workhouses of Dublin*, John Robins, 1999
[2] *Letter to Hannah Lecky from her father, Mr Lecky* – Historical Library of the Religious Society of Friends, Dublin
[3] Dublin Castle was at that time the seat of British administration in Ireland.
[4] *Chambers' Edinburgh Journal*, 25 September 1850

8 – Claremont, Glasnevin
[1] *Written by a deaf lad in America, copied from a Report of the Deaf and Dumb Asylum at Hartford* – reproduced in *The Dublin Penny Journal, Vol. IV* – April 2, 1836
[2] *A Topographical Dictionary of the Parishes, Towns and villages of Dublin City and County* - Samuel Lewis (1837)
[3] *A History of the County Dublin* - Francis Elrington Ball (1920)
[4] *The History of County Dublin* - John D'Alton (1838)
[5] Chief Secretary's Office Papers - 1822/623

9 – The Early Years of the Institution
[1] Minutes of the House of Industry, Volume 2
[2] *The Richmond, Whitworth & Hardwicke Hospitals, St. Laurence's Dublin, 1772-1972* – J.D.H. Widdes (1972)
[3] Joseph Lancaster, an English Quaker, developed a system of teaching which was designed to supplement a lack of teachers by encouraging the pupils to pass on such learning as they get through the use of a monitorial system. This tackled the problems of illiteracy and educational deprivation of the poor, and was designed also to disregard sectarianism and denominational differences. This was so designed that any committee members introducing proselytising ambitions would lose their places.
[4] *The Lost Children* – Joseph Robins, 1980
[5] Annual Report of the Institution, 1820
[6] Annual Report of the Institution, 1821
[7] The American Asylum for the Deaf and Dumb was established in 1817, exactly one year after the Irish Institution. For further details, see H. Lane's *When the Mind Hears*.
[8] Minutes of the Claremont Institution, September 1822
[9] Annual Report of the National Institution, 1822
[10] *Dublin Evening Mail*, 8 October 1830
[11] When Magee became Archbishop of Dublin, he found the archdiocese in 1822 in a shocking condition. On 24 October of that year, he made a stinging comment in his charge to the ordinands in St Patrick's Cathedral, 'the parson was to consider himself the true *parish priest*, in continual contact with his flock, as their adviser, their friend, the moderator of their disputes, the careful instructor of their children'. To most Roman Catholic critics this read like an open declaration of religious war – the

beginning of a 'Second Reformation'. [*The Protestant Crusade in Ireland*, D. Bowen (1978)]

[12] Census of Ireland, 1851, Part III, p.33 – *The Establishment and Operation of Institutions for the Education of the Deaf in Ireland, 1816-1889*, Patrick McDonnell (1979)

[13] *Saunders Newsletter*, 14 December 1840

[14] The Rev. Mortimer O'Sullivan was the most important of the Protestant controversialists of the pre-Famine period, and the most intelligent and interesting of them. He had been converted to Protestantism while at the Clonmel school of Dr Richard Carey. He attended Trinity College, was ordained and held various curacies before he moved north to become rector of Killyman, Co. Armagh. [*The Protestant Crusade in Ireland*, D. Bowen (1978)]

[15] Robert Daly, only son of the wealthy Rt Hon. Denis Daly and of his mother, heiress of the first Earl of Farnham. He entered the Church in 1803, and some years later, his conversion to the Evangelical Movement resulted from meeting Evangelical luminaries such as B.W. Mathias. He became rector of Powerscourt, Co. Wicklow, and his wife, Lady Powerscourt, helped him to advance in Evangelical circles. He was also assisted by the Hon. and Rev. Edward Wingfield, another renowned controversial preacher. In due course, Daly became prominent among the Evangelical clergy, and assumed the 'position and bearing of a Protestant Pope'. (*ibid*)

[16] Minutes of the Institution, 2 December 1825

[17] *Dublin Evening Mail*, 2 January 1829

[18] Annual Report of the Institution, 1822

[19] Annual Report of the Institution, 1835

[20] Minutes of the Institution, May 1832

[21] It is difficult at this point to ascertain whether this refers to the hearing boys, from wealthy families, who were members of the Juvenile Association. This was a charitable society with branches set up in private schools and seminaries across the country where pupils would use collecting cards to raise funds to support deaf children of the poor. This Association held its annual meetings and election of pupils at Claremont on the Easter Monday of each year, and in 1851 it amalgamated with the Committee of the Institution (which had hitherto been known as 'Parent Society').

[22] Annual Report of the Institution, 1835

10 – Claremont – The 1840s

[1] *Topographical Directory of Dublin* – Samuel Lewis, 1832

[2] Annual Report of the National Institution, 1843

[3] Annual Report of the National Institution, 1820

[4] ibid

11 – Claremont: The 1850s to 1880s

[1] *St Mary's School for Deaf Girls: 1846-1996* – Terri Broderick and Regina Duggan, 1996

[2] For further information on the Cabra Institution, see Crean (1997), Matthews (1996), McDonnell (1979), and O'Dowd (1955).

[3] Legal papers, 20 November 1852 – *Administration Papers of the Claremont Institution*

[4] *Report of a Deputation from the National Association for the Education of the Deaf and Dumb Poor of Ireland* – John Ringland and John Gelston, 1856

[5] ibid

[6] ibid

[7] *Edward James Chidley: In Memoriam* – The Deaf and Dumb Magazine, Vol. 9, No. 101, May 1881

[8] Annual Report of the Institution, 1858

[9] *Our Portrait Gallery* - Ephphtata, May 1896

[10] *British Links with Claremont* – Anthony J. Boyce, 2000

[11] *Mr Vere Henry Wintringham Huston* – Geoffrey Eagling, 2000

12 – Claremont: The 1890s to 1940s

[1] *Irish Times*, 16 May 1936

[2] In 1887, the Institution became an Incorporated Body under the Educational Endowment Commission, which eased the process of co-opting the successor for one of the trustees who either resigned or died, without enduring legal expenses. From this point, the title of 'Committee' is replaced by the 'Board of Governors'.

[3] Mrs. C.F. Alexander was renowned for her famous hymns, *There is a Green Hill Far Away* and *All Things Bright and Beautiful*. All the profits from sale of her book, *Hymns for Little Children*, went towards the building of the new school for the deaf on Derry Road, Strabane.

[4] *Britain's Worst Deaf School Tragedy* – P. & M. Jackson, *British Deaf History Journal*, December 2001

[5] *Irish Times*, 22 August 1893

[6] Thom's' Directory, 1914

[7] For further details, see the chapter *Going Abroad for Good.*

[8] Leinster, Munster and Connaught

[9] *Irish Times*, 12 May 1915

[10] *Irish Times*, 20 May 1925

[11] *Irish Times*, 3 May 1928

[12] *Irish Times*, 19 May 1935

[13] Annual Report of the Institution, 1928

[14] Minutes of the Institution, 1942

13 – The Monkstown School

[1] *A Glorious Extravaganza: the history of Monkstown Parish Church* – Etain Murphy (2003)

[2] *Personal communication* – Henry Pollard, 2006

[3] Annual Report of the Claremont School, 1977

14 – Teaching the Deaf

[1] *An Historical Guide to the City of Dublin* – G.N. Wright (1825)

[2] *Philocophus: or, the deafe and dumbe man's friend* - Bulwer, I. (John), (fl. 1654)

[3] ibid

[4] *On the Physical, Moral and Social Condition of the Deaf and Dumb* – W. Wilde (1854)

[5] *A Silent Minority: Deaf Education in Spain 1550-1835* – Susan Plann (1997)

[6] *Irish Times*, 20 August 1880

[7] *Damned for their Difference* – John Branson and Don Miller (2002)

[8] Petrus Pontius, a Benedictine monk, taught the deaf to speak by instructing them first to write, then pointing out to them the objects signed by the written characters, and finally guiding them to those motions of the tongue and lips which corresponds to the characters. This method had been generally adopted in Germany, hence the name 'German method'.

[9] *The Deaf and Dumb* – The Bray and Rathmichael Parish Magazine, July 1868

[10] *Church of Ireland Gazette*, 8 May 1903

[11] *The British Deaf Times* - 1911

[12] www.oghamdesign.ie, 2006

[13] *Visual-Kinetic Communication in Europe before 1600* - Lois Bragg (1997)

[14] *Moral Condition of the Deaf & Dumb* - Sir William Wilde (1856)

[15] Minutes of the Institution, May 1871, Volume 4

[16] Annual Report of the Institution, 1835

15 – Pictures in the Mind

[1] *An Investigation into the Principles, Management and Deficiencies of the National Institution at Claremont, near Dublin, for the Education of the Deaf and Dumb Poor of Ireland, 1822*

[2] Thomas Collogan, from Collon, Co.Louth - admitted in 1816

[3] William Brennan, from Rathgar, Dublin - admitted with Thomas Collins on 15 May 1816. He accompanied Thomas Collins on the deputation tours with Mr Humphreys in England.

[4] *George the Fourth* – Roger Fulford (1932)

[5] In 1817, the American Asylum for the Deaf and Dumb was established in Hartford, Connecticut, by the Rev. Thomas H. Gallaudet, with assistance from Laurent Clerc, deaf assistant teacher from the Institution for the Deaf in Paris.

[6] Founder of the American Asylum for the Deaf and Dumb in Hartford, Connecticut in 1817.

16 – Life at School

[1] This was featured on a RTÉ television programme, *Secret Sights*, on Irish history, in 2006.

[2] For further information on William Pagen, see the chapter, *Going Away for Good.*

[3] The Rev. Nangle, of the Irish Church Missions, established at Dugort in Achill, Co. Mayo, a self-supporting colony for those converted to the Protestant faith.

[4] *Saunders Newsletter,* 6 April 1847

[5] Personal recollection of D. J. Stanton, communicated to Henry Pollard, c.1965

[6] *The British Deaf Mute,* June 1893

[7] 'Exercises to develop strength and grace' (Oxford Dictionary)

[8] This is now known as Eskimo. 'The Proprietor of the Exhibition of the Labrador Indians wishes to exhibit the surprising feats of the Esquimaux in his canoe, on the Royal Canal Basin in Blessington Street. The male will give a real proof of the admirable dexterity of his countrymen, and will heave his dart, kill his game and perform other astonishing feats' – *Saunders Newsletter,* 15 May 1822

[9] obedience, submissiveness (English Thesaurus)

[10] *Irish Times,* 3 June 1864

[11] Annual Report of the Institution, 1834

[12] Annual Report of the Institution, 1858

[13] *Dublin Evening Post – 1826,* M.J. Tutty, Dublin Historical Record, Vol. XXIV, No.2 (March 1971)

[14] Annual Report of the Institution, 1841

[15] *Saunders Newsletter,* 17 June 1826

[16] *Dublin Evening Mail,* 28 April 1830

[17] *Daily Express,* 1 May 1861

17 – Leaving Claremont

[1] Annual Report of the Institution, 1834

[2] Annual Report of the Institution, 1863

[3] His father, a soldier, had died, and his mother, with a family of four children, resided at Portobello Barracks, Rathmines of Dublin. His application for admission to Claremont was supported by four ladies, members of the Young Women's Christian Association. Prior to his admission, he was maintained by the Protestant Orphan Association.

[4] *Daily Express,* 13 April 1887

[5] *Saunders Newsletter,* 10 June 1857

[6] *Genealogical and Biographical History of the Molyneux Families,* N.Z.R. Molyneux, 1904

[7] *The Silent Messenger,* January 1897, Vol. 2, No.12

[8] *The Morning Register,* 2 December 1823

[9] *The First British Deaf Juror,* A.J. Boyce et al, British Deaf History Journal, December 2001

[10] *Leinster Express,* 16 December 1843

[11] *Leinster Express*, 8 January 1848

[12] *Downpatrick Recorder*, 6 September 1851

[13] *Downpatrick Recorder*, 10 March 1852

[14] He might have been a brother or a relative of a 'William Blow', admitted into Claremont, aged nine years, in March 1834, having been from Hillsborough, Co. Down, and supported by the Juvenile Association for the Education of the Deaf).

[15] *Downpatrick Recorder*, 13 March 1852

[16] Report of the Select Committee on Administration of Relief of the Poor in Ireland, 1861, House of Commons 1861 (408) XX, Appendix 11 – *The Lost Children*, Joseph Robins, 1980

[17] *Irish Times*, 9 May 1939, p.3

[18] *Magazine for the Deaf and Dumb*, October 1875

[19] *Report of the Royal Commission for the Deaf, Dumb, Blind and the Imbeciles, 1889*

[20] *The Messenger*, July 1899

18 – Six Shillings and Six Pence

[1] *Cork City Quakers: A Brief History 1655-1939* – R. Harrison (1991)

[2] Cork Constitution, 5 August 1828

[3] Minutes of the Institution, September 1825

[4] *Slater's Directory of Ireland, 1858*

[5] *Breaking the Silence: Education of the Deaf in Ireland* – E. Crean (1997)

[6] *How to Educate the Deaf and Dumb – the Proposed Plan for the Establishment of Day Schools* – J.Copleston (1866)

[7] *Daily Express*, 13 April 1887

[8] Minutes of the Institution, 10 May 1854

[9] Chief Secretary Office Papers, CSO1825/26

[10] *The Liverpool Mercury*, 4 October 1822

[11] Deputation Letter book, Administration documents of the Institution

[12] Annual Report of the Juvenile Association, 1845

19 – Faith Cometh by Seeing

[1] Minutes of the Institution, 20 October 1820

[2] *Saunders Newsletter*, 22 April, 1851

[3] Chief Secretary was the most senior position in the British administration, based in Dublin Castle, reporting to the Lord Lieutenant, who represented Great Britain in Ireland until 1921

[4] *Daily Express*, 26 November, 1858

[5] *Saunders Newsletter*, 22 April 1851

[6] The Institution referred to was the male branch of the Catholic Institution for the Deaf and Dumb, in the Prospect seminary, near Glasnevin, Dublin, managed by the Carmelite monks. When the numbers of male pupils increased, a complex of build-

ings was erected in Cabra, and the Institution moved there in 1857.

[7] Minutes of the Institution, 25 August 1852

[8] Annual Report of the Institution, 1859

[9] Minutes of the Institution, 2 January 1849

[10] There was a class of females of correct morals, from 14 to 35 years of age, who, having lost one or both parents, or are without employment and without support. On 11 August 1838, a Society had been formed, and called 'The Dublin Providence Home' for the purpose of providing a temporary home, with support and employment, for such females until some permanent situation can be found them. On occasions, a few female former pupils had been sent to this Institution when all efforts of sourcing apprenticeship or tracking down their relatives and friends to take them had failed. The last resort taken by the Committee taken for such cases - that applied also to male former pupils - was removal to the workhouse.

[11] Letter-book of the Juvenile Association of Education of the Deaf and Dumb, 31 May 1849

[12] *Saunders Newsletter*, 6 and 7 May 1850, and 21 June 1850

[13] *Clonmel Chronicle* – 9 February 1905

[14] *British Links with Claremont* – Anthony J. Boyce (2001)

[15] *Daily Express*, 18 May 1853

20 – Working for Themselves

[1] *Deaf Heritage in Canada: A Distinctive, Diverse & Enduring Culture* - C.F. Carbin (ed. L. Smith, 1996)

[2] *Daily Express*, 1 April 1880

[3] *The Palatine Families of Ireland* – Henry Z. Jones, Jr. (1990)

[4] *The British Deaf Mute*, December 1893

[5] *The British Deaf Mute*, September 1894

[6] *Leinster Leader*, 19 August 1899

[7] *Letter from Patience Pollard*, Edenderry Historical Society

[8] *Brief Lives of Irish Doctors* - J. B. Lyons (1978)

[9] *Concise Dictionary of Irish Biography* – John S. Crone (1928)

[10] *David John (Jack) Stanton* – Henry Pollard, Dun Laoghaire Borough Historical Society, No. 11, 2002

[11] *Flying High!* - A.J. Boyce et al, British Deaf History Journal, December 2004

[12] *Succession List of Clergy in Dublin* - J. B. Leslie (1904)

21 – Messengers of the Gospel

[1] *When the Fire Fell* – G.T.B. Davis (www.revival-library.org)

[2] Annual Report of the Institution, 1834. Edward Whitfield was a private pupil of Mr Joseph Humphreys.

[3] *Daily Express*, 26 November 1858

[4] Minutes of the Institution, 3 July 1834

[5] *Ephphatha*, March 1899, p.47

[6] *Magazine for the Deaf and Dumb*, January 1875

[7] *Railway Incidents* – Peter W. Jackson, Deaf History Journal, December 1999

[8] *The Reverend Edward Rowland* – Raymond Lee, *Deaf Lives*, British Deaf History Society, 2001

[9] *The Deaf and Dumb Herald*, October and November 1876

[10] *Daily Express*, 1 April 1890

[11] *Irish Ecclesiastical Gazette*, 13 March 1891

[12] *Irish Ecclesiastical Gazette*, 31 March 1888

[13] *Church of Ireland Gazette*, 2 September 1904

[14] *A Missionary Chronicle*, Otto B. Berg, 1982

[15] *The Bible War in Ireland* – Irene Whelan, 2006

[16] Minutes of the Mission to the Adult Deaf and Dumb (Dublin), December 1942

[17] Letter from Mr Lyons, 9 June 1885, *Gallaudet Archives*

[18] *The Deaf and Dumb Times 1890*, Vol. 1, p.89 – cit. *Francis Maginn*, B. Grant – *Looking Back: A Reader* (1993)

[19] *Proceedings of Conference of Headmasters of Institutions for Education of the Deaf and Dumb, 1881*

[20] *The Messenger*, October/November 1911, Vol. 10, no. 10

[21] *The Messenger*, February 1898, Vol. 2, no. 2

[22] *The Messenger*, May/June 1902, Vol. 1, no. 3

[23] *Samuel Bright Lucas* – Peter W. Jackson, British Deaf History, 2001

[24] *The Messenger* – February 1905, Vol. 7, no. 7

22 – Talent for Drawing

[1] *Report of a Deputation from the National Association for the Education of the Deaf and Dumb Poor of Ireland* – John Ringland and John Gelston, 1856

[2] *Samuel Close*, David Breslin - *Deaf Lives*, British Deaf History Society, 2001

[3] Private collection of Trevor Neill, Lisburn Historical Society

[4] *Francis McDonnell*, David Breslin – *Deaf Lives*, British Deaf History Society, 2001

[5] Minutes of the Institution, November 1848

[6] *Lawrence Fagan 1825-1898, Draughtsman, Sketcher and Copyist* – David Breslin, 2000

23 – Deaf Women

[1] *Charlotte Elizabeth Tonna* - Doreen Woodford, British Deaf History Journal, April 2001

[2] Annual Report of the Institution, 1857

[3] *The Silent Worker, Vol. 11, No. 6.* February 1899, pp.82-83

[4] *The Deaf & Dumb News & Juvenile Instructor*, July 1889

[5] *Report of the Royal Commission for the Deaf, Dumb, Blind and Imbecile*, 1889

[6] *Banton* - Peter Brown, British Deaf History Publications, 1994

[7] *The Silent Messenger, p.58* (1897)

[8] *Frederick John Rose: An Australian Pioneer,* Jan Banson and Don Miller - *Collage: Works on International Deaf History,* 1996

[9] Personal communication with David Platts, 2001

[10] Written account from Sean Magee, 2000

[11] Letter-book of the Juvenile Association for the Education of the Deaf and Dumb

[12] *Daily Express,* 30 March 1880

[13] Braidwood's Academy in Edinburgh and the London Asylum for the Deaf and Dumb

[14] *Cork Constitution,* 11 August 1829

24 – Going away for Good

[1] *The Deaf and Dumb Times* – 1875 (undated)

[2] Annual Report of the Institution, 1862

[3] *A Founding Father of the Australian Deaf Community* - communication from Stanislius Foran, 2001

[4] Annual Report of the Institution, 1866

[5] *The MacDonald Brothers Dynasty* - Davina Merricks, British Deaf History Journal, August 2004

[6] *Letter to Mr Taylor from E. Simpson,* 3 March 1917 - Administrative Papers of the Institution

[7] Headmaster's Letter-book to the Committee - 5 January 1918

[8] *Torpedoed!* - Philip Lecane (2005)

[9] *Britain's Deaf Heritage* - Peter W. Jackson, 1990

25 – History of the Dublin Working Boys' Home

[1] *Irish Ecclesiastical Gazette,* 24 July 1876

[2] Annual Report of the Dublin Working Boys' Home, 1906

Index

Page numbers in italics indicate end-notes (Chapter number and end note number).